Lynda Weinman's | Hands-On Training

Includes CD-ROM with Exercise Files and Demo Movies

Adobe®
After Effects® 6

H·O·T ™

Hands-On Training

lynda.com/books

By Lynda Weinman
and Craig Newman

Design: Ali Karp

Adobe After Effects 6 | H·O·T
Hands-On Training
By Lynda Weinman and Craig Newman

lynda.com/books | Peachpit Press
1249 Eighth Street • Berkeley, CA • 94710
510.524.2178
510.524.2221 (fax)
http://www.lynda.com/books
http://www.peachpit.com

lynda.com/books is published
in association with Peachpit Press,
a division of Pearson Education
Copyright ©2004 by lynda.com

ISBN: 0-321-22854-5

0 9 8 7 6 5

Printed and bound in the
United States of America

H•O•T | Credits

Original Design: Ali Karp, Alink Newmedia *(alink@earthlink.net)*

Editor: Jennifer Eberhardt

Copyeditor: Darren Meiss

Compositors: Rick Gordon, Deborah Roberti

Beta Testers: Scott Cuzzo, Laurie Burress-Myers

Additional Writing: Jay Laird

Cover Illustration: Bruce Heavin *(bruce@stink.com)*

Indexer: Larry Sweazy

Proofreader: Beth Trudell

H•O•T | Colophon

The original design for *After Effects 6 H•O•T* was sketched on paper. The layout was heavily influenced by online communication–merging a traditional book format with a modern Web aesthetic.

The text in *After Effects 6 H•O•T* was set in Akzidenz Grotesk from Adobe and Triplex from Emigré. The cover illustration was painted in Adobe Photoshop 7.0 and Adobe Illustrator 10.

This book was created using QuarkXPress 4.1, Adobe Photoshop 7.0, Microsoft Office 2003, and After Effects 6 on a Macintosh G4, running Mac OS X (10.3). It was printed on 50 lb. Utopia Filmcoat at Phoenix BookTech.

Dedication

To the awesome team at lynda.com.

After Effects 6 | H•O•T _____ **Table of Contents**

Introduction

H·O·T

After Effects 6

A Note from Lynda Weinman

It's been a great pleasure to dig back into my After Effects roots. While many people know me as a Web graphics specialist, I started my creative life in filmmaking—specifically by creating special effects and motion graphics for television, music videos, industrial films, commercials, and motion pictures. My professional life in animation began around 1980, when my then-boyfriend owned an animation camera service. He introduced me to a world that I have never wanted to leave. I hate to sound old, but I remember the days before personal computers, when people actually made physical artwork and shot it with analog cameras. While that might seem like a lifetime ago, the truth is that within the past 24 years, a lot has changed. I don't think I could have fathomed that one little computer program named After Effects would one day replace an animation camera, optical printer, Moviola, and light box.

I started teaching After Effects with CoSa version 1.0, and the first place I taught it was at Art Center College of Design in 1991. It's quite possible that you've never heard of ACCD, but it is among the top art colleges in the world. It was amazing to see students from different disciplines create wonderful projects set to sound with moving graphics. I've been hooked on After Effects ever since, and the good news is that the program keeps getting better and better. To write a book on this software has been a dream of mine since those early days when I was first captivated by the magic and power of this product.

I created the Hands-On Training series of books because I believe there is a need for this type of training in the computer book field. In my opinion, most people buy computer books in order to learn, yet it is amazing how few of these books are actually written by teachers. In this book, you will find carefully developed lessons and exercises to help you learn After Effects 6. There are many excellent books out on After Effects, but most, if not all, are for intermediate to advanced users. This book will help you build the strong foundation you need to approach the more difficult projects that you'll find in those books. (Many other books are listed in the "*Resources*" appendix at the end.)

This book is written for beginning After Effects learners who are looking for a great tool to make motion graphics for the Web, CD-ROM, DVD, video, or film. The premise of the hands-on exercise approach is to get you up to speed quickly in After Effects while actively working through the book's lessons. It's one thing to read about a product and another experience entirely to try the product and get measurable results. Our motto is, "Read the book, follow the exercises, and you will know the product." We have received countless testimonials to this fact, and it is our goal to make sure it remains true for all of our Hands-On Training books.

Many exercise-based books take a paint-by-numbers approach to teaching. While this approach works, it's often difficult to figure out how to apply those lessons to a real-world situation, or to understand why or when you would use the technique again. What sets this book apart is that the lessons contain lots of background information, advice, and insights into each given subject, designed to help you understand the process as well as the exercise.

At times, pictures are worth a lot more than words, and moving pictures are even better! When necessary, I have also included short QuickTime movies to show any process that's difficult to explain with words. These files are located on the **H•O•T CD-ROM** inside a folder called **movies**. It's my style to approach teaching from many different angles, since I recognize that some people are visual learners, others like to read, and still others like to get out there and try things. This book combines a lot of teaching approaches so you can learn After Effects 6 as thoroughly as you want to.

I didn't set out to cover every single aspect of After Effects in this book. The manual and many other reference books are great for that! What I saw missing from the bookshelves was a process-oriented tutorial that taught readers core principles, techniques, and tips in a hands-on training format.

I welcome your comments at **ae6hot@lynda.com**. Please visit our Web site at **http://www.lynda.com**. The support URL for this book is **http://www.lynda.com/books/hot/ae6**.

It is my hope that this book will increase your skills in After Effects and motion graphics. If it does, I will have accomplished the job I set out to do!

–Lynda Weinman

> **NOTE** | **About lynda.com/books and lynda.com**
>
> **lynda.com/books** is dedicated to helping creative professionals understand tools and design principles. **lynda.com** offers hands-on conferences, on-site training, training CDs, and an online movie-training library. To learn more about our training programs, books, and products, be sure to give our site a visit at **http://www.lynda.com**.

About the Author, Lynda Weinman

Lynda Weinman graduated from Evergreen State College in Olympia, Washington, in 1976. She owned two retail stores named Vertigo until 1982, when she left retail to pursue a career in special effects and animation. She has worked on many animation projects, from *Return of the Jedi* to Dodge commercials to Howard Jones videos and industrial films for Apple and Momenta computers. She purchased the first model of the Macintosh computer in 1984, and her life forever changed.

In 1987, Lynda created animatics on a Macintosh FX for the motion picture *Star Trek V*, using Macromind VideoWorks (the predecessor to Macromedia Director) and Super 3D. From that point on, she has never left the personal computer graphics platform. After having a daughter in 1989, she left film and video production and began teaching full time.

Lynda has written for numerous magazines, including *MacUser*, *MacWeek*, *MacWorld*, *DV*, *Diem*, *Step-by-Step Graphics*, and *HOW Design*. She wrote her first book, *Designing Web Graphics*, in 1995 (published in 1996) and has been writing books and teaching ever since. A teacher at Art Center College of Design for seven years, she also taught at UCLA Extension, American Film Institute, and San Francisco Multimedia Studies Program.

lynda.com began as a Web site for her Art Center students and has grown into a business that supports a full-time staff, and multiple locations in Ojai, California. The focus of lynda.com is to provide education to those who want to work and be creative in the digital arts. lynda.com produces training materials in the form of books, CD-ROMs, an online movie training library, on-site training, and events such as FlashForward2000–2004, and After Effects West.

Lynda's Acknowledgments

This book is the culmination of the work of many! Sincerest gratitude to:

My husband, Bruce Heavin. Thank you for insisting that I get back to my After Effects roots after a long detour. I feel very lucky to have found you and to share my life with you.

My daughter, Jamie. I love you and am very proud to be your mom.

Garo Green, my partner in crime. It's such a pleasure to work together—thanks for sharing my vision for this book series and making stuff happen 'round da clock!

The beta testers, Laurie Burress and Scott Cuzzo. Thanks for seeking out and destroying the errors. Laurie, your sage teaching advice was invaluable. Scott, the level of detail of your work was awe inspiring. You two made a huge contribution to the book!

Jay Laird for helping with the new features—paint and text. You were instrumental in getting this book to market faster and helping out with some great exercises and instructional writing. Looking forward to working with you some more!

The team at lynda.com. Thank you for all your contributions to our company and making me proud to have my name at the helm.

The team at Peachpit and New Riders. It's a joy to work with a company that really cares. Jennifer and Stephanie—you've been great to work with! Thanks so much for working with us!

Chris and Trish Meyer. Thanks for your moral support and your friendship over the years. It's been great to reconnect, and I respect what you have done for the After Effects community enormously. You guys go!

The team at Adobe—Erica, Kevin, Steve, Dave H., Dave S., Dan—and everyone else. You rock so many people's worlds—thank you for making this amazing product.

David Rogelberg. Thank you for making this book series dream come true. Your support and contributions are appreciated beyond measure.

> **NOTE** | **The Formatting in This Book**
>
> This book has several components, including step-by-step exercises, commentaries, notes, tips, warnings, and movies. Step-by-step exercises are numbered, and filenames and command keys are shown in bold so they pop out more easily. Captions and commentary are in italicized text: *This is a caption.* Filenames/folders, command keys, and menu commands are bolded: **images** folder, **Ctrl+click**, and **File > Open**. Code is in a monospace font: **<html></html>**. And URLs are in bold: **http://www.lynda.com**.

The After Effects 6 Upgrade

If you have worked with past versions of After Effects, the upgrade to After Effects 6 is a must-have! Of most significance is the introduction of native text layers and paint effects. Here's a short list of feature enhancements:

- Text animation tools that are native inside After Effects
- Many impressive performance gains
- Non-destructive Vector Paint tools that work on layers over time
- Better integration with Adobe products
- Better masking, such as Auto-Trace for alpha channels

What Is the Production Bundle?

There are two versions of After Effects 6—one that ships with the Production Bundle and one that ships without it. Both versions have a full-featured version of After Effects 6; the only difference is that the Production Bundle version includes a lot more advanced and sophisticated effects and is therefore more expensive. As you'll learn in the hands-on exercises in this book, effects offer ways to add extra features to your After Effects movies, such as drop shadows, blurs, lighting, or warping effects. An effect is also called a plug-in and is similar to filter effects in programs like Photoshop or Premiere.

Once you learn After Effects by reading this book and following its step-by-step tutorials, you'll learn the process of working with effects. Some of the Production Bundle effects have settings that are unique to those specific plug-ins. Since this is a beginning-level book, I chose not to cover the Production Bundle effects packages. At the end of this book, in the "*Resources*" appendix, you'll find a lot of other books and resources that will help you advance your After Effects skills beyond this book. I highly recommend that you purchase the Production Bundle if you are serious about working as an After Effects professional. If you can't afford it just yet, however, don't fear! The standard version of After Effects has the same core product as the Production Bundle version.

Macintosh and Windows Interface Screen Captures

Most of the screen captures in this book were taken on a Macintosh using OS X. The only time I used Windows shots was when the interface differed from that of the Macintosh. I made this decision because I do most of my design work and writing on a Macintosh. I also own and use a Windows system, so I noted important differences when they occurred, and took screen captures accordingly.

Mac and Windows System Differences

Adobe has done a great job of ensuring that After Effects looks and works the same between the Macintosh and Windows operating systems. However, there are still some differences that should be noted. If you are using this book with one of the Windows operating systems, please be sure to read the following section, "Making Exercise Files Editable on Windows Systems," carefully.

WARNING | "Open" for Mac and "Select" for Windows

Throughout this book, you will be instructed to click the **Open** button. This is the correct way to do it on the Macintosh with OS X. On a PC running Windows, you will instead see a **Select** button. The two buttons are interchangeable and do the same thing.

Making Exercise Files Editable on Windows Systems

By default, when you copy files from a CD-ROM to your Windows 2000/NT/XP hard drive, they are set to read-only (write protected). This will cause a problem with the exercise files, because you will need to write over some of them. You will notice that the files have a small lock next to them, which means they have been set to read-only. To remove this setting and make them editable, follow this short procedure:

1. Drag the files from the **H•O•T CD-ROM** to a location on your hard drive. **Ctrl+click** on each of the files that has a lock next to it.

---

2. Once you have all of the files selected, choose **File > Turn Off Read Only**.

After Effects 6 System Requirements

Macintosh

- PowerPC® processor (multiprocessor G4 recommended)

- Mac OS X v10.2.6

- 128 MB of RAM installed (256 MB or more recommended)

- 150 MB of available hard-disk space for installation (500 MB or larger hard disk or disk array recommended for ongoing work)

- CD-ROM drive

- 24-bit color display adapter

- Apple QuickTime™ software (recommended)

Windows

- Intel® Pentium® III or 4 processor (multiprocessor recommended)

- Microsoft® Windows® 2000 or Windows XP Pro or Home Edition

- 128 MB of RAM installed (256 MB or more recommended)

- 150 MB of available hard-disk space for installation (500 MB or larger hard disk or disk array recommended for ongoing work)

- CD-ROM drive

- 24-bit color display adapter

- Apple QuickTime™ 6.1 software recommended

- Microsoft DirectX 8.1 software recommended

WARNING | Windows XP and QuickTime

Unfortunately, Windows XP may disable QuickTime. If this happens, try going to the Apple site and downloading the latest QuickTime plug-in. Make sure that After Effects is not open while you do this. If you are using Windows XP, make sure you have installed the latest updates. This is accomplished by choosing **Start > All Programs > Windows Update**. There have definitely been some updates that have affected QuickTime compatibility, so don't neglect to try this!

What's on the CD-ROM?

Exercise Files and the H·O·T CD-ROM

Your course files are located inside a folder called **exercise_files** on the **H·O·T CD-ROM**. These files are divided into chapter folders, and you will be instructed to copy the chapter folders to your hard drive during many of the exercises. Unfortunately, when files originate from a CD-ROM, the Windows operating system defaults to making them write-protected, meaning that you cannot alter them. You will need to alter them to follow the exercises, so please read the previous section, "Making Exercise Files Editable on Windows Systems," for instructions on how to convert them.

Demo Files on the CD-ROM

In addition to the exercise files, the H·O·T CD-ROM also contains free 30-day trial versions of After Effects 6 and QuickTime 6.1 software applications for the Mac or Windows. All software is located inside the **software** folder on the **H·O·T CD-ROM**.

I.

Background

| What Is After Effects? | What's New in After Effects 6.0? |
| What Are Animation & Motion Graphics? |
| File Formats | AE & Photoshop | AE & Flash |
| AE & Editing Tools | Video into AE | Other Tools |

No exercise files

After Effects 6
H•O•T CD-ROM

This chapter provides background information related to After Effects and motion graphics. If you are anxious to get into hands-on exercises, feel free to skip ahead. This is not a required chapter; instead, it is here to help readers who are not familiar with After Effect's capabilities or who want an overview before getting started. Even if you're a seasoned After Effects veteran, you might want to read the "What's New in After Effects 6.0?" section on the next page to see what new exciting and creative features are in store!

What Is After Effects?

You've already seen footage developed in After Effects, in movies such as *The Matrix* (the title sequence with the raining text), though you might not have been aware of it at the time. After Effects is used professionally throughout the motion picture and video industry for title sequences, identity campaigns for television stations, TV commercials, industrial videos, CD-ROMs and DVDs, Web animations, and much, much more. One of the coolest things about After Effects is that you can make a single project, yet publish it to a variety of formats that support video, film, and CD-ROM, DVD, or Web content.

After Effects allows you to compose moving images in the same way an artist might compose a drawing or a painting. It gives you the ability to create relationships between images, sounds, and moving footage. You can compose an animation by positioning images in locations on the screen and moving them or changing their characteristics (such as opacity, scale, and rotation) over time. As well, After Effects includes the capability of synchronizing audio to play back with your moving images.

What's New in After Effects 6.0?

For those of you have who worked with a previous version of After Effects, you are surely eager to know what new features have been added to this version. Here's a short list:

- Overall performance enhancements for editing and rendering.

- OpenGL support, which is an open standard that allows for very quick rendering of compositing, effects, and 3D. Although you won't need to learn about OpenGL (it is the behind-the-scenes reason for why these processes are faster), you will get hands-on experience with compositing, effects, and 3D throughout the book.

- Rendering automation through scripting. You'll learn about rendering and automation in Chapter 18, "*Rendering Final Movies*."

- New text engine. In the past, you had to bring text into After Effects from another application or work within a filter to create headline text. The new text engine allows you to type directly into After Effects and create paragraph text and headline text on a whim. With the text engine being more integrated into After Effects, an entire new world of typographic control is at your command. You'll specifically learn how to work with these new features in Chapter 9, "*Text Layers*."

- Integrated vector paint engine that allows you to paint directly in After Effects with Photoshop-style brushes. This is an important and exciting enhancement because you can make artwork in After Effects rather than relying on outside applications for artwork import. The ramifications are not only felt for convenience and more efficient workflow, but for animation purposes. That's because you can animate with the paint tools (imagine paint strokes drawing themselves on the screen and that sort of thing). You'll learn all about this in Chapter 12, "*Paint.*"

- New distortion tools that allow you to liquify or warp images and text over time.

- Eighteen new effects. This book doesn't have space to cover all the new effects, but once you learn how to create a single effect, the same skills apply to all other effects. You'll have a chance to use some new and old effects in Chapter 10, "*Effects.*"

- Enhanced masking. You can now use alpha channels from Photoshop and convert them to After Effects vector masks. You'll learn how to do this in Chapter 13, "*Masks.*"

- Improved Integration with Photoshop, Illustrator, and Premiere.

- Photoshop integration enhancements include the capability to edit Photoshop text layers in After Effects. You can now bring in multiple Photoshop documents as a sequence, and each PSD file will retain layers (in the past, all the layers were flattened). When you import a layered Photoshop file, a new feature allows you to make all the layers the same dimension automatically, which can be critical for using these files as compositions. You'll learn about compositions in Chapter 4, "*The Composition.*" If you rename or reorder layers of a PSD file in After Effects, the links to the original Photoshop document remain intact. Guides are preserved from PSD files. You'll learn about Photoshop integration in numerous chapters within this book.

- Illustrator integration enhancements include the capability to resize layers within After Effects to match the same dimensions for compositing reasons. You'll learn about compositions in Chapter 4, "*The Composition.*" More information on general Illustrator integration is found throughout the book in numerous exercises.

- Premiere integration (Windows only) will now accept After Effects compositions and nested compositions. This book is committed to a cross-platform audience, so we will not be covering a Windows-only feature.

What Are Animation and Motion Graphics?

The word "animation" comes from the Latin word *anima*, which means "life" or "soul." As an artist working with images, you bring them to life when you make them move. Still images can appear to move by arranging them in a specific order and changing from one image to the next in a fairly rapid sequence.

A flipbook is a simple form of animation, but live-action filmmaking and video also bring still images to life. Although not all films and video are classified as being "animated," they all share the same principal of animation.

The term "motion graphics" is used quite a bit in conjunction with After Effects. Motion graphics usually refers to taking a static image and making it move. In this context, the term "animation" would contrast with motion graphics, because animation might involve creating new artwork for each frame within a sequence. Often, the terms "motion graphics" and "animation" are used interchangeably.

NOTE | Why Does Animation Appear to Make Still Images Move?

Our eyes have sensors that retain an image for a moment. Stare at a high-contrast image for a while and then close your eyes. You'll see a ghost image although your eyes are closed. This is called "persistence of vision" or an "after effect" of vision. The name of the computer program, After Effects, comes from this sensory phenomenon.

The whole trick in animation is to have a series of related images and move them quickly enough that our eyes do not perceive the difference between separate images. It takes about 24 individual images per second to overcome the tendency for images to appear to separate and gain an illusion of fluid motion.

What Formats Does After Effects Produce?

After Effects can be used for film, video, digital video, CD-ROMs, Web, and print output. It produces a wide variety of file formats that are specifically tailored for each medium. After Effects provides ample options to meet the demands of artists and media professionals.

The most common format to output from After Effects is QuickTime, which can be published at a variety of resolutions that support everything from Web content to feature film quality. In addition to QuickTime, however, it supports all the following formats:

- Macromedia Flash (SWF)
- AIFF
- AVI
- DV Stream
- FLC
- Image Sequence
- Interframe Compressed VR Object Movie
- MPEG-4
- QuickTime Movie (MOV)
- Wave
- μLaw

How Does After Effects Differ from Photoshop?

Photoshop is designed to work with still images. If your project demands high-quality still images, Photoshop is probably the best tool for the job. Photoshop images can be used in After Effects projects with great results, so many people use Photoshop and After Effects together. A good rule of thumb to differentiate the two tools is that Photoshop is great for still images and After Effects is great for moving images.

How Is After Effects Different from Avid, Final Cut Pro, and Premiere?

The tools Avid, Final Cut Pro (Apple), and Premiere (Adobe) are used for nonlinear editing. They are geared toward putting finished video shots together as a single short-form or long-form movie. They don't focus on creating frame-by-frame animation, sophisticated title effects, or the manipulation of special effects. You can do some similar work in these programs, but After Effects has far more features for creating professional animation and motion graphics. You wouldn't want to cut a movie in After Effects, and you wouldn't want to do a title sequence in a nonlinear editing program.

How Is After Effects Different from Macromedia Flash?

Flash is a tool that combines still images, video, and sound, just like After Effects. Flash also offers, through its native scripting language called ActionScript, the capability to create interactive presentations. After Effects does not offer any ActionScript, and can only be used for animation and sound. Flash writes files with vectors and bitmaps; After Effects writes movie files that are converted entirely to bitmaps, even if the movie contains vector artwork to begin with. **Vector artwork** is composed of mathematically generated lines and shapes; **bitmap artwork** is generated by turning pixels on or off. The key advantage to vector artwork is its crisp and pristine appearance, whereas bitmap artwork can look more realistic with shadows, gradients, glows, and blurs.

Another key difference is that After Effects can render at any resolution—all the way up to IMAX! It has much more sophisticated effects and keyframe manipulation than Flash. You could bring an After Effects sequence into Flash, but After Effects does not offer any interactive features like Flash does. As well, Flash is time based, whereas Flash is frame based. This makes it possible to change the timing of an After Effects piece easily and stretch it from two seconds to two minutes without losing any of the animation relationships. This is not true in Flash.

What Is Compositing?

Compositing is the process of combining multiple sources of images, film footage, animation, text, or sound. Just like in Photoshop, After Effects uses *layers* (stacks of content that lay on top of each other) to create compositing. Compositing can be as simple as using two layers or as complex as hundreds of layers. After Effects has wonderful features that support sophisticated masking with alpha channels. (You'll learn more about alpha channels in Chapter 13, "*Masks*.")

How Do I Get Video Content into AE?

Getting video into After Effects can be done in a number of different ways. The first method involves digital video (DV) and FireWire. For this method, you would need the following:

- A DV camera or playback deck with a FireWire port

- A computer with a FireWire port

- A FireWire cable to connect the camera with your computer

- Software that controls the transfer of digital video into your computer (Premiere is an Adobe tool that enables this type of transfer)

Most computers that have FireWire ports also include the software to transfer digital video. Software products that support this process include Adobe Premiere, Apple iMovie, Apple Final Cut Pro, Apple Final Cut Express, and Sony MovieShaker. Transferring the footage from camera or video deck to computer is usually a simple process using this method.

In the second method, using analog video, you must convert analog video into digital format as part of the process. This can be done by using numerous tools, including the following:

- An analog video camera or playback deck

- A computer that has video digitizing hardware

- An appropriate cable to connect the camera with the digitizing hardware

- Software that allows you to control the digitizing process

Digitizing analog video is generally not a simple process and can require a fair amount of time and technical knowledge to ensure success. In general, we recommend using digital video (DV) and FireWire rather than analog video as source footage for your video projects. The image quality is usually higher with DV, and today's technologies make it easy to bring DV directly into your computer.

In the third method, video that has already been transferred to a computer may be available to you on CD-ROM, portable hard disks, or other computer storage media. This video can be copied directly into your computer system and used by After Effects.

Ultimately, all of the footage content that After Effects requires must be in digital format.

What Tools Do I Need Besides After Effects?

If you are using After Effects to produce animation for the Web, you may only need an image scanner and your computer. For a video project, you'll need access to appropriate hardware for your chosen video system. A motion picture film project might require that you utilize an outside service to scan your film images into digital form and provide the recording of your finished output onto film.

The extra software tools, if you need any, depend mostly on the type of media that you plan to create. After Effects can import a wide variety of file formats, allowing you to work with many types of computer art, such as bitmaps (from programs such as Photoshop), vectors (from programs such as Illustrator), or 3D content (from programs such as 3ds max). You don't need extra programs, but it's great to know that if you create artwork in them, you can use these images easily in After Effects.

How Do I Learn More About Animation, Video, and Compositing?

This book provides a good introduction to all of these subjects, and you'll get a strong foundation that will make the process clear. In the Resource Appendix, at the end of the book, you'll find a reference section of books, videos, and CD-ROMs that you can use to further your knowledge.

In summary, this chapter has offered an overview of some of the concepts and features of After Effects and related pursuits. I'm sure you're anxious to move from passively reading to hands-on exercises, so see you at the next chapter!

2.

Interface

| First View | Project Window |

| Composition Window | Timeline |

| Time Controls Palette | Audio Palette | Info & Tool Palettes |

| Shortcut Keys | Using the Interface |

chap_02

After Effects 6
H•O•T CD-ROM

Adobe provides a consistent interface throughout its products. If you've used Photoshop or Illustrator, many of the tools in After Effects will be familiar to you. On the other hand, After Effects is based on some concepts and features that might be new to you, and for this reason the interface is distinct as well.

Because the program requires assets, such as movies, sounds, and images (called "footage"), it has a Project window that stores all these types of items. It also has a Timeline window for setting up the motion for your moving images and a Composition window that acts as a stage where you can build, preview, and edit your projects. When working in After Effects, you'll primarily use these three windows. This chapter gives you a quick overview of these windows and walks you through a simple project so you can see how the interface changes in relation to your content. Other chapters will go into much more detail. As you'll see later, the After Effects interface gets a lot deeper when you start to build projects and moving pictures.

First View of After Effects

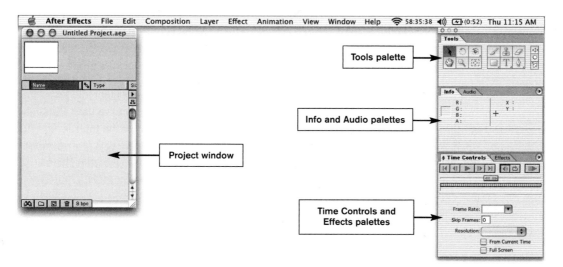

This is what you'll see the first time you open After Effects and create a new project. On Mac, the windows and palettes that open by default include the Project window, the Tools palette, the Info and Audio palettes, and the Time Controls and Effects palettes. In Windows, the default palettes are Tools, Info and Audio, and Time Controls and Effects. None of these windows and palettes do anything until you bring content such as movie footage, Photoshop files, Illustrator files, or other supported document types into the program. You'll learn how to bring in footage very soon!

> ### Tip of the Day #4
>
> For a list of keyboard shortcuts go to Help > After Effects Help and search for "shortcuts".
>
> ☑ Show Tips at Startup   (Next Tip)   (OK)

*Tips appear by default each time the program opens. Reading them can be incredibly useful, and you can cycle through more than one tip by clicking the **Next Tip** button. If you don't want to see tips on startup, uncheck the **Show Tips at Startup** check box, and they will disappear. You can always get them back by choosing **Help > Tip of The Day**.*

The Project Window

After Effects is different from many other programs that you might be familiar with because it uses something called the **project** to organize content and store the settings you create to produce animation and output audio. When you bring artwork into Photoshop, for example, that artwork is saved with the Photoshop document. The project file in After Effects is quite different because the project file only maintains pointers to whatever artwork you import. For this reason, After Effects project file sizes are quite small. They are also incredibly important because without a project, you can't work in After Effects at all.

The **Project window** is one of the three primary windows you use in After Effects. Think of it as where you store all the media you'll be working with—from still images to video footage to sounds. The word **footage** is an umbrella term for most media, even still images or audio. Importing or adding footage into your project creates references in the Project window. This means that the footage isn't actually copied into After Effects; instead, the project maintains pointers to where the footage resides on your hard drive.

Whenever you open a new After Effects project, a new empty Project window appears. When you import footage, it appears in the Project window. When you save your work, you save a project file—hence the file extension .aep (**A**fter **E**ffects **P**roject). The project file memorizes all kinds of things, including, but not limited to, the footage references of content you've imported. Think of After Effects as "linking" to the footage, whereas programs such as Photoshop or Illustrator "embed" content. This process will become much clearer as you work through the book.

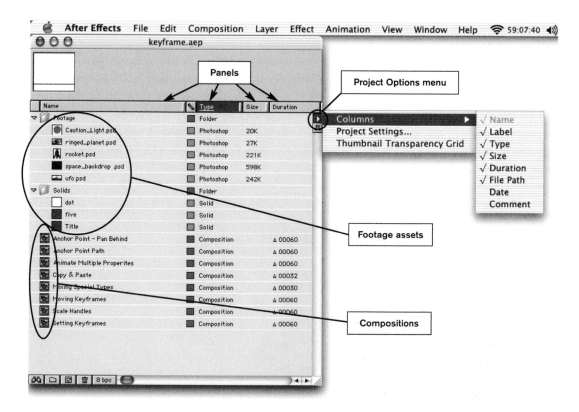

*Here's an example of a **Project window** that is filled with content. In order to see all this content, you would need to expand the Project window by dragging on its lower-right corner. Footage assets and compositions show up as a list in the Project window. This window can be stretched wider by dragging on the lower-right corner.*

Panels in the Project window allow you to view details about your footage or composition. A composition in After Effects is a type of file in which you combine all your layers of content and set it to animate over a Timeline. (You'll learn all about compositions in Chapter 4, "*The Composition*.") Panels form columns of information showing the name, label, size, type, file path, comments, date, and duration of each item. You can make a panel wider or narrower, and you can rearrange the order of panels simply by clicking and dragging the panel you want to move.

The Composition Window

The **Composition window** is the second of the three primary windows. Whereas the Project window contains a list of files and folders, the Composition window is where the visual preview or playback of your project appears. It's the equivalent of a screen area in a movie theater, except that you can have multiple compositions within a single project. A project is more like the movie theater complex where they are showing lots of movies, and each movie is represented by a composition! That's a silly analogy perhaps, but you are not limited to one composition per project—you can have hundreds of compositions per project, in fact. You can even nest compositions within compositions. The Composition window does not appear until you create a composition. You create a composition file from the Project window. You will see how to open a composition later in this chapter.

The **Composition window** is the equivalent of a stage or movie screen. It is where the visual preview of your work appears. The Composition window does not appear until you create and/or open a composition. You'll learn how to do this later in this chapter. You'll learn more about the features of this window in Chapter 4, "The Composition."

The Timeline Window

The **Timeline window** is the third primary window you use in After Effects. Like the Composition window, the Timeline window does not appear until you have opened a composition. It will be missing from your screen until you do this in Exercise 1, later in this chapter.

The main function of the Timeline window is to give you the ability to control time relationships between the various footage elements in your composition.

Footage elements are arranged in layers in the Timeline window. The length of each layer represents its duration in time. You can cause each layer to start or stop (be visible or invisible) at any point in the composition by adjusting it in the Timeline. You will learn more about the Timeline in Chapter 5, "Keyframes, Animation, and Timeline," as well as throughout the entire book.

Palette Organization

The palettes in After Effects can be pulled apart, reorganized, and restored easily. What distinguishes a palette from a window? A palette includes a tab; a window does not. This tab can be used to view or move a palette.

For example, the following palette group opens by default in the After Effects interface: Tools, Info, Audio, Time Controls, and Effects. If you select **Window > Tools**, all the palettes open that are connected together with Tools (Info, Audio, Time Controls, and Effects). If you separate Tools away from the group, it can be accessed independently.

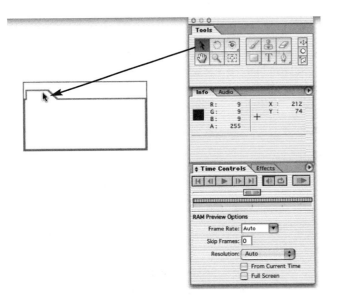

*Palettes can be separated and re-attached by dragging them on and off palette groupings by their tabs. To reset all your palettes to their default positions (which comes in handy if your screen gets too chaotic!), choose **Window > Reset Palette Locations**.*

Time Controls Palette

The **Time Controls palette** allows you to preview the compositions you create as moving images. You can play back the entire piece or select a specific frame.

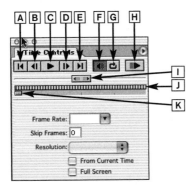

*The Time Controls palette: **A**. First Frame **B**. Previous Frame **C**. Play/Pause **D**. Next Frame **E**. Last Frame **F**. Audio **G**. Loop **H**. RAM Preview **I**. Shuttle **J**. Jog **K**. Time Indicator. These terms are defined in Chapter 5, "Keyframes, Animation, and Timeline."*

Audio Palette

On Mac, by default, the **Audio palette** is located in the same window as the Time Controls palette. On Windows, it is grouped with the Info palette. You can separate the Audio palette into its own window by clicking and dragging the **Audio** tab.

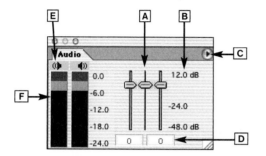

*The Audio palette: **A**. Level controls **B**. Level units **C**. Audio Options menu **D**. Level values* *E**. Audio Clipping warning icons **F**. VU (**V**olume **U**nit) meter. The audio level controls allow you to set the volume for each audio layer. The VU meter displays audio levels during playback. You will learn about these terms in Chapter 17, "Audio."*

Info Palette

The **Info palette** gives you information about images in the Composition window.

The Info palette offers color, alpha transparency, and coordinate information. You'll learn more about these topics throughout the book.

Tools Palette

The **Tools palette** provides a number of tools for drawing in the Composition window or for selecting elements and objects.

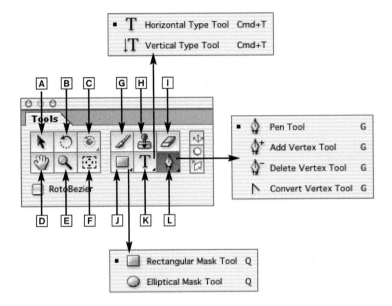

*The Tools palette: **A**. Selection **B**. Rotation **C**. Orbit Camera **D**. Hand **E**. Zoom **F**. Pan Behind **G**. Brush (new!) **H**. Clone Stamp (new!) **I**. Eraser (new!) **J**. Mask **K**. Type (new!) **L**. Pen. Note that some of these tools are new and reflect the capability of After Effects 6.0 to paint and type directly (rather than using external programs). You will learn about these different tools in future chapters.*

Shortcut Keys

There are many shortcut keys in After Effects, and all of them are listed in your program manual. The following chart lists the ones we find most useful. The book will refer to specific shortcut keys throughout the chapters as you encounter reasons to use them, so don't spend too much time memorizing them here. Consider copying this list and taping it to your monitor! This list will prove invaluable to you after you have learned the program.

Shortcuts in After Effects		
Command	**Mac**	**Windows**
Import file	Cmd+I	Ctrl+I
Project settings	Cmd+Option+Shift+K	Ctrl+Alt+Shift+K
Suspend window updates	Caps Lock	Caps Lock
Display/hide palettes	Tab	Tab
Step forward one frame	Cmd+right arrow	Ctrl+right arrow
Step backward one frame	Cmd+left arrow	Ctrl+left arrow
Start/pause playback	Spacebar	Spacebar
RAM preview	0 on numeric keypad	0 on numeric keypad
Nudge layer one pixel in specific direction	Arrow key	Arrow key
Select next layer back	Cmd+down arrow	Ctrl+down arrow
Select next layer forward	Cmd+up arrow	Ctrl+up arrow
Zoom in	. (period)	. (period)
Zoom out	, (comma)	, (comma)
Zoom in and resize window	Option +. (period)	Alt + . (period)
Zoom out and resize window	Option + , (comma)	Alt + , (comma)
Switch from Selection tool to Pen tool	Hold down Cmd	Hold down Ctrl

I._____Using the After Effects Interface

This exercise introduces you to the three primary windows in After Effects and lets you explore the basic functionality of each. In this exercise you will open an After Effects project file that has been prepared for you in advance.

1. Launch After Effects and open **interface.aep** from the **chap_02** folder that you have transferred to your hard drive from the **H•O•T CD-ROM**.

Note: It's very important that you transfer these files to your hard drive so that you can edit them in the future.

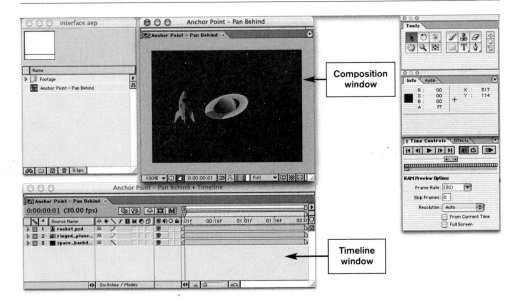

Notice that the Composition window and the Timeline window are open. Inside the Composition window, you'll see a preview of some artwork. Inside the Timeline window, you'll see a number of layers with a lot of settings. These settings will be described in detail in later chapters.

Note: If your palettes are unorganized because of moving them in the last chapter, choose ***Window > Reset Palette Locations.***

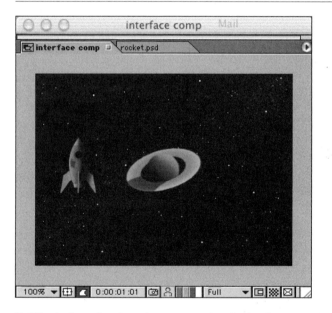

2. In the **Time Controls** palette, locate the **Play** button and click it. You can accomplish the same thing by pressing its shortcut key, the **spacebar**.

3. Watch the animation play as a preview in the **Composition window**. Click the **Play** button again in the **Time Controls** palette or press the **spacebar** to pause the animation.

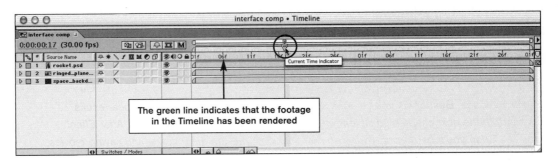

The green line indicates that the footage
in the Timeline has been rendered

4. In the **Timeline** window, locate the **Current Time Indicator**. Drag the **Current Time Indicator** left and right, and observe how its position affects the preview in the Composition window. This process is also known as "scrubbing" in the video editing industry.

Notice the green line in the Timeline window? This appears as After Effects "renders" the content to preview and play back. This green line will become a familiar cue to you as you work through the book's exercises. As you add things such as effects and 3D, playback can take longer because it takes longer to render the footage. It's helpful that you can position the Current Time Indicator to a specific frame, because sometimes you want to check a certain part of the Timeline but don't want to watch the playback of the entire composition.

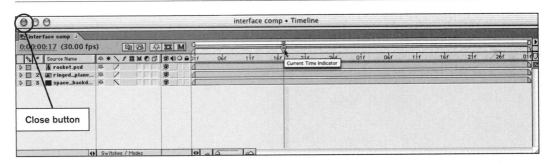

Close button

5. Click the **Close** button to close the Composition window. ***Note:*** The Close button for Windows users is in the upper-right corner of the Composition window.

*Observe that the Timeline window also closes. Without an open composition, the Timeline will not appear. To get the Timeline and the Composition windows back, simply double-click **interface comp** in the Project window.*

6. Close the project and don't save your changes. You can either quit After Effects or leave it open for the next chapter. You might want to choose **Window > Reset Palette Locations** to make sure that your palette positions in After Effects look the same for future chapters as they do in the book's examples.

Congratulations! You've completed your first exercise, and you got a good look at the After Effects interface. Best of all, you've been able to interact with After Effects and see results firsthand. In the next chapter, you'll learn more of the details involved in creating After Effect projects. Soon you'll be making your own compositions, making them move, and saving movies. Keep reading on!

3.

The Project

| What Is a Project? | Setting Up a Project |
| Importing Assets | Importing a Folder of Files |
| Organizing Your Project |

chap_03

After Effects 6
H•O•T CD-ROM

Animation, motion graphics, and visual effects often require a large number of individual images that make up a finished piece. Programs such as Photoshop and Illustrator store all the artwork for a picture on layers or flattened inside a single layer. After Effects is different in that it keeps art, video, and audio elements separate, allowing you to combine different kinds of documents in unrestricted ways. That is why an After Effects document is called a project instead of a file.

The **Project window** is where the program stores references to all the footage and image elements for your project. You were introduced to the Project window in the previous chapter. This window helps you organize images, movies, audio tracks, and compositions used by your project.

In this chapter, you'll learn exactly what a project is, and you'll see how to set up a project, import images, and organize items using the tools provided in After Effects.

What Is a Project?

An After Effects **project** is a single file that holds references to all of the images, video, and audio files that you'll need for your work. A **reference** is a pointer to the location of a file on your hard drive. After Effects uses references instead of copying the images, video, and audio files into the project file. Your project knows where to find the files it needs because After Effects automatically creates a reference to each file as part of the process of setting up your project.

In After Effects, all images, video, and audio elements—any media that After Effects uses inside a project—are called **footage** items.

In addition to holding references to footage, the project holds one or more **compositions** that you create in After Effects. You'll learn about compositions in detail in the next chapter. For now, think of compositions as the editing environment where all the action happens. You can't edit inside the Project window. The project holds all the footage and compositions that go into the final product that you create. In live-action filmmaking, a **shot** is the viewpoint from a single camera that is edited into film. In After Effects, you can think of a shot in the same way. You can create many versions, or **takes**, of the same shot, and keep all the takes in one project file. This is valuable, for instance, when working with clients. You can automatically maintain a record of exactly what you did in each take during the course of the project or easily show multiple versions of the same assignment.

It's also important to understand that when you save an After Effects document, that you are saving the project, not the individual footage items or compositions. The only way you can save a composition or compositions is to save the project file. Because an After Effects project file can contain multiple compositions, this is important to understand. Each time you save in After Effects, you're saving the reference to where all your footage items reside on your hard drive, and you're saving the updated the composition file or files. For this reason, project files are very small in file size, whereas the footage items that they reference might be huge.

Because saving is sooooo important, After Effects puts an asterisk by the filename every time the project has not been saved. Get in the habit of looking to see if the asterisk is showing. If it is, SAVE.

Only one project can be open at a time. Closing a project will close all windows associated with it and leave only the palettes open.

I. _____Creating and Setting Up a Project

Setting up a project in After Effects is quite simple. In this exercise, you'll create your first project, set basic project options, and learn to save the project.

When you open After Effects, in most cases an **untitled.aep** window will appear in the upper-left corner of your screen. This is the Project window that holds your footage items and compositions. Right now it is empty and untitled because you haven't saved it yet, and you haven't imported any footage or created any compositions. If this doesn't open automatically upon startup, choose **File > New > New Project**.

1. Create a new project and choose **File > Save As**. In the **Save Project As** dialog box, click the **New** button (Mac) or the **Create New Folder** icon (Windows) to create a new folder with the name **AE6 HOT Projects**.

This will be the place where you store all the exercises that you work on in this book. Saving your exercises in a different folder is important so that you don't write over the originals.

2. Navigate inside the new **HOT AE Projects** folder that you just created. Name the file **Space Project.aep** and click **Save**.

*Note for Window users: Name the files with no spaces, using an underscore instead— for example, **Space_Project.aep**.*

You've now successfully created a project and saved it. It's time to import footage into your project. You'll learn how to do this next.

3. Leave this file open for the next exercise.

Importing Assets (Also Known As Footage!)

As stated earlier, images, video, and audio tracks that are used in a project are called **footage items**. All footage items are considered to be **assets** for your project. Think of assets as valuable items necessary to create new compositions. Given how long it can take to create images, video, or sounds, they are truly assets!

Remember, when you import assets into After Effects, you don't actually copy the files into your project. With the import process, After Effects creates references inside your project to files that reside on your hard drive. In the following exercises, you will learn to import several different types of footage assets into your new After Effects project. Each type of footage asset has its own characteristics, and After Effects offers many options to take advantage of various file formats.

After Effects is a very forgiving program. It will import almost anything—Photoshop, TIF, EPS, Illustrator, AIF, WAV, MOV, and so on. Many other animation and nonlinear editing software applications are very picky about file formats and types of medium—not so with After Effects.

2. ————————Importing Photoshop Documents

In this exercise, you will learn to import a series of Photoshop files that have already been prepared for you. The files are located in the **chap_03** folder of the **exercise files** folder that you should have transferred to your hard drive from the **H•O•T CD-ROM**. If you haven't transferred these files yet, please do so now.

1. Choose **File > Import > File** and navigate to the **chap_03 > 01_space scene** folder that you transferred to your hard drive from the **H•O•T CD-ROM**.

2. Select all the items that end in **.psd** by holding down the **Shift** key as you click on each file. The **Import As: Footage** option should be selected. Click **Import** (Mac) or **Open** (Windows).

*Note: Using the **Shift** key allows you to select multiple files that are next to each other in the same folder. To select multiple files that aren't next to each other, use the **Cmd** key (Mac) or **Ctrl** key (Windows). This is referred to as a* contiguous *or* discontiguous *multiple selection.*

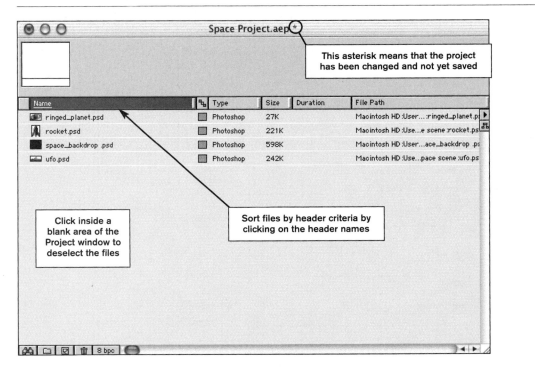

3. For each item that contains multiple layers, you'll see a prompt box like this. Click **OK** for each item.

*Photoshop files can have multiple layers. This import process ensures that all layers are flattened or "merged" for this particular project. New to After Effects 6.0 is the capability to choose the Footage Dimensions. The default setting is Layer Size. For now, click **OK** to choose the defaults. You will learn to work with more complex layered Photoshop files in future chapters.*

4. Click inside a blank area of the Project window to deselect the **PSD** file listings. Widen your Project window and observe the additional information available. You can click on any of the panel headings (**Name**, **Label**, **Type**, **Size**, **Duration**, or **File Path**) to sort the project by those criteria. Narrow the Project window to return it to a smaller view, and make sure that the **Name** header is selected.

In the Project window title bar, an asterisk appears at the end of the filename. This means that you've made changes to your After Effects project that have not been saved.

5. Save your project now, either by choosing **File > Save**, or by pressing **Cmd+S** (Mac) or **Ctrl+S** (Windows). Leave the file open; you will continue to work with it in the next exercise.

Notice that the asterisk goes away as soon as you save the file. The asterisk is a handy message from After Effects to remind you to save your work.

Note: There are many ways to import Photoshop files, including the capability to work with all the layers of a file. Before you learn to import this way, you'll need to understand what a composition is. You'll learn about this in Chapter 4, "Composition."

NOTE | Lost Footage

After Effects is pretty powerful when it comes to locating footage on your hard drive. Even if you move or rename footage after you've quit the program, After Effects can often locate it without any effort on your part. If you ever want to give your After Effects project to a client or coworker (or your grandmother or whomever!), there is a handy feature that lets you collect all the footage into one neat folder. You'll learn how to do this in Chapter 18, "*Rendering Final Movies.*"

Meanwhile, what to do if After Effects can't find your footage? The files will appear in your Project window as aliases, and the names will be in italics. Double-click on the alias name, and the Import File dialog box opens. Navigate to the lost footage, and it will reconnect.

3. ————————————Importing Illustrator Documents

Illustrator files are great to work with in After Effects. That's because they are resolution independent, unlike Photoshop files. This means that if you zoom into an Illustrator file during an animation, it will stay crisp and in perfect focus. A Photoshop file would get progressively pixelated, depending on how high the magnification of your zoom into the artwork was. For this reason, After Effects and Illustrator work really well together. Importing Illustrator files is quite simple, as you'll soon learn.

Note: Unfortunately, if you're not an Illustrator user, the support for Adobe tools is better than for Macromedia FreeHand, CorelDRAW, or other vector applications. If you use another kind of application, save the file as an EPS and import it that way. Sadly, you lose the advantage to work with layers this way.

⊖ ⊖ ⊖	Space Project.aep		
Name		Type	S
🖼 ringed_planet.psd		▫ Photoshop	▶
🖼 rocket.psd		▫ Photoshop	🔒
▪ space_backdrop .psd		▫ Photoshop	
🖼 ufo.psd		▫ Photoshop	

> **Double-click anywhere in a blank part of this window, and the Import File dialog box will appear! This technique is faster than going to the menu to select File > Import > Import File.**

1. Double-click on a blank area of the Project window. Notice that this action also brings up the **Import File** dialog box. This is easier than choosing **File > Import > Import File** and is the way I prefer to import footage.

2. Navigate to the **chap_03** > **illustrator files** folder. Select **monkey1.ai** and click **Import** (Mac) or **Open** (Windows).

3. In the prompt window, click **OK** to accept **Merged Layers** and **Layer Size**.

*New to After Effects 6.0 is the capability to choose the footage dimension of **Layer Size** or **Document Size**. For now, this decision is unimportant, and its significance is lost until you learn to work with compositions (Chapter 4) and setting keyframe properties (Chapter 5).*

Notice that the Illustrator file is added to the Project window, and the asterisk in the title bar indicates that you have changed your project and have not yet saved.

4. Save your project. Leave the file open—you will continue to work with it in the next exercise.

4. ——————————Importing QuickTime Movies

QuickTime movies are easy to import into an After Effects project. The efficiency and portability of QuickTime is truly a timesaver when working with moving images because QuickTime movies contain a sequence of images in a neat package. In this exercise, you'll learn how to import QuickTime movies.

1. Double-click inside a blank area of the Project window to open the **Import File** dialog box.

Import File

Show: [All Acceptable Files ▼]

From: [📁 01_ space scene ▼]

📁 01_ space scene ▶	📄 flames.mov
📁 illustrator files ▶	📄 ringed_planet.psd
	📄 rocket.psd
	⬛ space_backdrop .psd
	📄 ufo.psd
	📄 waving_monkey.mov

Format: QuickTime Movie

Import As: [Footage ▼]

☐ Sequence not available
☐ Force alphabetical order

(Find)   (Find Again)   (Import Folder)

Go to: [ ]

(Add to Favorites)   (Cancel) (Import)

---

2. Browse to the **chap_03 > 01_space scene** folder. Select both QuickTime movies by holding down the **Cmd** key (Mac) or **Ctrl** key (Windows) while you click on the files. These shortcut keys allow you to select files that are not right next to each other (a discontiguous selection). Click **Import** (Mac) or **Open** (Windows).

3. The QuickTime footage has been added to your Project window. In the Project window, click in a blank area to deselect the files that you just imported. Double-click on the **waving_monkey.mov** file inside the Project window, and press the **spacebar**. This plays the movie. If you double-click on any of the footage that you've imported so far, you can view it in its own window.

4. Close the **waving_monkey.mov** file by clicking on the **Close** button (upper left on Mac, upper right on Windows). Notice again that the title bar shows an asterisk after the filename. Save your project and leave the file open—you will continue to work with it in future exercises.

NOTE | What Is a QuickTime Movie?

Think of a QuickTime movie as an extremely handy container. Rather than having many different image files and a separate audio file, a QuickTime movie allows you to place all of the frames and synchronized audio into one neat package. With the QuickTime player installed on your computer, a single QuickTime file will play back hundreds or thousands of images with synchronous sound. Many other settings are available as well. Many of QuickTime's options are covered throughout this book.

NOTE | What About Macromedia Flash, Windows Media, and Real Networks Movie Formats?

QuickTime is used as the exclusive movie format while authoring content in After Effects. You can export final movies in many other formats, including Macromedia Flash, Microsoft Windows Media, and Real Network Movie files. You'll learn how to do this in Chapter 18, "*Rendering Final Movies.*"

5. Importing a Folder of File Types at One Time

In the past few exercises, you imported Photoshop, Illustrator, and QuickTime files separately. You don't have to work this way—you could have chosen to import all the different file types at once, and After Effects would have figured out what type of files they were automatically. In this exercise, you'll learn how to delete the files you've imported thus far from the Project window and import all the files in one fell swoop. Sound better? It is.

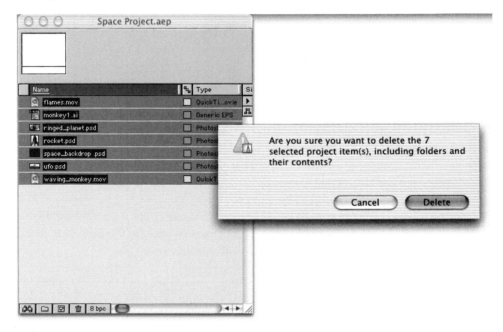

1. Shift+click to select all the files in the Project window. Press the **Delete** key to delete them. You will be prompted to confirm that this is what you really want to do. Click **Delete**.

Note: You are only deleting the reference to these files in the After Effects project. The files are still on your hard drive, so don't worry!

2. Double-click inside a blank area in the Project window to bring forth the **Import File** dialog box. Navigate to the **chap_03** folder and select it. Click the **Import Folder** button. Click **OK** multiple times to accept the merged layer version of the files.

3. All the files will come in at once in the same folder container that you selected on your hard drive. Click on the **arrow** to the left of the folder to easily reveal the folder contents.

It was a deliberate decision to have you learn to open the different types of files in separate exercises to have an opportunity to focus on each file type. In reality, importing all the footage at once is much faster!

Another neat feature of importing the folder is that you can organize your content so you can find it more easily. As you progress with your project, you may have hundreds of files in the Project window. Using folders is a great way to get organized.

4. Save the project, and leave it open for the next exercise.

6. _____Creating Folders

By creating folders and organizing project assets, you can access footage in a way that makes the most sense to you. This can be a real aid when you have a deadline and you're desperately looking for something that you need right away. After Effects allows you to create folders in the Project window. This is a great way to organize footage items. There are two ways to create folders. You'll learn both methods in this exercise.

1. Choose **File > New > New Folder**.

This creates a new folder inside the Project window. The folder name will be highlighted and ready to accept a new name

2. In the Project window, name the new folder **Stills** and press **Return** (Mac) or **Enter** (Windows).

*Note: If you need to rename the folder for any reason, select the folder and press the **Return** key (Mac) or **Enter** key (Windows). This allows you to type a new name.*

3. Drag the Photoshop files into the **Stills** folder.

Notice that the arrow to the left of the Stills folder can be clicked to hide or show the contents of the folder.

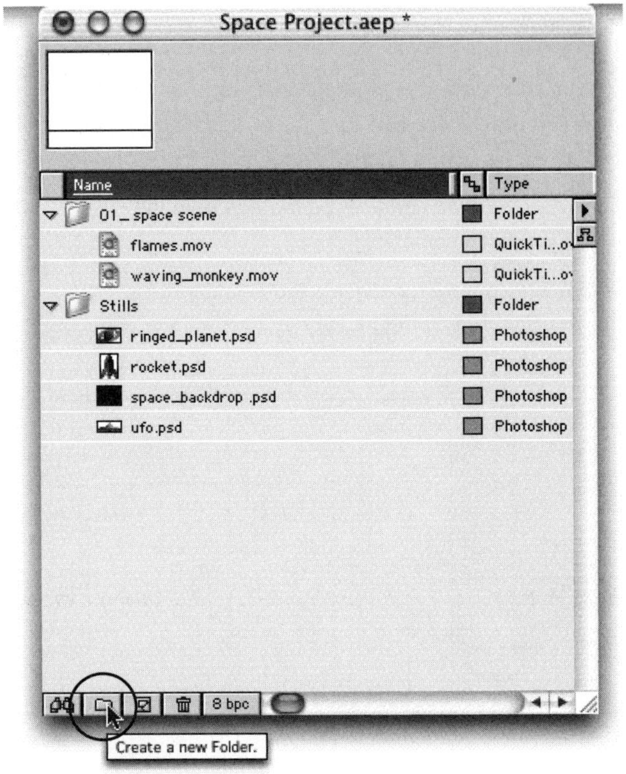

4. At the bottom of the Project window, click the **folder** icon.

This is another way to create a new folder.

---

5. Name your new folder **Movies**.

---

6. Drag all of the QuickTime (**.mov**) documents into the **Movies** folder. The project is now much more nicely organized.

---

7. Now that you're finished with the **01_ space scene** folder, select it in the Project window and press the **Delete** key to remove it.

---

8. Save and close the project file. You've finished this chapter!

Test Yourself on This Chapter!

You might not realize that you learned a lot of new procedures in this chapter. See if you can remember how to do the following on your own, without looking at the book.

A. Save and name a new project.

B. Import Photoshop, Illustrator, and QuickTime footage. You can use the footage from the **chap_03** exercise files, or try your own files if you have some!

C. Create folders to organize your footage and place your footage inside those folders.

D. Save the project.

If you don't remember how to do some of these procedures, reread the exercises and then try again on your own.

You've now successfully completed everything you need to do to set up, organize, and import footage assets into your first project! You'll learn some of the deeper nuances to working in the Project window as you work though other exercises later in this book.

If you feel ready, move on to the next chapter—or feel free to pick the book up again after taking a break.

4.

The Composition

chap_04

After Effects 6
H·O·T CD-ROM

Up until now, you have learned how to create a project file. The project file holds references to all your footage, but the composition is where you put this footage to use. Without a composition, you cannot create animation, video, graphics, or audio. Think of the composition as the instructions that tell After Effects what to do with your footage and as the preview that shows you how those instructions are being executed.

In this chapter, you'll get to know exactly what a composition is. You'll also see how to work with the Composition window—your main visual window that provides many options for working with the images you compose.

What Is a Composition?

A **composition** is where you make your footage come to life through animation, filters, combining of footage, masking, and all kinds of other efforts that you will learn about throughout this book.

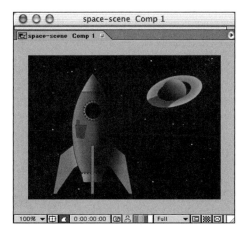

Compositions appear within your Project window along with other footage items. They have their own special icons. When you open the composition, by double-clicking on it from the Project window, you'll see two windows. The first is called, appropriately enough, the **Composition** window.

In the Composition window, you can graphically interact with the images in your composition. You can think of this window as being similar to a painter's canvas, because you visualize your design in it. You can also preview animation in the Composition window to see your animation move.

The second window associated with a composition is the **Timeline** window. Your composition settings are visible in this window.

Think of the Timeline window as the equivalent of a musical score that will be interpreted to create your finished piece. The settings you make here are like musical notations, and your finished piece will be your final animation. Note that the Composition and Timeline windows are separate, but one will not open or close without the other. If you are working and you lose your Timeline and Composition windows, you need to reopen them from your Project window.

Compositions are your frame-by-frame instructions to After Effects. Ultimately, After Effects will read your instructions, interpret them for each frame, and perform an output of your final product based on the settings you specify in your composition.

Unlike footage items that are created outside of After Effects in programs such as Photoshop, Illustrator, or Premiere, compositions can be made only from within your After Effects project. Compositions reside inside the project file, and cannot be saved separately on your hard drive, as other footage items can.

Your project can have as many different compositions as you wish. You can try out multiple versions of an idea by creating multiple compositions and keep all of them in the project file, or you can choose to delete compositions that you no longer need.

I. ————————Composition Settings

Starting a composition requires that you define a few settings. In the following exercises, you will learn to define settings by using the Composition Settings window. When you set up a new composition, you'll automatically see the Composition Settings window. It's best to decide on all the options in the Composition Settings window early in your composition. Most of the options are obvious, and we'll explain any terms that may be new to you.

1. Create a new project by choosing **File > New > New Project**.

2. Choose **File > Save As** and navigate to the **AE6 HOT Projects** folder you created in the previous chapter. Save this new empty file as **Composition Chapter.aep**. You'll be filling it soon with footage and a composition.

3. In the Project window, click on the **Create a new composition** button. The **Composition Settings** window will appear.

4. In the **Composition Settings** window, change the **Composition Name** to **First Comp1**. Make sure that you set the **Start Timecode** to **0:00:00:01** and end it at **0:00:02:00**.

Naming your composition appropriately is important. Because most projects go through several versions, it's a good idea to give each version a number. If you should have to output to two different media types (such as video and film), you'll want different names for each set of compositions to distinguish the two output types. Another reason to name composition versions carefully is that your client may make changes as the project moves along. Giving each composition its own name or number will allow you to keep track of version changes.

5. Match the remaining settings to the picture you see in Step 4, and visit the chart that follows this exercise to learn more about what the different options are. Click **OK** to accept the settings.

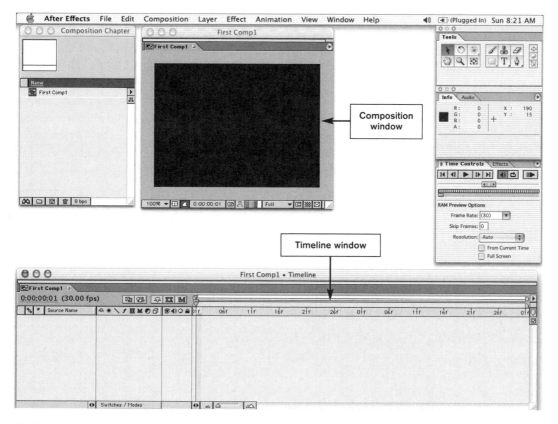

Notice that two things happen: a Composition window and Timeline appear. You'll get to work with these two windows in the next exercise—hold tight!

---

6. Make sure **First Comp1** is highlighted in the Project window, and choose **Composition > Composition Settings**, or use **Cmd+K** (Mac) or **Ctrl+K** (Windows).

The Composition Settings window reopens. If you ever need to change your composition settings, you can change them at any time. Leave them alone for now, and be sure to read the upcoming chart so you understand what they mean.

---

7. Save the project, and leave it open for the next exercise. You'll be taking a short break to do some reading before getting going again so you can better understand the significance of what you just did.

Composition Settings

One of the best things about composition settings is that they can always be changed at a later date. This means that you can work one way as you're brainstorming and creating, and output a different way when you're finished. Few programs offer the level of flexibility that After Effects does, and the composition settings are at the hub of many critical choices that are sometimes hard to determine until you're further along in the creative process. Sometimes a client has been known to change his or her mind, too! Once you've created a composition and fixed its settings, you can always bring back the Composition Settings dialog box to edit by choosing **Composition > Composition Settings**. Here's a handy chart to help you better understand what all those settings mean.

Composition Settings Chart	
Setting	**Description**
Preset	The Preset menu contains many choices for common sizes and resolutions. It contains settings for video, film, Web, and many others. Because you are learning After Effects in this book, the 320×240 size is small enough to render quickly but not so big that it gets in the way of learning. As you take on personal or professional projects, you will likely choose to use a different preset to match your output goals.
Width, Height, Aspect Ratio	As you change presets, the width and height settings will change depending on your needs. You can use the **Preset** menu to change these settings, or you can type custom values into the field. If you leave **Lock Aspect Ratio to 4:3** checked, you can type in a width, and After Effects will automatically calculate the height. A 4:3 aspect ratio is correct for many video, multimedia, and film format sizes. It ensures that the shape of your screen will be wider than it is tall, kind of like a TV screen or movie theater screen.
Pixel Aspect Ratio	Computer screens are composed of perfectly square pixels; however, video screens are composed of pixels that are rectangular (wider than they are tall)—referred to as "nonsquare pixels" in the video editing world. Because this book has the goal to teach you After Effects and has you working on your computer screen instead of a video screen, working with square pixels is fine. If you take on any projects that go to video, you will want to change this setting to one of the many video options that this menu offers, such as **DV**, **D1 NTSC**, **D1 PAL**, and so on. Note that when you change the format from square pixels to a nonsquare format, your footage may look slightly squished. It will unsquish once you output the final material to video. In the latest version of Photoshop (Photoshop CS), you can actually create images in nonsquare pixel formats so that they don't appear squished as you work on them. The nonsquare pixel format will look unsquished on your screen, but it will still scale properly when output to video.

continues on next page

Composition Settings Chart *continued*

Setting	Description
Frame Rate	Different kinds of output require different frame rates. An upcoming section in this chapter covers the different frame rate choices and describes in more detail what they mean and when to use them. Video runs at **30 frames per second**, and this number is fine for the purposes of this chapter. You'll soon learn firsthand that these settings are not set in stone and can be changed easily at a later time.
Resolution	You can choose to work at **Full**, **Half**, **Quarter**, or **Custom** resolution. This means that you will preview the footage at 1:1, 1:2, 1:4, or a custom setting. When working on large formats for film or using intense effects filters or 3D (which take extra time to render), many After Effects artists scale down the resolution so they can get a quick preview. You can always change this setting when you render the final movie. You'll learn more about rendering in Chapter 18, "*Rendering Final Movies.*" The great thing about this setting is that it is not permanent. You can choose to work at half resolution, but your full resolution footage isn't altered. That means you can always output full resolution at a later date, and none of the quality will be lost.
Start Timecode	Frame **0:00:00:01** means that it is the first frame of the duration of this particular composition. Sometimes, when dealing with footage that gets combined later with a film or video product, After Effects artists want to have their numbers match an edited sequence that has a very specific timecode. If you were to change this setting to not start on Frame 1, it could be set to match the timecode of external video footage. Most people, especially beginners, start on Frame 1. By the way, Frame 0:00:00:01 is the same as Frame 1. The zeros stand for hours, minutes, seconds, and frames—hence the different sets of zeros.
Duration	In this case, the duration of the composition is set for 2 seconds (or 0:00:02:00 in timecode-speak). You can always change the duration of a composition, which you will learn to do in later exercises in Chapter 5, "*Keyframes, Animation, and Timeline.*"

NOTE | Determining Duration

Frames per second (fps) refers to the number of frames changed sequentially before your eyes each second to create the illusion of moving pictures. To compute the number of frames for your composition, divide the duration by the number of frames per second.

For example, you might be using a standard video frame rate of 30 frames per second. If you have 300 frames in your composition, the calculation would be 300 / 30 = 10. Thus, your composition would be 10 seconds long.

Or you might be using a standard motion picture frame rate of 24 frames per second. If you have 240 frames in your composition, the calculation would be 240 / 24 = 10. Here too, the length of time for your composition would be 10 seconds.

NOTE | Determining Pixel Aspect Ratio

Most display devices in computer graphics use square pixels. This means that the height and width of the pixels are exactly the same. However, many video systems and anamorphic film projects (shot with a special lens) use display systems that are not square. The height of a non-square display system is not the same as its width, and these pixels are rectangular in shape.

How do you determine when you need to use square pixels or choose another option? The basic rule is this: If you are working on a project that will not be output to video or film, use square pixels.

If you are working on a video project, determine which video format you are using and select it from the menu. In the United States, the most common video format is D1/DV NTSC. In Europe, the most standard video format is D1/DV PAL.

If you are working on a film project, talk to your supervisor or client before deciding to use square pixels or Anamorphic 2:1. Unless you are a multimillionaire making your own film, you will have a supervisor. If you are a multimillionaire making your own film, hire someone who has a great deal of experience in motion picture visual effects as a consultant before making a determination. Although there are standard operating procedures, many film productions have special ways of doing things. Motion picture production is very expensive, and making assumptions can lead to formidable difficulties.

NOTE | More About Timecode

The Start Frame and Start Timecode settings can be critical when working on a video project. Video editors, for example, use timecode as a system to log all editing decisions. You may be asked to start a sequence or animation at a certain point in time, based on timecode numbering. Timecode specifies the exact hour, minute, second, and frame within a video piece.

0:00:00:01

Here is a starting point displayed as timecode. Notice the colons separating the numbers. The first number is the hour (0), followed by a colon; the second number is the minute (00), followed by a colon; the third number is the seconds (00), followed by a colon; the last number is the frame (01).

The Project Settings

In the last chapter, you learned about a project and its significance to the After Effects workflow. That chapter didn't cover the project settings because they relate more to compositions, even though they also relate to the project. The composition settings you just learned about affect individual shots within your project. It still might not be clear that a single project can contain numerous compositions. This will become more clear as you continue through this chapter. The project settings affect all the compositions you create, and they create global settings to the entire project. The composition settings create local settings to an individual composition.

To see the project settings for this (or any other) project, choose **File > Project Settings**. Don't change the settings, because you want to be on the default Timecode Base setting for the duration of this book. Still, it's important to understand that these settings are here, and what they mean, for future projects.

A handy chart on the next page describes what these settings mean.

Project Settings	
Setting	**Description**
Timecode Base	This is the setting to choose when you are authoring for video, Web, DVD, or multimedia. Most video is set to 30 fps, but the menu here offers other choices in the event you want something different.
NTSC	Unfortunately, NTSC video drops frames every so often, making it very difficult to count frames in a linear fashion. Most people leave their settings to **Non-Drop Frame** so that the frame numbers will advance sequentially in After Effects' Timeline. The reality is that when you output to video, you will be working with 29.97 frames per second. For this book's purposes, you'll leave this setting to Non-Drop Frame. Frankly, most After Effects artists leave this setting to Non-Drop Frame in order to count frames more easily. It doesn't affect the final output to video and is really there for preview and editing purposes.
Frames	If you choose this setting, After Effects will count frames instead of hours, minutes, seconds, and frames. Most animators doing cel or character animation are accustomed to working this way, because animators typically number their drawings sequentially and refer to their artwork by its frame numbers. This setting will not be used in this book, but it is here if you want it.
Feet + Frames	This is the setting to choose if you are authoring for film. Film is measured by feet and frames, and 35 mm film runs 24 frames per second. Therefore, with 35 mm film, a foot is 24 frames. If you were looking at Frame 120 in this context, you would divide the number into 24, and it would result in a measurement of 4ft, 6 frames. It's a confusing way to measure time to anyone who isn't a filmmaker, so I don't advise using this setting unless you are working on an actual film project. You have the choice here of **35mm** or **16mm.** The **Start Numbering Frames** setting refers to the numbering for the first frame. Typically, filmmakers call the first frame number 1, but this setting allows you to enter any value you want.
Color Depth	For most projects, **8 bits** per channel is the correct setting. The only systems that accept **16 bits** per channel are film systems that are expensive beyond the needs of most After Effects artists. It is great that you can use After Effects on a high-end film production project if you need it, though!

2. ——————Getting Footage into the Composition

Now that you've created and opened a composition, you're probably wondering how to get it to do something. The first step is to bring some footage into it, and the next step is to learn to animate that footage. In this exercise, you will learn to bring footage into a composition. In the next chapter, you'll learn how to animate footage in a Composition window. You cannot animate footage without a Timeline, and you cannot gain access to a Timeline without a composition. Understanding the relationship among the project, composition, and Timeline is key to understanding After Effects. This exercise should be a great help in unfolding the mystery of why you need all these things!

1. Double-click inside the blank area in the Project window. This causes the **Import File** dialog box to open.

2. Navigate to the **chap_04** folder and click **Import Folder**. This will import the entire folder of footage in one action. Click **OK** to the multiple dialog boxes that ask you to merge the PSD layers and accept the layer dimensions.

You learned in the last chapter that there's no need to import the footage items separately; however, you can import individual footage items or an entire folder of footage at once, depending on your needs.

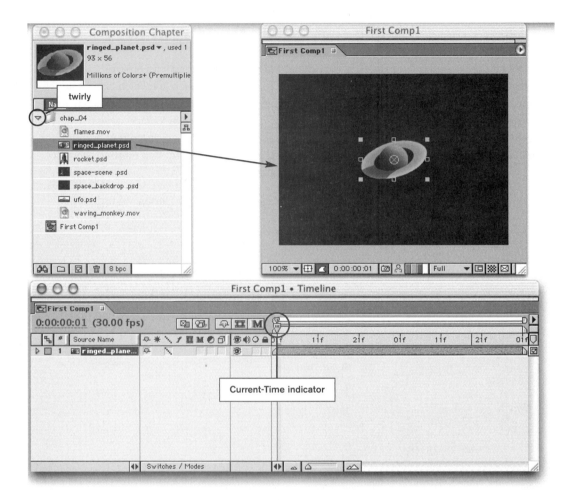

3. In the **Project** window, click on the **chap_04** twirly (a "twirly" is the official and affectionate After Effects term that describes the triangle to the left of the folder) to reveal the footage you just imported. Drag the file **ringed_planet.psd** into the **Composition** window.

There are several noteworthy events to observe once you complete this task. Notice that the file appears in the Timeline at the same time? The Timeline and the Composition window are tied together—nothing can happen in one window without affecting the other. Notice that the duration in the Timeline is the full two seconds, represented by the pink bar that stretches across the Timeline window. By default, a still picture will stretch as long as the duration of the composition if the Current Time Indicator is set to the first frame.

4. With **ringed_planet.psd** selected, either in the Composition window or the Timeline, press **Delete**. It will disappear from both the Composition and Timeline windows.

Notice that it has been deleted only from the composition and Timeline, and not from the project. This is significant. Your footage exists in the project whether it is in a composition or not.

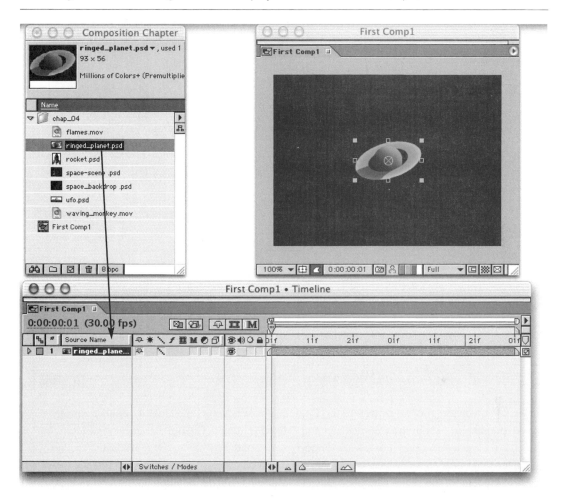

5. This time, drag **ringed_planet.psd** from the **Project** window directly into the **Timeline** window. It will appear in both the Composition and Timeline windows.

The benefit of using this technique is that the footage is automatically centered in the middle of the Composition window. This centering thing is a big deal. Get into the habit of dropping footage into the Timeline whenever you need it centered. Other than that, either method works fine.

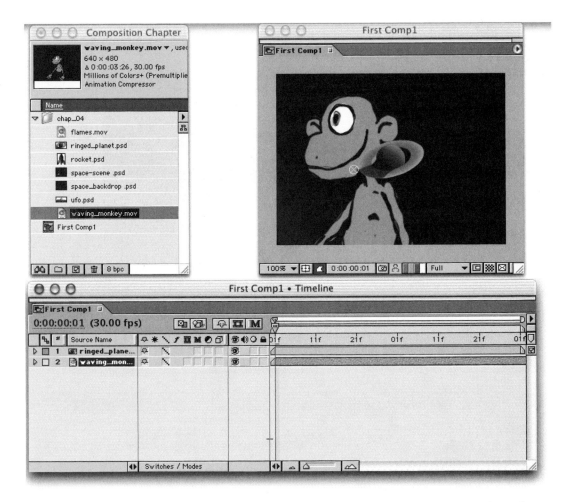

6. Next, drag **waving_monkey.mov** into the Composition window. Notice that it appears above the **ringed_planet.psd** in both the Composition and Project windows. Change its stacking order in the Timeline window by dragging it below the **ringed_planet.psd**. You can easily move layers around within the Timeline window by simply dragging them into different positions. The topmost files are visible in the foreground of the Composition window and have lower numbers in the Timeline.

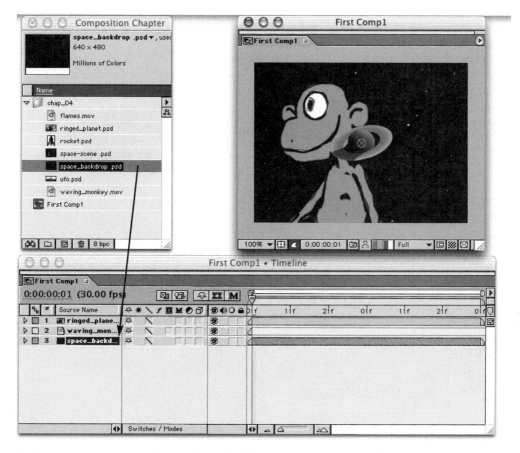

7. Next, drag **space_backdrop.psd** into the Timeline window, but position the file at the bottom of the stack. The stars will appear behind the monkey—no problem!

8. Press the **spacebar** to watch the contents of your composition and press it again to stop the preview. This is a fast way to observe your work. You'll learn a lot more about previewing work in future chapters.

9. Click the **Close** box of the Timeline window to close both the Composition and Timeline windows. These two windows are tied at the hip! Close one, and the other closes, too.

10. Double-click the **First Comp1** listing inside the Project window. This reopens the Composition window. It's good practice to recognize that you can reopen these windows easily in the event you accidentally close one of them.

11. Choose **File > Save**. When you save the project, it saves all the footage references and the composition, so there's no need or way to save those things separately. Leave the project open for the next exercise.

3. ————————Importing a Photoshop File as a Composition

So far, you have learned how to create a composition from scratch and how to import footage into a composition. Next, you'll learn a great technique related to Photoshop files. The After Effects Timeline has layers, and Photoshop files have layers. Wouldn't it be cool if you could compose the layers in Photoshop and have them appear that way inside After Effects? Well, you can, and this exercise shows you how.

1. Double-click inside the blank area of the Project window to open the **Import File** dialog box.

2. Navigate to **chap_04** folder and open it to look inside. Select the file called **space-scene.psd**. From the **Import As** drop-down menu, choose **Composition** and then click **Import**.

*In past exercises, you've chosen **Import As: Footage**. When you choose to import a file as a composition, the layers of the Photoshop file are preserved. The other choice, **Import As: Composition – Cropped Layers**, is new to After Effects 6. A cropped composition will look at the Photoshop transparency in the different layers and will crop in tight on each layer's content. This is helpful once you start to animate, because the center of each layer is dictated by the size of the layer, not the overall Photoshop document size. It used to be that After Effects would make each layer—regardless of content—the same size (which is what it has done in this example). You'll get to work with the new cropping choice in Chapter 5, "Keyframes, Animation, and Timeline."*

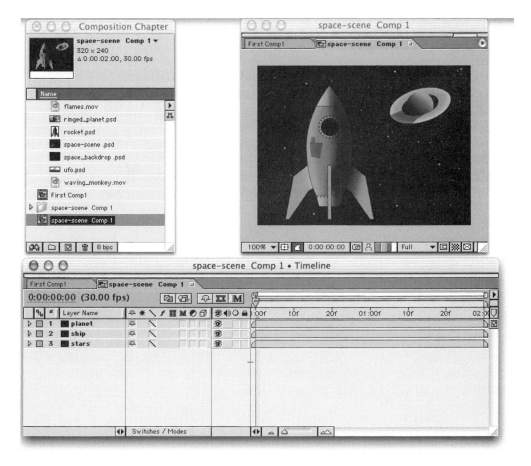

3. Notice that two files appear inside your Project window—a folder called **space-scene Comp 1** and a brand-new composition named **space-scene Comp 1**. Double-click on the **space-scene Comp 1** composition to open it. It's okay that your other composition is still open.

Whenever you import a Photoshop document as a composition, After Effects produces two files in the Project window: the footage folder and a composition. Both files take on whatever name the Photoshop document had. It's a little confusing that they're both named identically, but you can see that one displays a folder icon and the other a composition icon.

In the Composition window, also notice that you can have two (or more!) compositions open at once. Tabs appear in the Composition and Timeline windows with the name of each composition. This illustrates that you can also have multiple compositions inside a project. Often, when you're working on a big project, you might choose to separate elements into individual compositions or keep different versions active within a single project.

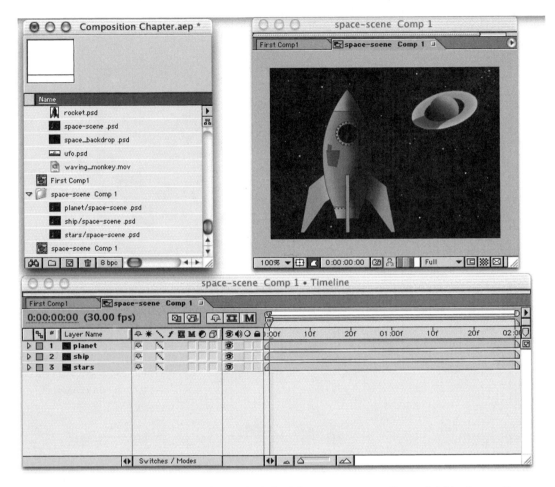

4. In the Project window, click the **twirly** to the left of the **space-scene Comp 1** folder to see its contents. It contains the three layers of the composition as three separate footage items. If you import Photoshop footage as merged layers, as you've done in past exercises, you won't be able to access individual layers as you can now. Also notice that the same Photoshop layer names appear inside the Timeline window. Way cool, eh?

5. Save and keep the project open for the next exercise.

4. ────────Creating a Composition from Footage Settings

There's another way to create a composition in After Effects, and it can be a great timesaver. In this exercise, you will learn to make a composition from a footage file. You'll see firsthand how and why this will be a valuable skill in your After Effects arsenal.

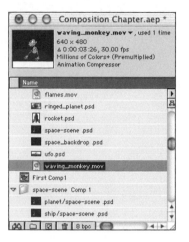

1. In the Project window, click on **waving_monkey.mov** and observe the information about this footage that appears at the top of the window. Notice that the file is 640×480, that it's 0:00:03:26 long, and that it was recorded at 30 frames per second. You could create a composition that size and duration with that setting and drag in this file. Or…

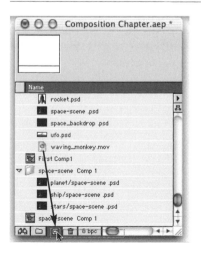

2. Drag the **waving_monkey.mov** file on the **Create a new composition** icon at the bottom of the Project window.

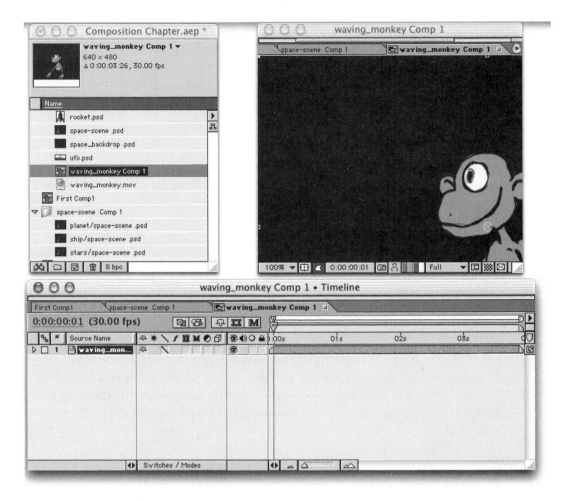

Notice that this action produced the instant creation of a new composition and Timeline that are named after the footage item.

3. The item **waving_monkey Comp 1** should be automatically selected in the **Project** window. If not, make sure it is selected and choose **Composition > Composition Settings**. The Composition Settings dialog box will appear for this composition. Notice how the settings match the footage properties. Click **OK**—you're not really changing anything, just looking!

This is a great technique when you want one footage item to dictate the settings for a composition. It's especially useful with movie footage, which can vary in frames per second, timecode, and duration.

4. Since the **waving_monkey.mov** was 640×480, so is this composition. You might want to expand the Composition window to see the difference.

5. Save and close the project—you won't be needing it any more for this chapter.

Test Yourself on This Chapter!

Try this short review of this chapter and the previous one to be sure that you know how to set up a project and a composition without reading our directions. The following suggested steps are intentionally vague to allow you to test your new knowledge. If you need a refresher on how to do any of these tasks, reread the pertinent exercises in this chapter and Chapter 3, "*The Project*."

A. Create a new project and save it to the **AE6 HOT Projects** folder you created in Chapter 3.

B. Import the artwork from the folder called **chap_04**.

C. Import a Photoshop file as a composition.

D. Create a composition using any of the methods taught in this chapter.

E. Drag the footage you imported from your Project window into the Timeline window.

F. Save and close the project.

That's a wrap for this chapter. You've learned how to make a composition, which might not seem like much but is a very important part of learning After Effects. These steps were necessary skill builders to get you ready to create animation. In the next chapter, you'll be at the point where it all comes together in the form of a moving composition! See you there.

5.

Keyframes, Animation, and Timeline

| What Is a Keyframe? | Setting Keyframes |

| What Is a Property? | Animating Multiple Properties |

| Using Bézier Handles with Motion Paths |

| Mixing Spatial Interpolation | Types | Anchor Points |

chap_05

After Effects 6
H•O•T CD-ROM

Because After Effects is a motion graphics tool, creating motion is at the heart of its power. A professional animator and motion graphics artist needs to know how to create movement that is deliberate and oftentimes complex. Some kinds of motion projects require the use of subtle movement, and others require the use of wild and erratic movement. You can achieve this kind of control over your motion by mastering the use of keyframes.

Keyframe action is set up using the Timeline interface of After Effects. You won't believe how deep the science of keyframes is until you read this chapter and work through its exercises. You'll see that some kinds of keyframes can create movement that speeds up or slows down, other kinds of keyframes can create curved paths, and still other kinds can smooth movement or make it jerky. Once you complete this chapter, you will have set a foundation for creating motion that will last your entire professional life.

Viewing the Timeline

This chapter focuses on using the Timeline for setting keyframes and animating properties of layers. The Timeline interface has a few features you haven't seen yet that will be useful to understand before proceeding.

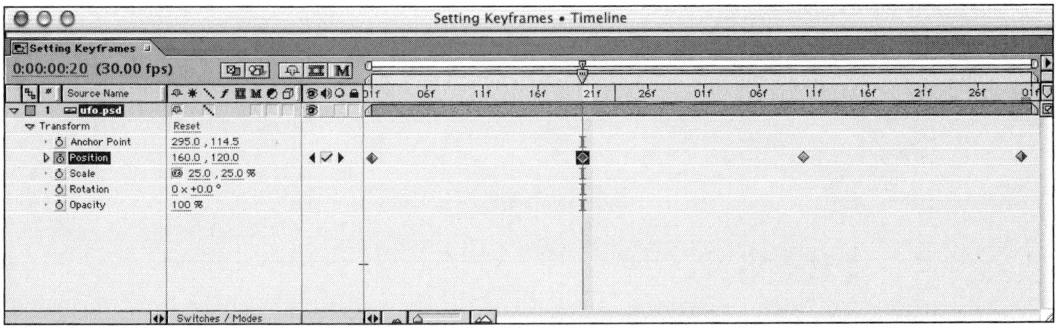

The Timeline window can be opened wider, which enables you to see more content. People with large monitor displays love this!

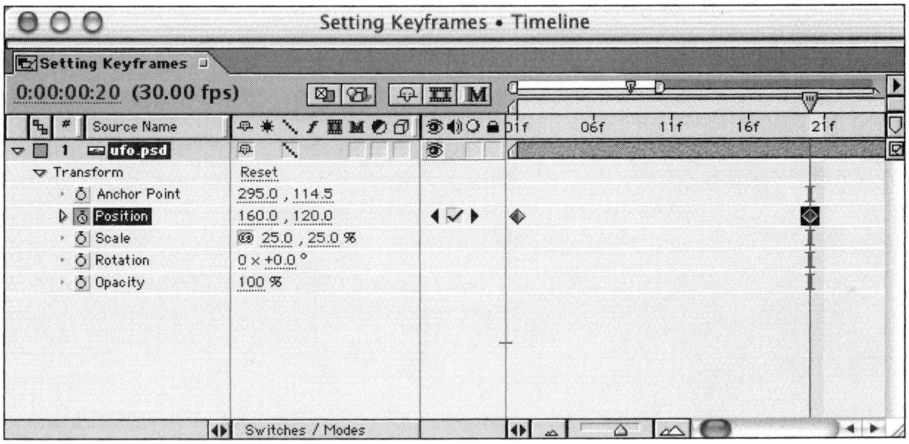

People working on laptops and smaller displays might have to shrink the Timeline. Doing so after stretching it causes the Timeline to get clipped, as you see in the above screen shot.

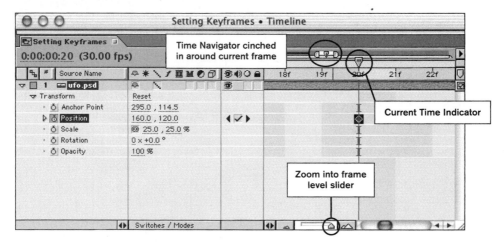

If this happens, you can shrink the Timeline back to fit the smaller window by using the **Time Navigator** slider. Simply stretch it to the location you want the Timeline content to fill.

You can also use the Time Navigator to zoom into the specific part of the Timeline where the **Current Time Indicator** resides. This is useful to check a frame you are working on or to the close surrounding frames. To do this, use the **Zoom into frame level** slider. Moving it to the right zooms in.

Moving the Zoom into frame level slider to the left widens the Time Navigator and reveals the entire Timeline again.

What Is a Keyframe?

Keyframe is an animation term that's been in existence since animation was first invented. It usually describes a point at which something changes.

The best way to plan and design animation is to determine the start point and end point for a particular action. These start and end points are keys to your animation. If the action is complex, you might need to indicate other points of change as well.

Animators use the concept of keyframes to describe key points of action, such as when an image moves from the left to the right side of the screen. In this example, there would need to be two keyframes: one set on the left side of the screen and another set on the right. Once keyframes are created, the frames in-between the keyframes can be created. For example, in traditional hand-drawn animation, an animator can draw two keyframes and then an assistant can draw the in-between frames. If artwork moved from the left to right of the screen in 30 frames with 2 keyframes, then 28 in-between frames would need to be drawn. The keyframes act as a guide for all the frames in-between.

In computer graphics, you can define the keyframes and have the computer draw the in-between frames for you. Again, the keyframes act as guides for the in-between frames created by your computer.

MOVIE | keyframes.mov

Please watch the movie entitled **keyframes.mov** located in the **movies** folder on the **H•O•T CD-ROM** before proceeding to the next exercise. It will serve as a quick guide to help you grasp the fundamentals of setting keyframes.

I. _____Setting Keyframes

You've learned to import footage into your project, create a composition, and import artwork from the project to a composition. Now it's finally time to start animating! In this exercise, you will learn how to set keyframes. You will learn how to create start and end points as keyframes, and you'll preview the results of your animation.

1. Launch After Effects, if it isn't already launched, navigate to **chap_05 > Keyframe Animation.aep**, and click **Open**.

This is a project file, just like the project files you learned to make on your own in Chapter 3, "The Project."

2. Navigate to your **AE6 HOT Projects** folder and save a copy of the document there so you won't alter the original.

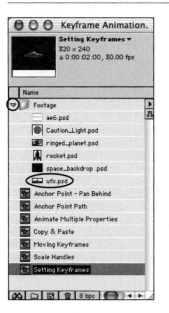

3. In the **Project** window, double-click the **Setting Keyframes** composition to open it. The Project window contains numerous compositions as well as a Footage folder. Twirl down the arrow next to the **Footage** folder in the Project window, and notice that it contains a file called **ufo.psd**. Look at the Timeline window, and notice that it contains a single footage item called **ufo.psd**, which was imported from the project into the Setting Keyframes composition as a merged Photoshop file.

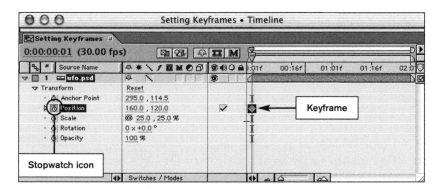

4. In the **Timeline** window, locate the small arrow to the left of the layer named **ufo.psd**. Click on the arrow and notice that it twirls down to display the **Transform** setting for the layer. This will reveal its properties: **Anchor Point**, **Position**, **Scale**, **Rotation**, and **Opacity**.

As a nickname, the triangle used to display properties is affectionately called the "twirly." Every layer in any Timeline has a twirly, with the exact same Transform properties you see for this layer. These properties are part of the After Effects interface, and you don't have to do anything special to make them appear.

Note: *For After Effects users of previous versions, the Properties interface has changed. It used to contain Transform, Mask, and Effects properties. Now, you have to add a mask or effect to see those specific properties appear. I think the decision to change this part of the interface was good and probably makes it easier to learn After Effects, because seeing the multiple properties at once can get pretty overwhelming until you get the hang of things.*

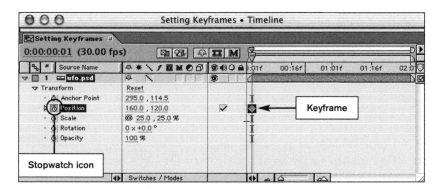

5. Locate and click the **Stopwatch** icon for the **Position** property. Notice that clicking the Stopwatch causes a **keyframe** icon to be placed in the **Timeline** at the current **Current Time Indicator** position (**Frame 0:00:00:01**).

Clicking the Stopwatch icon not only inserts a keyframe at the current Current Time Indicator, but it also turns on the capability to set keyframes for that property at other locations in the Timeline, as you'll do shortly.

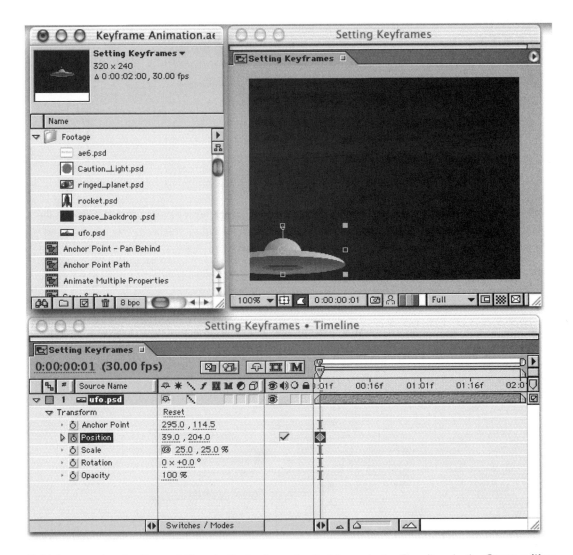

6. Make sure that the **Current Time Indicator** is on the first frame in the **Timeline**. In the **Composition** window, click and drag the **UFO image** to the position shown in the preceding screen shot. This sets the **Position** property of the image in the first keyframe.

7. In the **Timeline** window, move the **Current Time Indicator** to the last frame (02:00). Notice that the **Current Time** display in the upper-left corner changes based on the **Current Time Indicator** position.

WARNING | The Dreaded Gray Frame

If you manually move the Current Time Indicator to the last frame in the Timeline window, you may see a blank, gray frame. This means you've dragged the indicator too far. There are a few methods to get it to go to the true end. You could click on the **Current Time** display and type the correct value, use the **Time Controls** palette and click the **Last Frame** button, or press the **End** key. Or if you have a laptop that doesn't have an End key, you could use the shortcut **Cmd+Option+right arrow** (Mac) or **Ctrl+Alt+right arrow** (Windows). Or, you can readjust the playhead manually. Whew! That was a mouthful.

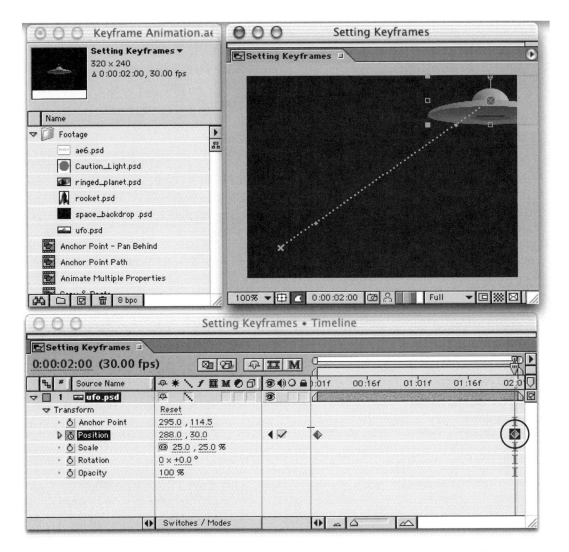

8. In the **Composition** window, drag the **UFO image** to the position shown in the preceding screen shot. A new keyframe will appear. Notice that a motion path is created between the two keyframe points.

When the Stopwatch is turned on for the Position property, moving the position of artwork in the Composition window will cause a keyframe to be set automatically at the location of the Current Time Indicator in the Timeline.

9. Drag the **Current Time Indicator** back and forth to preview your animation.

Dragging the Current Time Indicator back and forth is also called "scrubbing" the Timeline.

To review, the steps to create keyframe animation follow: You must click the Stopwatch icon to establish that a property will accept keyframes. Once you activate the Stopwatch to accept keyframes, move the Current Time Indicator and then make a change. A new keyframe will automatically appear. A motion path will appear if the change is to the Position property. If the change is to some other property, such as opacity or scale, you would not see a motion path.

10. Save your project and leave it open for the next exercise.

What Is a Property?

In the previous exercise, you set keyframes for the Position property. But what exactly is a property?

Transform properties are inherent to all footage layers. When a footage item is brought into the Timeline, it is referred to as a "layer." Think of layers as the individual components that make up your composition.

Each layer has properties you can access and change on a frame-by-frame basis to cause it to animate. Think of properties as options for a layer. **Properties** provide the means to change the color, size, position, and many other attributes associated with a layer. The variety of properties in After Effects is impressive, and they are organized into groups to make them easy to find.

Besides the Transform properties, there are a few primary groups of properties: **Masks**, **Effects**, **Text**, **3D**, and **Expressions**. Transform properties are automatically assigned to all footage layers. To access some of the other types of properties, you need to take other steps or create other types of layers. You'll learn about other types of properties throughout the rest of the book.

The good news is that all property values can be animated by setting keyframes. Once you learn how to set keyframes for a Transform property, the same process can be used on other types of layer properties. This chapter will be concerned only with setting keyframes for Transform properties. Other chapters will address the other types of properties.

2. ——————————Using RAM Preview

A significant part of creating animation is being able to preview the results. In the previous exercise, you watched the motion you created using a technique called "scrubbing." In this exercise, you will learn to preview your motion using the Time Controls and RAM Preview button.

1. If the **Time Controls** palette is not visible, choose **Window > Time Controls** to display it. You can also press **Cmd+3** (Mac) or **Ctrl+3** (Windows).

2. In the Timeline, set the **Current Time Indicator** to **Frame 0:00:00:01** to manually rewind your animation, or press the **Home** key on your keyboard. If you have a laptop without a **Home** key, use **Cmd+Option+left arrow** (Mac) or **Ctrl+Alt+left arrow** (Windows).

3. In the **Time Controls** palette, click the **Play** button to preview your animation.

4. Click anywhere or press any key to stop playing the looping animation.

*Note: I rarely use the Play button, because the spacebar shortcut is so much faster. Press the **spacebar** once to play and again to stop. It doesn't get any easier!*

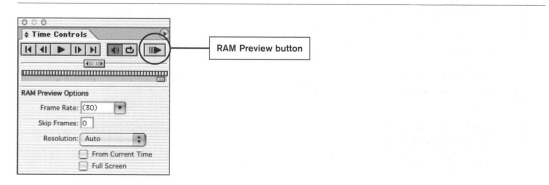

5. In the **Time Controls** palette, click the **First Frame** button to rewind your animation. An alternative way to get to the first frame is to press the **Home** key on your keyboard.

RAM Preview button

6. Click the **RAM Preview** button to preview your animation. Click anywhere or press any key to stop the preview.

*The RAM Preview function causes your computer to store the movie in its memory (RAM) in order to give you a real-time preview. The term "real-time" refers to the timing that would occur in video or film. When you click the **Play** button without using **RAM Preview**, After Effects has to render each frame, which can cause the preview to slow down. The **RAM Preview** is very useful for getting a sense of what the final timing of your movie will look like. If RAM Preview doesn't work well, it might be because you don't have enough RAM in your computer system. In that case, use the **Play** button or **spacebar** to preview your motion.*

7. Go to the last frame, by pressing **End** on your keyboard. Leave this composition open for the next lesson.

3. ————————————Editing the Motion

Remember (if you're old enough) how typewriters didn't have "undo" keys, so if you made a mistake you sometimes had to retype everything? Fortunately, computers are great for editing, and the old days of worrying about changing your mind are gone forever. What good would setting keyframes be if you couldn't make a change? In this exercise, you will learn the basics of editing keyframe animation. You'll learn to select individual keyframes and add more keyframes. You'll also learn how to change keyframe values. Nothing is ever cast in stone in After Effects—you can always change your mind (and so can your clients!).

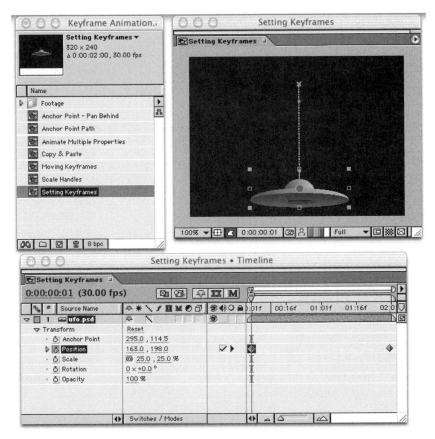

1. Make sure that your **Current Time Indicator** is on the last keyframe (press **End** to go there quickly). In the **Composition** window, click and drag the **UFO image** to the position shown in the preceding illustration. Notice that the motion path has changed because you altered the last keyframe. In the **Timeline** window, notice that the **Position** property values of the **ufo.psd** layer have changed.

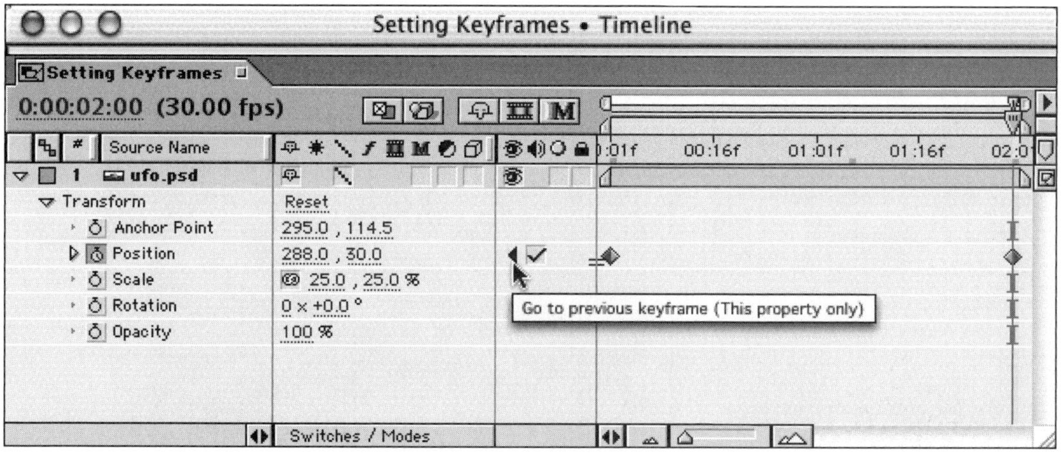

2. In the **Timeline** window, locate the **Keyframe Navigator** (shown above). Click the **left arrow**. Once you do this, notice that the **Current Time Indicator** moves to the previous keyframe (**Frame 0:00:00:01**).

The Keyframe Navigator appears whenever you have more than one keyframe set in the Timeline. Using the right arrow will take you forward to the next keyframe; using the left arrow will take you to the previous keyframe. Note that the right and left Keyframe Navigator arrows will appear only if there are keyframes present to the right or left of the Current Time Indicator's position. Using the Keyframe Navigator arrows is a great way to locate existing keyframes. The only way to change a keyframe is to go to it first, so you'll find the Keyframe Navigator to be invaluable.

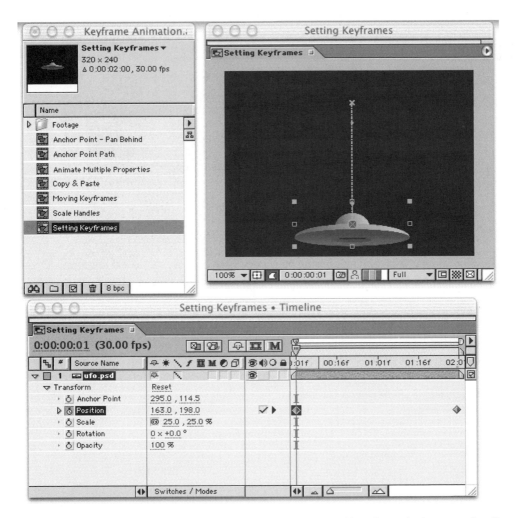

3. In the **Composition** window, drag the **UFO image** to the position shown in the preceding illustration. You've changed the motion path again by editing the keyframe for the end position.

4. Set the **Current Time Indicator** to **Frame 20**. There is no keyframe at Frame 20, but you'll learn how to set one next.

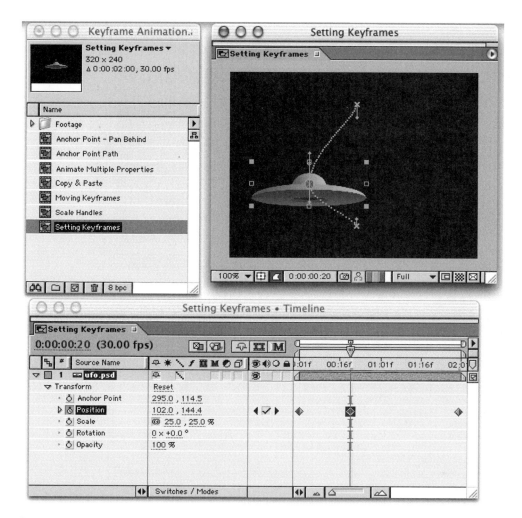

5. Drag the **UFO image** to the left, as shown here. Notice that this adds a new keyframe to your animation at **Frame 0:00:00:20**.

When you want to create a new position keyframe, go to a frame that does not have a keyframe and simply move the object, as you did in this step. This requires that you activate the Stopwatch icon as you did in the first exercise. From that point on, when you want to change an existing keyframe, go to that keyframe and move the object. Going to an existing keyframe is very easy with the Keyframe Navigator arrows.

6. Set the **Current Time Indicator** to **Frame 0:00:01:10**. If you notice tiny green marks next to the frame numbers in the Timeline, they represent frames that have been rendered. It's not important to this exercise to understand the green marks yet; they will be explained fully in Chapter 7, "*Previewing Movies.*"

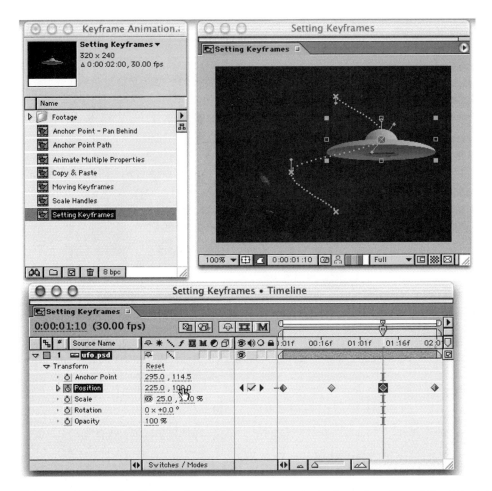

7. Locate the **Position X-axis** value, which represents the horizontal position of the object. Hold your cursor over the **X-axis** value (horizontal position) until the cursor changes into a hand with a double arrow (shown above over the Y-axis value). Click and drag to the right to increase the value. Set the value to approximately **225 pixels**.

8. Locate the **Position Y-axis** (vertical position) value. Use the **double-arrow cursor** and drag to the left to decrease the Y-axis value. Set the value to approximately **100 pixels**.

Moving this slider in the Timeline moves the physical object in the Composition window and is another way to set a position keyframe (as an alternative to dragging).

Observe the resulting motion path in the Composition window. It's curved by default. You'll learn ways to alter the shape of this path soon.

9. Press the **spacebar** or click the **RAM Preview** button to view your edited animation.

10. Choose **File > Save** to save your **Keyframe Animation.aep** project. Your **Setting Keyframes** composition will be saved automatically along with the project. Close the **Setting Keyframes** composition by clicking the upper-left **Close** icon (Mac) or upper-right **Close** icon (Windows). Notice that the **Keyframe Animation.aep** project does not close with the composition. Leave this project open for the next exercise.

*You may be confused at this point about the relationship between the project and the composition. The composition you've been working with in this exercise is inside the project file. The composition name is **Setting Keyframes**, and the project name is **Keyframe Animation.aep**. The only way to save the composition is to save the project. This is one of the distinctive things about After Effects—the project is what you open and save, not individual compositions. In fact, you cannot open a composition without being in an open project. You'll get used to this, but in the beginning it is confusing to most new users.*

TIP | Typing Property Values

In addition to dragging or using the sliders, you can type **Property** values directly into the **Timeline**. Click the value and type in the value box that appears. Press **Return** (Mac) or **Enter** (Windows) to enter the value.

TIP | Double-Clicking a Keyframe Icon to Adjust Values

You can also adjust keyframe values by double-clicking a **Keyframe** icon. This opens a **Position** dialog box in which values can be entered.

TIP | Adding a Keyframe via a Check Box

You can add a keyframe by clicking the **Keyframe Navigator** check box. This adds a keyframe wherever the Current Time Indicator is without changing the value of the frame. In effect, it copies the information from the previous keyframe and makes a new keyframe with the same information. This check box can come in handy when you want to hold a value for a specific frame. It's easier to show you how this technique works than it is to tell you, so please watch the following movie!

MOVIE | HoldKeyframes.mov

We've prepared a short movie that demonstrates how to set hold keyframes using the Keyframe Navigator in the Timeline. You'll find **HoldKeyframes.mov** in the **movies** folder on the **H•O•T CD-ROM**.

4. ——————Copying and Pasting Keyframes

Just as you copy and paste text in a word processor, you can copy and paste keyframes in After Effects. This technique is useful if you've set up a repetitive motion and want to continue with it. In this exercise, you'll use this process to make a light flash on and off.

1. In the **Project** window, double-click the **Copy & Paste** composition to open it. This is an empty composition you will set up yourself.

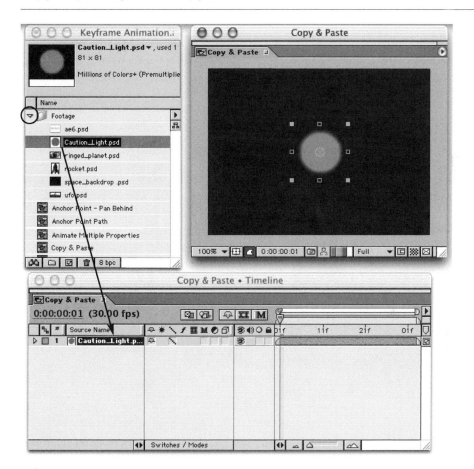

2. Make sure the **Current Time Indicator** is on the first frame in the **Timeline**. In the **Project** window, click the twirly of the **Footage** folder and locate **Caution_Light.psd**. Drag this file into the **Timeline**. The image of a circle appears centered in the **Copy & Paste Composition** window.

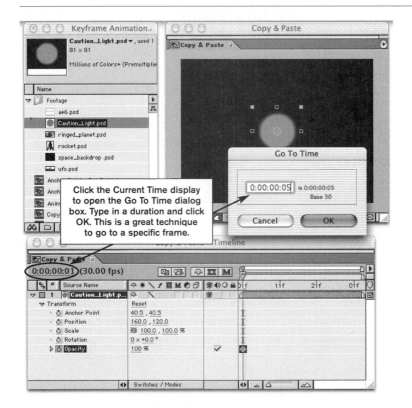

3. In the **Timeline** window, click the twirly next to the layer **Caution_Light.psd**. Click the twirly next to **Transform** to reveal the **Transform** properties for that layer. Click the **Stopwatch** icon for the **Opacity** property. This sets a keyframe for the opacity of the circle at the current **Current Time Indicator**, which should be on Frame 1. The circle is currently set to 100% opacity, which makes it fully visible.

4. Click the **Current Time** display in the **Timeline**. Another way to access this dialog box is **Cmd+G** (Mac) or **Ctrl+G** (Windows). This opens the **Go To Time** dialog box. Enter the value **Frame: 5** and click **OK**. This moves the **Current Time Indicator** to **Frame 5**.

*You can either move the **Current Time Indicator** to the desired frame in the **Timeline** window or use this more precise method of specifying the frame in the **Go To Time** dialog box in the future. Either technique achieves the same result.*

It's important to move the Current Time Indicator before you make a change to the property. This might take some getting used to, but you will eventually get the hang of it! In the next step, you'll change the property value and a new keyframe will be set.

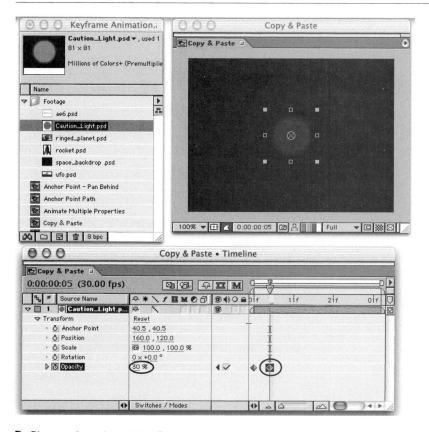

5. Change the value of the **Opacity** property to **30%**. Notice that the light appears less opaque in the Composition window. Also notice that a new keyframe has been set at Frame 5! Once you set a property to contain one keyframe, which is done by clicking the Stopwatch icon for that property, keyframes will automatically be set any time you move the Current Time Indicator and change that property's setting.

6. Scrub the **Current Time Indicator** over the first few frames and observe the existing keyframe animation. The light fades out quickly. This effect was created by changing the **Opacity** property from **100%** to **30%** over two different keyframes.

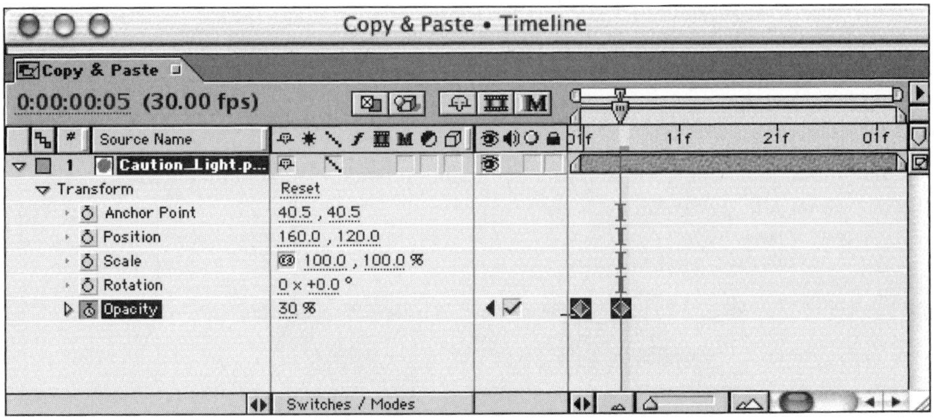

7. Hold down the **Shift** key and click the two **Opacity keyframes** to select them both. You will copy these two keyframes so that the fading effect will repeat itself.

---

8. Choose **Edit > Copy**. Or, press **Cmd+C** (Mac) or **Ctrl+C** (Windows).

---

9. Move the **Current Time Indicator** to **Frame 10**.

It's important to move the Current Time Indicator before you paste the keyframes into the new location. Keyframes are always pasted wherever the Current Time Indicator resides.

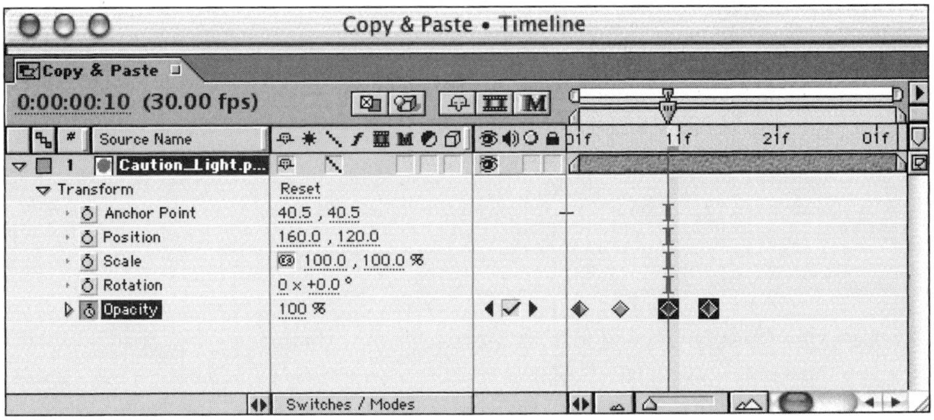

---

10. Choose **Edit > Paste**. Or, press **Cmd+V** (Mac) or **Ctrl+V** (Windows). Notice that the keyframes are pasted at the current Current Time Indicator position on Frame 10.

---

11. Move the **Current Time Indicator** to **Frame 20**. Press **Cmd+V** (Mac) or **Ctrl+V** (Windows) to paste the keyframes again.

Once the keyframes are in the computer's memory, they can be pasted indefinitely!

12. Press the **spacebar** to preview the animation. The action will repeat three times!

13. Save your project and close the **Copy & Paste** composition. Leave the project open for the next exercise.

5. _____Moving Keyframes

So far, you've set keyframes at the position of the Current Time Indicator. This is the only way to create a keyframe, because the keyframe appears wherever the Current Time Indicator is positioned in the Timeline. Sometimes, after you've created keyframes, you might change your mind about where in time you wanted them to occur. The good news is that once you've made a keyframe, you can always move it to other frame positions. Moving keyframes farther apart makes movement or property changes slow down, and moving them closer together makes movement speed up. In this exercise, you'll learn how to move keyframes, and you'll see the effect that has on animation.

1. In the **Project** window, double-click the **Moving Keyframes** composition. This composition was made ahead of time, and keyframes have been set for both the **Position** and **Scale** properties already.

2. Press the **spacebar** to preview the movement and observe the animation of the rocket moving up through the Composition window and growing smaller.

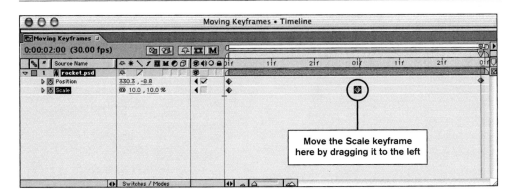

Move the Scale keyframe here by dragging it to the left

3. Select **rocket.psd** in the **Timeline** window. Press the letter **P**, which is a shortcut key to reveal only the **Position** property! (A list of other shortcut keys is found later in this chapter.) Next, hold down the **Shift** key and press the letter **S**. Holding the Shift key with the shortcut keys allows you to reveal the **multiple** properties without using the twirlies. Click the last **Scale** keyframe (at **0:00:02:00**) to select it and drag it on the **Timeline** to **0:00:01:00**.

4. Press the **spacebar** and observe the results of moving the Scale keyframe. The rocket now gets smaller more quickly and then continues to traverse the Composition window.

You can move the first or last Scale keyframe wherever you want on the Timeline to change the timing of scaling in your composition. The closer together the keyframes are, the faster the scaling; the farther apart they are, the slower the scaling.

5. Save your project and close the **Moving Keyframes** composition. Leave your project open for the next exercise.

TIP | Moving Multiple Keyframes

You can also move multiple keyframes at once. Using the cursor, drag a selection box around the keyframes you want to move, or hold down the **Shift** key to select multiple keyframes. Once the keyframes are selected, simply drag them to the new location and release.

Shortcut Keys for Properties

You've seen that you can press keys on the keyboard to display individual layer properties. The following table lists all the shortcut keys for displaying Transform properties. Individual properties are hidden unless you use these shortcut keys or click the twirly to reveal all the properties at once.

Let's say that you wanted to change the scale and rotation of a layer, and you wanted to know the shortcut to show those specific two properties. There's a way to add only the properties you want to see. To display more than one layer property in the Timeline, you must first show a single property. Then, hold down the **Shift** key and press the shortcut key for the property you want to add to the display. The following table lists all the shortcut keys for adding Transform properties to the Timeline display.

Shortcut Keys for Individual Transform Properties	
Shortcut Key	**Property**
A	**A**nchor Point
P	**P**osition
R	**R**otation
S	**S**cale
T	Opacity

Shortcut Keys to Add Transform Properties	
Shortcut Key	**Action**
Shift+A	**A**nchor Point
Shift+P	**P**osition
Shift+R	**R**otation
Shift+S	**S**cale
Shift+T	Opacity

Automatic Keyframe Shortcuts

If you want to set a keyframe automatically while you display a property, press **Option** (Mac) or **Alt+Shift** (Windows) along with the shortcut key for the property. This reveals the property you want and sets a keyframe in one shortcut key.

Shortcut Keys for Setting a Keyframe with a Transform Property		
Mac Shortcut Key	**Windows Shortcut Key**	**Action**
Option+A	**Alt+Shift+A**	**A**nchor Point
Option+P	**Alt+Shift+P**	**P**osition
Option+R	**Alt+ Shift+R**	**R**otation
Option+S	**Alt+ Shift+S**	**S**cale
Option+T	**Alt+Shift+T**	Opacity

MOVIE | Display_Properties.mov

A short movie that demonstrates how to use shortcut keys to display properties is called **Display_Properties.mov** and is located in the **movies** folder on the **H•O•T CD-ROM**.

6. ─────────Animating Scale Using Control Handles

When working with the **Scale** property, you have two ways to access its settings: by altering values in the Timeline for the Scale field or by working with its control handles. Sometimes you may want to change the proportions of an object by making it taller, wider, shorter or narrower than the original artwork. This exercise will show you both ways, so that you can choose which one you want to use.

1. Double-click the **Scale Handles** composition to open it.

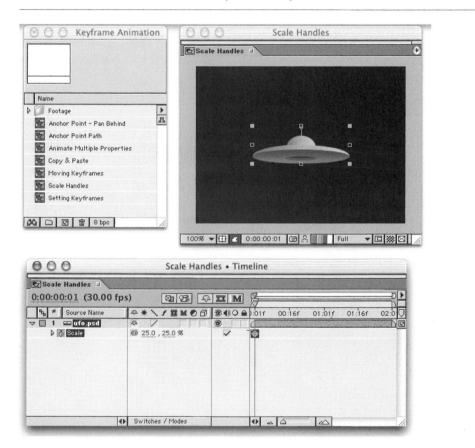

2. Make sure the **Current Time Indicator** is at the first frame in the **Timeline**. Select the **ufo.psd** layer in the **Timeline** window. Press **Option+S** (Mac) or **Alt+Shift+S** (Windows) to display the **Scale** property and automatically add a keyframe at the **Current Time Indicator** position (**Frame 0:00:00:01**). Adding the **Option** or **Alt** key to the shortcut key **S** not only reveals and isolates the **Scale** property from the others, but it also automatically activates the **Stopwatch** to set keyframes.

3. In the **Timeline** window, change the value of the **Scale** property to **30%**. Note that if you change one value, the other changes. That's because the **Link** icon (to the left of the values) is set to constrain the **X-axis** and **Y-axis** proportionally.

4. Move the **Current Time Indicator** to **Frame 0:00:01:00**. In the **Composition** window, drag the upper-right **control handle** of the UFO image up and to the right. Notice that you are able to scale the object differently in the **X-axis** and **Y-axis** using this technique? This is a great way to override the **Link** icon that is set to constrain the scale.

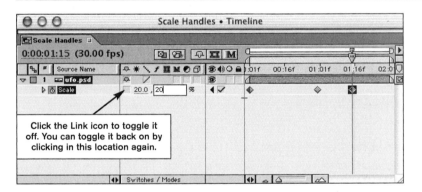

5. Move the **Current Time Indicator** to **Frame 0:00:01:15**. Type **20** into the first field of the **Scale** property. Notice that even though the **Link** icon is still turned on, the two numbers are no longer linked. Once you use the scale handles, you disrupt the relationship between the X and Y values. That's fine if you want them to be disproportional, but what if you want to resynchronize them?

6. Click on the **Link** icon to deselect it. Type **20** into the second field. Once these two values match again, click the **Link** icon to turn it back on. Now anytime you type a new value in here, the X and Y values will match.

Note: You can use the scale handles to scale proportionally as well. Holding down the **Shift** *key causes both the X-axis and the Y-axis values to scale identically. You have to first select the object in the* **Composition** *window and then press* **Shift** *for this to work. This is different from most programs, such as Photoshop, for example, where you have to hold down the* **Shift** *key to scale proportionally before you select the object.*

7. Save your project and close the **Scale Handles** composition. Leave your project open for the next exercise.

7. ————————Animating Multiple Properties

Most professional animation is obviously more complex than what you've created so far. To achieve more complex motion, you'll want to animate several properties for an individual layer. In this exercise, you'll learn to animate the Position, Scale, Rotation, and Opacity properties for a simple title graphic.

1. Double-click the **Animate Multiple Properties** composition to open it.

2. In the **Timeline** window, select the **ae6.psd** layer and click on the twirlies to reveal the **Transform** properties.

*Note: The **Scale** property in After Effects 6.0 shows both X and Y scale percentage values, and they are currently each set to 50%. When a value other than the default (in the case of Scale, a default value would be 100%) is entered without a keyframe, it simply changes that value throughout the composition as a held value. This is great when you want a value to stay the same throughout the animation, but you want it to be different from the default.*

3. Go to the end of the **Timeline** by pressing the **End** key on your keyboard, or **Cmd+Option+right arrow** (Mac) or **Ctrl+Alt+right arrow** on laptops that don't have an **End** key. This positions the **Current Time Indicator** at **0:00:02:00**. Check the **Stopwatch** icons for **Position, Scale, Rotation,** and **Opacity.** This will set a keyframe at the last frame for all those properties. Nothing will have changed in the **Composition** window because all you've done is set keyframes—you haven't changed their values.

This is a very common technique for setting keyframes. It allows you to set the final frame first and then animate the beginning keyframes so that the animation will resolve where you set the final frame. It's animating in reverse, which is often easier than animating forward.

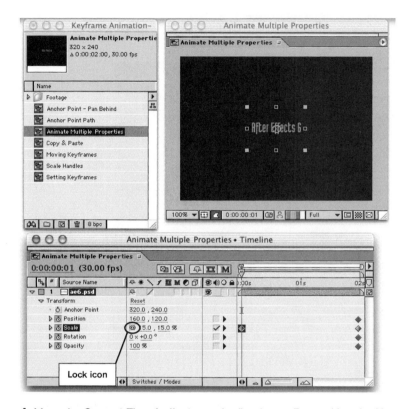

4. Move the **Current Time Indicator** to the first frame. Press either the **Home** key, or **Cmd+Option+left arrow** (Mac) or **Ctrl+Alt+left arrow** (Windows), or drag it into place. Set the **Scale** value to **15%**. Entering a value in either the X or Y field will set both fields if the **Link** icon is present. (You will learn how to unlock the **Scale** properties in a future exercise.) This will set a new keyframe for **Scale** at **0:00:00:01**.

5. Set the **Rotation** value to **−15 degrees**. Note that the keyframe was automatically set for **Frame 0:00:00:01**. Any time you activate the **Stopwatch** for a property, move the **Current Time Indicator** (which was done a few steps ago), and then change the property value, a new keyframe will be set.

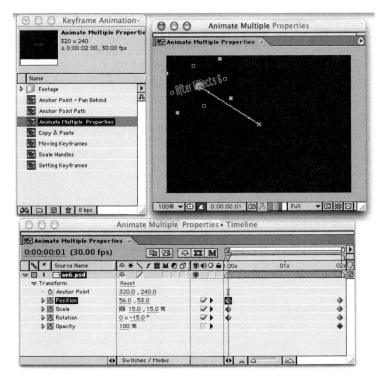

6. Click and drag the artwork in the composition to the location you see in the preceding illustration. Notice that a **Position** keyframe is automatically set at the same location where the **Current Time Indicator** resides in the **Timeline**. Press the **spacebar** to see what you've done so far. To get rid of the motion path in the **Composition** window, simply click off **the ae6.psd** layer in the **Timeline** and preview again. It might be sluggish—if so, press the **RAM Preview** button on the **Time Controls** palette.

The add or remove current keyframe check box

7. Move the **Current Time Indicator** to **0:00:01:14**. Click the **add or remove keyframe at current time** check box next to the **Opacity** property. This automatically inserts an **Opacity** keyframe at this frame. Why would you want to do this? To maintain the value of 100% between this keyframe and the last keyframe. This might make more sense after you complete the upcoming step.

8. Move the **Current Time Indicator** to **Frame 0:00:00:01**. Change the **Opacity** value to **30%**. A new keyframe will be set. If you press the **spacebar**, you'll see that the logo fades all the way up to 100% once it hits the second keyframe and then maintains its value of 100% from the second to the third keyframe.

*Tip: I taught you an interesting workflow here, though it might not be that obvious. You could have set the keyframes for the **Opacity** property in order, starting at **30%**, then setting another at **100%**, and another at **100%**. By clicking the **Stopwatch** icon when the **Current Time Indicator** was on the last frame, it set the **Opacity** to **100%** automatically. By clicking the **add or remove keyframe at current time** check box, you set another keyframe at **100%** without entering any value into the **Opacity** property. This allowed you to enter only one value, with the **Current Time Indicator** at the first frame. It sounds lazy (and it is!), but when you're working on a real-world project with a real-world deadline, these subtle shortcuts add up.*

9. Next, you'll learn another interesting workflow trick. Click the **Go to next keyframe** arrow (also referred to as the **Keyframe Navigator** arrow). This will position the **Current Time Indicator** on the second keyframe precisely.

10. Click on the last keyframe of the **Rotation** property and copy it by pressing **Cmd+C** (Mac) or **Ctrl+C** (Windows). Notice that this process causes the **Rotation** property to become selected in the **Timeline**. Paste the keyframe—by pressing **Cmd+V** (Mac) or **Ctrl+V** (Windows)—to the location of the **Current Time Indicator** on the **Rotation** property. The value of the last keyframe in the **Rotation** property has been pasted into the same location in time as the second keyframe for the **Opacity** keyframe.

Two different ideas are at play here. First, you can use keyframe locations from one property to set a keyframe for another property in the same location. Second, you can paste the value of a keyframe into another keyframe location based where the Current Time Indicator is positioned. This kind of copy-and-paste action will become second nature to you eventually, and it saves lots of time! As well, using the Go to next or previous keyframe arrows are a great timesaver over trying to manually position the Current Time Indicator right on the keyframe location.

11. Press the **spacebar** to preview the motion. If it's sluggish, there are a couple different techniques to try to speed up the preview:

- Click the **RAM Preview** button on the **Time Control** palette instead of the **spacebar**. This might take a moment to render, but once it does, the preview will be much faster.

- Change the quality to **Draft** by clicking on the **Quality** button in the **Timeline**. Basically, high quality looks the best but takes the longest to render. By changing the quality setting to **Draft**, the **spacebar** technique of previewing the footage will work much faster. You'll learn more about the quality settings in Chapter 7, "*Previewing Movies*."

12. Save your project and close the **Animate Multiple Properties** composition. Leave your project open for the next exercise.

What Is the Anchor Point?

The **anchor point** of an image is a designated point that is used for positioning, scale, and rotation. It is displayed as a circle with an X through it. Each footage item has its own anchor point. By default, After Effects places the anchor point at the center of each footage item. If the object rotates or scales, it will do so around the anchor point.

It is often necessary to move the anchor point to make an object rotate or scale around a point other than the center of the image. Another reason to move the anchor point is to rotate an object around another object. You'll get to move the anchor point in the exercise that follows.

8. ——————Animating the Anchor Point Using the Pan Behind Tool

This exercise will give you a real-world example of why you would change the **anchor point** in an animation. You're going to make the rocket ship rotate around the planet. This sounds like a simple idea, but it will require the use of the anchor point. Why? Because the default rotation axis of the rocket ship is in the middle of the rocket ship. By moving the anchor point, you'll move the axis to the planet, which will cause the rotation to occur around the planet instead of around the rocket itself. If it sounds confusing, trying the exercise will clarify things!

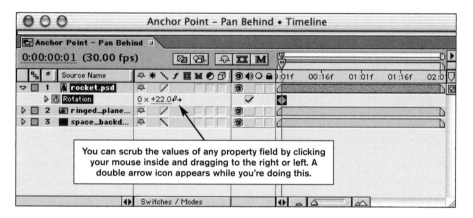

1. Double-click the **Anchor Point – Pan Behind** composition to open it. Notice the rocket and planet images in the **Composition** window. Select the **rocket.psd** layer. Press **Option+R** (Mac) or **Alt+Shift+R** (Windows). This reveals the **Rotation** property for this layer and activates the **Stopwatch** for keyframes at the same time.

*There are two values in the **Rotation** property. The first is how many full 360-degree rotations are being set, and the second is the degrees of rotation other than 360. Scrub the value of the **degrees rotation** field, and notice that the rocket rotates on its own axis. This is great for spinning knobs and gears, but rockets generally do not spin around their own axis. You'll want to change the axis to the center of the planet in order to get the rocket to have the motion that is needed in this animation.*

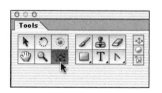

2. Select the **Pan Behind** tool from the **Tools** palette. If for some reason your Tools palette isn't open, choose **Window > Tools**.

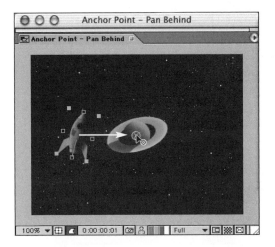

3. In the **Composition** window, click the **rocket** (if it isn't already selected) to display its anchor point and drag the rocket's **anchor point** to the center of the planet. Notice that the cursor changes to a four-pointed arrow shape when you use the **Pan Behind** tool.

Note: The Pan Behind tool moves the anchor point of the rocket but doesn't alter the position of the rocket. If you did not use this tool and simply changed the anchor point position in the Transform properties, the rocket would move along with the anchor point. The Pan Behind tool is very popular for moving the anchor point because it moves the anchor point without moving the object to which the anchor point is attached.

4. Reset the **Rotation** property to **0 rotations** and **0 degrees**, if necessary. Make sure the **Stopwatch** icon is activated.

5. Move the **Current Time Indicator** to the last frame and then set the **Rotation** value to **1**. Press the **spacebar** to watch the rocket rotate around the planet instead of its own axis.

6. Close this composition, but leave this project open for the next exercise.

WARNING | Pan Behind Alters the Motion Path

If you attempt to use the Pan Behind tool to move the anchor point on a layer with an existing motion path, your motion path will be altered. These alterations can be significant. We recommend that while you are learning After Effects, you use the Pan Behind tool to move an anchor point only when the selected layer does not have a motion path.

NOTE | What About Animating the Anchor Point Property?

In this last exercise, you worked with moving the anchor point, but you didn't set values in the Anchor property to do so. Using the Pan Behind tool, you moved the anchor point to a new location. By doing so, you changed the axis of the rocket artwork from its middle point to an outside location. When animating the Anchor Point property, you change the center location of your object. The center of an object is what all kinds of other properties are based on, such as Scale, Position, and Rotation. You can animate the Anchor Point by setting keyframes and changing its value if that's the effect you want. Let's say you want something to rotate from the center for part of the animation but then you want it to pivot from a corner point later. This would be accomplished by animating the Anchor property. Often, After Effects artists use the Pan Behind or Parenting techniques (see Chapter 11, "*Parenting*") instead of animating the Anchor property because of the impact it has on so many other properties (Scale, Position, and Rotation).

What Are Bézier Curves and Handles?

The title of this section might sound scarier than it is. Bézier curves and handles are something that digital artists love because they give the artists artistic control. Those of you who are familiar with Illustrator or FreeHand will likely be familiar with Bézier curve editing. In After Effects, Bézier curves are used to influence the shape of motion paths. They are also used for other purposes, such as for mask shapes and speed graphs, which you'll learn about in future chapters. If you are not familiar with Bézier curves and points, there's no need to worry—this section will help you out!

A **Bézier curve** contains points with control handles. To see the Bézier handles in the Composition window, you must click on a keyframe in the Timeline to select that keyframe. The **control handles** influence the curves around the Bézier point.

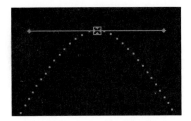

In this image, the series of tick marks represents the animation path. By dragging the Bézier handles, you affect the Bézier curve and influence the motion path.

Bézier points have two handles: one for the portion of the curve that precedes the Bézier point and another for the portion of the curve that follows the Bézier point.

The scary-sounding term **Bézier** comes from the name of a French mathematician, Pierre Bézier. He developed a mathematic formula used to describe curves. After Effects and many other computer graphics programs use this formula. Luckily, you don't have to worry about formulas. All you have to do is click and drag to get the curve you want.

MOVIE | Bézier_Points.mov

The short movie **Bézier_Points.mov** demonstrates the use of Bézier points. It's located in the **movies** folder on the **H•O•T CD-ROM**.

9. ——————Using Bézier Handles with Motion Paths

In this exercise, you will learn to select Bézier points and adjust Bézier handles to influence the motion path. This gives you added control over the way your objects move and, for that reason, is an invaluable skill.

1. In the **Project** window, double-click the **Setting Keyframes** composition to reopen it.

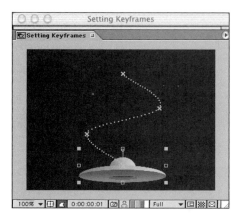

2. In the **Composition** window, click the **UFO image** to select it. The motion path will appear as an outline with little dots (the dots represent frames and speed, which you'll learn more about in the upcoming Chapter 6, "*Playing with Time*"). Press the **spacebar** to preview the motion and witness how the artwork indeed travels along this exact path.

3. Return to **Frame 0:00:00:01**. In the **Composition** window, click the second **Bézier point** in the motion path to select it. Notice that its handles appear? These handles influence the curve of the motion path.

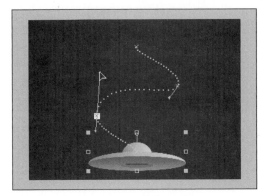

4. Pull upwards on the **Bézier handle** and observe the influence on the motion path. The curve becomes rounder and less angular.

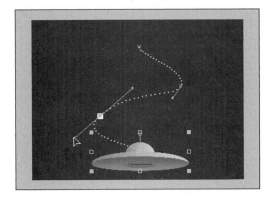

5. Drag the bottom **Bézier handle** outward and to the left. This bends the curve and alters its appearance even more.

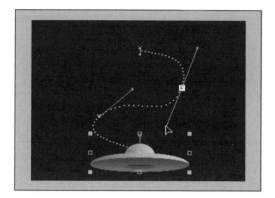

6. Click the third **Bézier point** in the motion path to select it. Drag its handles to be longer (this widens the curve) and angled to the left.

7. Press the **spacebar** to see the new animation. Getting used to pulling on handles to influence the motion path takes practice, but once you get the hang of it you'll gain a lot more control over the way your artwork moves.

8. Save your project, and close the **Setting Keyframes** composition. Leave your project open for the next exercise.

TIP | Auto Orientation

To make the UFO, or any object for that matter, orient to the path as it moves, choose **Layer > Transform > Auto Orient**.

> **Auto-Orientation**
>
> ┌─ Auto-Orientation ───────────────┐
> │ ○ Off   │
> │ ⦿ Orient Along Path   │
> └───────────────────────────────────┘
>
>   (Cancel)   (OK)

The **Auto-Orientation** dialog box appears. If you choose **Orient Along Path**, the object's orientation in space will follow the shape of the motion path. Sweet!

Spatial Interpolation Types

The next section will teach you how to control a motion path by learning how to give the path straight lines and curves. This is accomplished with a feature in After Effects called **spatial interpolation**. Spatial interpolation types are visible in the Composition window because they influence the appearance of the motion path.

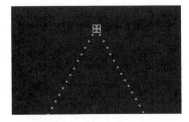

Linear interpolation can be identified by a sharp curve and even distribution of tick marks. There are no Bézier controls in a Linear type. Placing the **Pen** tool over any point in the curve in the Composition window and clicking will toggle the shape between a straight path (like this) and a curved one.

Auto Bézier interpolation can be identified by the smooth curve. There are control handles, but *without* handlebars. If you attempt to move a control point on an Auto Bézier type, it will be converted to a Continuous Bézier type. You'll get to try this in the next exercise.

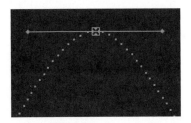

Continuous Bézier interpolation can be identified by the straight handlebars. The handlebars may be of different lengths, but they are always straight.

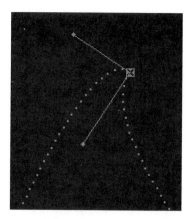

Angled handlebars identify the **Bézier** interpolation type. The angle and length of the handlebars can be adjusted independently. Using the **Selection** tool, if you hold the **Cmd** key (Mac) or **Ctrl** key (Windows) on any Bézier handle, you can create this type of path by pulling on the handles in different directions. In order to change a control point from a smooth to a corner point (or vice versa), press **Cmd** (Mac) or **Ctrl** (Windows) as you click the point with the **Selection** tool.

Mixing Spatial Interpolation Types

After Effects sometimes uses intimidating terms to explain common tasks. In this exercise, you'll be introduced to a big dose of new, intimidating-sounding terms. We'll explain all of the terms, but we hope they don't get in the way of your understanding. Remember that they are only words. This exercise will teach you something more important than new terms or strange words—it will show you how to make an object move exactly the way you want!

Take the term **spatial interpolation**, for example. The word "spatial" refers to the way an object moves in physical space, such as a Position property. "Interpolation" is what After Effects does to create fluid movement between keyframes. If you set a keyframe to move its position from screen left to screen right, you are affecting its spatial appearance. Interpolation is what makes it move from point A to point B. You may be familiar with the terms "tweening" and "in-betweening"; interpolation is the same thing.

The UFO moves from the top of the frame to the bottom using spatial interpolation. The default type of movement is Auto Bézier, which you learned to control manually in the preceding exercise. Other types of spatial interpolation methods are possible in addition to Bézier curves. Often you will need to create straight lines and complex curves within the same motion path. To accomplish this, you must use both linear and Bézier spatial interpolation types on the motion path.

IO. _____Following a Complex Motion Path

In this exercise, you will create a series of keyframes and make a small object follow the shape of a graphic number 2. When you create a keyframe, the default interpolation type used is Auto Bézier. You will change the interpolation type for each point to make the motion path follow the desired shape.

1. In the **Project** window, double-click in an empty area to launch the **Import File** dialog box. Navigate to the **chap_05 > Footage** folder and select **two.psd**. Before you click the **Import** button, be sure to select **Import As: Composition – Cropped Layers**. Click **Import**.

This is a multilayered Photoshop file. You are choosing to import it as its own composition with cropped layers. What does that mean? Once the file comes into After Effects, a composition will automatically appear with this layered file inside. All the Photoshop layers will automatically become layers in the After Effects Timeline. The **Cropped Layers** setting is new to After Effects 6, and it means that if there is transparency on a Photoshop layer, the layer will crop it to cinch in around the nontransparent pixels. A bounding box area will be defined to crop the artwork, instead of matching the size of the Photoshop document. You'll learn more in upcoming steps about why and how this is important.

2. Once the import is accepted, two new files appear inside the **Project** window: a footage folder called **two Comp 1** and a composition called **two Comp 1**. The names are automatically generated because the PSD file was called **two.psd**. Click the **twirly** on the footage folder to reveal that there are three different footage files. Double-click the **two Comp 1** composition to open it.

3. Once the composition is open, note that it contains three layers. These layer names match the layer names in the Photoshop document. (If you have Photoshop, open the file there and you'll see!) Click the layer visibility **eye** icons on and off for each layer to see what they look like, but make sure you turn them all back on. This will familiarize you with the content of this composition. Make sure the **Current Time Indicator** is on the first frame and select the layer named **dot**. Press the letter **P** to reveal the **Position** property. This is the only property you'll animate in this exercise. Once you start working on compositions with lots of layers and properties, using the shortcut keys to isolate a single property makes your screen a lot less cluttered and easier to use. Click the **Stopwatch** icon for the **Position** property, and you'll be ready to start animating this puppy!

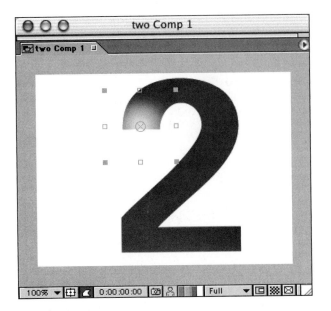

4. In the **Composition** window, move the **dot** layer to the position you see in this screen on top of the number two. This sets the first keyframe's position.

*Notice that the **dot** layer is smaller than the composition. That's the result of the cropped layer setting you chose upon import. It's extremely helpful because the center of the **dot** layer is the center of the actual artwork. In past versions of After Effects, you could bring a Photoshop document into After Effects as a composition, but all the layers would be the same size as the original Photoshop document. Here, each layer size is based on the nontransparent areas for each individual layer.*

5. Move the **Current Time Indicator** to frame **0:00:00:20**. In the **Composition** window, move the **dot** to the position you see here. You'll adjust the path later; for now, you're just blocking out the rough keyframe positions.

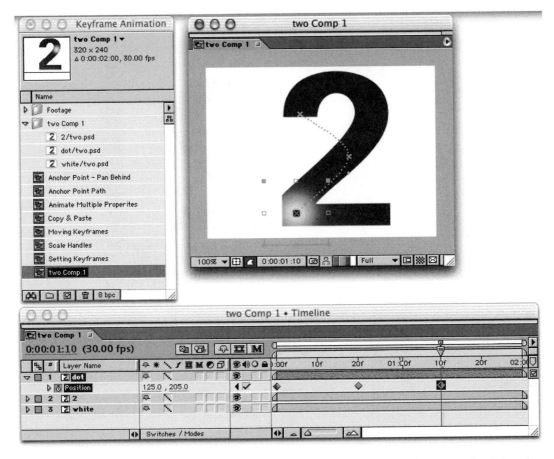

6. Move the **Current Time Indicator** to **0:00:01:10**. In the **Composition** window, move the **dot** to the position you see here. You just set the third keyframe.

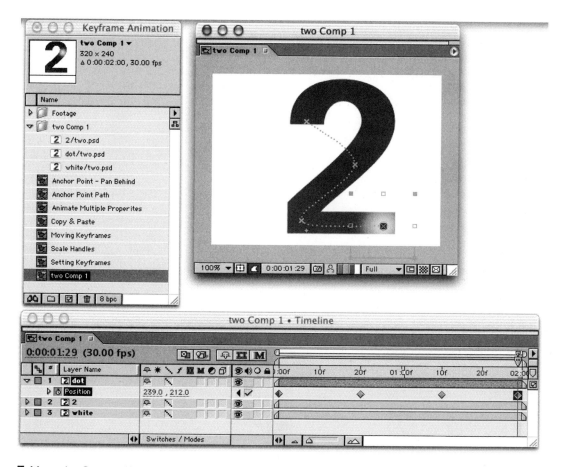

7. Move the **Current Time Indicator** to the **last frame,** and in the **Composition** window move the **dot** artwork to the position you see here. The last keyframe has been set. Now for tweaking that dang motion path!

8. Locate the handle of the **start** keyframe and drag it upwards to the position you see here. This new position is going to have an effect on the motion path curve of the second keyframe. You'll see in a minute.

9. In the **Composition** window, pull the **Bézier handle** of the second keyframe to the position you see here. See how the path is more closely resembling the shape of the **two** artwork?

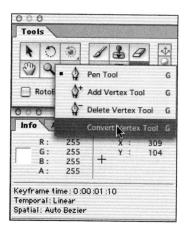

10. In the **Tools** palette, click and hold on the **Pen** tool and select the **Convert Vertex** tool from the drop-down menu.

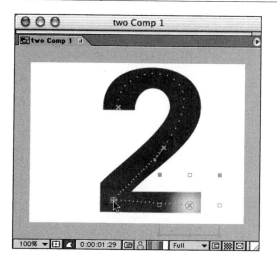

11. Click on the **third keyframe point** and notice that it shifts from a curve to an angle. Adjust all the points and curves to best fit the number two.

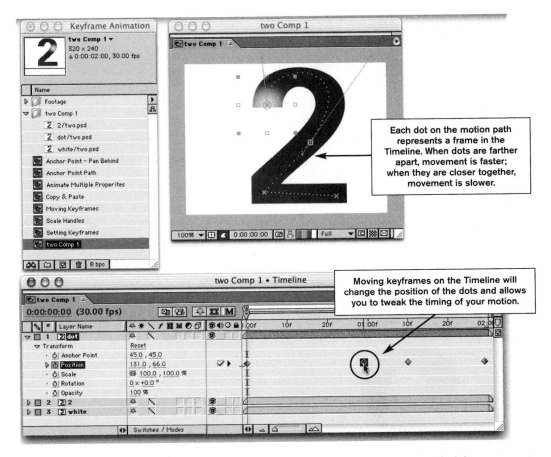

Each dot on the motion path represents a frame in the Timeline. When dots are farther apart, movement is faster; when they are closer together, movement is slower.

Moving keyframes on the Timeline will change the position of the dots and allows you to tweak the timing of your motion.

12. Press the **spacebar** to preview the animation. You might notice that the speed of the movement is faster at the beginning than the end. Notice that the dots are farther apart between keyframes one and two than between the other keyframes. Although the keyframes are evenly spaced over time in the Timeline, the actual time that it takes to move evenly around the two shape is not equal between these keyframes. In the **Timeline** window, drag the **second keyframe** over to the right and notice that the dots are more evenly spaced out. Press the **spacebar** again, and the acceleration between the four keyframes will seem more even, though they are no longer evenly spaced in time.

Why, you might wonder? When you're first roughing out motion, you rarely know how it will look until you preview it. It's hard to calculate how long it will take to move around the shape of the number 2 until you try different ideas. It's wonderful that After Effects offers the feedback of these dots to help you visualize the speed of the movement. It's also wonderful that the speed is so easy to change. The upcoming Chapter 6, "Playing with Time," offers other techniques to achieve this same result. The best part about After Effects is that it lets you change your mind about everything you'd ever need to change—it's just a matter of learning how to access these controls.

> **NOTE | Previewing Without the Dots**
>
> As mentioned before, the dots in the Composition window represent time—with each dot representing a single frame. The dots are incredibly useful because they're offering visual feedback about the timing of the movement. Still, when you preview the artwork, seeing the dots and the motion path can be very distracting. You can turn them off by deselecting the layer that the Position keyframes are on—just click anywhere in the Timeline window that is not directly on a layer.

13. Save your project, and close the **two Comp 1** composition. Save and close this project—the chapter has ended!

Test Yourself on This Chapter!

This was a critical chapter, in that you've combined the skills you've learned in the past three chapters to create animation—finally! Check your knowledge by trying the following. We're being intentionally vague about how to do these tasks, so you can make sure you have really learned how they are done. If you need to go back to any of the exercises, feel free. This stuff is new, and it really does require practice.

A. Create a new composition and drag some footage into it.

B. Set two position keyframes to make some artwork move from one part of the Composition window to another.

C. Add two more keyframes to the middle of the animation so that you can move the artwork around on the stage, creating curved and straight paths.

D. Change the opacity and scale of this animation over time.

E. Move the anchor point of one of the objects and create some rotation keyframes so that it spins on an axis other than its own.

Congratulations! You've completed a very important chapter in your work as an After Effects artist. Setting keyframes is a fundamental skill you'll use for the rest of your career with After Effects.

6.

Playing with Time

| Spatial Versus Temporal Interpolation |
| Using the Keyframe Assistant | Editing the Speed Graph |
| Using the Hold Temporal Interpolation Method |
| Using Roving Keyframes |

chap_06

After Effects 6
H·O·T CD-ROM

This chapter deals specifically with time, or the features that control time in After Effects. As you become more experienced with creating animation, you'll start to recognize the nuances of motion and see how timing plays a critical role. The term "timing" refers to whether objects move quickly, slowly, or change speed in the middle of an animation. During an animation, an object that takes 10 seconds has the potential to move at the same speed over the entire 10 seconds, or to start slow, maintain a constant speed, and then go faster at the end, and still occupy only 10 seconds of time. The tools described in this chapter will help you learn how to finesse the timing of your animation. After Effects is one of the most powerful desktop motion graphics tools because of its capability to give you, the animator and motion designer, the utmost control.

Spatial Versus Temporal Interpolation

As you'll soon see, the After Effects interface distinguishes between spatial and temporal keyframes and keyframe interpolation. **Spatial** means space, **temporal** means time, and **keyframe interpolation** describes the types of changes that occur between keyframes. Although those terms might sound a little technical or intimidating, their meanings are really that simple.

In After Effects, you can set footage to change in both space and time. Distinct tools are used to adjust the spatial and temporal aspects of your compositions. In the previous chapter, you worked primarily with spatial issues in the Composition window. By learning to change the curves of your motion paths, for example, you adjusted the spatial qualities of your animation. In this chapter, you will work with temporal issues in the Timeline window.

The **Timeline** window is the primary tool for playing with time. Just as you adjust spatial interpolation in the Composition window, you can adjust temporal interpolation in the Timeline window.

All properties have temporal interpolation. In other words, you can adjust the timing of any property. After Effects contains sophisticated tools that allow you to affect time in both subtle and dramatic ways. How you use these tools is up to your imagination and artistic sensibility.

It's been said that timing is everything. Timing is perhaps the most important aspect of animation. Although books can provide information, as an artist you develop a sense of timing through experience. A musician must practice to develop a full sense of rhythm. The same is true for an animator. You develop the subtlety of timing and rhythm through a commitment to the art form.

I. _____Using the Keyframe Assistant

In this exercise, you will learn to use the **Keyframe Assistant** to ease the timing of objects. **Easing** the timing means creating a smooth transition in timing. Rather than having something start moving and continue moving at the same speed, an ease will slowly build acceleration or deceleration.

Imagine an animation of a car slowing down at a stop sign. It is not like the car goes 40 miles per hour continuously between its starting and stopping points. First it accelerates, reaches a constant maximum speed and then gradually slows down. Newton's laws of physics apply here, too. Gravity and friction affect all objects moving on Earth.

The Keyframe Assistant offers **ease tools** that provide an automated way of creating speed acceleration and deceleration for the appearance of more natural movement. You'll learn to use the **Easy Ease In** and the **Easy Ease Out** tools to smooth timing changes.

You can see timing changes in the Timeline window by observing the graph associated with time. Through the use of the Keyframe Assistant, you will be introduced to the **Speed graph**, and you will learn to interpret changes in the graph.

1. Open the **Time.aep** project from the **chap_06** folder. Save a copy of this file in the **AE6 HOT Projects** folder that you created in Chapter 2. This allows you to make changes, and still be able to return to the original if you should ever want to.

2. In the **Project** window, double-click the **Ease In and Out** composition. This composition was prepared to teach you the principles of this exercise.

3. Click the **RAM Preview** button on the **Time Controls** palette to view the animation.

Observe that the rocket and the UFO move at a steady, consistent speed. This is called "linear timing." There is no acceleration or deceleration in speed with linear timing.

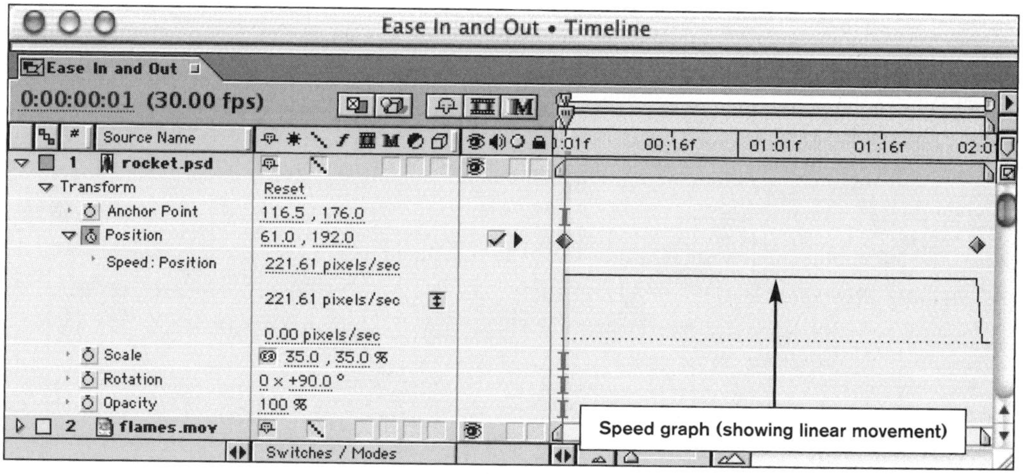

Speed graph (showing linear movement)

4. In the **Timeline** window, click the **rocket.psd Position twirly** to display the **Speed graph** for the **Position** property. Observe the straight line in the graph. This straight line reflects the linear timing of the rocket. This graph is part of the built-in After Effects interface called the **Value graph**, and it exists on any layer that has keyframed motion in the Position, Rotation, Scale, or Opacity properties.

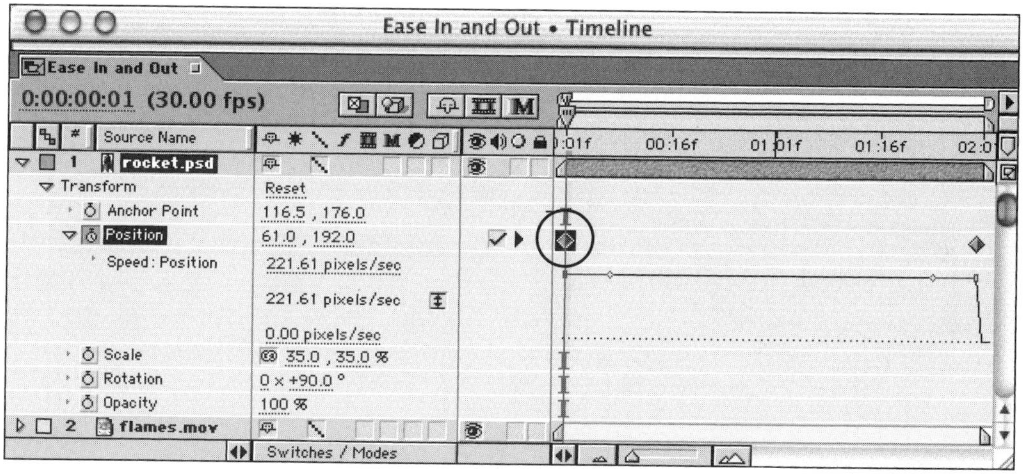

5. Select the keyframe on **Frame 0:00:00:01** of the **rocket.psd** layer.

6. Choose **Animation > Keyframe Assistant > Easy Ease Out**.

Note: A keyframe must be selected to use the Keyframe Assistant feature.

Observe that the Speed graph is now curved. This indicates that the movement is no longer linear. At the lower part of the curve, the timing of the object (in this example, the rocket artwork layer) is slowed down. At the higher part of the curve, the timing of the object is faster.

7. Click **RAM Preview** to see the results so far. Notice that the rocket starts slowly and gains speed.

8. In the **Timeline** window, click the **rocket.psd twirly** up to hide that layer's properties. Click the **ufo.psd Position twirly** down to display the **Speed graph** for that layer. The linear graph reflects the steady, linear timing of the UFO. Click the last keyframe to select it.

9. Choose **Animation > Keyframe Assistant > Easy Ease In**.

Observe that the Speed graph now curves downward. This means that the object starts out moving faster and slows down over time.

The dots get closer and closer together until they touch the last keyframe.

Observe in the Composition window that the dots get closer and closer together as they reach the last keyframe (circled).

10. Click **RAM Preview** to see the animation.

Notice that the UFO slows down at the end of the move. If you can't see the entire animation in RAM Preview, you may not have enough RAM in your computer. Adobe recommends 256 MB or more. If RAM Preview doesn't work, use the spacebar instead to preview everything. Unfortunately, the spacebar preview won't show you a real-time preview, which is what you need in order to judge the timing of your motion.

*So, when do you use Ease In and when do you use Ease Out? Use the **Ease In** function when you want movement to start fast and end slow. If you think of a car pulling "in" to a driveway, that might be an easy way to remember that Ease In means to slow down. Use the **Ease Out** function when you want movement to start slow and end fast. Think about a car pulling "out" of a driveway to remember that an Ease Out means to speed up. If you want something other than slow and fast or fast and slow, you'll have to learn how to adjust the timing curves on your own. (You'll learn how to do that in the next exercise!)*

---

11. Save your project and close the **Ease In and Out** composition. Leave the project open for the next exercise.

NOTE | Speed Dots

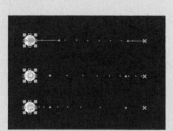

After Effects offers a visual way to see the timing of your animations. When you select an object in the Timeline or Composition window that already has Position keyframe properties set, dots will appear in the Composition window. Each dot indicates a frame in time. The spacing between the dots indicates how fast or slow or evenly paced the keyframed movement is. In the example above, the top circle has evenly spaced dots associated with its motion. This indicates **linear movement**. The middle circle is using an **Ease In**, shown by dots that are spaced farther apart at the beginning and closer together at the end. This means that the movement will start out fast and then slow down. The bottom circle is using an **Ease Out**, and the dots are spaced closer together at the first keyframe and get farther apart at the end. Dots that are closer together mean slower movement, and ones that are farther apart mean faster movement.

The only way to see these dots is to select artwork (that has Position keyframe properties set), either in the Timeline or Composition window. One way to affect the spacing between the dots is with the Speed graph, which you just learned about!

2. ——————Editing the Speed Graph

In this exercise, you will learn to work with the Speed graph. You've seen that the Easy Ease In and Easy Ease Out tools will automatically ease timing for you. However, it's often preferable to set the timing exactly as you want it. Here you'll learn to ease animation timing manually.

1. Double-click the **Time Graph** composition to open it.

2. Click **RAM Preview** and observe the linear timing of the rocket lifting off.

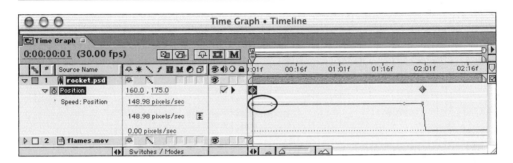

3. In the **Timeline** window, select the **rocket.psd** layer and press the letter **P** to reveal the **Position** property by itself. Click its **twirly** to reveal the **Speed graph**. Click on the first keyframe for the **rocket.psd** layer. Once the keyframe is selected, control handles will appear on the Speed graph.

4. Locate the **control handle** for the keyframe on the graph. Drag the handle down to slow the speed of the rocket. Notice that the graph adjusts as you drag and release the control handle.

Dragging the handle down on the graph slows the timing. Dragging the handle up speeds up the timing.

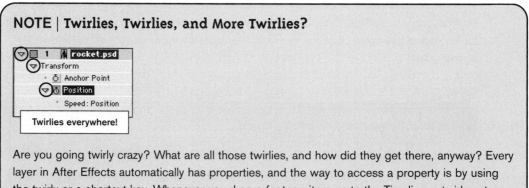

5. Drag the **control handle** to the right to influence more outgoing frames. Notice that the graph adjusts as you drag and release the handle.

Dragging the control handle away from the point influences more frames. Dragging it toward the point influences fewer frames.

6. Click **RAM Preview** and notice that the rocket now lifts off slowly and then speeds up.

7. Save your project, and leave this composition open for the next exercise.

NOTE | Twirlies, Twirlies, and More Twirlies?

Are you going twirly crazy? What are all those twirlies, and how did they get there, anyway? Every layer in After Effects automatically has properties, and the way to access a property is by using the twirly or a shortcut key. Whenever you drag a footage item on to the Timeline, a twirly automatically appears next to it. Chances are that whenever you encounter a twirly and click it, you might find some hidden treasures or properties to explore. Twirlies will be discussed and demonstrated throughout the book, so get used to them now!

3. ——————————Using the Hold Temporal Interpolation Method

In this exercise, you'll learn to use the **Hold interpolation method**. This method is useful when you want movement in an animation to stop and hold. In the process of learning how to use the Hold interpolation method, you'll get more experience building a new composition and setting keyframes.

1. Create a new composition. You haven't made a new composition for a few chapters, so here's a refresher on how to do it. In the **Project** window, click the **Create a new composition** button. This opens the **Composition Settings** window. Name this **Hold Comp**, match the settings to what you see here, and click **OK**.

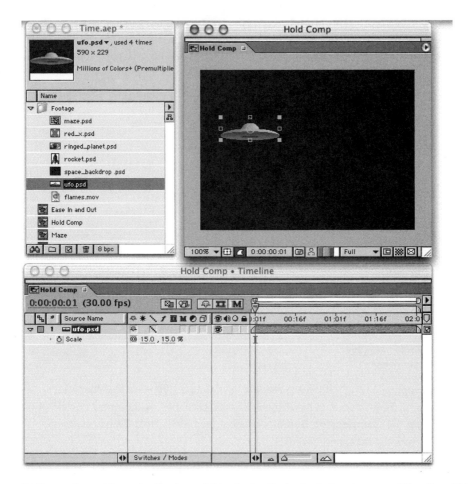

2. Drag **ufo.psd** from the **Footage** folder in the **Project** window into your **Timeline**. This artwork is way too big, so set the scale to **15%**. (**Hint:** The letter **S** on your keyboard will show you the **Scale** properties, or you can use the twirly in the **Timeline** to locate the **Transform > Scale** properties.) Move the UFO into the position that you see here by dragging it into place in the **Composition** window.

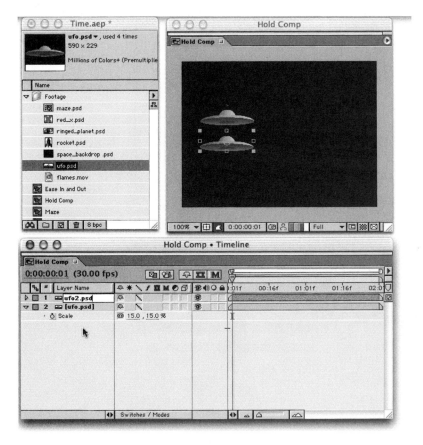

3. Duplicate the layer so you can have two identical UFOs in the **Composition** window. This is a little easier said than done, so here's how to accomplish it. Select the **ufo.psd** layer in the **Timeline** window, and choose **Cmd+D** (Mac) or **Ctrl+D** (Windows) to duplicate the layer. A new layer will appear in the **Timeline** with the same filename. Next, with the copy selected (it appears above the original), use the arrow keys on your keyboard to nudge the copy of the UFO image down in the **Composition** window until it matches what you see in the screen shown here. Change the filename to **ufo2.psd** by selecting the layer in the **Timeline**, using the **Return** key (Mac) or **Enter** key (Windows) to access the editable name field, and typing new a name. The bracket around the new name indicates that you've made a change to its original name.

*You may not realize what you've just accomplished. By changing the scale in Step 2 and not setting a keyframe by not clicking the **Stopwatch** icon, you created a global change for the object. This means that it will be 15% scale throughout any animation unless you change your mind, set keyframes, and make changes to the scale between keyframes. By duplicating the object with the global scale change, you now have two identical small UFO images. After Effects professionals often use this duplicate-and-rename technique to save time.*

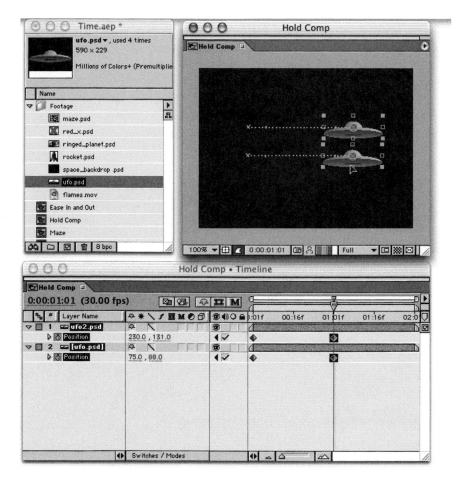

4. Next you'll set position keyframes to make the UFO layers move across the screen. You can do this to both layers at once—joy! Here's how: Select both layers, using your **Shift** key, and press **P** on the keyboard. This causes the **Position** property to appear on both layers. Or, you could twirl all the twirlies down, but what a hassle! Then click the **Stopwatch** icon to set start keyframes for both layers. Move the **Current Time Indicator** to **Frame 0:00:01:01**. Select both UFO objects in the composition by using your **Shift** key and move one to the right. They should both move together, and two identical keyframes will be set.

You could have done this keyframe animation to one UFO layer and then duplicated the layer. There are always multiple ways to do things in After Effects. You'll find that sometimes you think through the most efficient workflow, and other times you'll change your mind as you're working. After Effects will let you work easily either way.

5. Deselect all the layers by clicking in a blank area in the **Timeline**. Select the keyframe on **Frame 1** in the **Timeline** for the layer **ufo2.psd**. Choose **Animation > Keyframe Interpolation**. You can also press **Cmd+Option+K** (Mac) or **Ctrl+Alt+K** (Windows).

6. In the **Keyframe Interpolation** dialog box, select **Hold** as the **Temporal Interpolation** type. Click **OK**.

This sets the first keyframe as a Hold interpolation keyframe. You'll see the result when you preview the motion in the next step. As you can see, the Keyframe Interpolation dialog box is rather complex. Be sure to read the chart at the end of this chapter to understand its settings.

7. Click **RAM Preview** or press the **spacebar**, and observe the change in timing between the two UFOs. In particular, notice that the **ufo2.psd** layer holds in time before appearing at the next keyframe. The Hold interpolation keyframe type is used to make objects stop or jump from frame to frame. If you wanted to make **ufo2.psd** move on the first frame, you could change the keyframe interpolation type back to **Linear** or another type of interpolation. You can also mix and match interpolation types within an animation if you set numerous keyframes.

8. Save your project, and close this composition.

NOTE | Temporal Interpolation Icons

When you change the timing of your animation using the Speed graph, different icons for keyframes show up in the Timeline window. It is not necessary to memorize these icons, but if you are curious about what they mean, read through the following chart.

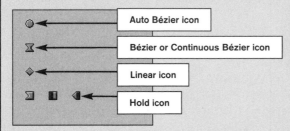

The shape of the Keyframe icon in the Time graph represents the temporal interpolation type. If you ever want to change a temporal keyframe interpolation type, select the keyframe you want to change and choose **Animation > Keyframe Interpolation**. This will cause a dialog box to appear, in which you can choose another temporal interpolation type.

It's not important to memorize what these icons look like. You'll probably be more interested in making your artwork move the way you want it to visually than in worrying about what icon is on your Timeline. Still, you might notice that the icons for keyframes change, and this is a handy chart to refer to if your curiosity gets aroused.

Interpolation Icons and Functions	
Icon	**When to Use**
Auto Bézier	This type of interpolation maintains a smooth transition between different keyframes. The Speed graph will show handles, and automatic curves will be applied.
Bézier or Continuous Bézier	Any time you change the curves on the Speed graph, manually or through the Ease In or Ease Out functions, the icon changes to reflect a Bézier or Continuous Bézier interpolation type. The difference between the two is that Continuous Bézier handles adjust both sides of the curve, whereas Bézier handles adjust each side of the curve separately.
Linear	This is the default temporal interpolation type. Use this interpolation method when you don't want the speed of movement to change.
Hold	Use the Hold interpolation method when you want movement to stop or pause.

4. ————————Using Roving Keyframes

When you set multiple keyframes, it can be hard to get the speed of the movement to be equal and even. This exercise demonstrates this issue. To make the X shape go around the maze in this example, you would have to set numerous keyframes. The trouble is, the physical distance that the X has to travel from keyframe to keyframe varies. Some of the moves are very short, and others are longer. It's hard to know where to set the keyframes on the Timeline because you aren't going to spend the time to measure the distance, divide it into frames, and figure out where to set your keyframes. Wouldn't it be cool if After Effects provided a way to mathematically figure out even timing for you?

It does, of course! The roving keyframes feature addresses this issue. **Roving keyframes** ensures that the speed from keyframe to keyframe is consistent, even if you didn't set it up that way to begin with. In this exercise, you will learn to use roving keyframes by applying the Roving Keyframe command to a prepared composition. If you don't have a good sense of when you'd want to use roving keyframes, this exercise will give you an example.

1. Double-click the **Maze** composition to open it.

2. Click **RAM Preview** and observe the X moving through the maze. Notice that the timing of the movement is not even. The X speeds up and slows down.

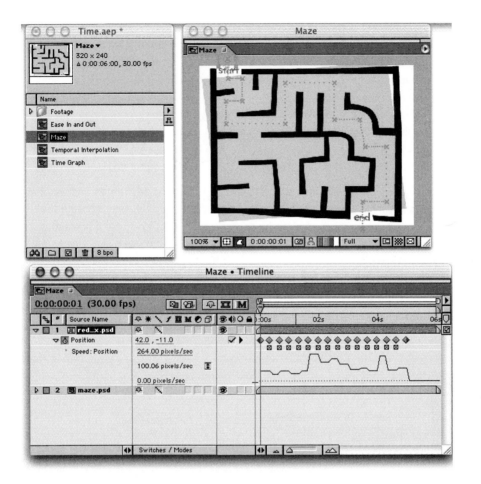

3. In the **Timeline** window, select the **red_x.psd** layer and press **P** to reveal the **Position** property. Note that keyframes have already been set. Click the **Position** twirly to see the **Speed graph**. The high portions of the graph are where the **red_x.psd** layer is moving faster. The low portions of the graph are where the **red_x.psd** layer is moving slower. Also observe that all the keyframes except the first and last have little check boxes beneath them.

*Note: You might wonder how the check boxes got here. If you click the twirly for **Position** to reveal the **Speed graph**, any time that keyframes have been set, these check boxes appear because they are a default part of the After Effects interface. A check box that is marked indicates that the accompanying keyframe is frozen and cannot move across time. You'll learn what this means in the following steps.*

4. With your cursor, drag a selection around all the keyframes that have the little check boxes underneath. This should select all of these keyframes at once. You can also hold down the **Shift** key to select each keyframe, but the dragging method is faster.

All of the keyframes with check boxes should now be selected.

5. Choose **Animation > Keyframe Interpolation**, or press **Cmd+Option+K** (Mac) or **Ctrl+Alt+K** (Windows). In the **Keyframe Interpolation** dialog box, locate the **Roving** option and select **Rove Across Time**. Click **OK**.

As you can see, the options in the Keyframe Interpolation dialog box are rather complex. Be sure to read the chart at the end of this chapter for an explanation of the various options.

6. In the **Timeline** window, observe that the selected keyframes have been moved and the check boxes are now cleared. Also observe that the **Speed graph** is flat and even. This kind of timing would have been really difficult to figure out manually!

Clearing the little check box allows a keyframe to "rove across time." This means that After Effects will move the keyframes that you set manually to mathematically adjust itself to even increments of time. The position of the keyframes on the Timeline will not look even, but After Effects will even out the timing that it takes to get from each point in the composition. This smoothes the timing of movement when the distance of travel between points is varied.

7. Click **RAM Preview** to see the result of the roving keyframes.

8. Save your project, and close After Effects.

What Is Keyframe Interpolation?

The term "interpolation" refers to the process of creating changes between keyframes. It's often referred to as "tweening" in animation terminology.

The **Keyframe Interpolation** dialog box is where temporal and spatial attributes can be set for keyframes. You can access this dialog box by choosing **Animation > Keyframe Interpolation**. You must select single or multiple keyframes before you access this dialog box. Any changes you make in the dialog box will be applied to the selected keyframes. You can mix keyframe interpolation types on different keyframes on a Timeline.

In the Keyframe Interpolation dialog box, you can choose whether you want to use temporal interpolation or spatial interpolation. All properties have temporal interpolation. Of the Transform properties, Opacity is the only one that doesn't have spatial attributes because its changes are marked by time only, not by space. Here's a chart that explains all the complex settings in this dialog box.

Keyframe Interpolation Dialog Box Settings	
Category	**Option**
Temporal Interpolation: Affects the shape of the path in the Composition window.	**Linear:** Creates a uniform rate of change between keyframes. Linear keyframes can be used to form a corner or sharp turn in the graph line. This is useful for giving a mechanical or rhythmic feel to animation timing.
	Bézier: A completely manual type. The two control handles operate independently of one another in both the motion path and Value graph. Use this type when you want manual control of the timing in and out of the keyframe.
	Continuous Bézier: Creates a smooth rate of change through a keyframe, but you set the positions of the control handles manually. Use this type where you want smooth change in time and you need specific control.
	Auto Bézier: Creates a smooth rate of change through a keyframe. You cannot manually adjust the handles of an Auto Bézier point. The handles adjust automatically based on the nearest keyframes and create smooth transitions through the Auto Bézier point. Use it when you want a smooth change in time and do not need manual control. **Note:** If you do adjust the Auto Bézier handle manually, that action will convert it to a Continuous Bézier keyframe.
	Hold: Creates an abrupt change. Use it when you want an image to appear or disappear suddenly. It's also useful when you want a strobe effect. It can hold any point in time steady until the next keyframe.
Spatial Interpolation: Affects how a property changes over time in the Timeline window.	**Linear:** Creates a straight motion path.
	Bézier: Identified by angled handlebars. The handlebars can be adjusted independently in both angle and length.
	Continuous Bézier: Identified by the straight handlebars. The handlebars may be of different length, but they are always straight.
	Auto Bézier: Identified by the smooth curve. There are control handles, but without handlebars. (If you attempt to move a control point on an Auto Bézier type, it will be converted to a Continuous Bézier type.)

continues on next page

Keyframe Interpolation Dialog Box Settings *continued*

Category	Option
Roving: Roving keyframes rove across time to smooth out the Speed graph. The first and last keyframes cannot rove.	**Lock to Time:** The default setting for Roving. This setting allows you to set the keyframe position on the Timeline. **Rove Across Time:** Changes the position of the keyframe on the Timeline to mathematically smooth out the speed of motion. Use this when you want After Effects to create a consistent speed between multiple keyframes.

TIP | Cycle Through Temporal Keyframe Types

You don't have to invoke the complicated Keyframe Interpolation dialog box to change the temporal keyframe setting in your Timeline. Simply **Cmd+click** (Mac) or **Ctrl+click** (Windows) on a keyframe, and you'll see the icon change. You can cycle through all the different temporal and spatial keyframe interpolation types this way, which is much easier than going to a dialog box!

That's it! This chapter is done. Remember that learning the tools of timing is a skill, but the real talent is how you apply your skill to the art of animation. This takes experience, but you have now taken your first steps towards gaining it!

7.

Previewing Movies

| The Time Controls Palette | Types of Previews | Play Modes |

| Skipping Frames | Lowering Preview Resolution |

| Changing Resolution in the Composition Window |

| Defining a Region of Interest | Setting a Work Area |

| Wireframe Previews |

chap_07

After Effects 6
H•O•T CD-ROM

You've already had a little experience previewing your animations using the spacebar shortcut and the Play and RAM Preview buttons in the Time Controls palette, as well as learning to scrub the Current Time Indicator in the Timeline window. It's hard to believe that there's much more to previewing than what you've already learned, but surprise—there is! Numerous options for previewing exist that vary depending on whether you want to save time and see a very quick playback or you want to see every detail possible during playback.

Between these two extremes of fast or accurate are mix-and-match settings within the preview features of After Effects that can be tuned to maximize the type of detail you're looking for and minimize the time it takes to see the results. This chapter demonstrates a number of scenarios that will help you understand when and how to use different preview settings.

The Importance of Previewing

To preview animation in the olden days of filmmaking, you had to photograph your hand-drawn cells, send the film from the camera to a lab, and wait until the following day just to see what you had created! After Effects has made life much easier, but there is a science involved with previewing.

When you create animation and keyframe settings in After Effects, the program has to render what each frame should look like. The rendering process can take a long time if you have a lot of layers, effects, or property settings. Although this is barely noticeable when you're looking at a single frame, it is possible that After Effects will have trouble keeping up with rendering complicated compositions that contain many frames. For this reason, the speed of your previews can become a problem. This chapter covers a lot of techniques to speed up the preview and rendering process.

The Time Controls Palette

You've already worked with the Time Controls palette in previous chapters. Like most things in After Effects, the Time Controls palette is a lot deeper than you might think at first glance. This chapter gives you the opportunity to really learn its features. The following chart describes the various controls on this palette. If your Time Controls palette is not open, choose **Window > Time Controls**.

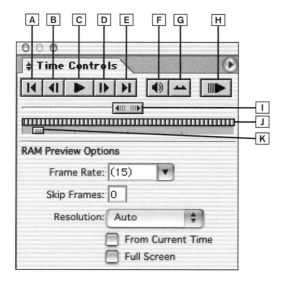

The Time Controls palette is the main tool for controlling previews (see the handy chart on the next page for explanations of the options). As you'll see in this chapter, settings in the Composition and Timeline windows also affect the previewing of movies.

The Time Controls Palette

Option	Description
A. First Frame	Like a rewind button on a VCR, this button will always quickly jump the Current Time Indicator to the first frame.
B. Previous Frame	Allows you to view the composition in single-frame increments in reverse.
C. Play/Pause	Plays the composition. It doesn't play in real time, but it plays as fast as it can—which is sometimes slow. :-)
D. Next Frame	Allows you to view the composition in single-frame increments going forward.
E. Last Frame	Moves the Current Time Indicator to the last frame in the composition.
F. Audio	This button needs to be depressed to hear audio. (Audio is audible only using the RAM Preview button, not the Play button.)
G. Loop	Allows you to watch the same composition over and over (and did I say over?). Clicking this button makes After Effects repeatedly access the Play Once and Palindrome (play forward and then play in reverse over and over) play modes.
H. RAM Preview	Causes After Effects to do its best job to show you the composition at its true speed. It might take a moment for the program to render the preview, but once it does, it will play back faster than using the Play button. The green bar that appears in the Timeline indicates what your computer can play in RAM.
I. Shuttle control	Move this slider forward or backward to view many frames quickly. It doesn't play smoothly, but it gives you a big picture idea of what your composition looks like.
J. Jog	A reference bar that equates to the entire length of your composition.
K. Time indicator	Like the Jog control, this slider lets you view more frames of the composition at once, so you can get a better idea of what is in it. It offers more precise control than the Jog control, however, in that you can move the slider in smaller increments.

> **NOTE | You Need RAM for RAM Preview**
>
> It's very common to have problems with the RAM preview stopping before it has finished display-ing your entire composition. This can be due to a few causes. First, you might not have enough RAM in your computer to run the entire composition. You can solve this problem by buying more RAM (a total of 256 MB is recommended by Adobe, but more is much better!) or by using some of the workarounds you'll learn about in this chapter, such as skipping frames or lowering the pre-view resolution. Another option is to render a final movie, which you'll learn how to do in Chapter 18, "*Rendering Final Movies*."

Types of Previews

There are four different types of previews: **manual**, **standard**, **RAM**, and **wireframe**. The following chart gives an in-depth description of each type and tells how to access these features.

Preview Types and Uses	
Preview Type	**Use**
Manual	Manual preview is used primarily when you want to step through your anima-tion a frame at a time to analyze motion or when you want to set the current time to a specific frame. The Current Time Indicator playhead in the Timeline window, the Shuttle playhead, and the Previous Frame/Next Frame and Play/Pause buttons in the Time Controls palette are all Manual preview types.
Standard	Standard preview is accessed by either clicking the Play button in the Time Controls palette or pressing the spacebar on your keyboard. This mode is use-ful if you want to see every frame. You can use it to analyze motion at slower than real-time playback. You can also choose to use standard preview when you are running low on available RAM and you need to see the entire anima-tion play from beginning to end.
	continues on next page

Preview Types and Uses *continued*	
Preview Type	**Use**
RAM	RAM preview is most useful when you need to see real-time playback. It is located on the Time Controls palette. You can set up two RAM preview modes and switch between them to optimize your workflow. The best use of the two modes is to set one for high image detail and the other for low image detail. Using higher image detail will cut down on the number of frames that can be played back from RAM. Based on your available system RAM, you may also choose to skip frames to optimize the playback.
Wireframe	Wireframe preview should be used when you need real-time preview, and image outlines will provide enough detail to allow for broad compositional choices. Wireframe previews use relatively little RAM and can be valuable when you have numerous frames and very little available RAM. This method can enable you to view a long animation piece in its entirety. You access wireframe settings by choosing **Composition > Wireframe Preview.**

NOTE | Comp or Composition?

Many After Effects professionals use two terms: **comp** and **composition**. They are the same thing. The term "comp" is short for "composition." "Composition" is used in the more formal context, such as when referring to the Composition window. "Comp" is used in the more informal context, such as when you are creating a new comp, opening a comp, or closing your comp.

I. _____ Play Modes in the Time Controls Palette

Three **play modes** are available in the Time Controls palette. These three modes determine whether you see your animation preview once, in a continuous loop, or playing forward and backward continuously.

Although you probably won't need to change play modes often, each of the play modes in After Effects is necessary at times. In this exercise, you'll see how to access the three play modes, and you'll learn the reasons to use each one.

1. Copy the **chap_07** folder from the **H·O·T CD-ROM** to your hard drive.

2. Open the **Preview.aep** project from the **chap_07** folder. Choose **File > Save As** and navigate to the **AE6 HOT Projects** folder that you created in Chapter 2 to save a copy there.

3. Double-click **clown.psd comp** in the **Project** window to open it.

*This composition was made in advance for you. It is 0:00:04:28 long and contains a different layer for each feature of the clown. The layers are animated using Scale, Position, and Rotation properties. It also contains a live-action layer of grass called **grass.mov**. This footage was shot in my front yard with a digital video camera and imported into After Effects. If you want to practice making compositions, feel free to reconstruct this composition at another time, using the contents of the **clown.psd** folder.*

4. In the **Time Controls** palette, click the **Loop** button until it displays the **Loop** icon (shown in the screen shot). As you click this button, it cycles through different icons. You will learn about them all in the course of this exercise. Make sure you click until you see the icon for the loop feature. Click the **RAM Preview** button to play your animation.

Choosing the Loop icon causes your animation to continue to loop until you click on the screen or press a key on the keyboard. This play mode is generally the most useful for analyzing motion.

5. Click the **Loop** button until it shows the **Play Once** icon (shown in the screen shot) and click **RAM Preview.**

In Play Once mode, your animation plays through once and stops on the first frame. This mode is good if you are the type who likes to see something once through and quickly get on to making changes. It can also be useful for presenting work to a client for a first impression.

6. Click the **Loop** button again to display the **Palindrome** icon (shown in the screen shot) and press the **spacebar** on your keyboard. Pressing the **spacebar** is a shortcut for pressing the **Play** button to preview an animation.

The Palindrome mode plays forward and backward continuously. This mode can be good for analyzing complex motion. It can sometimes help to see an action in reverse, perhaps running slowly, to understand the subtleties of the motion.

7. When you're finished watching the animation, press any key to stop the preview. Return the icon to the **Loop** mode, which is the default setting for the Time Controls preview.

8. Close the Composition window for the **clown.psd comp**, but leave the **Preview.aep** project open.

2. ————————Skipping Frames for Faster RAM Previews

You'll sometimes find yourself creating huge, ambitious projects that take a long time to preview. This exercise focuses on a great method for speeding up preview playback: skipping frames.

The Continuous Rasterization icon means that Illustrator footage will always be crisp, no matter how large it is scaled.

The Best quality setting renders all the layers at the highest possible quality so they look as good as possible.

1. Open the **fire-text comp** from the **Project** window.

This composition was created in advance for this exercise. It contains Illustrator and QuickTime footage items. All of the footage is set to Best quality, so it looks as good as it possibly can. The Best quality setting is located in the Switches panel and is discussed in Chapter 8, "Layers." Although this setting makes the artwork look great, it makes the composition take longer to render in RAM preview. The Illustrator items are set in the Timeline to Continuous Rasterization, which means that they'll look crisp even if the artwork is scaled large. This also makes the composition more difficult to render. This composition was designed to demonstrate what happens when you have artwork that is difficult to preview using RAM preview.

2. Move the **Current Time Indicator** to any frame in the **Timeline** and notice that the arrow cursor animates with black and white for a moment. This is a visual indicator that After Effects is rendering and cannot show the final frame. Moving the **Current Time Indicator** to any other point in the **Timeline** will cause the same result.

3. Move the **Current Time Indicator** to the first frame of the composition (or press the **Home** key). Click the **Play** button. You'll see that After Effects struggles to play this animation. This is what happens as you start to work on larger and more complicated compositions, and it is a common issue for every After Effects artist.

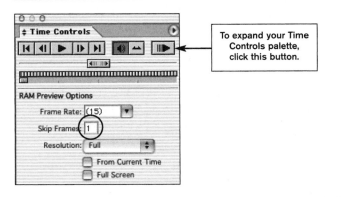

RAM Preview button

4. Click the **RAM Preview** button. It will take After Effects a while to build the preview. Once it is ready to play, it will likely not play all the way through, unless you have a lot of RAM.

See that green line at the top of your Timeline window? That is After Effects' visual display of how many frames it can play in RAM. That green line will appear, disappear, and redraw itself every time you preview a change in your Timeline. It indicates that those frames have been rendered.

To expand your Time
Controls palette,
click this button.

5. Enter a value of **1** into the **Skip Frames** field of the **RAM Preview** options. Click the **RAM Preview** button again. It should take only half as long to prepare this preview. It should also play all the way through now. If it doesn't, enter a value of **2** into the **Skip Frames** field.

The Skip Frames feature is a way to help you see an entire composition, even if you don't have enough RAM to play every frame. This preview technique is useful when you want to see a real-time preview but you don't care about seeing each individual frame. It gives you an accurate sense of timing but not a completely accurate sense of appearance.

6. Set the **Skip Frames** option back to **0**. Save your project and leave this composition open for the next exercise.

NOTE | More About the Skip Frames Option

Setting the **Skip Frames** option to **1** causes the preview to display one frame and then skip one frame. This process continues for the length of the preview.

Skipping frames can help preserve RAM. Every frame skipped preserves memory. However, the more frames you skip, the less smooth the preview. If you need to preserve RAM, it is best to start by skipping one frame and seeing whether this preserves the amount of RAM necessary for your playback.

Another reason you may choose to skip frames is that this option will speed the time it takes to render your preview. Just setting the option to skip one frame will cut the preview rendering time in half.

NOTE | More RAM Questions

You might be curious about other RAM limitations. If RAM is such a big problem, how does it affect your ability to create After Effects projects or the ability for your audience to see your final movies? It is easiest to separate some of these issues to clarify these matters.

First of all, insufficient RAM can affect your RAM preview, but there are several ways around this problem. RAM preview is simply a very handy feature that helps you see your animations quickly as you're working. If you don't have enough RAM in your computer, however, there are other options. The Play/Pause button, the Time indicator control, and the Shuttle control on the Time Controls palette will all allow you to preview your work; they just won't play as fast as the RAM preview will.

The amount of available RAM won't have much of an impact on your ability to create and render After Effects compositions. You can create very complicated movies in After Effects using the minimum RAM requirement of the program. You can also render final movies in After Effects without much RAM. The real issue with RAM is related to using the RAM preview only (and to some of the 3D features that you'll learn about in Chapter 15, "*3D Layers*").

3. _____Lowering Preview Resolution

After Effects treats resolution a little differently from programs that are geared toward outputting files for print. Everything that you bring into After Effects should be prepared at 72 dots per inch (dpi), or it will be converted to that resolution automatically once it is brought into a composition. Instead of dots per inch, After Effects measures resolution in **pixels per inch**. You set the resolution for a composition in the Compositions Settings dialog box. Whatever resolution is set there is considered to be full resolution by After Effects. In our example for this exercise, the full resolution is 320×240 pixels per inch.

In the following steps, you will learn about the **RAM Preview Resolution** option. This option allows you to preview your animation at a lower resolution than the full resolution assigned to the composition. It increases playback speed, so it's another method for speeding things up. You can combine skipped frames with lowered resolution settings, but we're showing you these features one at a time so you'll understand them better.

1. Make sure **fire-text comp** is still open. In the **Time Controls** palette, make sure that **Skip Frames** is set to **0**. Set the **Resolution** to **Quarter**. This takes whatever resolution After Effects is set at (in this case, 320×240) and reduces it by 75 percent.

2. Click the **RAM Preview** button.

All frames are rendered at quarter resolution and previewed in real time. This setting is good for previewing all the frames in your composition while preserving RAM. It also speeds up preview rendering time because lower-resolution images are quicker to render. The downside is that the moving footage doesn't look nearly as good at quarter resolution. It does give you a good indication of motion, but it gives a bad indication of appearance.

3. Save the project and close this composition.

TIP | Frame Rate Settings Can Speed Rendering, Too

Occasionally, you will want to preview your movie faster or slower than the composition settings. To do this, use the **Frame Rate** option. This technique can provide another way to analyze motion.

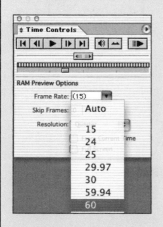

In the **Time Controls** palette, the **Frame Rate** option can be set to **60** frames per second. The animation will play back at twice the speed of the composition setting if the RAM Preview button is used.

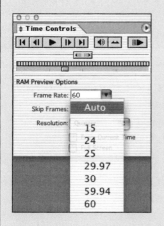

The **Auto Frame Rate** option automatically adjusts the frame rate to match the composition settings.

TIP | Using the Shift+RAM Preview Option

Now that you've learned how to set up the RAM preview with all of its different settings, you might want to take advantage of **Shift+RAM preview**. This option allows you to work with two different kinds of RAM previews. You can set the first RAM preview to be full resolution, not to skip frames, and to use a high frame rate. Do this by setting the RAM Preview options accordingly.

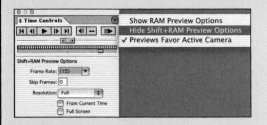

If you want, you can then set up a second type of RAM preview, called **Shift+RAM Preview**. You access this setting by clicking the arrow at the top right of the Time Controls palette and choosing **Show Shift+RAM Preview Options**.

Once you've done this, the **Time Controls** palette will indicate that you are setting the **Shift+RAM Preview** options. Make your changes to the **Frame Rate**, **Skip Frames**, and **Resolution** options. Once you're finished, click the arrow at the top right of the Time Controls palette again and choose **Show RAM Preview Options**. Now you'll have two different options set for previewing.

You can access the standard settings simply by clicking the **RAM Preview** button. If you want to access the **Shift+RAM Preview** settings, hold down the **Shift** key and click the same button. Voilà—you've got two groups of settings with which to preview. Sweet!

4. ——————————Changing Resolution in the Composition Window

You can change the **Resolution** setting in the Composition window as an alternative to changing the RAM Preview resolution in the Time Controls palette. When you make this change in the Composition window, it affects the way the Composition window appears all the time, until you change it back to full resolution. When you change the setting in the Time Controls palette, the Composition window will look normal, but the RAM preview will display with the lower resolution. Why change the resolution in the Composition window? If your composition has a lot of render-intensive filter effects, such as Blur or Motion Blur, and the Composition window is set to full resolution, After Effects will take a long time to render a still frame. This gets very cumbersome when you're trying to position objects and set keyframes. For this reason, knowing how to use the Composition window's Resolution setting is an important skill.

1. Open **large space comp** from the **Project** window.

This composition was created at 640×480 pixels and is larger than other compositions you have worked with so far in this book. After Effects can create compositions with resolutions as high as 30,000×30,000 pixels, which is well beyond anything you would ever need! The 640×480 resolution is a common one that is often used for video and CD-ROM development. The trouble is, a 640×480 composition is difficult to render at times. This particular composition has some Motion Blur and Best quality settings added to it, which make it challenging to render as well. You will learn about Motion Blur in Chapter 10, "Effects."

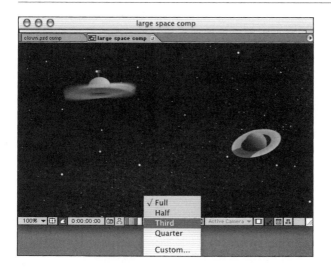

2. Press the **spacebar** to play the composition. Notice how slow it is. In the **Composition** window, click the **Resolution** drop-down menu and choose **Third** from the available options. Press the **spacebar** to play the composition. Notice that the image looks noticeably degraded but that the animation plays more quickly.

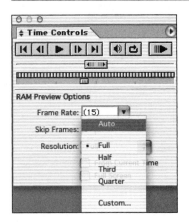

3. In the **Time Controls** palette, set the **Resolution** option to **Full**. Click the **RAM Preview** button.

Your animation plays back at full resolution, even though it is still changed in the Composition window to the Third resolution setting. The RAM Preview Resolution option is independent of the Composition window's Resolution setting. You can make a resolution change in either spot—in the RAM Preview options of the Time Controls palette or the Composition window. That way, when you press the space-bar, the Composition window setting will play (currently set to Third). If you click the RAM Preview button, the composition will play at its current setting, which is Full resolution. RAM preview may not be able to play the entire Composition because you may not have enough RAM in your computer.

4. In the **Time Controls** palette, choose **Auto** as the **Resolution** setting. Click the **RAM Preview** button.

The animation plays back at Third resolution. The Auto setting allows the RAM preview to use the same resolution as the current Resolution setting in the Composition window.

5. In the **Composition** window, choose **Full** as the resolution setting. Click the **RAM Preview** button.

With the RAM Preview Resolution set to Auto, the preview adjusts to full resolution. Now the playback will be slower, and it might not be able to play all the frames again.

6. Save your project and leave this composition open for the next exercise.

MOVIE | resolution.mov

If you still have questions about changing the resolution in the Time Controls palette versus the Composition window, please watch the movie entitled **resolution.mov**, located in the **movies** folder on the **H•O•T CD-ROM**.

5. ———————Previewing a Region of Interest

Defining a **region of interest** allows you to preview a specific area of the image. By specifying a smaller area for preview, you decrease the rendering time and speed up your workflow. This method also allows you to visually concentrate on the details of a limited area.

A region of interest is very easy to use. Once you've set it up, it is always available and can be toggled on or off at the click of a button. In this brief exercise, you'll learn everything about the Region of Interest option.

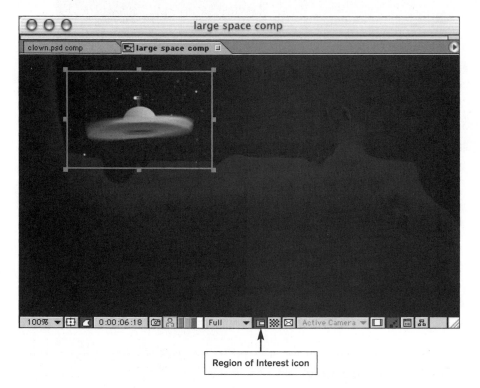

Region of Interest icon

1. Make sure **large space comp** is still open. In the **Composition** window, click the **Region of Interest** icon. The cursor changes to a **Marquee** tool. Drag in the upper-left corner to define a region of interest. Use the control handles on the resulting bounding box to adjust the size of the region. Once you complete the shape, everything else will disappear except the area you selected.

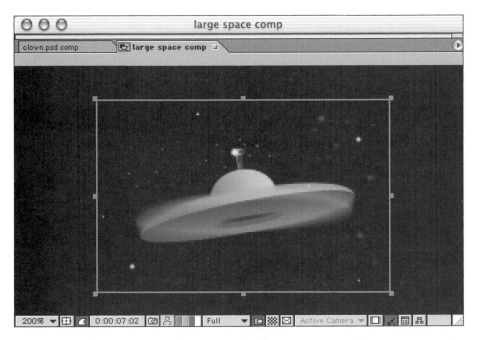

2. In the **Composition** window, set the **Magnification** to **200%**. Hold down the **spacebar**, and the **Hand** tool will appear if you place your cursor in the **Composition** window. Click the **Hand** tool and drag the image to position the region of interest in the center of the window.

*Note: You can also use the **Zoom** tool from the **Tools** palette to zoom into a document and look at a specific area. Holding the **Option** (Mac) or **Alt** (Windows) key will cause the **Zoom** tool to zoom out and decrease magnification. Press the **spacebar** to view your animation.*

3. Set the **Magnification** to **100%**. Click the **Region of Interest** icon to toggle the region of interest off.

4. With the region of interest toggled off, hold down the **Option** key (Mac) or **Alt** key (Windows) and click on the **Region of Interest** icon at the bottom of the Composition window. This clears the region of interest. The **Marquee** tool appears again so you can draw a new region of interest.

5. Save your project, and leave this composition open for the next exercise.

NOTE | When Should You Use RAM Preview?

RAM preview is preferable to using the spacebar or Play button on the Time Controls palette because it gives you a better sense of how fast your animation plays in real time. You won't always need to know that, however. There are times when you'll just want to check movement, not timing. It's fine to use any preview method you want—RAM preview simply offers the fastest preview of them all.

6. ——————Limiting Previews with Work Area Settings

Sometimes, if your animation is long, you might want to preview only a small section that you are in the process of refining. You can do this by using the **work area** settings in the Timeline window. In the following exercise, you will learn to use the work area. First, you'll learn the keyboard shortcuts, and then you'll learn to set the work area by simply dragging the handles.

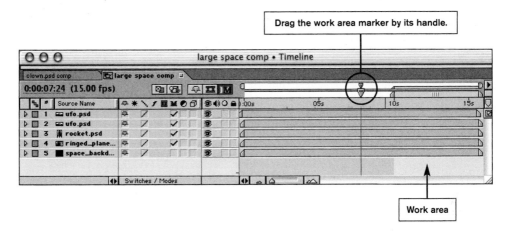

Drag the work area marker by its handle.

Work area

1. Make sure **large space comp** is still open. Drag the left side of the **work area** marker in the **Timeline** to begin the work area at **10 seconds**.

---

2. Click the **RAM Preview** button in the **Time Controls** palette. You'll see that the preview includes only the frames within the work area. The animation should start playing at **00:10:00**, where the work area begins, instead of at **00:00:00**. This is useful if you want to preview a small section of your Timeline. If the animation won't play in full, try lowering the resolution in the **RAM Preview** options to **Half** or lower.

---

3. Drag the left **work area** marker to **00:00:00** and the right **work area** marker to **00:15:18** so that the work area begins on the first frame and ends on the last frame of the composition.

Tip: In addition to dragging the work area marker, you can use keyboard shortcuts to set these points.

Work Area Keyboard Shortcuts		
Action	**Macintosh**	**Windows**
Set beginning of work area to current time	B	B
Set end of work area to current time	N	N

4. Click **RAM Preview** in the **Time Controls** palette. You'll see a preview of the new work area. If the animation won't play in full, try lowering the **Resolution** in the **RAM Preview** options to **Half** or lower. Sometimes you have to combine techniques. If you make this change, be sure to set it back to **Auto** once you've finished this exercise.

5. Save your project and close the **large space comp** window. You won't need it again in this chapter.

7. ——————Wireframe Previews

Sometimes in a preview, you want to focus on the motion of your objects and not so much on their appearance. In such cases, you can use a more-specialized type of preview that allows you to see a wireframe of your artwork instead of the full-pixel version. A wireframe outline will typically conform to the shape of the different layers of artwork in your composition. This mode shows a white outline that gives you a quick impression of the shape of your artwork, but without the color, fill, effects, and texture.

Using a wireframe setting is useful for previewing motion quickly, because the computer doesn't have to render as much information as it does in other modes. There are two different types of wireframe previews: basic wireframe and wireframe with motion trails; you'll learn to use both in this exercise.

1. Double-click on the **clown.psd comp** in the **Project** window to open it.

2. Click the **Play** button in the **Time Controls** palette to view the animation. Click it again to stop the animation.

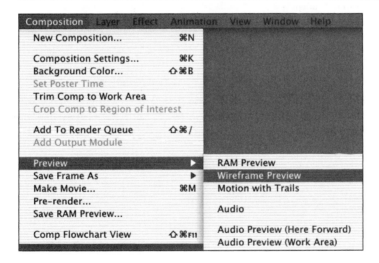

3. Choose **Composition > Preview > Wireframe Preview**.

This setting enables your composition to play in real time because After Effects doesn't have to render much content to the screen. In this preview, it's easy to see the compositional relationship between all of the objects while viewing the animation in its entirety. This setting is used when you have a complicated animation and you want to see parts that are hidden by other objects. It's also faster for the computer to generate than full frames, so it's used sometimes as a quick-and-dirty preview method.

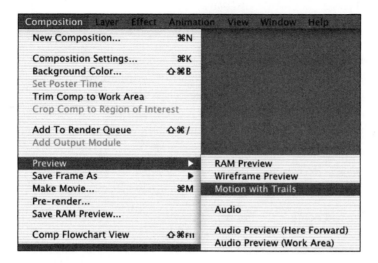

4. Choose **Composition > Preview > Motion with Trails**. This type of preview shows a wireframe view that repeats with every frame, leaving a trace of its motion. It's useful for observing the motion paths of your objects as they are moving.

5. Close this project—you're finished with it for this chapter.

That's all there is to previewing with wireframes. You won't use this feature all the time; you'll want it only when you have a complicated composition that takes a long time to render. If you want to go back to using the standard previewing options, simply click the Play or RAM Preview button, and the preview will return to normal.

Eeek! Which Setting Should You Use?

At this point, you've been introduced to a lot of different preview settings, and you might be confused as to which setting to use when. It's a good practice to be aware of the following items when previewing animation. You can use this chart as a checklist when setting up a preview. With a little time, this list will become second nature.

Summary of Preview Settings		
Location	Feature	Reason to Use
Timeline window	Set the **work area** in the Timeline and use RAM preview in the Time Controls palette.	Useful to reduce the number of frames shown during a preview when you have a long animation that takes too long to render.
Composition window	Select a **Resolution** option—Full, Half, Third, Quarter, or Custom.	Useful when the static preview takes a long time when you are trying to move an object.
Composition window	Set the **region of interest**.	Useful if you want to focus on one small part of your screen only.
Time Controls palette	Select a **play mode**: Play Once, Loop, or Palindrome.	Useful for choosing whether to watch something once, over and over, or forward and backward.
Time Controls palette	Select **RAM or Shift+RAM Preview** options	Helpful for previewing in real time. Being able to access a secondary group of settings with the Shift key is useful for easily toggling between an accurate or a fast preview.

Another chapter under your belt! Getting used to previewing movies and using the options takes time and working experience. You won't necessarily need everything you've learned right away, but it will come in handy as you work on larger projects. So give yourself some time to absorb everything here, and feel free to return to this chapter when you want to remember exactly how a preview option functions.

8.

Layers

Layer Basics	Labeling	Switches	Shy Layers
Solo Button	Quality Switch	Continuous Rasterization
Motion Blur	Moving and Trimming Layers	Trimming Layers
Splitting Layers	Time Stretching and Frame Blending
Time Remapping	Replacing Layers
Sequencing Layers	Solid Layers	Layer Modes

chap_08

After Effects 6
H•O•T CD-ROM

You might be used to the concept of layers from programs such as Photoshop and Illustrator. In After Effects, many of the same principles apply, yet its use of layers is much more complicated than in programs that deal only with still images.

Layers reside in the Timeline of After Effects, and they relate not only to what appears visually in your composition, but also to the timing of your graphics and animations. This chapter will expose you to the power that layers hold. Some of the things you'll learn to do here include moving layers, renaming layers, replacing layers, trimming layers, sliding layers, and organizing layers. It's a long chapter but an invaluable part of your After Effects education.

I. ————————Layer Basics

You've used layers throughout the preceding chapters. In the following exercise, you'll start with a couple of items you've seen before, and then you'll quickly move into new territory. You'll learn how to rename a layer and to change the stacking order of layers, using the keyboard to lock and unlock layers. In the process, you'll get practice in making a composition and importing a layered Photoshop file.

1. Choose **File > New > New Project** to create a new project. Choose **File > Save As** and navigate to the **AE6 HOT Projects** folder you created in Chapter 2. Save this new empty project file there as **Layers.aep**.

2. Double-click inside the empty **Project** window to bring up the **Import File** dialog box. Navigate to the **chap_08** folder and select the file called **gnometank.psd**. In the **Import As** list, select **Composition – Cropped Layers**, and then click the **Import** (Mac) or **Open** (Windows) button. Both a footage folder and a composition should appear in the Project window, both named **gnometank Comp 1** This is a way to bring a layered Photoshop file into After Effects as a composition. Twirl down the **arrow** on the **gnometank.psd** footage folder in the Project window to see that each layer in the Photoshop file has been imported as a separate piece of footage.

3. Select the composition icon **gnometank Comp 1** in the Project window and choose **Composition > Composition Settings**. How did these settings get in here, you might wonder? The Photoshop document was created at 320×240, so that is how it got the dimensions. All of the other settings are carried over from the last settings you created, the last time you made a composition. Click **OK**.

4. Double-click the **gnometank Comp 1** composition to open the Composition and Timeline windows. In the **Timeline** window, select the top layer, named **Layer 3**, and press **Return** (Mac) or **Enter** (Windows). Rename the layer **fish 1**. Now that you know how to rename layers, change the name of **Layer 2** to **fish 2** and the name of **Layer 1** to **fish 3**.

Sometimes you'll want to rename layers that get imported from Photoshop, or you'll simply change your mind about a layer's name you brought in from any source. Now you know how to do this.

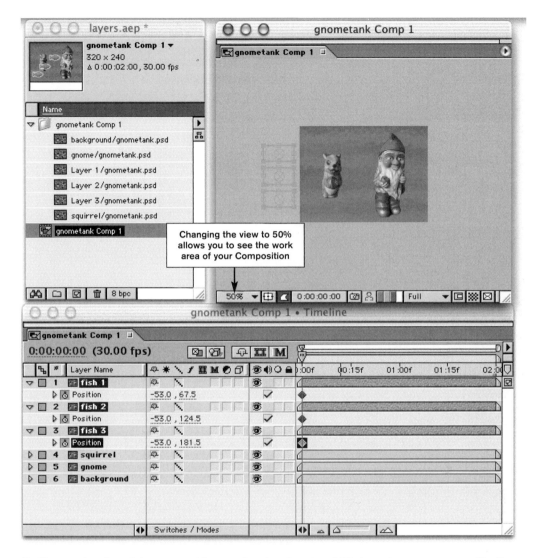

5. Change the size of the composition preview by choosing **50%** from the pop-up **magnification** menu. Click and drag each fish so it is in the work area of the Composition window. This is how you set artwork to a position that is out of view. The fish will animate eventually into view and exit out of view from left to right. This is the first step in accomplishing such an animation. Hold down the **Shift** key and select **fish 1**, **fish 2**, and **fish 3** in the **Timeline** window. Press the **P** key to reveal the Position property of each layer. Click the **Stopwatch** icon on any of the layers. Because all three layers were selected, this process should activate the Stopwatch for all the selected layers with a single click.

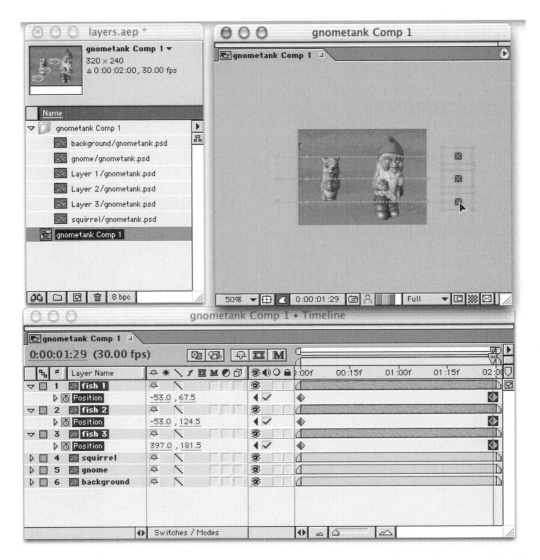

6. Move the **Current Time Indicator** to the last frame of the **Timeline**. All three layers should still be selected in the Timeline along with the three associated objects in the Composition window. If not, use the **Shift** key to select all three objects in your **Composition** window and move them to the other side of the **Composition** window, as shown here. You can do this by holding down the **Shift** key and dragging the items or by using the **arrow** keys. This should set the second keyframe on all three layers.

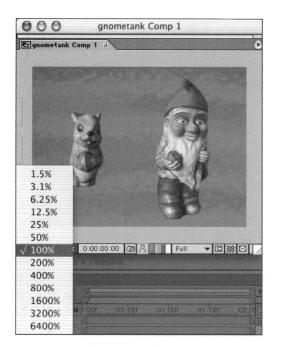

7. Change the scale of the **Composition** window back to **100%** and watch the animation you just created by pressing the **spacebar**. If you don't want to see the motion paths as you preview the movement, deselect the layers by clicking in an empty area of the **Timeline** window.

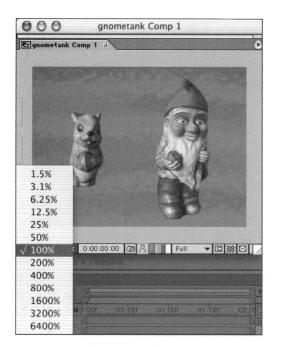

8. In the **Timeline** window click and drag the **squirrel** layer so that it is at the top of the stack. Move the **gnome** layer so it is above **fish 3**. Press the **spacebar** to watch the animation to see how the stacking order of the layers changes the preview in the Composition window. After Effects stacks its layers from bottom to top, with the topmost layer being in front of all other layers.

9. Since you wouldn't want the background layer to be animated, click in the **Lock** switch area of the **background** layer, as you see here. This is a great way to ensure that you don't accidentally move or bump a layer that you want to stay still.

10. Save the project, and leave this composition open for the next exercise.

TIP | Using the Keyboard to Change the Stacking Order

The following table shows keyboard shortcuts you can use to change the stacking order of the layers in a composition.

Stacking Order Keyboard Commands		
Stacking Change	**Mac**	**Windows**
Move down one level	Cmd+[	Ctrl+[
Move up one level	Cmd+]	Ctrl+]
Move to bottom of stack	Cmd+Shift+[	Ctrl+Shift+[
Move to top of stack	Cmd+Shift+]	Ctrl+Shift+[

2. ——————Labeling Layers

All layers have color-coded labels. You probably haven't paid too much attention to these labels; they are displayed in the Timeline window in the second column from the left and are just little squares. You can assign and control the color coding of each layer.

Labels can help you identify layers when you are working with large projects. For example, you could assign one label color to layers that contain type and another to layers that contain photographs. Once layers have color codes, they can be selected using the label color. Label colors can help you keep from losing your mind when you need some method of organizing a lot of content. In this exercise, you'll learn how to assign label colors and then select layers based on the label assignment.

1. With the composition still open from the last exercise, hold down the **Cmd** key (Mac) or **Ctrl** key (Windows) and click **fish 1**, **fish 2**, and **fish 3**. Clicking while holding down the **Cmd** or **Ctrl** key allows you to select noncontiguous layers.

Observe the column of color squares to the left of the Level # column. At the moment, they are all pink, which is the default color code for layers. You'll learn to change the color of selected layers in the next step.

2. Choose **Edit > Label > Red** and notice that the color codes on all the selected fish layers turn red.

3. Click the **squirrel** layer to select it. Choose **Edit > Label > Select Label Group**. Notice that all layers with the same label color are selected in the Timeline window. Also notice that a locked layer is not selected unless you unlock it, which is why the background layer is not selected.

4. Save and close the project.

NOTE | Label Color Preferences

You can change the available label colors and names by choosing **Edit > Preferences > Label Colors**. Label Preferences aren't under the **Edit** menu in OS X; they're under the **After Effects** menu. To rename a label, type in a color name. You can also use the eyedropper or click on a color field to access the color picker to change a label color.

What Are Switches?

Switches allow you to display layers in After Effects in different ways. Depending on your work process, you may want to use switches to hide layers from display in the Timeline, turn off the sound from an audio layer, or show only an individual layer in the Composition window. Switches give you options for working with After Effects to make your work process as efficient as possible. They affect the preview and final rendering of your movie.

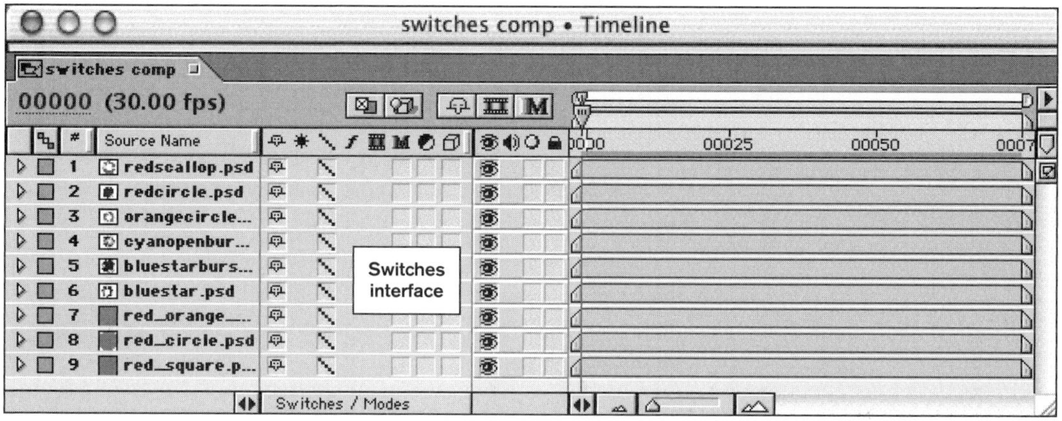

Switches are located in the Timeline window. Each layer has its own set of switches that affect only that layer.

Switches form columns of options for your layers. The preceding illustration shows some of the switch options you might use most often. You've already been introduced to the Lock switch. In the exercises that follow, you'll learn about more switch options, and we'll introduce you to others throughout the rest of this book.

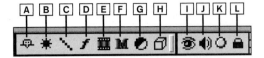

Here's a handy chart that explains the meaning of each switch. The letters correspond to the labels in the preceding illustration. **Tip:** If you forget what the name of a switch is, you can see its tool tip by hovering the pointer over any of the switch icons.

Switch Functions	
Switch Name	**Definition**
A. Shy Layers	Allows you to turn off a layer in the Timeline window, even though it will still be visible in the Composition window. This allows you to limit the number of layers that are visible to make it easier to work with a complicated Timeline. The shy layers can be turned on and off with the click of one button, making it easy to enable and disable them. You'll work with shy layers in the next exercise.
B. Continuous Rasterization	Allows vector artwork to rasterize when different transformations are applied, causing it to have a crisp appearance. You'll get to work with this switch a little later in this chapter.
C. Quality	Toggles to specify either Draft or Best quality. The default is Draft quality. You can click on this switch to see the effect that the two settings produce. The Quality setting is especially noticeable when artwork is transformed using scaling or rotation.
D. Effect	Allows you to turn off effects temporarily so they don't have to be rendered. You don't lose your effects settings when you turn them off. You'll work with this switch in Chapter 10, "*Effects.*"
E. Frame Blend	When you use the time mapping or time stretching features (you'll learn to do so later in this chapter), the result is that After Effects holds frames, which often results in jerky movement. Frame blending smoothes out the jerkiness by creating dissolves between different frames.

continues on next page

Switch Functions *continued*	
Switch Name	**Definition**
F. Motion Blur	Uses After Effects' built-in motion blur feature, which emulates a motion picture camera that uses a long exposure. You'll learn to use this feature later in this chapter.
G. Adjustment Layers	Allows you to apply effects to more than one layer at a time. You'll learn to work with adjustment layers in Chapter 10, "*Effects*".
H. 3D Layer	A 3D layer can move in three-dimensional space. You'll learn to work with 3D layers in Chapter 15 "*3D Layers.*"
I. Video	Available only if your layer contains movie footage. This switch toggles the video on or off.
J. Audio	Available only if your layer contains audio. This switch toggles the audio on or off.
K. Solo	Allows you to easily isolate one or more layers and turn all the other layers off. It saves you the effort of turning off the layers you don't want to see. This switch turns off the visibility of layers in the Composition window; the Shy Layers switch turns off the visibility of a layer or layers only in the Timeline window.
L. Lock	Allows you to lock a layer so it cannot be moved or edited. This is useful when you want to ensure that a layer doesn't change.

3. —————————————Using Shy Layers

When you have a composition with a lot of layers, it's sometimes helpful to turn off a layer or layers in the Timeline but to leave the artwork itself visible. This eliminates visual clutter in the Timeline when you're trying to focus on setting keyframes. When you mark a layer as shy, it can be hidden from display in the Timeline window until you're ready to display it again.

Shy layers are still active in your composition and display normally in the Composition window. They are just hidden from view in the Timeline window so you can concentrate on the task at hand without scrolling up and down in search of the layers that need attention.

When you have a layer or group of layers you're happy with, and you aren't planning on tweaking them any more, mark them as shy. You can use this technique as a checklist to remind yourself which layers still need work: The visible layers are the ones that need attention before you complete your composition.

In this exercise, you'll learn to mark shy layers and to hide or display all shy layers by using the Enable Shy Layer button.

1. Open the **Switches.aep** project from the **chap_08** folder. Choose **File > Save As** and navigate to the **AE6 HOT Projects** folder you created in Chapter 2 and create a copy of it there. In the **Project** window, double-click the **switches comp** composition to open it and its associated Timeline.

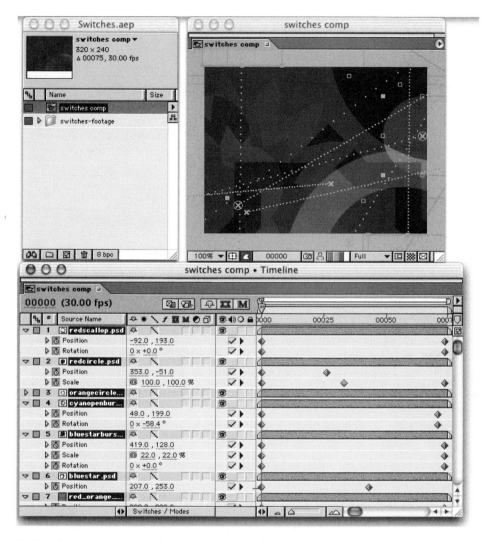

2. Play the composition to view the animation. There are lots of layers and keyframes for Scale, Rotation, Position, and Opacity in this composition. In the Timeline window, select all the layers with **Cmd+A** (Mac) or **Ctrl+A** (Windows). Press the letter **U** (the shortcut key to reveal all the properties that contain keyframes).

I like to remember the letter U as the Uberkey! It's a great shortcut key to know about when you want to quickly see what properties have been set to animate in an unfamiliar (or even complicated but familiar!) composition.

This causes quite a few layers and properties to open in the Timeline. Once your Timeline gets to this level of complexity, it becomes difficult to focus on an individual layer.

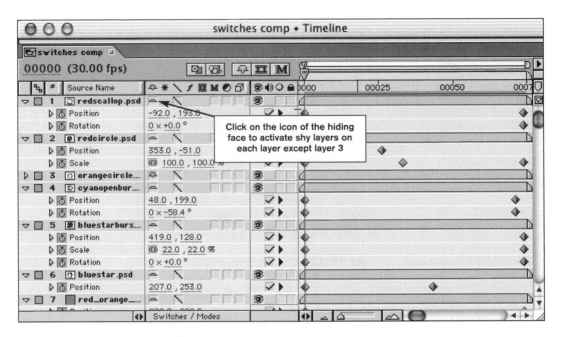

3. Deselect the layers by clicking in an empty area of the **Timeline**. Click the **Shy Layers** switch for all of the layers except **layer 3, orangecircle.psd**. Nothing noticeable will happen in the Timeline or composition yet, except that the icons for the Shy Layers switch will change to identify each of the layers as shy. When a layer is shy, the icon looks flat (as though the guy is hiding), and when it isn't shy, it shows a picture of him with his nose peeking out.

4. Click the **Enable Shy Layer** button at the top of the **Timeline** window. Observe that the shy layers you created in Step 3 are now hidden in the **Timeline** window. Click the **Enable Shy Layer** button again to toggle it off (so all of your layers are displayed).

*Why would you do this? In this example, the **orangecircle** layer is the only layer that doesn't animate. To add animation keyframes to it, you might want to isolate it so you aren't distracted by all the other layers in the Timeline window. Once you've worked on it and set keyframes, you'd want to see all the other layers again, which you could do easily by clicking the Enable Shy Layer button at the top of the Timeline window. Shy layers offer a way to organize your Timeline when it gets too cluttered with layers and property settings.*

5. Save this project, and leave **switches comp** open for the next exercise.

4. ──────────Using the Solo Switch

The **Solo switch** provides a quick way to hide certain layers temporarily and to leave selected layers turned on. Unlike shy layers, which remain visible in the Composition window when they're turned off in the Timeline, solo layers hide the artwork in the Composition window but leave it visible in the Timeline window.

Sometimes it's useful to see a few layers together. Fortunately, despite its name, soloing is not limited to displaying just one layer at a time. In this exercise, you will learn to solo individual and multiple layers. You'll also learn how to stop soloing layers and return to normal display.

1. You should still have the **switches comp** open from the last exercise. Click on the **Timeline** to make it active. Select all the layers by using the shortcut keys: **Cmd+A** (Mac) or **Ctrl+A** (Windows). Press the letter **U**. All the layer properties should disappear. If you press the letter **U** twice again, they will appear and disappear. This is a great technique to quickly collapse your Timeline!

2. Deselect all the layers by clicking in an empty area of the **Timeline** window.

When a Solo switch is used, all the layers remain visible in the Timeline window, but only the layer(s) that have been soloed appear in the Composition window.

3. In the **Timeline** window, locate the **Solo** column. Click the **Solo** switch for the **redscallop.psd** layer to solo the layer in the **Composition** window. Notice that the other layers are no longer displayed!

Why would you want to turn off all the other layers in the Composition window? You may want to work on this individual layer without the distraction of all the other artwork on the screen.

4. Click the **Solo** switch for the **bluestar.psd** and **red_circle.psd** layers. These layers turn on, and the previous solo layer stays on as well.

Tip: You can select multiple layers and then click the Solo switch of any of the selected layers to turn on soloing for all selected layers.

5. Click the **Solo** switch for the top layer (**redscallop.psd**) and leave your mouse button depressed. With the mouse button down, drag straight down the **Solo** switch column to clear all active Solo switches. Once they are cleared, the artwork for all of the layers will reappear in the Composition window.

The Solo switch is actually a toggle, meaning that you can also click each individual Solo icon to clear soloing for the corresponding layer.

6. Save and close the **Switches.aep** project. You won't be needing it again.

5. _____ Using the Quality Switch

In this exercise, you will learn to use the **Quality switch**. This switch toggles the quality for artwork on a layer between the Best and Draft settings. As a rule, Best quality looks better but takes longer to render.

Pixel-based images such as those originating from Photoshop, also known as "raster" images, are affected by the Quality switch setting. If you scale or rotate a pixel image, the Best setting will improve the quality of these types of images. This exercise demonstrates when to use the Best setting and how to do so.

1. Create a new project by choosing **File > New > New Project**. Choose **File > Save As** and navigate to the **AE6 HOT Projects** folder you created in Chapter 2. Save this new empty project file there as **Quality.aep**.

2. Double-click inside the empty **Project** window to launch the **Import File** dialog box. Navigate to the **chap_08** folder and select **small3.psd**. Click the **Import** (Mac) or **Open** (Windows) button and click **OK** to merge layers. The file will appear as footage inside the Project window. This is a Photoshop document, also known as a raster image.

Note that this import method brings in a flattened PSD file, whereas the method you learned in Exercise 1 brought in a Photoshop file as a composition. It's up to you to know the different importing methods and to choose accordingly, depending on whether you want a flattened footage element or layers brought in as separate footage items. In this exercise, a flattened PSD layer is all that's needed.

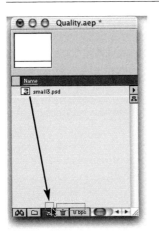

3. In the **Project** window, drag **small3.psd** onto the **Create a new composition** button. The composition is automatically named **small3 Comp 1**, and it opens right away. This is my favorite way to make a new composition because it always scales to the size of my content and automatically names itself. Laziness rules!

4. Choose **Composition > Background Color**. Click inside the **color swatch** to change the color from black to dark burgundy in any of the color pickers that appear. You can change the background color of any composition at any time. Now you know how! Click **OK**.

5. Click the **Quality** switch for the **small3.psd** layer to change it to **Best** quality (the line will slant up to the right). Switch it back and forth, and then return it to **Draft** quality (slanted up to the left). At this point, you shouldn't see a difference in the Quality settings. The next steps will show you when and why you would want to change this switch.

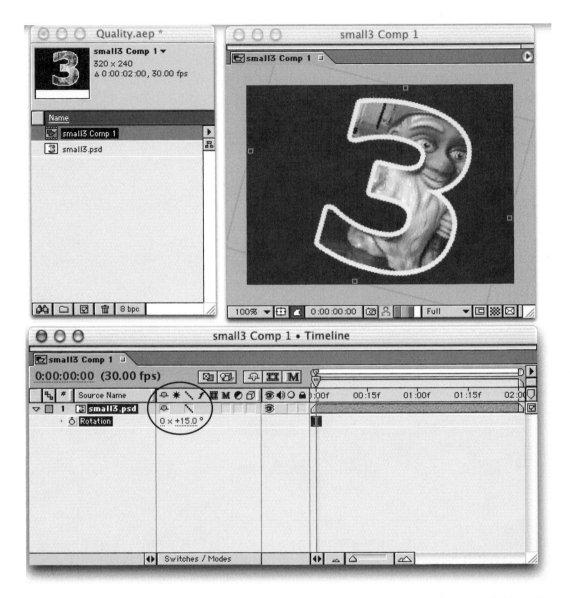

6. Select the **small3.psd** layer in the **Timeline**, if it's not already selected. Press **R** on your keyboard to display the **Rotation** property. Set the **Rotation** value to **15** degrees. Notice that the edges look jagged now.

7. Click the **Quality** switch to set the layer to **Best** quality. Notice that all the jaggedness disappears!

8. Hold the **Shift** key down and press the letter **S**. This should open the **Scale** property, while leaving the **Rotation** property visible. Change the **Scale** to **50%** and toggle the **Quality** switch back and forth. You'll see what a big difference **Best** quality makes when the scale or rotation properties change.

9. Change the **Scale** property to **200%** and toggle the **Quality** switch. You'll see that the **Best** quality setting makes the image look much better. Note, however, that whenever you scale a raster image larger than its original size, the image will look a little out of focus. It's always best to prepare your Photoshop artwork bigger than what you will need if you plan to animate the **Scale** property. The **Best** quality setting helps improve the appearance, but it can't totally compensate for a raster image that is scaled larger than 100%.

In summary, the Quality switch will make a difference to your source footage only if the footage is scaled or rotated. Many After Effects artists leave the Quality switch set to Draft mode to speed up rendering. When you make a final movie (which you'll learn to do in Chapter 18, "Rendering Final Movies"), you can set the overall Quality setting to Best quality and override the switch setting so that your movie will look the best it can. Otherwise, the Quality switch is usually toggled to Best quality occasionally to check the quality, but is left in Draft mode otherwise to allow the work to go faster.

10. Save this project, and leave it open for the next exercise. Close **small3 Comp 1**.

6. _____The Quality Switch vs. Continuous Rasterization

Vector images, such as the type created by Adobe Illustrator, do not consist of pixels. When After Effects displays vector images in the Composition window, it converts the display of the vector information to pixels. The Quality switch will determine whether the vector image is displayed in Draft or Best quality. The difference between the two settings is quite noticeable when working with vector images.

As you learned in the previous exercise, if you scale an image larger than 100%, the Best quality setting will improve its appearance, but it will still look out of focus. If you are working with raster images, there is no way around this problem except to remake your artwork larger than the composition size so you won't have to scale it larger than 100% in After Effects. With vector images, however, there is a solution to this problem—it's called **Continuous Rasterization**. The switch that controls this feature is located next to the Quality switch, and it allows vector artwork to scale to any size and always look perfectly crisp. You'll gain working knowledge of this important feature by following this exercise.

1. Import **starmonkey.ai** into your project from the **chap_08** folder. Click **OK** to merge the Illustrator layers as you did with the PSD artwork.

---

2. Drag **starmonkey.ai** onto the **Create a new composition** button in the **Project** window. This will automatically make the comp size match the artwork and will name the composition **starmonkey Comp 1**. You should know how to do this now without a lot of instruction. If you don't, please revisit the previous exercise. The background color is still set from the last composition. To change it (optional!), choose **Composition > Background Color**.

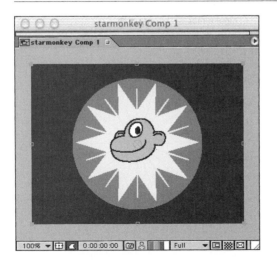

Notice that the monkey image looks jaggy?

---

3. Click the **Quality** switch in the **Timeline** for the **starmonkey.ai** layer, and the monkey will look crisp.

4. Change the scale of the monkey to **200%**. **Hint:** The **S** key on your keyboard will bring forward the **Scale** property setting.

Observe that the monkey image looks quite blurry at this point.

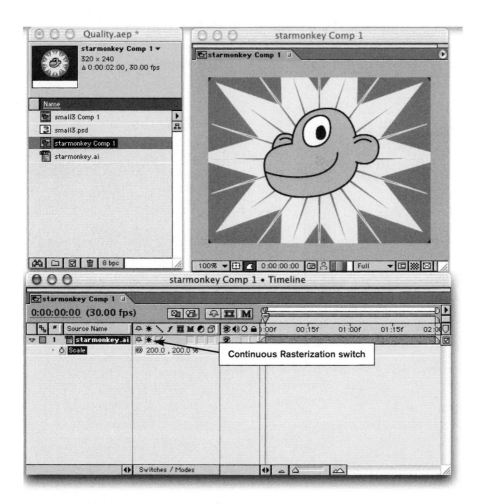

5. Click the **Continuous Rasterization** switch to improve the quality of the vector image. Presto chango; it's beautiful!

*The Continuous Rasterization switch is available only for vector-based footage items. If you reopen the **small3 Comp 1** composition you made earlier, you'll see that this switch is missing for raster images. This switch will cause a vector image to look pristine at any scale or rotation setting. It does slow down previews and work, however. You can test this by creating an animation in this composition using different scale settings on different keyframes and activating the Continuous Rasterization switch. If you preview your animation, you'll see that it takes quite a bit longer to render with continuous rasterization in effect. For this reason, most After Effects artists use the Continuous Rasterization switch sparingly until the composition is rendered to a final movie.*

6. Save and close this project.

What Is Motion Blur?

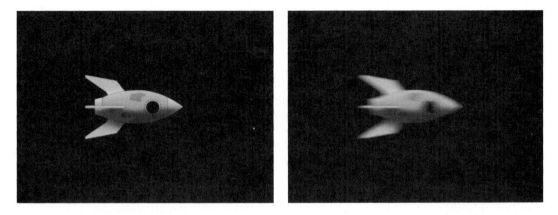

If an object is in motion when it is photographed, any recorded motion will be seen as blur. This is called **motion blur**. For example, if you take a picture of someone on a bicycle speeding past you on the street, the photograph may be blurred if the camera shutter is open long enough to record motion. In the images above, the rocket on the left shows no motion blur and the rocket on right has some blurring.

Cameras have shutters that expose film to light. When the shutter is open, the image is recorded onto film. When you use your snapshot camera, the clicking sound you hear while taking a picture is the sound of the shutter opening and closing. The shorter the time that the shutter is open, the less motion is recorded onto the film image. The longer the shutter is open, the more motion is recorded into the film image.

In motion picture photography, motion blur is useful and often desirable. In everyday life, we don't see the world as individual snapshots; we see continuous motion. Fast-moving objects are naturally blurred to our eyes. When a series of images is projected in a movie theatre, fast-moving action appears natural to our eyes because motion blur caught by the camera helps to blend images together and produce the perception of smooth action. Including motion blur can produce a natural feel to animation created in After Effects.

After Effects offers a very useful tool for smoothing motion by creating motion blur, as you'll see in the next exercise.

7. ——————————Applying Motion Blur

The **Motion Blur** switch can be used to make quick movements in your animations look more realistic. After Effects makes it easy to apply motion blur. In this exercise, you will learn to use the Motion Blur switch and the Enable Motion Blur button.

1. Open the **Motion Blur.aep** project from the **chap_08** folder. Choose **File > Save As** and navigate to the **AE6 HOT Projects** folder you created in Chapter 2. Save a copy into that folder so that you don't overwrite the original.

2. Double-click on **Space Comp 1** to open it. Scrub the **Timeline** so you can see how the motion looks before you apply motion blur. Move the **Current Time Indicator** back to the beginning frame of the **Timeline**.

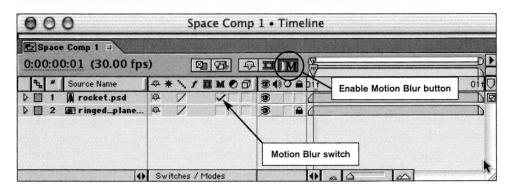

3. In the **Timeline** window, locate the **rocket.psd** layer, and then locate the column for the **Motion Blur** switch, indicated by a capital M icon. Click the **Motion Blur** switch to turn on motion blur for the **rocket.psd** layer. You won't notice any change in the composition yet. At the top of the **Timeline** window, locate the group of buttons to the left of the **Current Time Indicator** slider. The button with the capital M is the **Enable Motion Blur** button. Click on this button to enable motion blur. In the Composition window, motion blur is applied to the rocket image, which you will see if you move to a later frame in the Timeline.

Why are there two settings—the Enable Motion Blur button and the Motion Blur switch? Motion blur is render-intensive. Lots of people set it up, then turn off the Enable Motion Blur button while they're working and want speedier previews. It's nice to have a local switch on the layer and a master switch for the entire composition.

4. Move the current **Current Time Indicator** to frame **0:00:00:17**. Toggle the **Motion Blur** switch off and on, and notice that this turns motion blur off and on in the Composition window.

In After Effects, the Motion Blur switch is very intelligent. It applies more motion blur to objects that are moving faster.

5. With motion blur still on, click **RAM Preview** in the **Time Controls** palette to view your animation.

You'll probably notice that your animation takes longer to render than it did before you added motion blur. As stated, motion blur is render-intensive! Beautiful, but beauty has a price sometimes!

TIP | Motion Blur and Rendering

Motion blur slows down rendering to the screen. When you are designing a composition, it's generally best to enable motion blur only when you want to check the effect it has on the image. To speed your workflow, switch on all the layers that will need motion blur and then enable or disable motion blur with the Enable Motion Blur button.

---

6. Save and close your project.

Moving and Trimming Time in Layers

You can control two basic items when working with layer time. First, you can define where a layer starts in your composition, and second, you can control how many frames of a layer are actually used.

When you import footage and add it to your composition, by default, the new layer starts on the frame at the current Current Time Indicator position. Of course, you often need to change where the layer starts, which you can accomplish by sliding the layer duration bar to the right or left on the Timeline. This is called **moving** a layer.

The layer added to your composition has a default frame length, as well. Sometimes you need to shorten the length of a layer. This is known as **trimming** a layer.

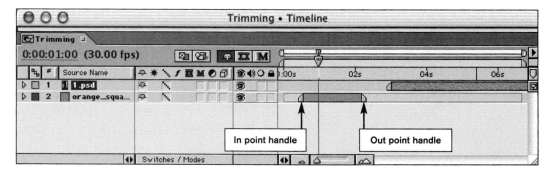

In this example, the top layer has been moved, and the second layer has been trimmed. Observe that the moved layer (the top one) has an **In point** *handle, but the* **Out point** *handle is off the screen in the Timeline window. You can move a layer in time to the right, but not to the left. That's because the In point can never move before the first frame of the composition. Notice that the trimmed layer (the bottom one) has a ghosted bar to its left and right. That is a visual cue that a layer has been trimmed. It indicates that the handles can be pulled back out to their original duration.*

After Effects provides several means to accomplish these two essential tasks. You'll learn some new tricks and shortcuts as you work through the next exercises.

8. ———————In and Out Points in Layers

In this exercise, you will first learn to move the point at which a layer starts and stops in the Timeline. The starting point is called the **In point**, and the stopping point is called the **Out point**. You'll learn to drag a layer in the Timeline to change the In and Out points.

1. Create a new project by choosing **File > New > New Project**. Choose **File > Save As**. Name the project **Sky Project.aep** and navigate to the **AE6 HOT Projects** folder you created in Chapter 2 to save a copy there. In the **Project** window, import the following footage items from the **chap_08** folder: **sky.mov**, **sky1.psd**, and **sky2.psd**. Click **OK** to merge the Photoshop layers as you import the PSD items.

2. Drag **sky.mov** onto the **Create a new composition** button. This creates a new composition with the same settings (and name) as the movie. Observe that the Composition and Timeline windows both open in the process and that the layer **sky.mov** already exists in the Timeline.

*This is a great technique for making a new composition if you have movie footage and you want the composition to be the same length in both frames and frame rate as the movie file. If you want to check out the composition settings, choose **Composition > Composition Settings**. You'll see that the settings are different from those of other compositions you've made. The composition got all these settings automatically from the movie footage.*

3. Drag **sky1.psd** from the **Project** window to the **Timeline** window. Make sure to place it above the **sky.mov** layer. Press the **spacebar** to watch the composition. Notice that the **sky1.psd** artwork is visible over the movie footage in the Composition window. This artwork was created in Photoshop and was saved on a transparent layer. The areas that were transparent in Photoshop are also transparent in After Effects. Also notice that there is an abrupt cut in the movie footage midway through and that a different moving cloud image appears. This abrupt change is built into the movie footage, and in the steps that follow you'll add a different title to begin when this new footage appears.

4. Scrub the **Current Time Indicator** to the point in time where the abrupt sky change occurs in the movie (**Frame 0:00:02:07**). Pull the right handle of the **sky1.psd** layer to the left to match the **Current Time Indicator**. You have just adjusted this layer's **Out** point, trimming the number of frames of footage in this layer. Press the **spacebar** to watch the composition so far. Notice that the lettering turns off at the same point as the abrupt change in the movie footage. Observe that there is a white bar to the right of the Out point. This means that you could drag the handle back to the right, and the footage would reappear all the way to the end of that bar.

5. Make sure the **Current Time Indicator** is still at **Frame 0:00:02:07**. **Hint:** You can easily see what frame the **Current Time Indicator** is on by looking at the readout in the upper-left corner of the **Timeline** window. An alternative to moving the **Current Time Indicator** to a specific frame is to press **Cmd+G** (Mac) or **Ctrl+G** (Windows) to see the **Go To Time** dialog box and type in a number.

6. Drag **sky2.psd** into the **Timeline** and make sure it is the top layer. Notice that it appears in the Timeline window at exactly the same position as the Current Time Indicator.

After Effects always sets the In point of any footage item in the Timeline to the same position as the Current Time Indicator when you bring the footage from the Project window. If you ever accidentally bring footage in at the wrong In point, you can always slide the layer's duration bar to the right or left to make a change.

7. Press the **spacebar** to preview the movie. You successfully trimmed a layer and set the In point of another. These are very useful features to learn and understand.

8. Save and close this project.

9. ————————Keyboard Methods for Trimming Layers

Trimming is a method that is useful when you want to shorten a layer within the composition. You can trim an Out point or an In point in After Effects. The neat thing about trimming is that you can always change your mind.

The difference between moving and trimming footage is that when you move footage, you don't change its physical length in the Timeline; you just move it. With trimming, you can shave off time from the beginning or end of a layer. You trimmed footage in the previous exercise by using the layer handles. In this exercise, you'll learn to trim footage using the **Current Time Indicator** and bracket keys.

1. Open the **trimming.aep** project from the **chap_08** folder and double-click the **Trimming** composition to open it. Choose **File > Save As** and navigate to the **AE6 HOT Projects** folder you created in Chapter 2 to save a copy of it there.

2. Click the **Options** menu arrow at the upper-right corner of the **Timeline** window and select **Columns > In**. Repeat this process and select **Columns > Out**. This will cause the **In** and **Out** panels to appear in your Timeline window. These panels are not necessary for performing trimming functions, but they give you numeric feedback about where your footage starts and ends. To make these panels go away, repeat the same process, and they will toggle off. Leave them on for now.

In the Composition window, notice the images. They don't move at all, even though they are on the Timeline for four full seconds. You're going to make the numbers and the monkey turn off and back on over time by using trimming methods.

3. Drag the right layer handle for the **1.psd** layer and set the **Out** point to **Frame 0:00:01:00**. Use the **Out** panel as a frame reference.

4. Drag the right layer handle for the **orange_square.psd** layer and set the **Out** point to **Frame 0:00:01:06**.

5. Drag the right layer handle for the **2.psd** layer and set the **Out** point to **Frame 00:00:02:00**. **Tip:** If you have trouble dragging the end point to an accurate frame, click on the **Out** point value. This will open the **Layer Out Time** dialog box in which you can type accurate values.

6. Select the **red_orange_square.psd** layer. Set the **Current Time Indicator** to **Frame 0:00:02:15**. Press **Option+]** (Mac) or **Alt+]** (Windows). Notice that the Out point is trimmed to the current Current Time Indicator position. This is a shortcut key to trim the Out point of any layer, based on the location of the Current Time Indicator.

7. Deselect the **red_orange_square.psd** layer. **Shift+click** to select the **monkey1.ai** and **orange_circle.psd** layers. Set the **Current Time Indicator** to **Frame 0:00:03:00**. Press **Option+[** (Mac) or **Alt+[** (Windows). This keyboard shortcut will trim the In point of any selected layer, based on the location of the Current Time Indicator.

The In points of both selected layers are trimmed to the current Current Time Indicator position. This is the quickest way to trim multiple layers to the same In or Out point.

8. Press the **spacebar** to see your animation.

9. Save and close your project.

TIP | Using the Bracket Keys

The left and right bracket keys are important in After Effects. You can use them to move layers, change the stacking order, and trim layers. Here is a chart that summarizes the different types of bracket key commands.

Bracket Key Commands			
Command Type	**Command**	**Mac**	**Windows**
Move	Move In point to Current Time Indicator	[	[
Move	Move Out point to Current Time Indicator	]	]
Stacking order	Bring forward	Cmd+]	Ctrl+]
Stacking order	Send backward	Cmd+[	Ctrl+[
Stacking order	Bring to front	Cmd+Shift+]	Ctrl+Shift+]
Stacking order	Send to back	Cmd+Shift+[	Ctrl+Shift+[
Trim	Trim In point to Current Time Indicator	Option+[	Alt+[
Trim	Trim Out point to Current Time Indicator	Option+]	Alt+]

NOTE | Using In and Out Panels

You can enter values into the In and Out panels, and your footage will move to the frame position you enter. The In or Out panels in the Timeline window cannot be used to trim footage. Although they will display the current trimmed points, the In and Out panels are useful only for *moving* layers or to display the numeric In and Out point frame values of footage.

In and Out columns

Access the Options menu to locate Columns > In or Columns > Out

IO. —————————Splitting Layers

Most of the time, when you drag a footage item into your composition, you want that footage to be used as a single layer in your composition. There are times, however, when that isn't the case. For example, let's say that you want an item to travel in front of a layer and then behind the same layer. You might, for instance, want a spaceship to go in front of a planet in one part of your animation and then behind the planet in another. The long way to do this would be to duplicate the spaceship layer, put it above and below the planet layer, and trim its In and Out points correctly.

After Effects offers a much simpler way of dealing with such a situation by **splitting** a layer. When you split a layer, the layer is split into two pieces. The two pieces contain all the properties that were originally on the single layer. Each piece is actually a whole layer that is placed in your Timeline window and trimmed automatically according to the Current Time Indicator position. This is a real timesaver. In the following exercise, you'll learn how to split a layer and when you'll need to split a layer.

1. Choose **File > Open Project**, navigate to **Split Layer Project.aep** in the **chap_08** folder, and click **Open**. Choose **File > Save As** and navigate to the **AE6 HOT Projects** folder you created in Chapter 2 to save a copy of it there.

2. If the **Composition** window is not open, double-click **Split Layer Comp** in the **Project** window. Press the **spacebar** to preview. Notice that the monkey goes behind the orange circle twice. This is appropriate for the first half of the movie. However, the monkey should go in front of the orange circle during the second half of the movie. You're going to learn how to split the layer to achieve this effect.

3. Set the **Current Time Indicator** in the Timeline to **Frame 0:00:01:20** and select the **monkey1.ai** layer. This frame was chosen because it is the first frame where you want the monkey to appear in front of the circle, instead of behind the circle.

4. Choose **Edit** > **Split Layer**.

After the split, your Timeline window will look like this. Notice that the layer automatically duplicated itself and set In and Out points to line up exactly on the frame at which you specified that the layer be split.

5. Drag the second half of the split **monkey1.ai** layer above the **orange_circle.psd** layer.

6. Press the **spacebar** and check out the split layer action. Sweet! That was so much more painless than duplicating and trimming, don't you agree?

7. Save your project and close it.

II. ————————————Time Stretching and Frame Blending

You've learned how to trim (shorten) layers, but what about stretching layers? There's hardly anything that After Effects can't do, so this is possible, of course! This exercise will show you how to define, set, and adjust the duration of layers.

1. Open **Time Stretch Project.aep** from the **chap_08** folder. It contains two footage items: a QuickTime movie and a Photoshop document.

2. Create a new composition that is one second long and name it **short comp**. You should know how to do this now without instruction. Make your settings match what you see here.

3. Drag the two footage items into this composition. Make sure that **walktitle.psd** is above **walk.mov** in the **Timeline** window. Play the composition by pressing the **spacebar**.

Notice that the Photoshop layer stops at Frame 0:00:01:00 and that the movie footage item extends beyond the Timeline and seems to get cut off by the short length of the composition. That's because a still footage item, such as a Photoshop or Illustrator document, is automatically scaled to the duration of whatever composition it is inserted into. The movie footage has a fixed time associated with it. You can change the length of the composition to fit the movie, or you can change the duration of the movie to fit the length of the composition. You'll learn to do both in this exercise.

```
┌─────────────────────────────────────────────┐
│                  Time Stretch                 │
│ ┌─ Stretch ───────────────────────────────┐ │
│ │ Original Duration: 0:00:05:06            │ │
│ │                                           │ │
│ │ Stretch Factor: [19.304348] %             │ │
│ │                                           │ │
│ │ New Duration: ( 0:00:01:00 ) is 0:00:01:00│ │
│ │                                  Base 30  │ │
│ └───────────────────────────────────────────┘ │
│ ┌─ Hold In Place ─────────────────────────┐ │
│ │ ◉ Layer In-point                         │ │
│ │ ○ Current Frame                          │ │
│ │ ○ Layer Out-point                        │ │
│ └───────────────────────────────────────────┘ │
│          ( Cancel )    ( OK )                 │
└─────────────────────────────────────────────┘
```

4. Select the layer **walk.mov**. Choose **Layer > Time Stretch**. This will open the **Time Stretch** dialog box, which makes it possible to alter the duration of the movie. Enter a **New Duration** of **0:00:01:00** and click **OK**. You will see that the **walk.mov** footage is now only one second long in the Timeline. If you play the composition by pressing the **spacebar**, you'll see the woman walking quite a bit faster than before. That's because the footage of her walking has been compressed to span a much shorter duration. How did After Effects do it? By dividing the original length by the requested length and temporarily discarding the frames that weren't needed. In this case, you've used Time Stretch to shorten the duration of the layer. It might not seem like the term "stretch" in "Time Stretch" should be appropriate, but Time Stretch can be used to shrink as well as stretch. You'll get to try both operations over the next few exercises.

You can stretch or shrink the duration of footage based on entering frame values or percentage values. Hold In Place means that After Effects will stretch or shrink the duration of the footage to make sure the In point is preserved, the Out point is preserved, or the current Current Time Indicator position (Current Frame) is preserved, depending on the option you choose.

5. Change the length of the composition by choosing **Composition > Composition Settings**. Enter **0:00:10:00** frames for the **Duration** setting. This will lengthen the composition to be 10 seconds. Click **OK**.

6. Move the **Time bracket** handle to the right to reveal all 10 seconds in the Timeline. You can always zoom in and out on your Timeline by using this handle. Try stretching it back and forth to try it. Move it back to the end of the composition when you are finished. Notice that the two layers are much shorter than the length of the Timeline. That's because the layers were automatically set to the original duration of the length of the original composition. Now that you've changed the composition's duration, the layers no longer fit to size.

7. Move the layer handle for **walktitle.psd** to the end of the length of the composition. If you press the **spacebar**, you'll see that the title now extends much longer than the walk movie. The PSD layer has a movable handle, but the **walk.mov** layer does not. That's because movie footage has to be time-stretched to change its duration. Still footage is always a lot more flexible than movie footage.

8. Select the **walk.mov** layer and choose **Layer > Time Stretch**. Enter a **Duration** value of **0:00:10:00** and click **OK**. Watch the composition by pressing the **spacebar**.

Now the walk is very, very slow. You would walk slow, too, if you'd been time-stretched! How is After Effects achieving this? It's repeating frames. Most of the frames are being repeated two to four times. A good way to see this is to step through the composition by clicking the Next Frame button on the Time Controls palette, as you'll do in the next step.

9. Click the **Next Frame** button on the **Time Controls** palette to step through the frames. Notice that many poses of the walk are held for more than one frame. After Effects has a solution for this, believe it or not. It's called **frame blending**, and you'll get to try it in the next step.

10. Click the **Quality** switch and the **Frame Blending** switch for the **walk.mov** layer and then click the **Enable Frame Blending** button. Step through the animation again, using the **Next Frame** button on the **Time Controls** palette. You'll see that After Effects has created soft opacity transitions between the held frames.

11. Press the **spacebar** and watch the final results. Turn off the **Frame Blending** switch and click the **Enable Frame Blending** button and watch again. The frame blending feature makes time-stretched footage look significantly better!

You can set up frame blending with the switch, but turn off the Enable Frame Blending button to speed up rendering while you're working on your project. **Note:** *Frame blending works only on moving footage—it has no effect on still frames.*

12. Save and close this project.

I2. _____Time Remapping

Time remapping is a feature in After Effects that lets you change the way time is interpreted for a live action movie. Using the same walk footage you worked with in the previous exercise, you'll see how time remapping lets you speed up and reverse the footage layer over time. This effect isn't used that often, but when you need something like this, there is no better tool to do the job!

1. Create a new project and save this to the **AE6 HOT Projects** folder you created in Chapter 2. Name it **timeremapping.aep**.

2. Import **walk.mov** from the **chap_08** folder. You should know how to do this now! After you've done this, in the **Project** window, drag this footage onto the **Create a new Composition** button. This creates a composition that's exactly the right length and frame rate. The composition is automatically named **walk Comp 1**, and the **Timeline** and **Composition** windows open automatically.

Whenever I work with live action in a project, I usually like to create the composition using this technique because of all the behind-the-scenes work that After Effects does automatically.

3. Select the **walk.mov** layer in the **Timeline** window and choose **Layer > Enable Time Remapping**. Nothing happens—or so you think. You won't see the effect of this feature until you twirl down some twirlies. Wheeeee!

4. A **Time Remap** property will appear. Your screen should look like the one here. Notice that a start and end keyframe has been set and that the Stopwatch icon is active. This happens automatically when you enable this feature. The Time Remap property shows a graph, called the **Time Map** graph, that represents the length of the layer. The graph shows a gradual incline, which means that the movie footage plays at the expected speed. You are going to add keyframes to this graph to change all that.

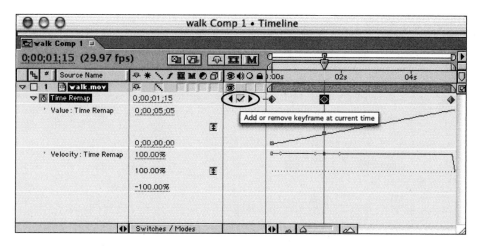

5. Move the **Current Time Indicator** to **0:00:01:15** and click the **Add or remove keyframe** check box. This inserts a keyframe at this frame. Nothing else happens (yet).

6. Now that you've placed a keyframe on **0:00:01:15**, you'll see a handle appear on the graph at that frame. Move the handle up to approximately the point you see here.

7. Add another keyframe by moving the **Current Time Indicator** to **0:00:03:19** and clicking the **Add or remove keyframe** check box. On this new keyframe, move the graph down to approximately the point you see here.

8. Play the animation, and you'll see that the time of this movie speeds up, then reverses, then slows down, and reverses. That's what time mapping does, folks! Feel free to add more keyframes and move the graph to new places. Time will just get more and more distorted!

NOTE | More About the Time Map Graph

You might be wondering what kinds of results you can get by making changes to the Time Map graph. Here are some visual examples that might help you out.

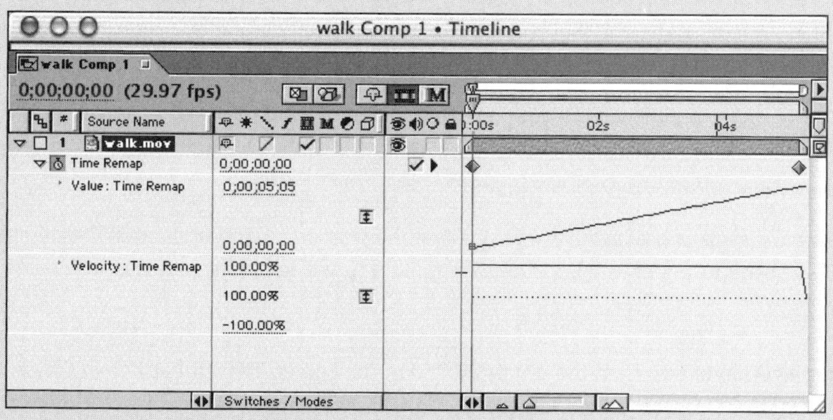

This Time Map graph will play at a constant speed.

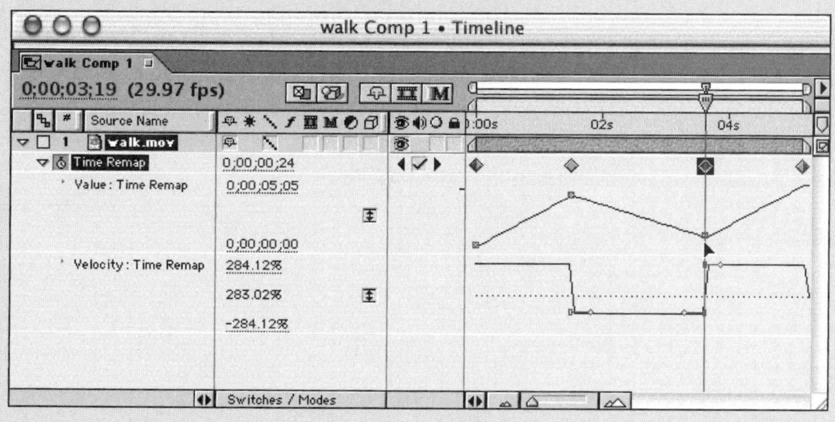

The steep incline at the beginning of this graph will speed the footage up. The decline in the graph will cause the footage to play in reverse. The gradual incline at the end will cause it to play at a constant speed.

9. Save and close this project.

I3. —————————Replacing Layers

As you well know, After Effects allows you to bring a layer into the Timeline, set keyframes, and change properties. What you may not realize is how easy it is to then swap out different footage for the layer. This new footage will retain all the animation and property settings of the layer it replaces. Why would you need to do something like this? Imagine that you are working for a motion graphics design company. Your job might be to design an English and a French version of a main title sequence.

Replacing titles could get rather complicated if you had to start from scratch and replace each English title with a French title. You would have to rework the position keyframes for each title, add mask properties, add effects properties, add the layer options, and so on.

Luckily, After Effects makes replacing a layer very easy. All of the properties and options of the original layer are automatically applied to the new layer. In this exercise, you will see how easy it is to replace a layer.

1. Open **Replace Layer.aep** from the **chap_08** folder you copied to your hard drive. Save this to the **AE6 HOT Projects** folder you created in Chapter 2 to create a copy of it there.

2. Press the **spacebar** to preview the animation.

In the next steps, you will learn to use the Replace Layer command. When a layer is replaced, all of the animation and keyframes applied to the original layer continue to work with the new layer.

3. In the **Timeline** window, select the **english_title.psd** layer.

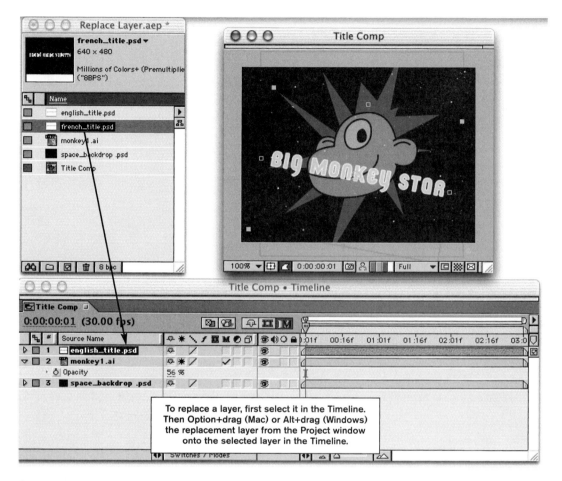

To replace a layer, first select it in the Timeline. Then Option+drag (Mac) or Alt+drag (Windows) the replacement layer from the Project window onto the selected layer in the Timeline.

4. In the **Project** window, select the **french_title.psd** footage. Press **Option** (Mac) or **Alt** (Windows) and drag the French title footage from the **Project** window to the **Timeline** window. Release the footage in the **Timeline**.

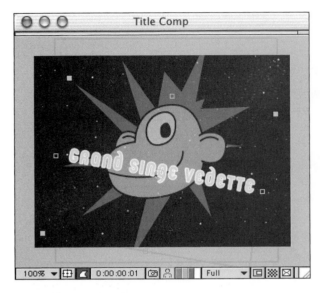

*Notice that the **english_title** layer is replaced by the **french_title** layer in the Timeline window.*

*It doesn't matter where you drop the **french_title.psd** footage in the Timeline, because After Effects knows that it should replace the **english_title** layer. Why? Because you selected that layer before you dragged the replacement layer into the Timeline.*

5. Press the **spacebar** to preview your work, and notice that the French title uses the original animation.

This technique is used for a lot of purposes besides language translations. You might design a template for a title sequence and just swap out the appropriate titles. If you have a commercial, you might make the same animation for different products and just swap them out.

*To review, here are the steps needed to replace footage: Select the layer you wish to replace in the **Timeline**, and **Option+drag** (Mac) or **Alt+drag** (Windows) the replacement footage from the **Project** window into the **Timeline**. Practice this on your own so you really understand how it works. You'll use this timesaving technique often in your real work.*

6. Save your project and close it.

Sequencing Layers

Quite often in motion graphics, you want to create a sequence of frames, in which the first piece of artwork shows on screen, followed by each successive piece of artwork playing in order. When you learned how to move and trim layers, you saw that you can accomplish something like this by having layers start and end on different frames. The manual method of sequencing layers would be to move each layer in the Timeline to sequentially follow another. However, After Effects provides a way to select multiple layers and sequence them automatically in the Timeline.

After Effects also provides options to overlap the layers rather than simply have one end and the next begin. When you overlap layers, a certain number of frames can be transitioned with crossfades, which is a term that means fading in on one picture while fading out on another. This is a lovely transitional device that filmmakers use all the time. In the following exercise, you'll learn to sequence layers, overlap them, and crossfade the overlapping layers.

1. Create a new composition by choosing **File > New > New Project**. Choose **File > Save As** and name the file **Sequence.aep**. Navigate to the **AE6 HOT Projects** folder you created in Chapter 2 and save it there.

2. Double-click inside the empty **Project** window to launch the **Import File** dialog box. Select the folder called **cloud photos** from the **chap_08** folder. Click the **Import Folder** button. This brings an entire folder of images into your project.

Sequence.aep *	**Composition Settings**
	Composition Name: cloud sequence comp
Name	**Basic** \ Advanced
▷ 🗀 cloud photos	Preset: Medium, 320 x 240
	Width: 320
	☑ Lock Aspect Ratio to 4:3
	Height: 240
	Pixel Aspect Ratio: Square Pixels Frame Aspect Ratio: 4:3
	Frame Rate: 30 Frames per second
	Resolution: Full 320 x 240, 300K per 8bpc frame
	Start Timecode: 0:00:00:01 Base 30
👓 🗀 🗗 🗑 8 bpc	Duration: 0:00:38:00 is 0:00:38:00 Base 30
	Cancel OK

3. Click the **Create a new composition** button in the **Project** window to create a new composition. Name it **cloud sequence comp**, and set the rest of the settings to match the screen shown here. Click **OK**. An empty **Timeline** and **Composition** window will open.

4. Click the **twirly** by the **cloud photos** folder to open its contents in the **Project** window. This reveals the list of images that are inside the folder. If you click on an image, you will see a thumbnail appear at the top of the Project window with some information about the document.

This folder contains 19 different cloud photos that were imported into Photoshop from a digital still camera. They were all sized identically in order to work well in a 320×240 After Effects composition, and you will soon learn how to create a slideshow from these still images using the sequence layers feature.

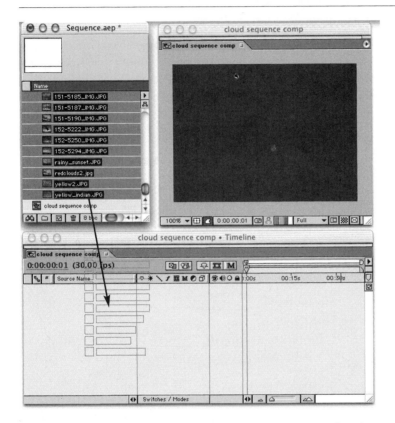

5. In the **Project** window, hold the **Shift** key down to select all 19 images in the **cloud photos** folder. Drag them all together into the **Timeline. Warning:** Make sure you don't select the **cloud sequence comp** you just made when you select these images. If you do, you won't be able to drag the images into the composition.

Notice that all 19 layers inside the Timeline are 38 seconds long. After Effects automatically creates a duration for still footage that is the length of the composition. As you have already learned, you can trim this footage to be a different length, and you can also stretch footage to be longer than a composition. For the purpose of this exercise, we want each layer to be two seconds long so that we can create a slideshow. You'll do this next.

6. Position the **Current Time Indicator** at **0:00:02:00**. If all the layers are not still selected, choose **Cmd+A** (Mac) or **Ctrl+A** (Windows) to select them. Press the keyboard shortcut **Option+]** (Mac) or **Alt+]** (Windows). This trims each layer to be two seconds long.

You can see why keyboard shortcuts for trimming are useful. Sure, you could have dragged 18 handles to Frame 14, but why do that when you can automate the whole process? Now that the layers are trimmed, you'll learn to automatically position each layer in a sequence on the Timeline.

7. With all the layers still selected, choose **Animation > Keyframe Assistant > Sequence Layers**. The **Sequence Layers** dialog box appears. Do not click the **Overlap** button. Click **OK**. The settings in this dialog box will be explained shortly.

*Notice that the layers are now perfectly positioned on the Timeline to create a 2-second sequence 19 times. Press the **spacebar** to preview the animation. It might be cooler if there were little crossfades between each pair of layers, don't you think? You've learned how to set Opacity property keyframes— can you imagine the labor involved in manually setting keyframes for this kind of animation on 18 frames? Of course, there's a better solution, which you'll learn next.*

Note: *The order in which you select the images is important. If you want to select which image comes first in the sequence order, you can use the **Cmd** key (Mac) or **Ctrl** key (Windows) to select images in a noncontiguous order. When you use the **Shift** key to select the images (as you did in the Project window when you imported these images), the order you select the images in will affect which image appears first in the layer sequence (top to bottom or bottom to top).*

8. All of the layers should still be selected; if not, select them. Choose **Animation** > **Keyframe Assistant** > **Sequence Layers**. This time, don't click **OK** when the **Sequence Layers** dialog box opens until you select the **Overlap** check box. Set the **Duration** to **0:00:00:10** frames and set **Transition** to **Cross Dissolve Front and Back Layers**. Check out the chart at the end of this exercise to understand all the possible settings in the Sequence Layers dialog box. Click **OK**.

9. Press the **spacebar** to play the composition, and notice the crossfades between the layers. Press the **T** key (to reveal the Opacity settings) and notice that each layer has keyframes automatically set for opacity changes. Move the **Zoom** slider to see a larger view of the **Timeline** content. After Effects has placed four keyframes per layer—to fade up and fade down on the image. Wow! After Effects has just saved you a lot of work, eh?

Notice that the composition is now too long for the animation. That's because, with the overlapping of each layer by 10 frames, the footage no longer takes up the entire 38 seconds. The last frame containing an image is Frame 202. Fortunately, you can also trim a composition! The next step will show you how.

10. Choose **Composition > Composition Settings** and change the **Duration** to **0:00:32:00** seconds. Click **OK**. When you do, you'll see that your composition has been shortened. Now when you play the slideshow, the composition will end at the same time that the images do.

---

11. Save and close your project.

NOTE | The Sequence Layers Dialog Box

In this last exercise, you worked with the sequence layers feature of After Effects. The Sequence Layers dialog box has many options. Here's a handy chart that outlines what they are.

Sequence Layers Dialog Box	
Option	**Description**
Overlap	Allows you to overlap two adjacent layers with a crossfade. This causes each layer to look as though it is fading in or out or both in and out. The crossfade is controlled by the Crossfade setting.
Duration	Indicates the number of frames over which the overlap of layers occurs. You can enter any value into this field that does not exceed the duration of the layer.
Crossfade: End Layer Only	Fades out at the end of the layer's duration. Opacity keyframes are automatically set that last for the duration of the overlap. For a layer that is 15 frames long with a 5-frame overlap, the fade-out will occur from frames 10 to 15.
Crossfade: Front and Back Layers	Fades the layer in at the beginning and out at the end of the layer's duration. Opacity keyframes are automatically set that last for the duration of the overlap. For a layer that is 15 frames long with a 5-frame overlap, the fade-in will occur from frames 1 to 5, and the fade-out will occur from frames 10 to 15.

What Is a Solid Layer?

A **solid layer** is exactly what it sounds like—a layer that contains a solid-colored shape. You can make a solid layer of any size, from a 1×1 pixel up to 32,000×32,000 pixels. The color can be any color of your choosing. Why would you want a solid layer? They are useful when you want a quick graphic in the shape of a rectangle. Later in the book, you'll also see that solid layers can be masked to create shapes other than rectangles.

At first it would seem that having a layer of a solid color would be of minimal use—say, only for a background color. However, because solid layers have all of the properties of a normal layer, you'll find yourself using them all the time. You can add effects, masks, and transformations to solid layers and make them useful in many ways.

In the following exercise, you'll learn how to create solid layers and change their color, dimensions, and settings. You can make solid layers smaller than the shape of your composition so they don't cover up other layers of artwork, or you can make them partially transparent so you can see through them. All of the properties of a solid layer can be animated as well.

15. _____Creating Solid Layers

In this exercise, you will create a solid layer, change the settings, and animate the properties.

1. Create a new composition by choosing **File > New > New Project**. Choose **File > Save As** and name the file **Solid Layers.aep**. Navigate to the **AE6 HOT Projects** folder you created in Chapter 2 and save it there.

2. Create a new composition and name it **Solid Layers Comp 1**. Set the duration to **0:00:01:00** seconds. Click **OK**.

3. Choose **Layer > New > Solid**. As an alternative method, press **Cmd+Y** (Mac) or **Ctrl+Y** (Windows).

4. In the **Solid Footage Settings** dialog box, accept **Dark Gray Solid 1** as the name for the solid layer. Make sure the **Width** is **320** and the **Height** is **240**. Notice the color in the **Color** block. This will be the color of your solid layer. Click **OK**.

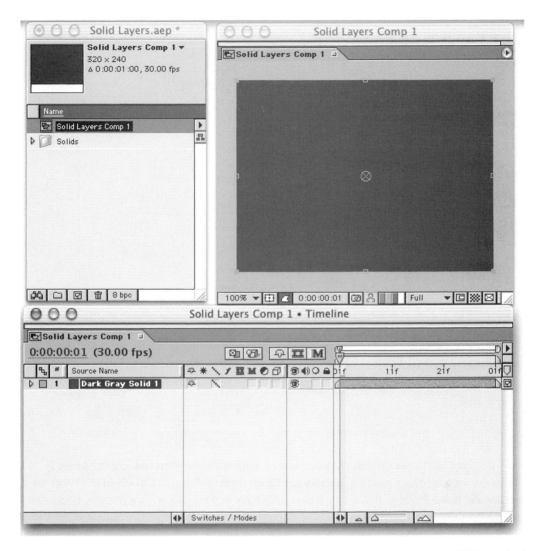

Your Composition window should look like this. Observe that when you create a solid layer, the layer appears inside the Timeline and inside a folder in the Project window called Solids. You cannot create a solid without a composition—it's a special kind of artwork that After Effects allows you to create for the purpose of working inside a composition's Timeline. Note that solids have changed a bit in this version of After Effects; the Solids folder is new, as is the default capability to name the solid by its color name.

Click here to open
the Color Picker

5. What if you want to change the color? With the solid selected in the **Timeline**, choose **Layer >
Solid Settings**. As a keyboard shortcut, you can use **Cmd+Shift+Y** (Mac) or **Ctrl+Shift+Y** (Windows).
This reopens the **Solid Settings** dialog box, which will enable you to make a color change. Click inside
the color swatch, and your operating system's color picker will open. Select a dark red color.

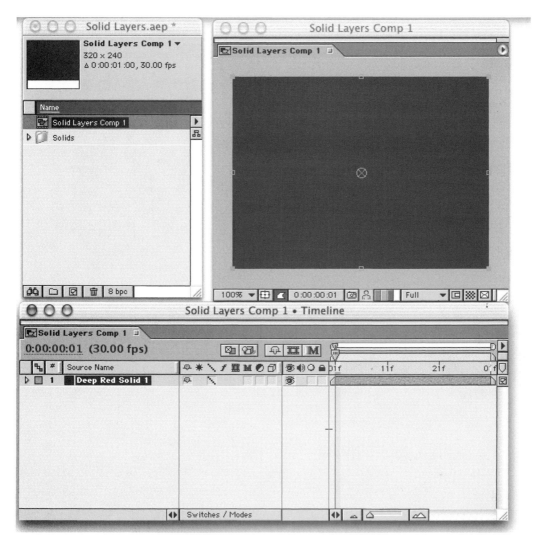

Observe that the Solid layer has changed color and has also assumed an automatic name of **Deep Red Solid 1**. This automatic naming system is new to After Effects 6. You can always change the name of a layer by selecting it first, and then pressing the **Return** (Mac) or **Enter** (Windows) key to edit its name. Leave the name at its default for now; it's a nice convenience to let After Effects do the naming for you.

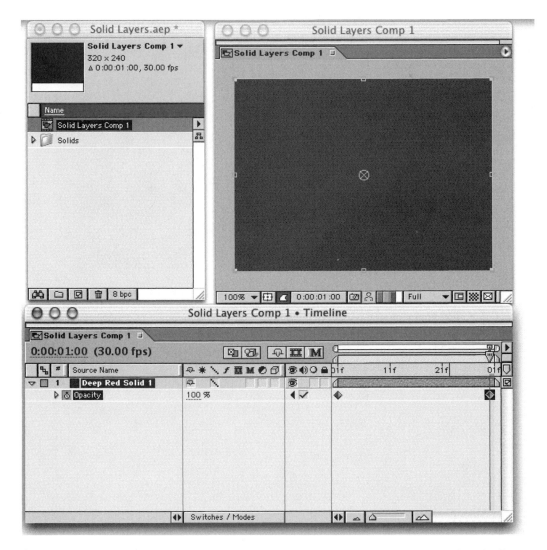

6. Make sure the **Current Time Indicator** is on **Frame 1**. In the **Timeline** window, select the **Deep Red Solid 1** layer and press **T** on your keyboard to display the **Opacity** property. Click the **Stopwatch** icon and set the **Opacity** to **0%**. Press **K** to move the **Current Time Indicator** to the last frame of the composition. Set the **Opacity** to **100%**.

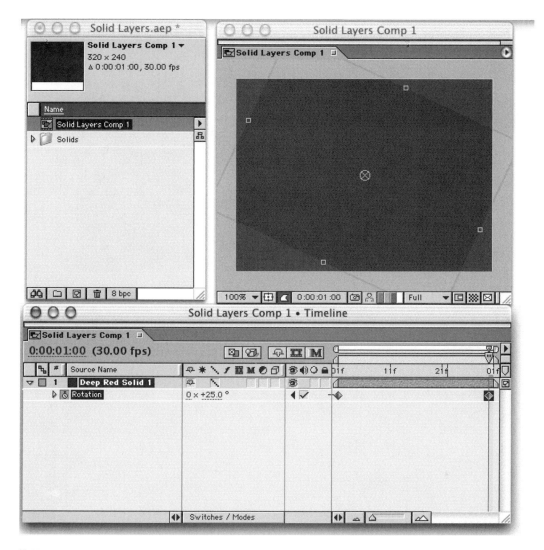

7. With the **Deep Red Solid 1** layer selected, press **R** to display the **Rotation** property. Press **J** to move the **Current Time Indicator** to the first frame. Click the **Stopwatch** icon. Press **K** to move the **Current Time Indicator** to the last frame. Set the **Rotation** to **25.0** degrees.

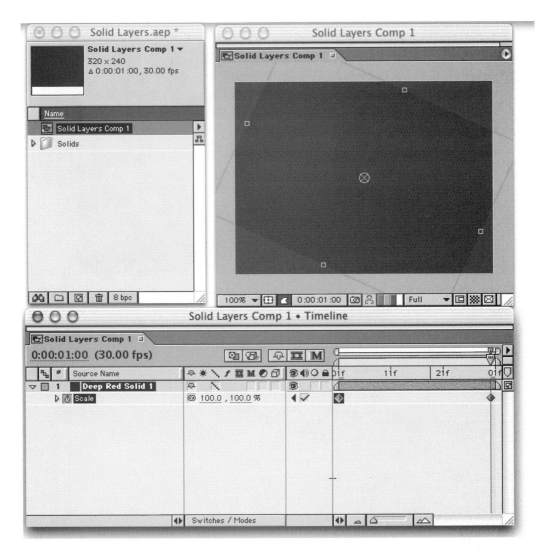

8. Press **S** to display the **Scale** property. Press **J** to move the **Current Time Indicator** to the first frame. Click the **Stopwatch** icon and set the **Scale** to **20%**. Press **K** to move to the last frame. Set the **Scale** to **100%**. Click the **Quality** switch to set it to **Best** quality. Solid layers preview much better at Best quality.

9. Press the **spacebar** to preview the animation. Notice that the solid layer responds to all property settings just as imported footage does.

In the following step, you will learn to change the dimensions of a solid layer.

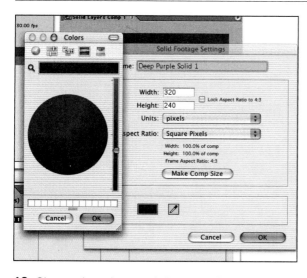

10. Choose **Layer > Solid Settings**. As a keyboard shortcut, you can use **Cmd+Shift+Y** (Mac) or **Ctrl+Shift+Y** (Windows). If it isn't already unchecked, uncheck the **Lock Aspect Ratio to 1:1** check box and type **Width: 200** and **Height: 200**. Click **OK**.

---

11. Press the **spacebar** to watch the animation and observe the square dimensions of the solid layer. Even though you changed the size, it retains all the animation properties you set in previous steps.

---

12. Choose **Layer > New > Solid**. As an alternative method, press **Cmd+Y** (Mac) or **Ctrl+Y** (Windows).

---

13. Change the color to a dark purple. Click the **Make Comp Size** button, and observe that the Width and Height settings change to match the composition size. Click **OK**.

14. In the **Timeline** window, drag the **Deep Purple Solid 1** layer under the **Deep Red Solid 1** layer. In the **Composition** window, notice that the new solid layer displays at the composition dimensions.

My hope is that this exercise has given you some idea of the capabilities of a solid layer. You'll work with these layers in other chapters as well, to get other ideas that demonstrate their usefulness. For now, you could make an abstract moving composition with lots of animating rectangles set to different scales, opacities, and rotations. In future chapters, you'll learn to combine solid layers with other footage, text, and effects elements.

15. Save and close this project.

Aligning and Distributing Layers

There will be times when you have multiple layers that need to be aligned mathematically. You could use a ruler and sit and calculate what constitutes perfect distribution and alignment, but it's much easier to let the computer do these sorts of tasks for you!

In After Effects, layers can be moved using the Align palette. You access this palette by choosing **Window > Align & Distribute**.

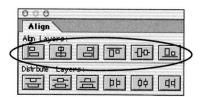

The top row contains the **alignment** icons. Alignment indicates that artwork on layers is lined up. The icons in this row represent left, vertical center, right, top, horizontal center, and bottom alignment.

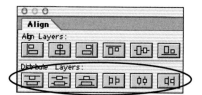

The bottom row contains the **distribution** icons. To distribute something means to space it evenly. You can space multiple pieces of artwork by using the icons in this row, choosing from vertical top, vertical center, vertical bottom, horizontal left, horizontal center, or horizontal right distribution.

16.——————————Using the Align Palette

In this exercise, you will get to use the alignment and distribution tools for the first time. This example, of a menu system, would be useful if you were doing a design for a DVD interface or for a title sequence. It is just one of numerous examples in which the align and distribute features of After Effects are useful.

1. Open the **Align_Distribute Project.aep** file from the **chap_08** folder. Save a copy to the **AE6 HOT Projects** folder you created in Chapter 2.

2. In the **Project** window, double-click on **menu comp**, if it isn't already open.

3. Choose **Window > Align & Distribute**, if it isn't already open from the last exercise. This opens the **Align** palette. **Warning:** Your **Align_Distribute Project** listing also appears under the **Window** menu. Be sure to click **Align & Distribute**, not the project name!

Study the Align palette. The top row contains the alignment icons. The bottom row contains the distribution icons.

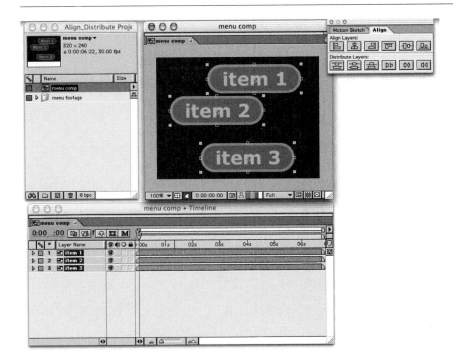

4. In the **Timeline** window, **Shift+click** to select all the layers. Notice that they also become selected in the **Composition** window. **Tip:** Alternatively, you could **Shift+click** on the images in the **Composition** window. This would also select them in both places.

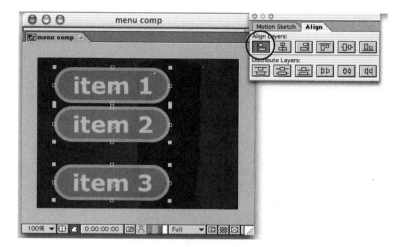

5. Click the **Left Align** button and notice that the menu items move to align with the left edge of the button shape.

Notice that when you specify left alignment, the selected layers align with the selected object that is farthest to the left. The far left edge does not move—it is used to identify the alignment edge.

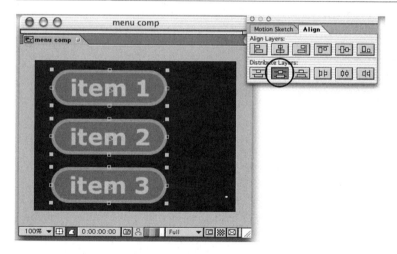

6. Click the **Distribute Vertical Center** button and notice that the menu items are distributed evenly from top to bottom. This button spaces the centers of the items evenly, starting from the most extreme vertical positions.

This sure beats aligning the objects by hand! This technique is useful for static or animated graphics. In the next few steps, you'll see how you can incorporate this alignment technique to create an animation of the menu items flying in the screen.

7. With all three layers still selected, press **Option+P** (Mac) or **Shift+Alt+P** (Windows) to reveal the **Position** properties. Notice that the **Stopwatch** is active and that a checkmark already appears in the **Keyframe Navigator** check box. This happens automatically when you use the **Option/Alt** shortcut keys. Move the **Current Time Indicator** to **0:00:01:00** and check the **Keyframe Navigator** check boxes for each layer. This inserts a keyframe of the current position for each layer at this point in the **Timeline**.

8. Move the **Current Time Indicator** back to the first frame (press the letter **J** to accomplish this).

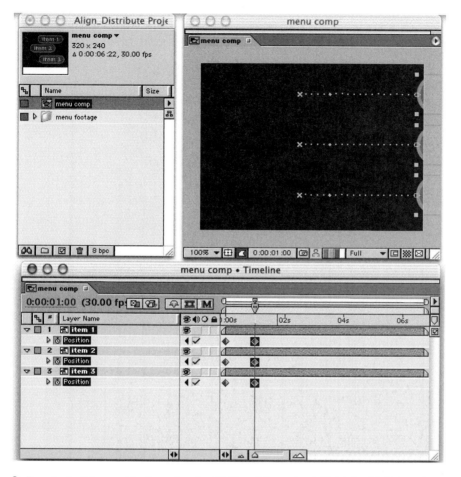

9. Reselect all three objects, using the **Shift+click** method. Hold the **Shift** key down and use your **right arrow** key to move the artwork to the right. This moves the artwork in larger increments than using the **right arrow** without the **Shift** key. Repeat this process until the artwork is moved off the screen. Since two keyframes have been set and the layers are selected, you should see the motion path of the animation you just created.

TIP | Using the Keyboard to Move an Object

You can move an object inside the Composition window by selecting its layer in the Timeline window and using the keyboard arrow keys. Pressing an **arrow** key moves the selected layer or layers one pixel in the direction of the arrow. Holding the **Shift** key down while pressing an **arrow** key moves the selected layers 10 pixels.

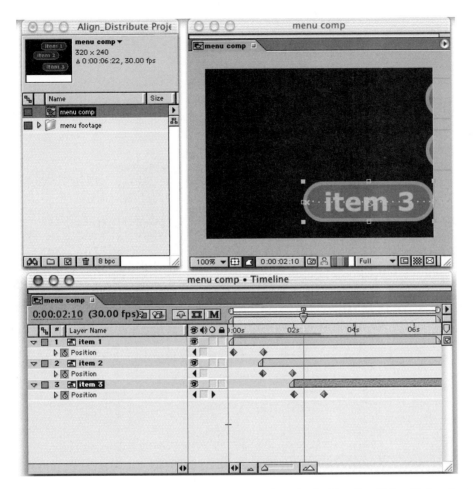

10. Deselect all the layers by clicking away from them in the Timeline. This will deactivate the motion path preview. Press the **spacebar** to view what you've done so far. Try moving the layers as you see here by dragging them, and watch the animation again. This staggers the timing of each layer.

11. Once you've seen the results of your efforts, save and close this project.

NOTE | Reversing Keyframes!

Let's say you wanted to reverse the direction of the position keyframes. Can you do it? Of course—this is After Effects! Simply select the keyframes you want to reverse by holding down the **Shift** key. Choose **Animation > Keyframe Assistant > Time Reverse Keyframes.**

What Are Layer Modes?

You may have worked with **layer modes** in Photoshop before, and if you have, you'll find that they are quite similar in After Effects. Layer modes affect the way that multiple layers in the Timeline appear when composited (or combined) in the Composition window. A normal layer, if put on top of another normal layer in the Timeline, will cover the lower layer completely. If set to a layer mode, however, the top layer will interact with the layer beneath it to change its appearance.

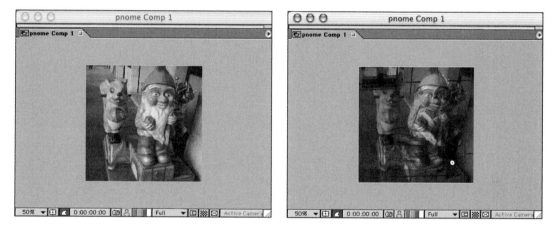

If the top layer is set to Normal mode, it obscures the layer(s) beneath it. If the top layer is set to Multiply mode, the layer beneath it shows through. Layer modes offer alternative compositing effects in multilayered After Effects documents.

Layer modes are created by mathematical formulas that add, subtract, multiply, and divide pixels. Depending on the formula used, a different result occurs. Most After Effects artists use layer modes in an experimental way. It's hard to remember what each layer mode does, and it's much easier to try different ones to search for a desired effect.

Here's a handy chart that explains what the different layer modes do.

Layer Modes		
Visual	**Mode**	**Description**
	Normal	Covers the layer(s) beneath it.
	Dissolve	In order for Dissolve to work, the layer to which it is applied must contain transparent pixels. This can be achieved with a mask or an alpha, or by lowering the opacity. The result is that random pixels of the layer(s) beneath this layer will appear. If you set keyframes with different values for the Opacity property for the top layer, this layer mode will animate in After Effects. It is actually the Opacity property that is animating, however, because you cannot set keyframes for layer modes.
	Dancing Dissolve	Looks identical to Dissolve, except that the random pixels will change over time. This creates an animated flicker effect. As with the Dissolve layer mode, the top image must have transparent pixels.

continues on next page

Layer Modes *continued*

Visual	Mode	Description
	Add	Combines the colors of the top and underlying layers, resulting in a lighter color than the original.
	Multiply	Multiplies and divides the color value from the layer beneath, resulting in a darker image than the original.
	Screen	Multiplies the inverse brightness of the colors for the top and underlying layers. The result is never darker than original.
	Overlay	Preserves the light and dark areas of the layer colors while mixing colors between layers.

continues on next page

Layer Modes *continued*		
Visual	**Mode**	**Description**
	Soft Light	Darkens or lightens colors, depending on the original layer color. Changes depending on whether the underlying color is lighter or darker than 50 percent gray.
	Hard Light	Produces different results depending on the lightness or darkness of the pixel values.
	Color Dodge	Results in a lot of pure whites and blacks and creates a brighter result than the original layer.
	Color Burn	Creates a darker result than the original layer; pure white does not change the underlying color, while pure black is preserved.
	Darken	Gives preference to the darker of the two images. Will cause color shifts.

continues on next page

Layer Modes *continued*		

Visual	Mode	Description
	Difference	Subtracts the values of the top layer's underlying color.
	Exclusion	Similar to the Difference filter but with lower contrast.
	Hue	Combines the luminance and saturation of the underlying colors with the hue of the layer colors.
	Saturation	Combines the luminance and hue of the underlying colors with the saturation of the layer colors. Has no effect on grayscale images.

continues on next page

Layer Modes *continued*		
Visual	**Mode**	**Description**
	Color	Combines the luminance of the underlying colors with the hue and saturation of the layer colors. Grays are preserved.
	Luminosity	Combines the hue and saturation of the underlying colors of one layer with the luminance of the layer colors. The effect is the opposite of what the Color mode achieves.

Note: Some of the layer modes were omitted from the Layer Modes chart because they relate more to the chapter on masking. Those left out include Stencil Alpha, Stencil Luma, Silhouette Alpha, and Silhouette Luma, as well as Alpha Add and Luminescent Premul. These other modes will be covered in Chapter 13, "*Masks.*"

17. ——————————Layer Modes

Layer modes add, subtract, divide, and multiply pixel values of different layers together. Because After Effects is programmed to do this in many different ways, you have a wide variety of blending modes to choose from. These modes are used to create special effects in the way images look when they are composited together. There really isn't a practical use for them; it is more of a visual effect you might choose to use when you want your movie footage to look different from normal. This exercise will let you experiment with layer modes.

1. Open **layermodes.aep** from the **chap_08** folder. Save a copy to the **AE6 HOT Projects** folder you created in Chapter 2.

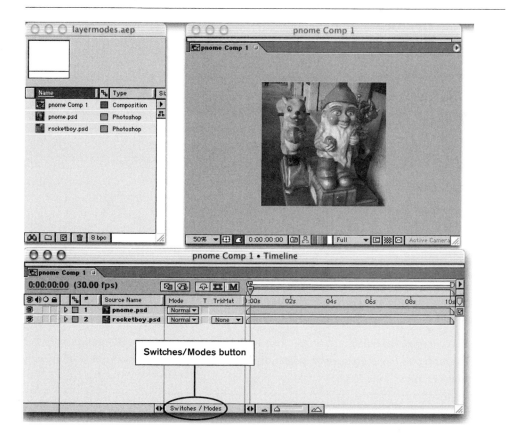

2. Click the words **Switches/Modes** to toggle to the **Modes** panel. This is a somewhat hidden button in After Effects (aren't ya glad ya got this book?). Try clicking it several times—you'll see that it toggles on and off. Make sure you leave it set to the **Modes** panel when you're finished clicking.

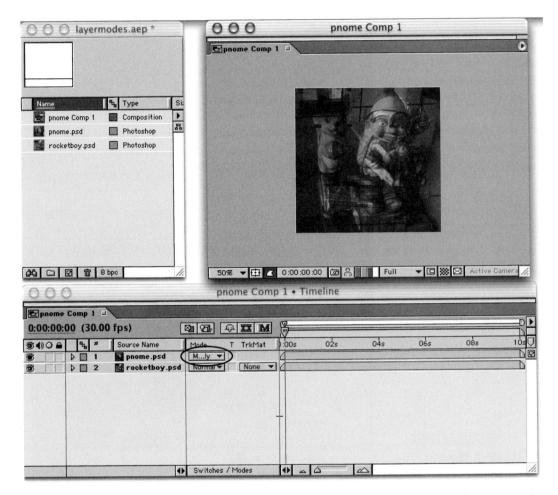

3. Change the **pnome.psd** layer from **Normal** to **Multiply** mode by displaying the **Mode** menu on the top layer. You always apply the layer mode to the layer above the one you want to affect.

*Tip: As an alternative method, select the layer and then choose **Layer > Blending Mode > Multiply**. This **transfer** mode menu contains the same list found in the Mode pop-up menu. (Layer modes are also known as transfer modes.)*

4. Experiment with other modes, and see what they do. There is no better way to learn which ones you like than to experiment. You might also try lowering the opacity on the **pnome.psd** layer, which will have varying effects with different layer modes. When you are finished, save and close this project.

TIP | Changing Layer Modes

Unlike layer properties, layer modes cannot be animated over time using keyframes. If you wish to use another layer mode on the same layer at any point in a Timeline, split the layer and apply a new layer mode. You learned how to split a layer earlier in this chapter.

This chapter was a biggie! As we said, layers are quite a bit more complex in After Effects than in other programs. I guess you believe me now! Have yourself a nice break before moving forward to the next chapter.

9.

Text Layers

Setting and Animating Text	Animating Selector Ranges
Advanced Selector Properties	Text Boxes and the Wiggly Selector
Using Multiple Animators and Selectors	Putting Text on a Path
Importing Text from Photoshop and Illustrator Files

chap_09

After Effects 6
H•O•T CD-ROM

The text layer is an exciting new feature in this release of After Effects. In the past, you either had to bring text in from another application, such as Photoshop or Illustrator, or create text with an effect. There was no possibility of typing directly into After Effects. That's all changed with After Effects 6's new feature called text layers.

With text layers, you can set your text with the same precision and ease you find in Illustrator and Photoshop. The advanced formatting options enable you to fuss over the layout of every character in a single word, or create a line- or paragraph-length text block. If you still prefer to completely develop your text layouts in the other applications before importing, your options have expanded: you can now retain the editability of text brought in from other Adobe applications such as Photoshop and Illustrator!

The new Animator properties enable you to create text transformations in new and exciting ways. With the Selector properties, you can increase or decrease the range of a transformation across your text. By combining multiple Selectors and Animators and by applying Wiggly Selectors and shape modifiers, you have an unlimited arsenal of text effects at your disposal! These new terms will be described and easily understood through hands-on exercises.

The exercises in this chapter will familiarize you with creating direct text, importing text from other applications, and putting text on a path. You'll also learn all about the Animator and Selector properties.

Text Layers and the Animate Text Menus

In previous versions of After Effects, you could create text by applying one of the built-in text effects to a layer, but all of the text on the layer had to be treated as a single unit. A similar problem occurred with text imported from Illustrator: if you wanted to animate a series of letters individually, you'd first have to convert the letters to outlines and then bring each one in a on a separate layer, which created a complex and difficult-to-edit animation setup.

With text layers, you can set text blocks of any length and apply changes in the Text properties to any character or set of characters over time. Using the **Animation > Animate Text** menu, you add Animators, which control changes in text properties over time. Using the **Animation > Add Text Selector** menu, you add Text Selectors that control which parts of the text blocks are affected by each Animator. You can apply multiple Animators, each with its own combination of animated Text properties, to a single text layer, and you can apply multiple Selectors to a single Animator. If this sounds like a lot of gobbledygook, don't worry. You'll get to try all of this and learn by doing, as usual!

I. ——————————Setting and Animating Text

Adding text to a composition is as easy as adding any other type of layer. In this first exercise, you will set a line of text and apply some basic transformations to an entire word, causing it to stretch and glow over time.

1. Open **textacy-1.aep** from the **chap_09** folder and resave it to the **AE6 HOT Projects** folder so you have a copy to work on. From the **Project** window, open **finished comp** to preview what you'll be doing in this exercise. Press the **spacebar** to view the contents. This composition was created entirely in After Effects—no artwork was imported. You'll be making this same composition on your own. Close **finished comp** once you've checked it out. Double-click **starter comp** to open the **Timeline** and **Composition** windows. They should be empty, but you'll change that soon!

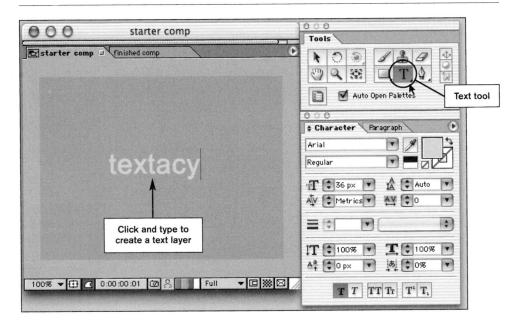

2. Select the **Text** tool from the **Tools** palette (If it's not already open, open it by choosing **Window > Tools**.) The **Character** and **Paragraph** palettes should open automatically. In the **Composition** window, click near the center of the composition and type the word **textacy**. Once you finish typing, a text layer named the same as its content will appear in the Timeline.

When you click into an empty part of the Composition window with the Text tool, a text layer is automatically created inside the Timeline. You can also create an empty text layer by choosing Layer > New > Text from the main menus. With this other method, the Text tool will automatically be selected, and the cursor will be placed in the center of the screen for you.

3. If it is not open already, open the **Character** palette by choosing **Window > Character**. Select all of the text in your composition by clicking and dragging across the word **textacy**, just as you would in any other text-handling program. In the **Character** palette, set the font to **Arial Regular** and the size to **36 px**.

Note that since After Effects is intended for screen-based output, fonts are measured in pixels instead of points. However, at 100% magnification, the pixels and points will appear roughly equivalent, so don't let the alternative measurement throw you.

NOTE | Font Usage and Collect Files

For these exercises, we've chosen standard fonts that almost everyone has on their systems, but feel free to jazz up these projects with more exciting fonts. The only caveat when working on your own projects is that you must make sure that the fonts are available on any system on which you'll edit or render your work. If you're passing on a project to someone else, you might want to check your font usage by choosing **File > Collect Files**. This feature will generate a report of the fonts, files, and effects that are necessary to render your project. Note that Collect Files does not do all the work for you: it gathers your media source files together in one place for ease of transfer, but it leaves the complexities of installing any fonts and effects to you.

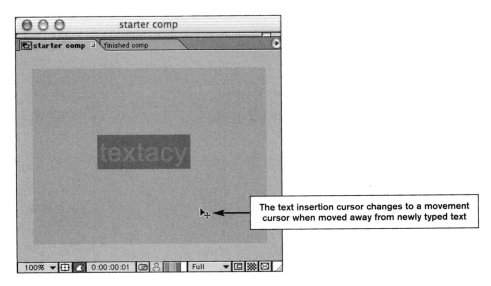

The text insertion cursor changes to a movement cursor when moved away from newly typed text

4. With the **Text** tool still selected, move the cursor away from the text until it changes from the **I-beam** text insertion cursor to the **Move Layer** cursor. Drag the layer until your text is centered on the stage. Note that the **Text** tool remains selected so that you can immediately return to editing text.

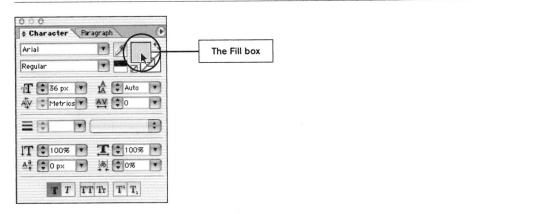

The Fill box

5. With the text still selected, click the **Fill** box in the **Character** palette. Select a **medium gray** from the color picker that pops up.

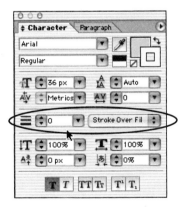

6. Click once to bring the stroke to the top; then click the **Stroke** box and select a **light yellow** color.

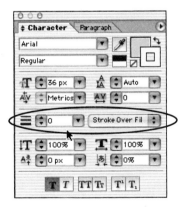

7. Enter **0** in the **Stroke Width** field of the **Character** palette. If it isn't already selected, choose **Stroke Over Fill** from the pop-up next to the **Stroke Width** field. Click inside of the type to deselect it. It's hard to see the color changes until the type is deselected.

8. Choose **Animation > Animate Text > Stroke Width. Animator 1** and **Range Selector 1** will be added to your Timeline, along with the **Stroke Width** property. Note that the initial value of **0** in the **Stroke Width** is taken from the setting you chose in the **Character** palette earlier.

In the Animate Text submenu, you might notice that the other options include animating the stroke color. You'll learn about this soon. Range Selector will also be explained in a forthcoming exercise.

9. Click the **Stopwatch** icon next to the **Stroke Width** property on the **Timeline**. Move the **Current Time Indicator** to **0:00:02:00** on the **Timeline** and set the value of the **Stroke Width** property to **6**. You should now have two keyframes set. Preview your animation and watch the text glow.

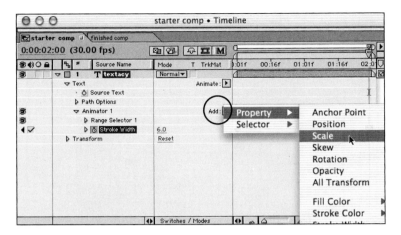

10. In the **Switches/Modes** panel of the **Timeline**, click the **Add** arrow next to **Animator 1.** Select **Property > Scale** from the pop-up menu. A new **Scale** property will be added beneath **Animator 1.**

*If your hierarchy of Animators and Selectors gets too complicated, you might want to rename them by selecting each one, pressing **Enter**, and typing in a new name—just like renaming any layer. Animated properties can't be renamed, but if you pay attention to the indentation, you'll be able to tell which properties belong to which Animators. Note that the layer-wide versions of the properties (which we're not touching in this exercise) are still in a separate Transform category for each layer and aren't part of the Animator hierarchy.*

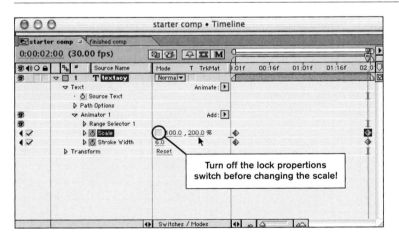

11. Click the **Link** icon next to the **Scale** values to remove the proportion constraints on scaling. Move the **Current Time Indicator** back to **0:00:00:00** in the **Timeline** and click the **Stopwatch** icon next to the **Scale** property beneath **Animator 1.** This will set a first keyframe with both **Horizontal** and **Vertical Scale** set to **100%.** Move the **Current Time Indicator** to **0:00:02:00** on the **Timeline,** and set the **Vertical Scale** to **200%.**

12. The scaled-up and glowing text is looking a bit cramped, now. Using the **Text** tool, select the word **textacy** by dragging across it in the **Composition** window. Enter **100** in the **Tracking** field of the **Character** palette.

Property changes made using the Character palette are applied to the selected text across the entire existence of the layer unless Animate Source Text is turned on. The change in tracking will not animate because you did not explicitly set up an Animator property for it.

13. Press the **spacebar** to play your animation. The text should now appear to stretch and glow. **Save** your project in the **AE6 HOT Projects** folder and close it.

Animator Properties	
Animator	**Description**
Position	Relates to the position of the characters. You can set values for this property in the Timeline window, or in the Composition window using the Selection tool, which changes to a Move tool when positioned over text characters.
All Transform	Allows all the Transform properties to be added at once to the Animator group. You will work with this setting in Exercise 4.
Skew	Allows you to set and animate the slant of the text characters. The skew axis specifies the axis along which the character is skewed.
Fill Color (RGB, Hue, Saturation, Brightness, Opacity)	Allows you to set and animate the color values of the text characters, based on the type of color Animator property you choose.
Stroke Color (RGB, Hue, Saturation, Brightness, Opacity)	Allows you to set and animate the color of the text character's stroke or outline. You worked with this setting in Exercise 1.
Stroke Width	Allows you to set and animate the width of the text character's stroke. You worked with this setting in Exercise 1.
Tracking	Allows you to set and animate the space between each text character in a word.
Line Anchor	Allows you to set the alignment for the tracking of each line of text. A value of 0% specifies left align, 50% specifies center align, and 100% specifies right align.
Line Spacing	Allows you to set and animate the space between lines of text in a multiline text layer.
Character Offset	Allows you to offset a number or letter by whatever value you enter. For example, if you used a value of 5 for the letter "a," it would become an "e." You get to work with this setting in Exercise 6.
Character Value	Allows you to substitute the value for selected characters, replacing each character with one character represented by the new value. You get to work with this setting in Exercise 6.
Character Range	Limits the range of the character. You get to work with this setting in Exercise 2.

2. _____Using the Range Selector

In the previous exercise, you practiced animating an entire text layer using Animator properties. In this exercise, you will apply the Animator properties to different portions of the text by animating the Range Selector property. Frankly, the Range Selector feature is better shown than explained. Basically, a Range Selector determines which characters in a text layer are affected by the Text Animator properties. If this explanation seems fuzzy to you, try this exercise and then read it again. It will make more sense!

1. Open **textacy-2.aep** from the **chap_09** folder and resave it to the **AE6 HOT Projects** folder so you have a copy to work on. From the **Project** window, open **finish comp** to preview what you'll be doing in this exercise. Use **RAM Preview** to view the contents. You'll be making this same composition on your own. Close **finish comp** once you've checked it out. Double-click **start comp** to open the **Timeline** and **Composition** windows. Press the **spacebar** to view this comp. It should be familiar to you; it's where you left off in the last exercise. Rewind the **Timeline** to the first frame before you begin.

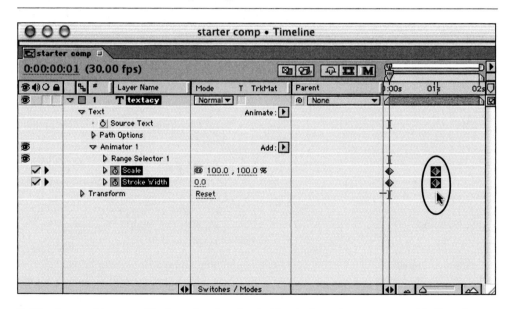

2. The first goal is to modify the animation that is identical to what you created in Exercise 1. The objective is to have the scale and glow ramp up over less amount of time than they do now, and then ramp back down. Use the **Shift** key to select the two end keyframes. Drag them to the **1s** mark on the **Timeline** as shown here. You can move keyframes after they're set, and you can even move multiple keyframes over multiple properties, as demonstrated here!

3. Next, use the **Shift** key to select the first two keyframes. When they are selected, choose **Edit > Copy**, or choose **Cmd+C** (Mac) or **Ctrl+C** (Windows).

4. Press the **End** key on your keyboard to move the **Current Time Indicator** to the last frame in the **Timeline**. Choose **Edit > Paste**, or **Cmd+V** (Mac) or **Ctrl+V** (Windows). The two keyframes should paste into the last frame. Press the **spacebar**. If all worked as planned, your animation should now ramp up to scale and glow, then fade down.

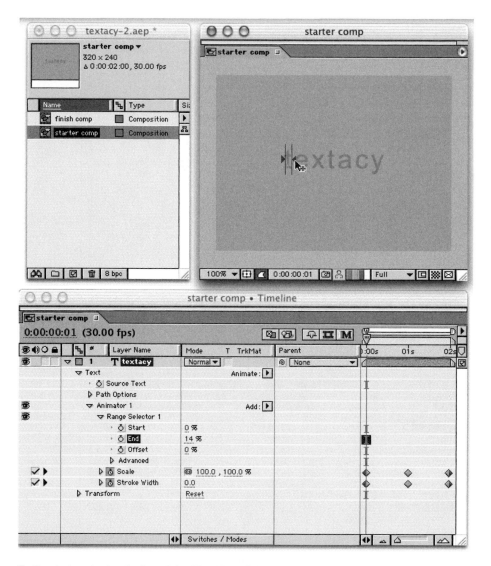

5. Rewind to the beginning of the **Timeline**. Click the **twirly** for the **Range Selector 1** settings. Change the **End** settings to **14%** or to where it brackets the first letter in the **textacy** type layer, as shown here. This is going to isolate a section of the type that encompasses the approximate width of a single character. If you press the **spacebar** right now, you'll only see the ramp of color and scale occur within the first letter of the **textacy** text. But wait, there's more!

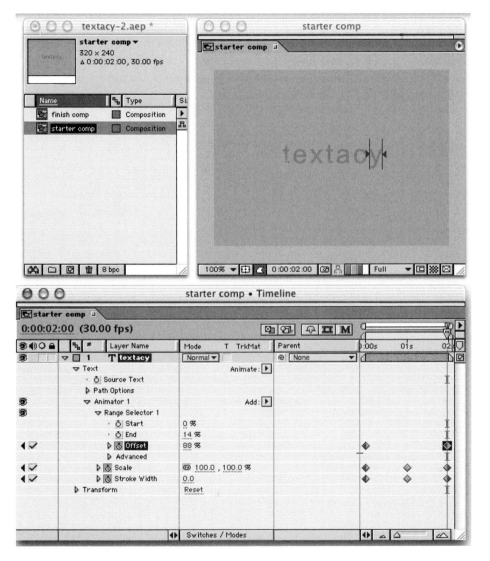

6. Click the **Stopwatch** icon for the **Offset** property. Leave it at **0%** on Frame **0:00:00:00**. Move the **Current Time Indicator** to the last frame and change the **Offset** to **88%**. Notice that the shape of the Range Selector brackets still bracket the approximate width of a single character? That shape has been offset to move to the end of the lettering.

7. Click off the layer so you don't see the Range Selector brackets. Click **RAM Preview** to view the results.

Pretty dang cool, eh? The next exercise will reveal deeper powers found within Range Selectors. It keeps getting better! Make way for the next wave of education.

8. Save your project in the **AE6 HOT Projects** folder and close it.

What Is Offset?

Offset is a part of the Range Selector, but it deserves a bit of special attention. The Offset value of a Selector moves the start and end points of the selection relative to the beginning of the text block. For example, an Offset of 0% leaves the start and end points exactly as you've set them, whereas an Offset of 100% moves the start and end points to the end of the text block.

The advantage of using Offset is the ability to move both start and end points at the same time, so that you can create the effect of a constantly sized selection moving over time. Like the start and end properties, Offset can be expressed in terms of percentages or in terms of an index by characters, words, or lines. The next project uses the Offset property to apply the same animated effect across different parts of a text block over time.

3. ————————— Multiple Animators and Selectors

In the last exercise, you saw how to use a Range Selector and have it isolate an animation within a text block. Would it blow your mind to imagine that you can use unlimited animation properties and Range Selector properties on a single text block? It impressed me when I first learned of it, and I hope you'll agree! Here's how you do it.

1. Open **textacy-3.aep** from the **chap_09** folder and resave it to the **AE6 HOT Projects** folder so you have a copy to work on. From the **Project** window, open **finish comp** to preview what you'll be doing in this exercise. Use **RAM Preview** to view the contents. Pretty wild, eh? This is the result of multiple Animator and Selector settings. You'll be making this same composition on your own. Close **finish comp** once you've checked it out. Double-click **starter comp** to open the **Timeline** and **Composition** windows. Press the **spacebar** to view this comp. It should be familiar to you; it's where you left off in the last exercise. Rewind the **Timeline** to the first frame before you begin.

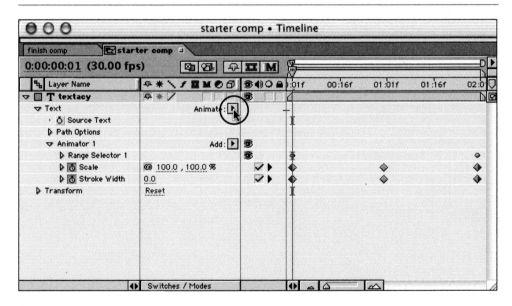

2. Click the **Animate** menu, and choose **Animate > Fill Color > RGB**.

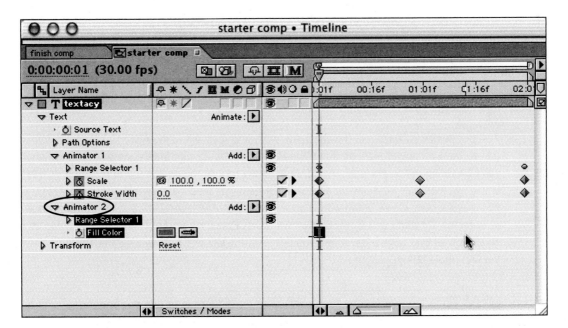

*This adds an **Animator 2** setting with its own Range Selector and properties for Fill Color.*

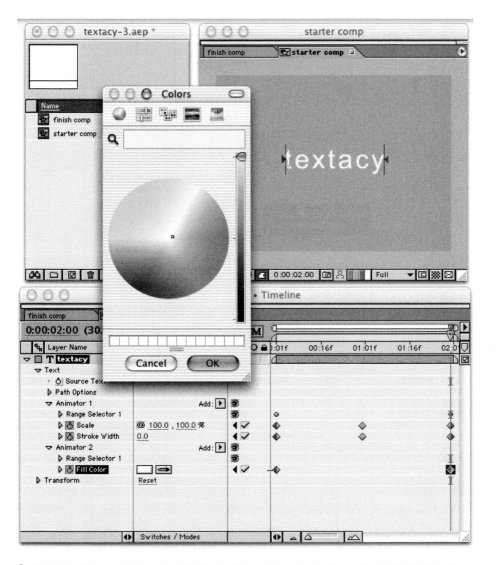

3. Click the **Stopwatch** icon for **Fill Color**. This will set the keyframe for **0:00:00:00** to its default setting: a **bright red**. Move the **Current Time Indicator** to the end of the **Timeline**. Click the **Fill Color** box and select a **light yellow** color. This will set two keyframes for color fill that animate from red to yellow. Press the **spacebar** to preview what you've done so far. The Fill color changes over the course of the composition; it is not restricted by the Range Selector that has been applied to Animator 1 that was set in a previous exercise. Notice that Animator 2 has its own Range Selector? You'll work with that next.

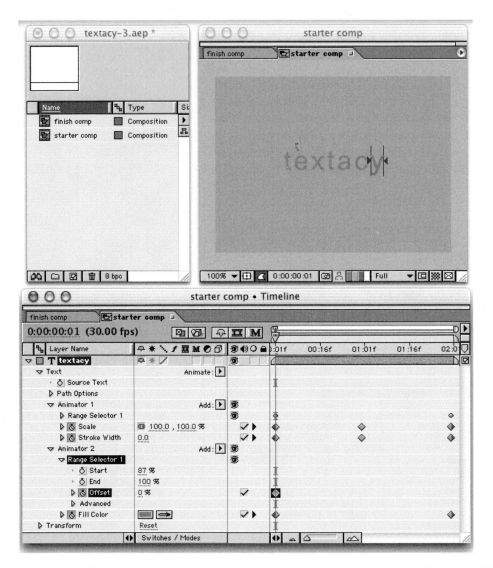

4. Click the **twirlies** for **Animator 2** and **Range Selector 1** to reveal the **Start**, **End**, and **Offset** properties. Change the **Start** position to **87%**. Leave the **End** position at **100%**. Click the **Stopwatch** icon for **Offset** to set a keyframe here in this position.

5. Move the **Current Time Indicator** to the end of the comp. Change the **Offset** position to **−88**. Press the **spacebar** to preview. Notice how the two Animators and Range Selectors interact? Cool, eh?

Notice how there is one Animate menu and two Add menus now? What is the difference between them? If you choose a new Animate property, you can set up an independent animation property with its own Range Selector. Using the Add menu instead will add to the Animator and Range Selector that currently exists. You'll do this next.

6. Click the **Add** menu button for **Animator 1** and select **Property > Position**.

7. Change the **Y Position** property to **13.0**. Press the **spacebar** to watch the position change occur within the existing Range Selector.

8. Click the **Add** menu for **Animator 2**. Choose **Property > Rotation**. Change the **Rotation** value to **−10**. Click **RAM Preview** to see your handiwork.

Congratulations—you've just animated multiple Animators and Range Selectors. The results are pretty wacky. Imagine the endless possibilities with these controls! It hurts to think about it!

9. Save your project in the **AE6 HOT Projects** folder and close it.

4. ——————————Advanced Selector Properties

In the last exercise, you explored the difference between adding a new Animator or using the Add feature to augment an existing Animator. You worked with the Range Selector and Offset setting. This exercise demonstrates the Advanced Selector properties that can cause an effect to vary in strength over time. You'll play with a couple of different ways that you can create animation via the Advanced Selector without changing its position, start, or end points—in fact, you'll create a complex effect while only setting a total of three keyframes!

1. Open the **advanced.aep** file from the **chap_09** folder and resave it to the **AE6 HOT Projects** folder so you have a copy to work on. View the finished comp to see what you're about to learn. When you're finished, open **starter comp**.

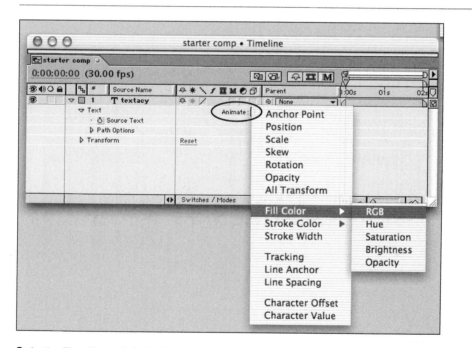

2. In the **Timeline**, click the **Animate** menu on the **textacy** layer and choose **Fill Color > RGB** from the pop-up menu. An Animator and a Range Selector will be added to the layer.

3. Click the **Fill Color** box and select a **light yellow**. The entire word will turn yellow.

4. Twirl down the arrow next to **Range Selector 1** and then twirl down the arrow next to **Advanced** to reveal the Advanced Selector properties.

5. Make sure the **Current Time Indicator** is at the beginning of the **Timeline (0:00:00:00)**. Turn on the **Stopwatch** icon next to the **Amount** property (within the **Advanced** properties of **Range Selector 1**). Change the value of the **Amount** property to **0%**.

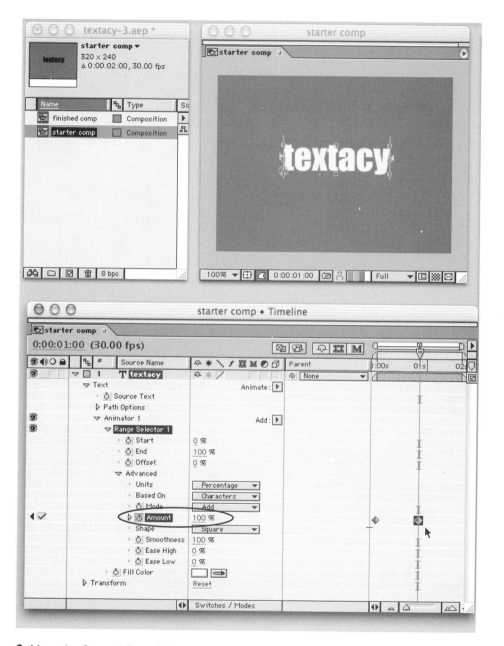

6. Move the **Current Time Indicator** to halfway through the animation (**0:00:01:00**). Change the value of the **Amount** property to **100%**.

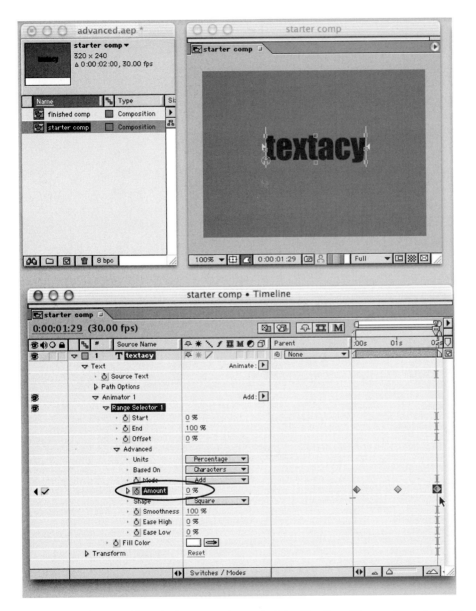

7. Move the **Current Time Indicator** to the end of the Timeline. Change the value of the **Amount** property back to **0%**. Press the **spacebar** to preview the animation.

At this point, a preview of the composition should look somewhat like the first exercise in this chapter: the entire word gradually changes color and fades back to its initial state. When the Amount property is set to less than 100%, it applies the property changes at a proportionally reduced strength.

8. In the **Advanced** properties of **Range Selector 1**, find the **Shape** property and choose **Triangle** from its pop-up menu. Press the **spacebar** to preview the animation.

Now you should see quite a change! Rather than the effect evenly fading in across the entire word, the effect will fade in from the middle out to the edges. What's going on here? The **Shape** *property determines how the effect is applied across the length of the text. The next step will show how the triangle shape can influence more than color.*

9. From the **Add** menu next to **Animator 1**, choose **Property > Position.** Change the value of the **Y** position to **-100**. Press the **spacebar** to preview the animation.

Now you can really see the "triangle" shape in action. See how the highest point in the triangle is also the section that glows brightest, while the lower end points of the triangle barely glow at all? Using this example, you can now think of the Shape property as setting up a graph that plots how much the effect should be applied across the length of the text, with the vertical axis of the graph representing the strength of the effect!

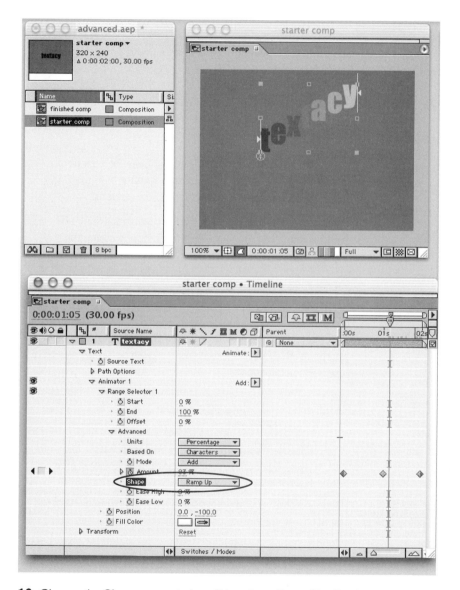

10. Change the **Shape** property from **Triangle** to **Ramp Up**. Preview the animation again and notice the change in the effect. Try playing with some of the other **Shape** options as well!

There is no stopwatch to turn on for the Shape property because it affects the interpolation of other properties, rather than being an animated effect itself.

11. Save your project in the **AE6 HOT Projects** folder and close it.

Range Selector Properties

The Range Selector is a powerful animation tool in its own right. This chart summarizes the options available when applying a Range Selector to an Animator.

Range Selector Properties		
Property	**Options**	**Function**
Start	Any number	Designates the start point for the Text Selector. Numbers greater than the length of the text or greater than the End property mean that the effect won't show up at all.
End	Any number	Designates the end point for the Text Selector. Numbers smaller than 1 or less than the Start property mean that the effect won't show up at all.
Offset	Any number	Designates how far from the beginning of the text the Selector should be set. An Offset of 0 means no modification to the Start and End properties.
Units	Index	Counts characters, words, or lines using absolute numbers starting with 1. Useful if the length of your text may change during the animation.
	Percentage	Counts characters, words, or lines by percentage. If the text is lengthened or shortened, the number of characters affected by the Selector will also be shortened.
Based On	Characters	Counts every character and unit of whitespace as a character. When using this option, your animation may seem to pause when it reaches a space.
	Characters Excluding Spaces	Counts individual characters but does not include whitespace (spaces, returns) in the count.
	Words	Counts groups of characters that are separated by whitespace as a single unit
	Lines	Counts groups of characters that are separated by carriage returns as a single unit
Mode	Add	Adds the characters within this Selector to any other active selections within this Animator.
	Subtract	Removes the characters within this Selector from any other active selections within this Animator.

continues on next page

	Range Selector Properties *continued*	
Property	**Options**	**Function**
Mode *continued*	Intersect	Modifies the selection to allow only characters that appear both within this Selector and any other active selection within this Animator.
	Min	Filters out all but the selection closest to the beginning of the word.
	Max	Filters out all but the selection closest to the end of the word.
	Difference	Filters out any characters that appear both within this Selector and any other active selection within this Animator.
Amount	−100% to 100%	Determines how much influence the Animator properties associated with the current Selector have on the overall text.
Shape	Square	Applies the Amount property from left to right across the text.
	Ramp up	Applies the Amount property from right to left, weighting the effect towards the right.
	Ramp down	Applies the Amount property from left to right, weighting the effect towards the left.
	Triangle	Applies the Amount property from the center outwards, weighting the effect towards the center.
	Round	Applies the Amount property in a gradually increasing and then decreasing amount, describing a half-circle.
	Smooth	Applies the Amount property from the center outwards, but in a smoother arc than when the Triangle shape is used.
Smoothness	0% to 100%	Determines the gradation with which the effect is applied across individual characters; 100% is the most gradual effect; 0% applies the full strength of the effect to each character in turn.
Ease High	−100% to 100%	Determines the weighting of influence of the text properties over time, decreasing the rate of change in an effect as its strength increases.
Ease Low	−100% to 100%	Determines the weighting of influence of the text properties over time, increasing the rate of change in an effect as its strength decreases.

5. ——————Text Boxes and the Wiggly Selectors

In the last four exercises, you've changed the properties of a single word over time. In this exercise, you will work with a longer piece of text and will explore not only transforming the "look" of the text but the text itself!

1. Open the **text-4.aep** project from the **chap_09** folder and resave it to the **AE6 HOT Projects** folder so you have a copy to work on. Check out the finished comp to see what the objective of this exercise is. This comp might take a while to render; use **RAM Preview**. The results are worth it; I promise! When you're ready to start, open **starter comp** to proceed.

2. In the **Timeline** window, click the **Text** layer's **twirly** down to reveal the **Source Text** property. With the **Current Time Indicator** at **0s (0:00:00:00)**, click the **Stopwatch** icon next to the **Source Text** property.

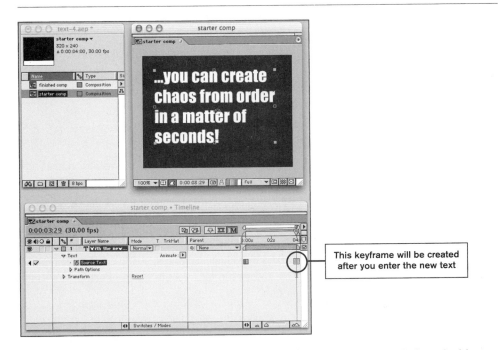

This keyframe will be created after you enter the new text

3. Move the **Current Time Indicator** to **0:00:02:15**. In the **Composition** window, double-click the text. If the text is not all automatically selected, drag across the text to select it all. Replace it with the following text: "...you can create chaos from order in a matter of seconds!"

Note that the Source Text keyframes are automatically created as Hold keyframes, which is represented by a different icon than keyframes for other properties. The text itself won't morph or transform itself letter by letter between keyframes.

> **TIP | Why Did the Text Just Fit into Place?**
>
> The text you just typed automatically fits into the same space that was filled by the initial text because this text was created using a text box. Just as in Illustrator, you can create a text box instead of a line of text by clicking and dragging out a box-shaped area using the Text tool. Text boxes are a great way to keep your text lined up across multiple screens of any presentation, from a public service announcement to film credits!

4. From the **Animation** menu, choose **Animate Text > All Transform**. This option simultaneously assigns all of the basic text transformations to a single Animator.

5. Modify the properties underneath **Animator 1** as follows: Set **Position** to **142** horizontal, **22** vertical. Set **Scale** to **212** horizontal, **212** vertical. Set **Rotation** to **10 x 0.0** (10 complete rotations). *DO NOT* turn on the stopwatches for these properties.

At this point, you should have kind of a mess on your screen. Fear not—the next steps will clean that up just fine!

6. In the **Timeline**, delete **Range Selector 1** by selecting it and pressing the **Backspace** or **Delete** key. You're going to add a new kind of Selector called a Wiggly Selector next instead.

7. From the **Add** menu, next to **Animator 1**, choose **Selector > Wiggly**.

Wiggly is another kind of Selector. It has to be tried to be explained! You'll do this soon!

8. Twirl down the options beneath the newly created **Wiggly Selector 1**. Move the **Current Time Indicator** to **1s (0:00:01:00)** and turn on the **Stopwatches** for the **Max Amount** and **Min Amount** properties. Make sure both properties are set to **0%**.

The setting of 0% essentially turns off all the wacky settings that you created in the previous step. Setting this keyframe at 0% allows the craziness to animate into insanity rather than popping on.

9. Move the **Current Time Indicator** to **1s 15f (0:00:01:15)**. Change the **Max Amount** property to **10%** and the **Min Amount** property to **−10%**.

The Wiggly Selector modifies the current selection (and the strength of Text Animators on the selection) by the given percentage. In this case, we're starting with no selection (since you deleted the original Selector), and you're gradually increasing the influence of the Wiggly Selector until it is affecting 100% of the text.

10. Move the **Current Time Indicator** to **2s (0:00:02:00)**. Change the **Max Amount** property to **100%** and the **Min Amount** property to **−100%**. Now the Wiggler can modify as much or as little of the text with each wiggle!

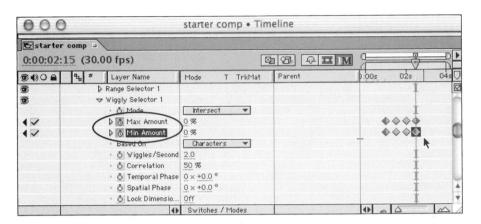

11. Move the **Current Time Indicator** to **2s 15f (0:00:02:15)**. Change the **Max Amount** property back to **0%** and the **Min Amount** property back to **0%**. Now the text will resolve itself into the new words.

12. Change the **Wiggles/Second** property to **5.0**. This means that the text affected by the transformations will change every 6 frames (30 frames/sec divided by 5 wiggles/sec).

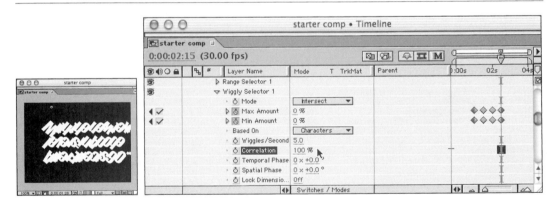

13. Change the **Correlation** property to **100%**. **RAM Preview** the animation. Cool transition, huh? And it's all from the chaos of a Wiggly selection!

14. Add a little more chaos to the piece by changing the **Correlation** property to **0%**. For an added touch of excitement, turn on **Motion Blur**. Hang on to your seat and **RAM Preview** the animation again.

The Correlation property tells the Wiggly Selector how much to vary its randomization between characters (or words or lines, if you choose those units). 100% causes all of the characters in the selection to vary in unison, and 0% causes each character to do its own thing. For more details on the Wiggly Selector, see the Wiggly Selector Properties chart.

15. Save your project in the **AE6 HOT Projects** folder and close it.

Wiggly Selector Properties

The Wiggly Selector can be used on its own or can be used to enhance the power of the Range Selector, as you'll see in upcoming exercises. This chart summarizes the properties unique to the Wiggly Selector; properties that work the same as they do with the Range Selector are not repeated here.

Wiggly Selector Properties		
Property	**Options**	**Function**
Max Amount	−100% to 100%	Determines the maximum amount that the Wiggler can randomly expand or contract the selection to which it is applied.
Min Amount	−100% to 100%	Determines the minimum amount that the Wiggler will randomly expand or contract the selection to which it is applied.
Wiggles/Sec.	Any number	Determines how many times per second the Wiggler changes the size of the Selector; a number greater than the frame rate or less than 0 will have no visible effect.
Correlation	0% to 100%	Determines the random individuality of characters (or words or lines, depending on your setting in the Based On property). 0% modifies each character randomly; 100% modifies all characters within the selection in unison.
Temporal Phase	Revolutions + degrees	Causes slight variations in the animation over time, based on the phase of the animation.
Spatial Phase	Revolutions + degrees	Causes slight variations in the animation per character.
Lock Dimensions	On or off	Instructs the Wiggly Selector to apply itself equally to both dimensions of multidimensional properties. For example, with this property set to "on," the Wiggly Selector will equally modify the horizontal and vertical components of the Scale property.

6. _____Using Character Offset

In this exercise, you will apply multiple Animators to a single text layer to create a complex effect. If you've seen any of the recent high-tech heist movies, you'll recognize the gadget readout that you'll be simulating. It runs through all of the possible numbers for each part of a safe combination until it "hears" the right combination. An extension of this technique can be used to create the "falling numbers" effect seen in the opening titles of the *Matrix* movies (which was created in After Effects!).

1. Open the **safecracker.aep** project from the **chap_09** folder and resave it to the **AE6 HOT Projects** folder so you have a copy to work on. Open **finished comp** to observe the project you'll be building. Open **finished comp2** and notice the same effect with a different font.

The font used here is Impact, and the font used in finished comp was Courier. Notice how the numbers seem to jump around a bit when set in Impact, versus Courier that seemed to work in perfect registration? Courier is a monotype font; Impact is not. **Monotype** *means that every character in the font is allotted the exact same width of space, including blank spaces. For effects like this safe-cracking effect, using a monotype font is more effective because it has better registration throughout the animation.*

When you're ready, open **starter comp** *to get going.*

2. If you press the **spacebar**, you'll see that the text layer has already been created for you and keyframes have been set in the **Source Text** property to change the numbers from the "unsolved" combination (all zeros) to the "solved" combination.

3. Rewind the **Current Time Indicator** back to the first frame. Click the **Animate** menu and choose **Character Offset**. Even though this is a new property, using it employs the same techniques you've been using throughout this chapter.

4. Make sure that the **Character Range** pop-up is set to **Preserve Case & Digits**. This ensures that numbers remain numbers and letters remain letters, so your animation will seem random within limits.

*The **Full Unicode** setting would allow the randomization of letters and numbers.*

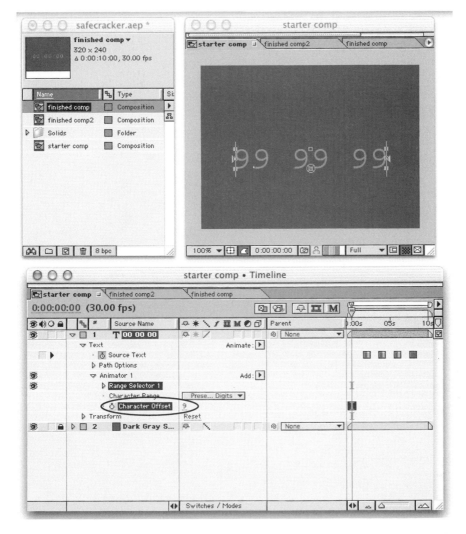

5. Increase the value of the **Character Offset** property to **9**. All of the digits in the "readout" will change from **0s** to **9s**. You have just set the threshold for how the numbers will randomize. Once you set the randomization, which you will do next by using a Wiggly Selector, the values will never go beyond 9.

---

6. You have new numbers, but no randomness. But in the last exercise, you learned about a great force of chaos: the **Wiggly Selector**. Using the **Add** pop-up menu next to **Animator 1**, add a **Wiggly Selector** to **Animator 1**.

Note: You can have a Range Selector and a Wiggly Selector in the same Animator.

---

7. Twirl down the **Wiggly Selector 1** options. Make sure the **Min Amount** is set to **−100%** and the **Max Amount** is set to **100%**. Change the **Wiggles/Second** to **7** (which will ensure that the randomization happens at a speed of 7 changes per second). Make sure the **Mode** is set to **Intersect**.

When a Selector is in Intersect mode, only the parts of its selection that intersect another selection will be affected. Right now, since you've made no changes to Range Selector 1, the Wiggly Selector can randomly change any part of the text layer. Later on, you'll constrain the Wiggly Selector using Range Selector 1.

8. Press the **spacebar** to preview the animation.

All of the numbers run randomly through the length of the animation, and the combination never gets solved. The numbers randomly increment, which is better than the unison increase you observed back in Step 2, but now there's no sense of an ordered solving sequence. You'll fix this next.

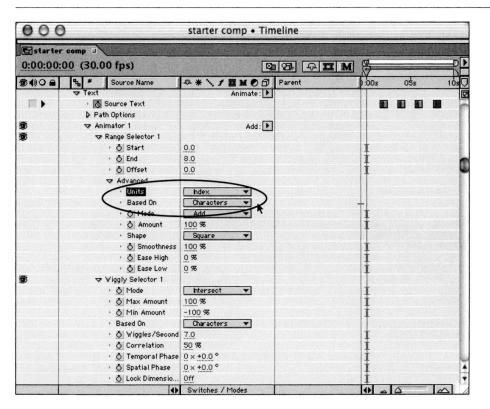

9. Wouldn't it be nice if you could get randomness and order at the same time? This is where multiple Selectors come in. Twirl down **Range Selector 1**, and then twirl down its **Advanced** properties. Choose **Index** from the **Units** pop-up menu, and make sure that the **Based On** property is set to **Characters**.

*The **Units** property lets you specify how you want to measure your selection: by characters or by percentages. The **Based On** property lets you specify whether you want to include spaces in your measurements or not, or whether you want to count by words or lines instead of characters. By changing the Units to Index, you're telling After Effects to treat each letter as a unit.*

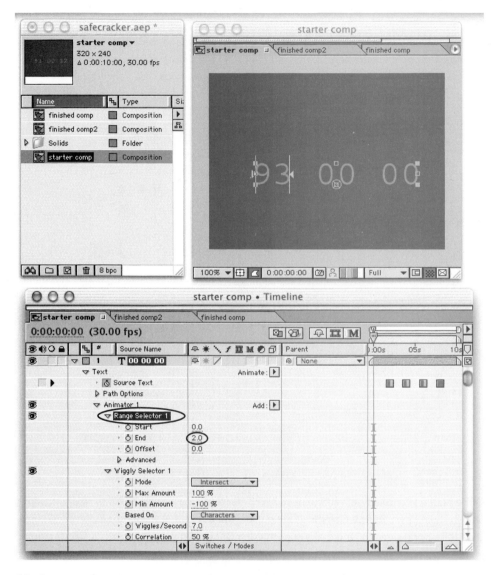

10. Observe that the **End** property of **Range Selector 1** is set to **8**? This demonstrates that After Effects recognizes that there are eight characters in the text block (six numbers and two spaces). Change the **End** value to **2** in the **Timeline**. Notice that the **End** property cinches in on the first two numbers? Cool, eh?

I want to take a moment to summarize what's happened so far. A set of six numbers was created in a text block. Keyframes were established that changed the source text three times to the final safe crack numbers. A Character Offset Animator was applied to the entire text block, allowing it to offset to nine numbers away from its origin. A Wiggly Selector was applied to randomize the numbers from 0 to 9. Now, a Range Selector has been set to a two-character width to limit the Wiggly Selector's effect on only two numbers. It's a lot of steps, but the effect is worth it, right? The next objective is to move the randomization away from each set of two letters so they can end on their real numbers that were set in the original source text.

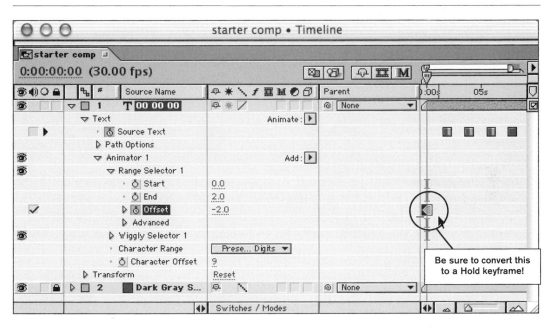

11. Make sure that the **Current Time Indicator** is still set at the beginning of the composition (**0:00:00:00**). Turn on the **Stopwatch** for the **Offset** property of **Range Selector 1**. Set its initial value to **−2**. This moves the Range Selector, which is set to the width of two characters, completely off the text to the left. Why? Because I wanted a pause before the computer appears to try to solve the problem. From the main menus, choose **Animation > Toggle Hold Keyframe**. This will cause the **Offset** to hold in its offscreen position until the next time I want it to change. If you don't set a Hold keyframe, the changes in the Offset value will gradually interpolate over time. I want the offset value to jump from keyframe to keyframe, hence my decision to use a Hold keyframe.

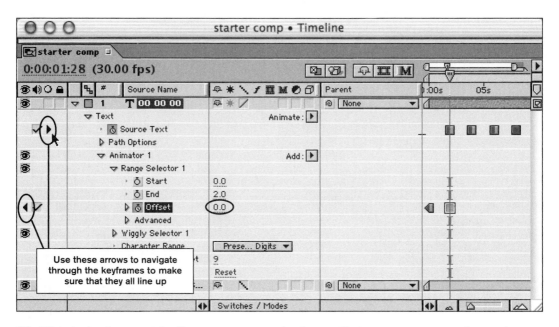

12. Click the **keyframe navigation arrows** next to the **Source Text** property once to advance the **Current Time Indicator** to the first Source Text keyframe (**2s**, or **0:00:02:00**). This keyframe icon is for a hold interpolation type, which is the only kind of keyframe allowed for source text. Set the **Offset** property to **0**. Moving the Offset to 0 causes the Range Selector to cinch in on the first two numbers of the text block.

Since you set the initial keyframe to a Hold keyframe, all subsequently created keyframes for the Offset property will be set up as Hold keyframes automatically, which is exactly what you want in this case. This will cause the Offset value to jump from keyframe to keyframe rather than gradually move over time from keyframe to keyframe. You learned about Hold keyframes and keyframe interpolation wayyyy back in Chapter 6, "Playing with Time." It might make more sense now that you have a bit more experience under your belt! Every keyframe from now on will be a Hold keyframe, unless you toggle your last Hold keyframe back to an interpolated keyframe.

13. Click the **keyframe navigation arrow** again for **Source Text** to advance the **Current Time Indicator** to the next Source Text keyframe (**4s**, or **0:00:04:00**). Set the **Offset** property to **3**. Click the **keyframe navigation arrow** again for **Source Text** to advance the **Current Time Indicator** to the next Source Text keyframe (**6s**, or **0:00:06:00**), and set the **Offset** property to **6**. Click the **keyframe navigation arrow** again for **Source Text** to advance the **Current Time Indicator** to the next Source Text keyframe (**8s**, **0:00:08:00**), and set the **Offset** property to **9**.

At each one of the Source keyframe's locations, you've moved the Offset value. It started offscreen to the left, then cinched in on the first two numbers, then the second two numbers, then the third two numbers, and then off screen to the right of the text block.

---

14. Press the **spacebar** to preview the composition. At this point, the combination appears to solve itself, but it's a little difficult for the casual viewer to tell what's going on. How about if the solved parts of the combination turn green? This is where the second Animator will come in.

Why a second Animator, not just a second Selector? The second Animator is required because you will be modifying both the selection and the attributes being applied to the selection for this next effect. If only one of these two things were changing, you could just add the new Selector or the new property to be changed to this Animator. But since they're both changing independently of this Animator, you'll need a second one to do the work.

15. Next to the **Text** layer, click the **Animate** menu and choose **Fill Color > RGB**.

16. Click the **Fill Color** box that appears beneath **Animator 2** and change its color to a **bright green**. All of your text in the Composition window will turn green as well.

17. Twirl down **Range Selector 1** beneath **Animator 2**. If you're running out of room on your **Timeline**, you can twirl up **Animator 1**, since you're done with it.

18. Click the **twirly** for **Advanced**. Change the **Units** to **Index**, and notice that the **End** setting in the **Range Selector 1** changes to **8** for the 8 characters in the text block (including spaces). In the **Timeline**, drag the **Current Time Indicator** back to the beginning of the composition (**0:00:00:00**) and click the **Stopwatch** icon next to the new Range Selector's **End** property.

19. In the **Composition** window, drag the Range Selector's **End** marker to the left until it meets up with the Selector **Start** marker and all of your text turns back to red. This dragging method is an alternative to entering values inside the Timeline window. It's a lot more intuitive to drag, isn't it?

20. Ctrl+click (Mac) or **right-click** (Windows) on the keyframe you just created and select **Toggle Hold Keyframe** from the pop-up menu.

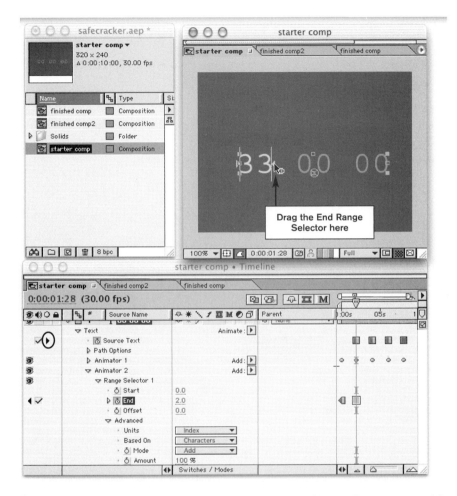

21. Using the **keyframe navigation arrows** next to the **Source Text** property of the text layer, advance to the first text change (the second keyframe). In the **Composition** window, drag the Selector **End** marker to the right until the first set of numbers turns green.

---

22. Using the **keyframe navigation arrows** next to the **Source Text** property, move to the next three keyframes. On the second keyframe, drag the Selector **End** marker to the right until the second set of numbers turns green. Do the same thing for the third set of numbers at the keyframe.

---

23. Press the **spacebar** to test the animation one last time.

Hey, if this After Effects thing doesn't work out for you, at least now you can crack a safe!

---

24. Save your project in the **AE6 HOT Projects** folder and close it.

7.————————Putting Text on a Path

After that last marathon exercise, you probably need a little breather. Here's a nice, quick effect that is new to text layers in After Effects 6.

1. Open the **pathtext.aep** project from the **chap_09** folder and resave it to the **AE6 HOT Projects** folder so you have a copy to work on. In the **Project** window, open **finished comp** to preview what you are about to learn. When you're ready, double-click the composition named **starter comp** to open the **Composition** and **Timeline** windows.

2. A text layer and a mask have already been created for you in this composition. The mask is partially clipping the text layer, but you'll fix this soon. To link the two together, click the text layer's twirly, and then twirl open the **Path Options**. Choose **Mask 1** from the **Path** pop-up menu.

Masks can be created on text layers just like any other layer by selecting the text layer and then simply drawing on the layer with After Effects' masking tools. You learned how to draw masks in Chapter 13, "Masks."

3. The text is currently running along the inside of the path. In the new options that appeared beneath the **Path** property, find **Reverse Path**, and change its value to **On**. Your text should disappear. Don't panic!

The text disappeared because the default behavior of a mask is to only reveal what is contained inside of the closed path, and you've just asked that the text attach itself to the outside of the path. This applies only to closed paths; open paths do not mask out any part of the image.

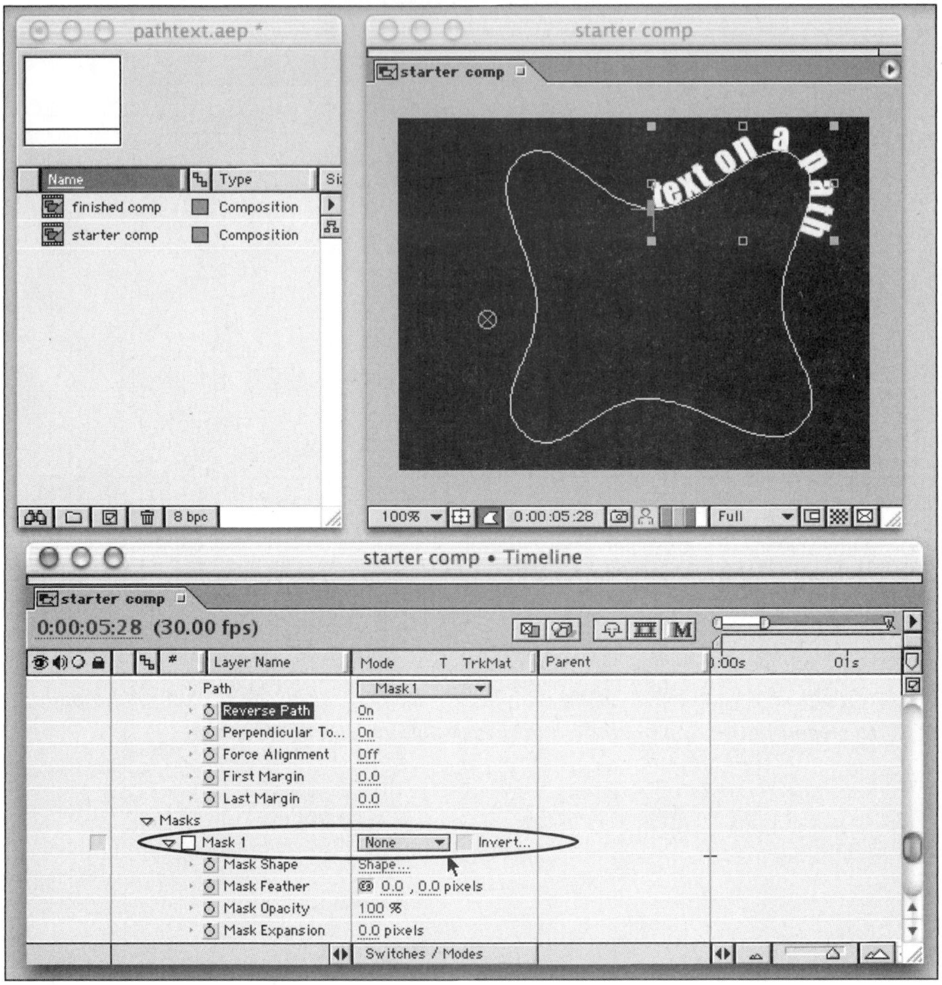

4. To fix the disappearing text, twirl down the **Masks** options. Change the Mode of **Mask 1** to **None** by using the pop-up menu that appears next to the mask name. Now the mask will have no effect on the layer except to serve as a path for the text.

---

5. Add a **Position** Animator to the text layer using any of the techniques you've learned already.

---

6. Make sure that the **Current Time Indicator** is at **0s (0:00:00:00)** and turn on the **Stopwatch** icon next to the **Position** property of **Animator 1**.

---

7. In the **Timeline**, go to the end of the comp (**6s**, or **0:00:06:00**). Drag across the first value of the **Position** property (the "horizontal" value) until the text makes its way one time around the mask shape (the value will be approximately **810**).

When attaching text to a path, the "horizontal" component of the position controls the text's movement parallel to the path, and the "vertical" component of the position controls the text's movement perpendicular to the path.

8. Press the **spacebar** to test your movie. It's that simple—really!

9. Save and close this project.

8. _____Importing Text from Photoshop and Illustrator Files

If you've used earlier versions of After Effects, you may know the pain of discovering that you made a typographic error in one of your source files and having to go back and change the text, reconvert it to an outline or graphic, and bring it back into After Effects. If you're new to After Effects, you'll never have to experience this pain at all. In this exercise, you'll import a graphic with a text layer attached to it, and then you'll correct a typo without ever leaving After Effects.

1. Create a new project by choosing **File > New > New Project**.

2. Double click the **Project** window to bring up the **Import File** dialog box. Navigate to the **chap_09** folder and click (but don't double-click!) on the file named **madcat.psd**.

3. Change the **Import As** pop-up menu to **Composition – Cropped Layers**. This will bring in all of the Photoshop layers as a single comp. Click the **Import** (Mac) or **Open** (Windows) button to complete the import.

4. Double-click **madcat Comp 1** in the **Project** window to open up its **Timeline** and **Composition** window. Maybe test your proofreading skills by looking for the typo before going on to the next step!

Note: If you do not have exactly the same fonts on your machine, a dialog box appears warning of that problem. After Effects will convert it to editable text, but changes it to a font that you do have on your system.

*Hopefully you spotted that the word **kat** should be **c-a-t**. If you try to use the Text tool to edit the word, though, you'll find yourself in a new text layer. It needs to be converted to an After Effects text layer first!*

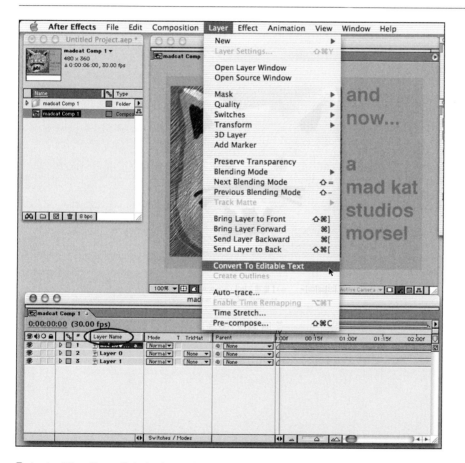

5. In the **Timeline**, click the layer that begins with "and now a." From the **Layer** menu, choose **Convert to Editable Text.**

If you have the same font used to create this text, it should change into a text layer without a problem. If you don't have the same font, After Effects will alert you about the missing font and will change the text to the default font.

6. Select the **Text** tool from the **Tools** palette and highlight the word "kat." Type **cat** in its place.

That wasn't so bad, was it? This works great with any Photoshop or Illustrator text that has not already been converted to outlines or rasterized in the other programs. Once that extra step has been taken, there's no going back in After Effects—so be sure to tell any designers you're working with that you have the new version of After Effects and that they should leave their text unrasterized… as long as you all have the same fonts, of course.

7. Save your project in the **AE6 HOT Projects** folder and close it.

NOTE | **Create Outlines**

In the last exercise, you might have noticed the **Create Outlines** option right beneath Convert to Editable Text. This option is similar to the options found in Adobe Illustrator and Macromedia Flash, and is the one way to share an After Effects file that contains a specific font with another After Effects user who doesn't have the same font. Unfortunately, there's a catch: when you create outlines from text in After Effects, all of its animated properties go away. You end up with a layer with a bunch of masks (one per shape in each letter), which you can then animate separately, but most of the value of the new text layers goes away with the conversion.

Whew! You've now made it through the most complicated and powerful new feature of After Effects 6.0. Hopefully, the awesome abilities you've gained here will turn you into a text junkie, if you weren't one already. Now reward yourself with a break before going on to explore the next chapter, which educates you about another exciting new feature—Dynamic Paint tools.

10.

Effects

Applying Multiple Effects	Drop Shadow Effect
Transition Effects	Favorites	Adjustment Layers
Precompose	Effects Palette

chap_10

After Effects 6
H·O·T CD-ROM

You might be familiar with the terms "filters" and "layer effects" in Photoshop. These are mini-applications, called plug-ins, that you can use to change the appearance of footage, such as brightness, contrast, color, blur, and so on. After Effects contains plug-in filters, just as Photoshop does, only they're much better! Why? Because you can animate them over time, and they have many keyframable settings that can add endless variations of visual alterations to your animations.

In this chapter, you'll learn to apply effects and control their settings. You'll see the interaction among multiple effects, and you will learn how to control this interaction.

On the other hand, there is no physical way that I could take you through all of After Effects' effects and settings. The book would be much fatter than the one you're holding, because the variations are practically endless. It's my hope that this chapter will open your eyes to the power of effects so that you become inspired to try them all on your own. It might take a lifetime, but hey, you'll enjoy yourself, so who cares?

What Are Plug-ins?

You can think of **plug-ins** as little programs that work within After Effects. After Effects is written to allow these special external programs to plug in to After Effects and work their magic.

All "effects" are actually plug-ins. They reside in a special folder within the **After Effects** folder called **Plug-ins** (strangely enough!) on your hard disk.

Adobe supplies a great number of plug-in effects that ship with After Effects. Other companies also create plug-in effects that can be used in After Effects. You can add any number of effects to your **Plug-ins** folder. Check the "*Resources*" appendix at the back of this book for plug-in suppliers.

Many Photoshop plug-ins also work with After Effects. If you are interested in learning more about plug-ins, consult the user guide that came with your program, or choose **Help > Effects Help**.

I. ——————————**Applying Effects**

During this exercise, you will create a new project and apply four effects: **Find Edges**, **Posterize**, **Hue/Saturation**, and **Bulge**. As you work through this exercise, notice how the effects are organized for easy identification. After Effects groups the various types of effects together to speed selection.

> **1.** Open **effects.aep** from the **chap_10** folder. Save a copy to your **AE6 HOT Projects** folder.

> **2.** In the **Project** window, locate the **effects folder** folder and open **Effects Finished Comp**. Press the **spacebar** to preview the composition. In the **Timeline**, turn off the effects temporarily to view the original by toggling the *f* symbol, which is the icon for the Effects switch.
>
> *Quite a difference, eh? Effects can dramatically alter boring footage and change the mundane to the outright psychedelic. How far you take effects is your own decision. You can easily create garish, over-the-top styles, or you can make subtle changes that trick the eye into not knowing what is real or unreal.*

3. Click the twirly for the **walk.mov** layer and you'll see that four different effects were applied to this layer. If you click their twirlies, you'll see more settings, and you will start to appreciate the number of options that Effects offers.

4. With the **walk.mov** layer selected, choose **Effect > Effect Controls**. This opens an auxiliary window—the **Effect Controls** window—that shows what effects have been applied to any layer. If you turn on and off any of the *f* symbols here, you can selectively turn on or off individual effects.

5. Turn on all the *f* symbols in the **Effect Controls** window, and then move the order around by dragging the names above or below each other.

It can be confusing to new After Effects users to know when to use the Timeline settings and when to use the Effect Controls window settings. They are both similar, and there's a lot of redundancy between them. It's a personal choice. You'll get to work both with the Timeline settings and Effect Controls window settings in this chapter, so you can develop your own preferences based on your own liking.

Effects Finished Comp • Timeline

Effects Finished Comp

0;00;03;12 (29.97 fps)

Source Name

▽ 1	🎬 **walk.mov**	
	▽ Effects	
	▷ Find Edges	Reset
	▷ Posterize	Reset
	▷ Bulge	Reset
	▷ Hue/Saturation	Reset
	▷ Transform	Reset

Click the individual Effects on or off here

You can reorder the Effects by dragging them above or below each other

Switches / Modes

You can also reorder the effects in the Timeline as well as turn on or off individual effects.

6. Close the **Effects Finished Comp** and open the **Effects Start Comp** from the **effects folder** folder in the **Project** window.

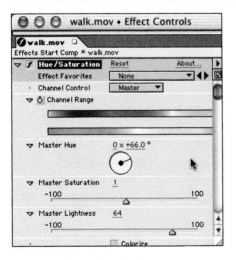

7. Select **walk.mov** in the **Timeline**. Select **Effect > Adjust > Hue/Saturation**. The **Effect Controls** window will open automatically with all the **Hue/Saturation** settings visible. Change the **Master Hue** to **66** degrees and the **Master Lightness** to **64**. Note that there is a **Stopwatch** icon for **Channel Range**. You can animate any of these properties! Hold off for now—you'll have your chance soon enough!

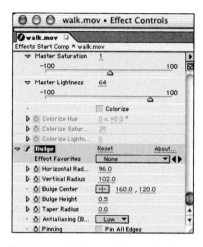

8. Choose **Effect > Distort > Bulge**. The **Bulge** effect will appear below the **Hue/Saturation** effect in the **Effect Controls** window. Notice the overwhelming number of choices here? For now, change the **Horizontal Radius** to **96.0**, the **Vertical Radius** to **102.0**, and the **Bulge Height** to **0.5**.

I can't possibly go into detail about all the properties in the different effects choices in After Effects. The best advice is to try everything and figure it out on your own. When you are bored and have nothing to do, experimenting with each and every effect in the menu can provide hours of diversion! There is no excuse to ever be bored again! For the sake of getting through this chapter, however, it's best if you follow the instructions and move on to the next step.

9. Choose **Effect > Stylize > Find Edges**. The effect is a little intense. Change the **Blend With Original** setting to **63%**. Nicer!

10. Choose **Effect > Adjust > Posterize**. Change the **Level** setting to **4**.

This exercise has given you a small inkling of what's in store regarding Effects. You have learned how to apply effects, and how to view them in the Effect Controls and Timeline windows. You could keyframe and animate any property on any of these Effects using the Stopwatch icon. You have done this so many times now that you already know how to use this interface even though you've never used it before. Woo hoo! That's all for this exercise—if you want to create some animation before moving on to the next exercise, or experiment with other settings or Effects, feel free. When you're ready, read on so you can keep building your skills and understanding.

NOTE | Resetting and Deleting an Effect

If you are ever unhappy with settings you've created, you can reset the effect to clear all your settings. To the right of every effect in the Effect Controls window is a **Reset** switch. Click this switch and voilà—your settings will disappear. If you ever want to delete an effect, simply select it in the Effect Controls window and press the **Delete** key.

2. ——————The Drop Shadow Effect

The **Drop Shadow** effect is one of the most commonly used effects in many graphics programs. In this exercise, you will add the Drop Shadow effect and learn to animate it as well.

1. Open **dropshadow Finished** from the **dropshadow folder** folder located inside the **Project** window. Click **RAM Preview** to observe that the drop shadow animates closer to the monkey as it shrinks, giving a natural effect of the lighting changes that occur when something gets closer to the ground. Check out the twirly action to view the keyframes and effects settings. When you're finished snooping around, close the comp and open **dropshadow Start** from the same folder.

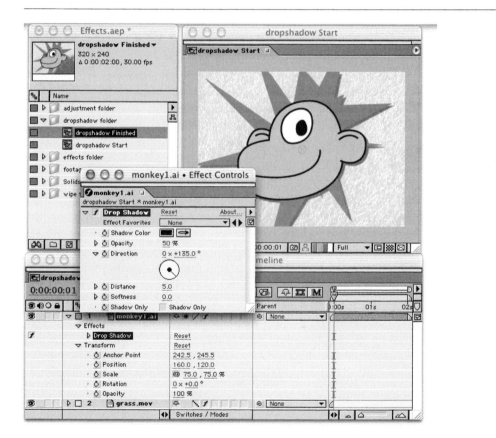

2. Select the **monkey1.ai** layer and choose **Effect > Perspective > Drop Shadow**. When you apply this effect, the Effect Controls window opens automatically. You have a choice to set the **Stopwatch** icon here or in the **Timeline**. I prefer using the **Timeline** because I can also animate other properties there besides Effects properties.

```
┌──────────────────────────────────────────────────────────────────────────┐
│  ⊙ ⊙ ⊙              dropshadow Start • Timeline                            │
├──────────────────────────────────────────────────────────────────────────┤
│ 🖼dropshadow Start ▫                                                        │
│ 0:00:00:01 (30.00 fps)          ⊠ ⊠  ⊡ ▦ M       ▫:00s    01s      02s▫   │
│ 🔊◐⚪🔒  🔲 #   Source Name    ⊞✳🔍∫▦M◉🔲 Parent     ▫:00s   01s    02s    │
│ 👁      ▽ 🔲 1  🖼monkey1.ai    ⊞✳╱∫        ◉ None  ▾ │                  │
│          ▽ Effects                                                          │
│ ∫        ▷ Drop Shadow      Reset                                          │
│          ▽ Transform        Reset                                          │
│          ▸ Ŏ Anchor Point   242.5 , 245.5                                  │
│          ▸ Ŏ Position       160.0 , 120.0                                  │
│ ✓        ▷ Ŏ Scale          ◎ 75.0 , 75.0 %              ◇                │
│          ▸ Ŏ Rotation       0 x +0.0 °                                     │
│          ▸ Ŏ Opacity        100 %                                          │
│ 👁      ▷ 🔲 2  🖼grass.mov   ⊞ ╲ ∫        ◉ None  ▾ │                   │
│                     ◀▶│ Switches / Modes    │        ◀▶ ⬠ △      ⬡       │
└──────────────────────────────────────────────────────────────────────────┘
```

3. Make sure the **Current Time Indicator** is on the first frame. In the **Timeline** window, click the twirlies to see the **Transform** properties and set the **Scale** property's **Stopwatch** icon. It is already set to **75%** on both X and Y, which is where I want it to begin its animation.

4. Move the **Current Time Indicator** to the last frame. Change the **Scale** to **19%**. If you preview the animation right now, the drop shadow looks pretty flat and unrealistic. That shall soon change!

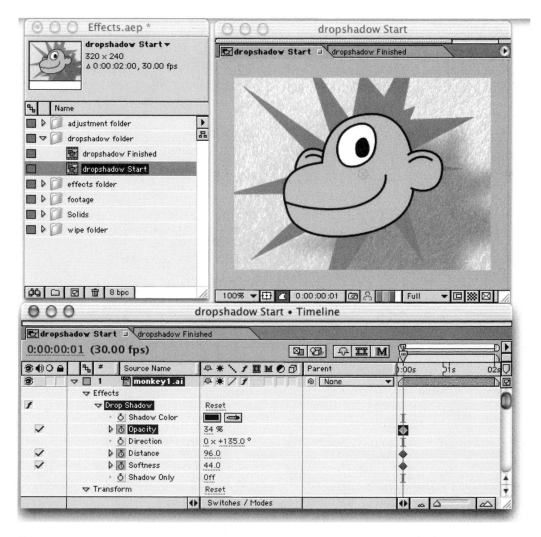

5. Rewind the **Current Time Indicator** to the beginning again. In the **Timeline**, click the **Stopwatch** icons for **Opacity**, **Distance**, and **Softness**. Change those settings to what you see here: **Opacity: 34%**, **Distance: 96.0**, and **Softness: 44.0**.

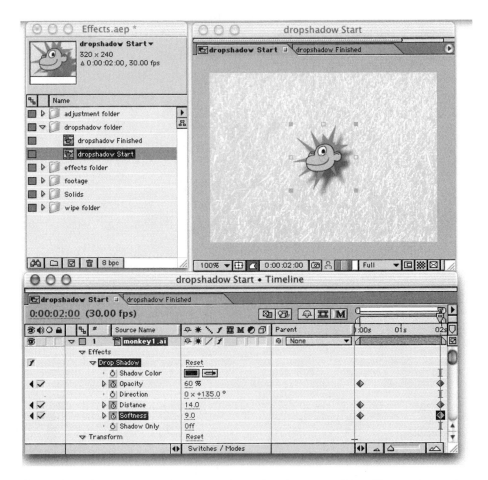

6. Move the **Current Time Indicator** to the end of the composition. Change the settings to **Opacity**: **60%**, **Distance**: **14.0**, and **Softness**: **9.0**. Click **RAM Preview**. Much better!

7. Close the **dropshadow Start** composition and get ready for the next exercise. Save your project.

TIP | Use Best Quality for Illustrator Files

When using Illustrator files or other types of vector graphics in your compositions, set the Quality switch to Best to ensure that the preview image is as detailed as possible. If you want to speed up rendering of previews, return to the Draft setting. In past versions of After Effects, the Continuous Rasterization switch could not be used on vector files that have effects applied. This has changed in this version—yay!

3. ──────────Transition Effects

The effects that After Effects offers are too numerous to mention, and if I were to cover each one of them, this book would be too heavy to hold in your hands! I do want to cover transition effects, however, because they are so commonly used, and aren't intuitive upon first glance. Transition effects always require at least two layers, because the purpose is to transition from one layer to another.

1. In the **Project** window, click the twirly for the **wipe** folder to open two comps: **Gradient_Wipe Finished** and **Radial_Wipe Finished**. Watch these two comps by pressing the **spacebar** or clicking **RAM Preview**. These effects are found in the **Transition** category of the **Effect** menu.

You'll get to practice learning how to create transitions in this exercise, and the techniques learned here will apply to other transition effects.

2. Open **Radial_Wipe Start**. This is a simple comp with two layers—one hiding the other.

3. Select the top layer in the **Timeline**. In this comp, the top layer is **walk.mov**. It's important to note, however, that you always want to apply the effect to the top layer in a composition when creating transitions. This will cause the top layer to wipe off to reveal the bottom layer. If you were to put the wipe effect on the bottom layer, you wouldn't see it because the top layer would be hiding it.

4. Choose **Effect > Transition > Radial Wipe**. The **Effect Controls** window automatically opens. I prefer to set this effect inside the **Timeline** because I can see the **Current Time Indicator** there and can see my keyframes. In the **Timeline**, click the twirlies for the **walk.mov** layer to reveal the properties for the **Radial Wipe** effect.

5. Make sure the **Current Time Indicator** is on the first frame. Click the **Stopwatch** icon for **Transition Completion**. This will set a keyframe on frame **0:00:00:01** for **0%**.

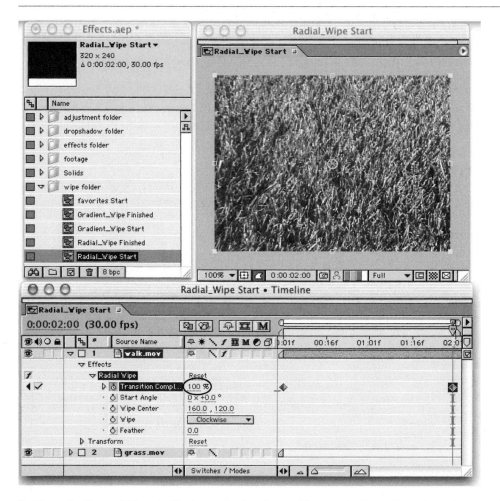

6. Move the **Current Time Indicator** to the last frame. Change the **Transition Completion** value to **100%**. You should see the bottom layer (**grass.mov**) appear in the **Composition** window.

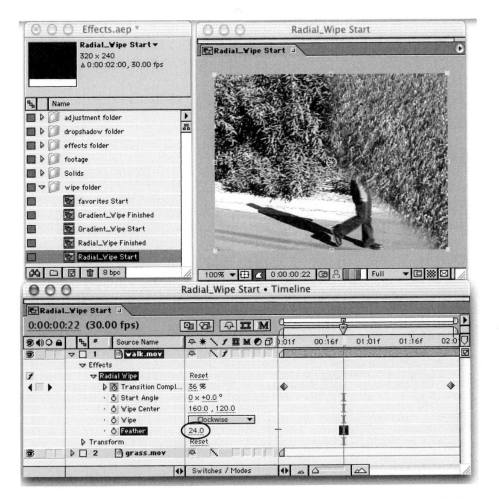

7. Scrub the **Current Time Indicator** to view the radial wipe effect. I think it would look better with a softer edge. Change the **Feather** property to a setting you find pleasing. Since you didn't set the **Stopwatch** icon for the **Feather** property, this change will be global to the entire comp. The only time you want to set keyframes is when you want something to change over time. To leave the feather set over the duration of this comp, just change the value and it will be done!

Next, you'll try another transition effect: Gradient Wipe.

---

8. From the **Project** window, open **Gradient_Wipe Start** from the **wipe folder** folder. In the **Timeline** window, select **walk.mov** and choose **Effect > Transition > Gradient Wipe**. The **Effect Controls** window will automatically open. Click the **About** link there.

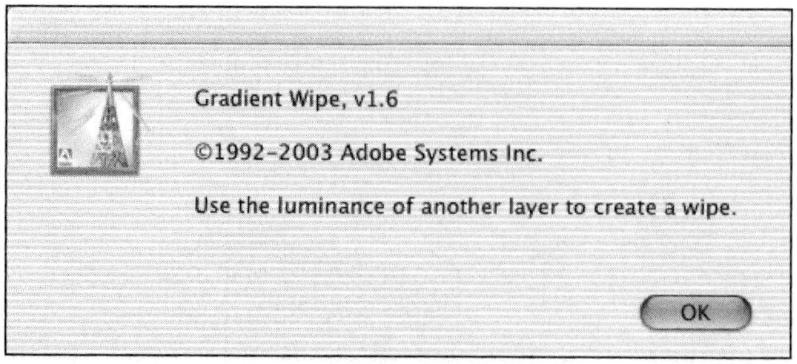

Gradient Wipe, v1.6

©1992–2003 Adobe Systems Inc.

Use the luminance of another layer to create a wipe.

OK

The About link (located in the Effect Controls window) offers a description of what the effect can be used for. This is useful for effects that don't have obvious names, like Gradient Wipe, for example!

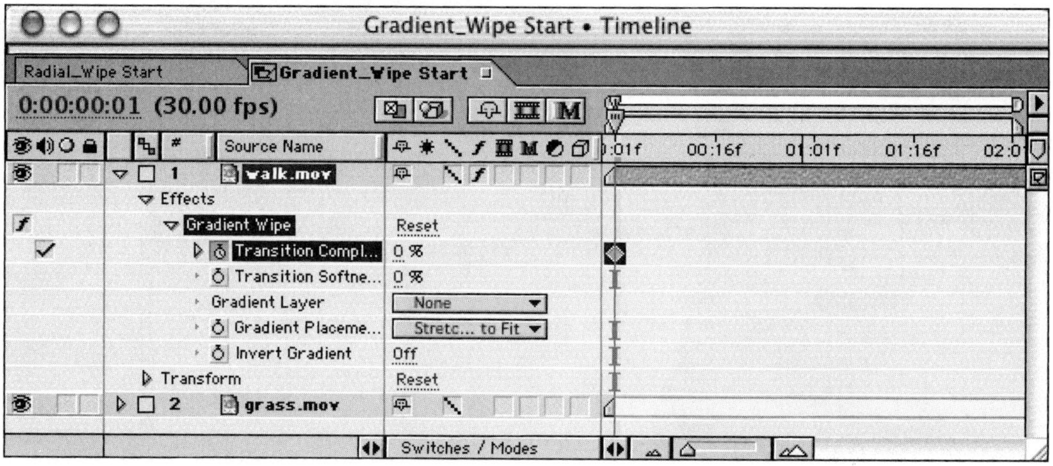

9. Return to the **Timeline** and click the twirlies for **walk.mov** to reveal the **Effects** properties for the **Gradient Wipe** effect. Make sure the **Current Time Indicator** is set to the first frame. Click the **Stopwatch** icon for the **Transition Completion** property. This will set the first keyframe.

10. Move the **Current Time Indicator** to the last frame. Enter **100%** into the **Transition Completion** value field. Scrub the **Current Time Indicator**. Nothing happens. Huh?

11. This particular effect requires that you assign a layer to it and doesn't assume that you want the effect applied to the **walk.mov** layer. Click the **Gradient Layer** menu and choose **walk.mov** to see the effect appear. I also increased the **Transition Softness** to **37%** once I saw the effect in action, because it felt too hard edged to me.

This exercise demonstrated how to work with transition effects. You should be well on your way to trying new effects on your own!

4. —————————Favorites

Favorites offer a way to save an effect and its keyframes for use on another comp. In this exercise, you'll make some favorites based on the two transition effects you just worked with, and then you'll apply those favorites to another comp.

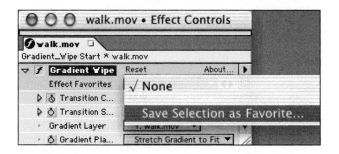

1. Open the comp called **Gradient_Wipe Start** you completed in Exercise 3. In the **Timeline**, click the twirlies for **walk.mov** if they aren't already twirled down, and double-click the **Gradient Wipe** effect. This opens the **Effect Controls** window (if it was closed) with **walk.mov** loaded. Click the **Effect Favorites** menu and choose **Save Selection as Favorite**. This automatically prompts you to save a file into the **Favorites** folder that ships with After Effects. Name your file **gradient.ffx** and click **Save**.

2. Open the comp called **Radial_Wipe Start** you completed in Exercise 3. In the **Timeline**, click the twirlies for **walk.mov** if they aren't already twirled down, and double-click the **Radial Wipe** effect. This opens the **Effect Controls** window with **walk.mov** loaded. Click the **Effect Favorites** menu and choose **Save Selection as Favorite**. This automatically prompts you to save a file in the **Favorites** folder that ships with After Effects. Name your file **radial.ffx** and click **Save**.

3. From the **Project** window, open the **favorites Start** from the **wipe folder** folder. This comp contains two still images. Select the top layer, called **redclouds2.jpg**. Choose **Effect > Apply Favorites**. This will open the **Favorites** folder on your hard drive. Select **gradient.ffx** and click **Open**.

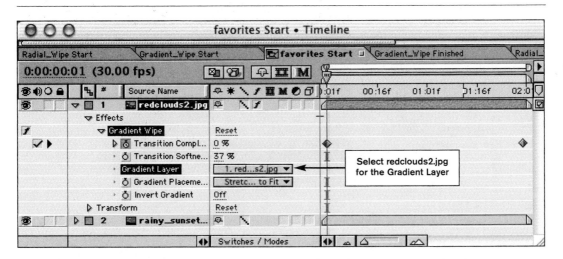

4. Scrub the **Timeline**, and it will look as if nothing happened. Not true! Click the twirlies for **red-clouds2.jpg** to reveal the **Effects** settings. Notice that keyframes have been set and the **Gradient Wipe** effect has been applied? You need to select a **Gradient Layer**, just like you had to the last time you used this filter. Click that menu and choose **redclouds2.jpg**. The transition will work now!

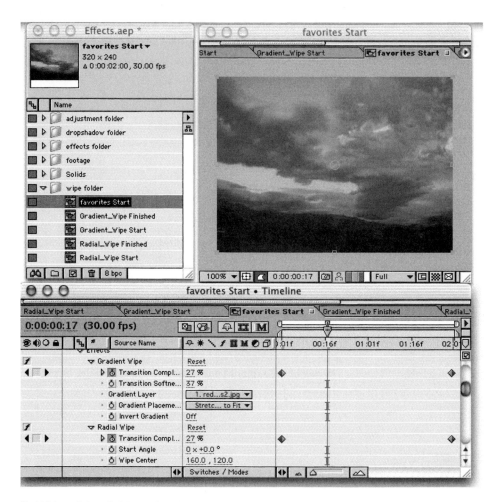

5. With **redclouds2.jpg** still selected, choose **Effect > Apply Favorite**. Choose **radial.ffx** and click **Open**. Notice that this effect and its keyframes were added. Play the movie and watch the two effects interact. Pretty cool? I sure think so!

Favorites are a great way to store your Effects settings for later use. They can save lots of time, especially on a project that reuses the same effects over and over.

5. ——————Adjustment Layers with Effects

In Chapter 8, "*Layers,*" I promised that we'd get to the subject of **adjustment layers** in the "*Effects*" chapter. I waited because adjustment layers are hard to show without using effects, since they work especially well together. You're probably wondering what the heck adjustment layers are, anyway. They are special layers that affect other layers. If you apply an effect to an adjustment layer, the effect will apply to any and all layers below it. It's best to show you what I mean, so dig in and learn!

1. In the **Project** window, open **adjustment finished** from the **adjustment folder** folder. This is a finished comp that includes an adjustment layer that contains a Gaussian Blur effect.

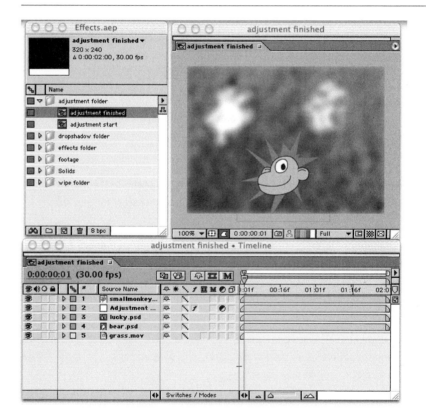

Notice the stacking order of the layers in the Timeline? The Adjustment layer has a blur filter attached to it, and all the layers below it are affected by this Effects setting. If you move the Adjustment layer below lucky.psd and bear.psd, you'll see that those layers are no longer blurry. If you move the Adjustment layer to the top of the stack, you'll observe that all of the layers in the comp are affected by it. This is the power of an adjustment layer. It's a way you can apply one effect to multiple layers.

```
●●●                    adjustment start • Timeline
🖫 adjustment start
0:00:00:01 (30.00 fps)        🖾 🖾   🖾 🖽 M
👁◀)○🔒    ⬚ #   Source Name    🖾 ✳ ＼ ✦ 🖽 M ⊘ ⬚  :01f   00:16f   01:01f   01:16f   02:0
👁        ▷⬚ 1   🖾 Adjustment... 🖾   ＼        ⊘
👁        ▷⬚ 2   🖾 smallmonkey... 🖾   ＼
👁        ▷⬚ 3   🖾 lucky.psd     🖾   ＼
👁        ▷⬚ 4   🖾 bear.psd      🖾   ＼
👁        ▷⬚ 5   🖾 grass.mov     🖾   ＼
                              ◀▶ Switches / Modes   ◀▶ ⌂ △      ⌂
```

2. Close the comp **adjustment finished** and open **adjustment start**. This composition has been set up with unaltered footage and does not yet contain an adjustment layer. Choose **Layer > New > Adjustment Layer**. An **Adjustment** layer has been added to this composition, but nothing will have yet changed because there is no effect associated yet with it.

---

3. With the **Adjustment** layer selected, choose **Effect > Blur & Sharpen > Gaussian Blur**. In the **Effect Controls** window that automatically opens, change the **Blurriness** setting to **6.0**.

Notice that all the layers in the composition became blurry. That's the power of an adjustment layer. Any layer below the adjustment layer that contains an effect is affected by the effect. Although I'm showing this with the Gaussian Blur effect, it works with any effect!

---

4. Move the **Adjustment** layer from the top of the **Timeline** to the number **3** position, so that it is above the **bear.psd** layer.

Notice that the layers above the Adjustment layer are unaffected, and the layers below it are still affected. That's how an adjustment layer works. Basically, any time you want to apply the same effect to multiple layers, use an adjustment layer.

---

5. Save the project and leave this composition open for the next exercise.

---

6. Using Precompose with Effects

In the last exercise, you learned how to use an adjustment layer with an effect. In this exercise, you'll see how to combine this with another technique called **precomposing**. You probably didn't know that you can put compositions inside compositions. That's right–a composition can be used as a footage item inside of another composition. Why would you ever want to do such a thing? This exercise will provide a good example of why.

1. Move the **Adjustment** layer back to the top position in the **Timeline** of the **adjustment start** comp. This will blur all of the layers below it.

Let's say that you wanted to blur the animals in this composition but not the background movie. How would you accomplish this? By putting the animal images and Adjustment layer in their own composition and then placing that composition inside this composition, that's how. You'll learn to do this next.

2. Holding down the **Shift** key, click to select the top four layers.

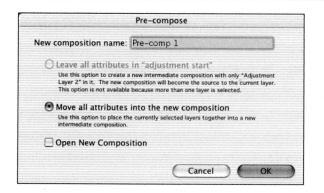

3. Choose **Layer > Pre-compose**. The **Pre-compose** dialog box appears, with **Move all attributes into the new composition** selected. The section at the end of this exercise explains all of the settings in this dialog box. The name **Pre-Comp 1** automatically appears in the dialog box, which you could change if you want to. For now, keep this default name, click **OK**, and watch what happens.

*The four layers you selected in the previous step disappeared and were replaced by a composition layer called **Pre-comp 1**. You are probably scratching your head, because this is a difficult concept to comprehend at first glance.*

When you choose Pre-compose, After Effects takes those layers, places them in their own composition, and places this new composition inside the original. The result is that the adjustment layer that affected all the layers now affects only the layers in Pre-comp 1. The grass.mov layer is unaffected by the Adjustment layer, because it is in its own composition.

4. In the **Project** window, double-click the **Pre-comp 1** composition.

5. Notice that the Adjustment layer is affecting all the layers below it. Move the **Adjustment** layer below the **smallmonkey.psd** layer. Notice that the **smallmonkey.psd** layer is now unaffected by the **Adjustment** layer.

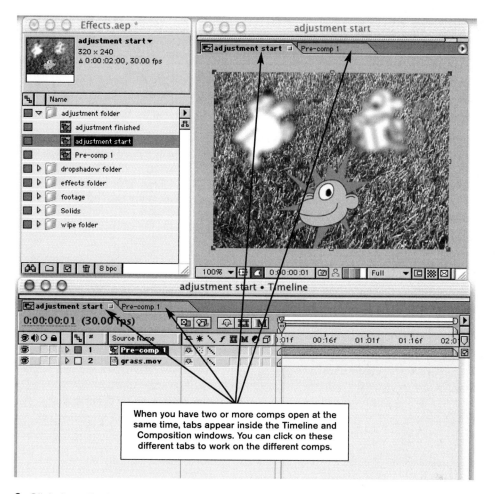

When you have two or more comps open at the same time, tabs appear inside the Timeline and Composition windows. You can click on these different tabs to work on the different comps.

6. Click the **adjustment start** tab in the **Timeline** window. Notice that the change you made inside **Pre-comp 1** is reflected in **adjustment start**. This is the nature of a nested composition, which is what the Pre-compose feature allows you to do.

7. Save and close this project.

The Pre-Compose Dialog Box

Since this dialog box is new to you, here's a handy description of its features:

Leave all attributes in "adjustment start": This option works only with a single layer. Since you had selected multiple layers before choosing Pre-compose, this option was grayed out. It places the single layer into its own composition and places that new composition into the original composition.

Move all attributes into the new composition: This feature is chosen most often. It moves layers, effects, masks, and keyframes into the new composition and places them into the existing composition.

Open New Composition: This setting can be used with either of the other choices. It simply means that the new composition will open. If you don't check this option, you stay in the existing composition and the new composition is nested in the original composition.

Parenting Versus Precomposing

You've already learned about parenting, and now you've learned about precomposing. You might wonder when to use which technique. This comparison chart should help.

Parenting Versus Precomposing	
Parenting	**Precomposing**
Parenting can affect all Transform properties except Opacity.	All Transform properties can be precomposed. However, parenting may prove more effective than precomposing much of the time.
Parenting is not useful for all effects or mask properties.	Effects and mask properties can be precomposed for selected layers.
Parenting is useful for creating complex, dependent animation such as the orbits of planets in a solar system or the linking of marionette parts for movement.	Precomposing is not always useful for anchor point–based animation. For example, linking the parts of a marionette would not be an effective use of precomposing.
	continues on next page

Parenting Versus Precomposing *continued*	
Parenting	**Precomposing**
Parenting does not affect the rendering order.	Precomposing can be used to change the rendering order. You learned about the rendering order in Exercise 2. In that exercise, you used the Transform effect to render the rotation before the drop shadow. You could also have also used precomposing to create a composition that rotated the monkey, and then nested that composition inside the composition with the Drop Shadow effect. This is an important use of precomposing.
Parenting does not affect adjustment layers.	Precomposing can control the effect of adjustment layers.
N/A	Precomposed items can be reused inside other compositions.
N/A	Precomposed animations can be updated in one step by editing the original composition.

This chart can help you identify where you might use parenting rather than precomposing. Parenting affects only the Transform properties (except Opacity). For this reason, parenting is used for animating the motion of objects. As its major strength, parenting provides a very effective way to create animation that is dependent on the motion of other objects within a composition.

Precomposing, on the other hand, provides the most effective means of applying complex changes to a multitude of properties and layers. Effects, masks, adjustment layers, and prerendering are all excellent reasons to use precomposing on a group of layers. Many people also use precomposing as a way to organize groups of layers in complicated projects.

The Effects Palette

The **Effects palette** (not to be confused with the Effect Controls window you used earlier) is a great tool for locating effects. There are many effects, and it can be difficult to remember where an effect is located in the menu, or even to remember the exact name of an effect. The Effects palette offers another way to search for and select any effect you want.

To display the Effects palette, choose **Window > Effects**.

The Effects palette contains all of the types of effects. Click the twirlies to display the individual effects available under each type.

Best of all, you can type in the entry field to display the name of any effect that has matching letters.

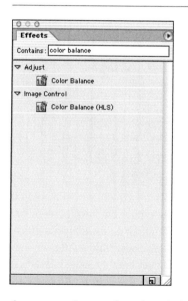

As you continue typing, the window will continue to display the items that match, making it easy to find exactly what you are looking for.

That's another chapter wrap. Be sure to experiment with effects on your own—we have barely scratched the surface. A great way to learn about effects is to visit discussion boards and learn from other After Effects users. The combinations of effects are literally endless, so don't stop with this chapter!

11.
Parenting

| Parenting Layers | Attaching Children to a Parent |
| Animating Children and Parents | Animating Null Objects |

chap_11

After Effects 6
H•O•T CD-ROM

In programs such as Photoshop or Illustrator, you might be familiar with "grouping," "linking," or "nesting" objects. These features allow you to address multiple objects as a single object in order to edit, move, or organize them. After Effects doesn't use these same terms, but it does offer some of these same functions in its parenting features.

Parenting allows one layer to inherit the Transform properties of another. This means you can animate the anchor point or the Position, Scale, or Rotation properties of one parent object, and the attached child object's properties will be animated in the same way. The only Transform property that does not work with parenting is Opacity.

This chapter covers how to use the After Effects parenting features and gives some examples that show why you would want to use them. Parenting was one of the new features introduced in After Effects 5, and it caused legions of users to upgrade because of its usefulness. Before After Effects 5, achieving similar effects required nesting compositions within compositions (which is still possible to do, and is covered in Chapter 10, "*Effects*"). Suffice it to say that the tasks you'll learn to do easily with parenting used to take much longer and were much harder to perform.

Parenting Layers

In parenting, one layer is assigned as a **parent**, and another layer or multiple layers are assigned to be the **child** or **children**. The Transform properties of the parent layer are inherited by any layer that you assign as a child. This might mean, for example, that if a parent layer had a Rotation property set to 30 degrees, the child layer would also rotate 30 degrees from its initial position, even though you hadn't set the child's Transform properties to do so. A child layer can have only one parent, but a parent layer can have any number of child layers within the same composition. Any composition may have multiple parent layers, each controlling a different set of children.

In this section, you will learn how to assign parenting to a layer. You'll also learn how to adjust the child layer to work appropriately with the parent. (This is beginning to sound like a psychology book! However, it's much easier than psychology.)

I. _____Attaching Children to a Parent

Assigning a parent layer to a child layer is very easy in After Effects. However, once you've attached a child layer to a parent, you may need to make adjustments to the child layer's anchor point to position the child properly with respect to the parent. For example, if you wanted an arm [child] to attach to a body [parent], you'd need to set the anchor point of the arm at the shoulder point. Often when you attach a layer to another as a child, its default anchor point (the center of the object) is not where you really want it to be.

In this exercise, you will assign the rocket layer as the parent and the flame footage as the child. Setting the rocket layer as the parent will allow the flames to follow the rocket's animation path. As you'll see, the Position, Scale, and Rotation properties of the flame layer will all be affected by the rocket layer's Transform properties.

The flame footage is a QuickTime movie that is 30 frames long. It is too short to play for the entire duration of the composition. However, the flames were designed to play as a continuous loop, and After Effects provides a way to loop movies.

Before assigning the parenting, you will first learn how to use the **Interpret Footage** dialog box to loop the flame movie. This dialog box provides options for each footage item in the Project window.

1. Open **Space Project.aep** from the **chap_11** folder. Save the project into the **AE6 HOT Projects** folder that you created in Chapter 2 so you have a copy to work on. Double-click **Space Comp 1**, if it is not already open This will open the **Timeline** and **Composition** windows.

2. In the **Timeline**, click the **Video** switch for **flames.mov** to display the flame footage. Scrub the **Current Time Indicator** and notice that the flame footage has fewer frames represented in the Timeline than the rocket footage.

In the next steps, you'll learn how to loop the flames for the duration of the shot, using the Interpret Footage dialog box.

3. In the **Project** window, select the **flames.mov** footage from the **Movies** folder inside the **chap_11** folder. In the following steps, you'll learn how to make this footage loop last longer. This process has to start in the **Project** window, where you select the footage you want to loop.

4. Choose **File > Interpret Footage > Main**. As an alternative method, press **Cmd+F** (Mac) or **Ctrl+F** (Windows).

5. At the bottom of the **Interpret Footage** dialog box locate the **Loop** option. Enter **8** as the number of times to loop and click **OK**.

Note: The value 8 was chosen to make the 1-second movie last 8 seconds. The options in the Interpret Footage dialog box is explained in the section and chart that follow this exercise.

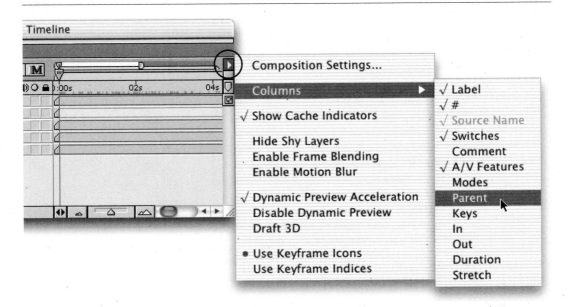

6. Notice that the duration of the **flames.mov** layer now matches the length of the other layers. Scrub the **Current Time Indicator** and notice that the footage now stretches for the duration of the shot. It does this by looping (repeating) itself eight times.

In the next steps, you'll assign the ***rocket.psd*** *layer as the parent of the* ***flames.mov*** *layer.*

7. Click the **arrow** at the top right of the **Timeline** and choose **Columns > Parent** to display the **Parent** column in the Timeline.

8. Locate the **Pick Whip** icons (the spiral icons) in the **Parent** panel. Click the **Pick Whip** icon and drag the resulting line from the **flames.mov** layer to the **rocket.psd** layer.

*This method of dragging the Pick Whip from one layer to another is an easy way to create a parent-child relationship. Everything in the child layer (**flames.mov**) takes on the Transform properties of the parent layer (**rocket.psd**). You establish which layer is the parent and which is the child through this tool. You always drag the child to the parent to establish this relationship.*

*Notice that the Parent panel pop-up menu now lists the **1.rocket.psd** layer as the parent for the* **flames.mov** *layer.* **Note:** *The **1.** in **1.rocket.psd** indicates the layer's stacking order in the Timeline. Layers are numbered from top to bottom.*

> ## NOTE | Pick Whip? What?!?
>
> You might wonder what the heck a Pick Whip is and why Adobe chose to use this funny term. The **"Pick"** in Pick Whip stands for picking a relationship between layers. The **"Whip"** part of the term was chosen because of how the line behaves between the layers if you change your mind and don't select anything. It animates, kind of like a whip at a rodeo. Hey, engineers have senses of humor, too!

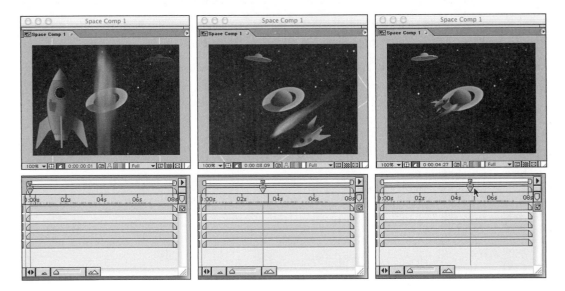

9. Scrub the **Current Time Indicator** and observe that the flame movie now follows along next to the rocket ship animation.

The Position, Scale, and Rotation properties of the rocket's layer are now applied to the flame's layer properties! That's what happens when you parent something—the Transform properties (except Opacity, sadly) are applied to the child layer. The fact that the flame and rocket are not positioned properly yet will be addressed in the following steps.

NOTE | Why Not Opacity?

It may seem bizarre that Adobe has missed adding support for Opacity to the parenting feature in the last three revisions of After Effects. This probably has more to do with the traditional uses of parenting features in animation than with an absent-minded programmer. The other four Transform properties—Position, Scale, Rotation, and Anchor Point—all affect the movement of your layers in one way or another, but Opacity affects the layer's appearance. Since parenting is traditionally used to create movement hierarchies, Opacity doesn't really fit in. So there *is* a reason—but having parental control of Opacity would still be nice!

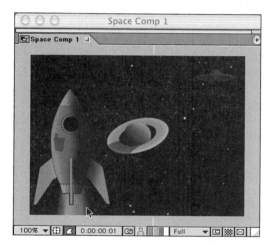

10. Move the flames below the rocket in the **Composition** window, as you see here.

---

11. Press the **spacebar** to play your animation. The flame should now track the rocket ship perfectly! By parenting the **flames.mov** layer to the **rocket.psd** layer, you avoided having to animate the flames to make them match the motion of the rocket.

---

12. Save and close this project; you won't be using it again.

TIP | Changing or Removing a Parent

To specify a different layer as a child's parent, drag the **Pick Whip** icon for the child layer to another layer. The new layer will be selected as the parent.

As an alternative method, use the **Parent** panel pop-up menu to select another layer. To remove a child's parent, choose **None** from the **Parent** panel pop-up menu.

The Interpret Footage Dialog Box

In the last exercise, you learned to loop the flame footage to make it last longer. This was done through the Interpret Footage dialog box. This dialog box is used when you want to change footage from the way it was originally imported. You can use it to change the number of times footage repeats (or loops) the frame rate, or the way After Effects interprets the alpha channel. You don't need to use this dialog box all the time—only when you want to change your footage in some way. Often you'll use it to make a change while you're in the middle of a project, as was done in the previous exercise when the footage wasn't long enough to last the duration of the composition (although in some projects you may not be lucky enough to have a seamlessly looping piece of footage to start from!).

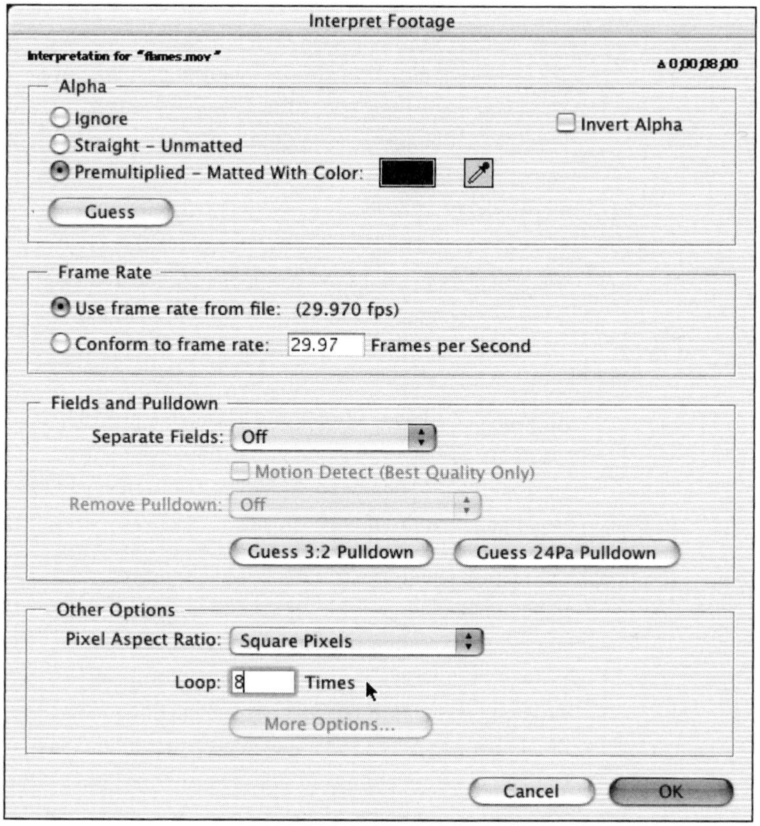

Interpret Footage

Interpretation for "flames.mov"   ▲ 0;00;08;00

Alpha

- ◯ Ignore   ☐ Invert Alpha
- ◯ Straight – Unmatted
- ⦿ Premultiplied – Matted With Color: ▮   ⧉

(Guess)

Frame Rate

- ⦿ Use frame rate from file: (29.970 fps)
- ◯ Conform to frame rate: [29.97] Frames per Second

Fields and Pulldown

Separate Fields: [Off ▾]

☐ Motion Detect (Best Quality Only)

Remove Pulldown: [Off ▾]

(Guess 3:2 Pulldown)   (Guess 24Pa Pulldown)

Other Options

Pixel Aspect Ratio: [Square Pixels ▾]

Loop: [8] Times ▸

(More Options...)

(Cancel)   (OK)

You can access the **Interpret Footage** dialog box by selecting any **footage** item in the Project window and pressing **Cmd+F** (Mac) or **Ctrl+F** (Windows). The following chart describes the options in this dialog box.

The Interpret Footage Dialog Box		
Category	**Option**	**Description**
Alpha	Ignore	When you import an image or movie that is partially transparent, that transparency information is stored in the footage's alpha channel. If Ignore is checked, After Effects will ignore the transparent parts of the image or movie, and they will appear as a solid color, generally the background color defined in the program used to create the image
	Straight–Unmatted	After Effects treats footage files that contain alpha channels in one of two ways: straight or premultiplied. When you import footage, After Effects makes a guess, and it almost always guesses right. The only time you need to use this option is when you want to alter the way After Effects has treated your alpha channel—for example, if you don't like the way your footage looks once it's in a composition and you want to make a change. For footage with a straight alpha channel, the program you used to generate the footage must have built a straight alpha. Few 2D programs use this kind of alpha channel. Many 3D programs generate straight alpha channels because these kinds of alphas can be placed over any background color without predisposition.
	Premultiplied–Matted with Color	Most alpha channels created in common graphics applications such as Photoshop and Illustrator are premultiplied. With a premultiplied alpha channel, a footage item keeps the transparency information in the alpha channel. A premultiplied alpha channel is also known as matted alpha with a background color. The colors of semitransparent areas, such as feathered edges, are shifted toward the background color in proportion to their degree of transparency. The background color, in this instance, is defined in the authoring program, such as Illustrator or Photoshop.

continues on next page

	The Interpret Footage Dialog Box *continued*	
Category	**Option**	**Description**
Alpha *continued*	Invert Alpha	This option will invert the alpha channel mask, so everything that was originally masked out will show, and everything that wasn't masked will be hidden.
Frame Rate	Use frame rate from file	This setting applies only to movie footage. It uses the original frame rate of the footage.
	Conform to frame rate	This setting applies only to movie footage. It changes the original frame rate of the movie to any new frame rate that you enter. A higher frame rate than the original will cause the footage to play faster (the same number of frames in less time).
Fields and Pulldown	Separate Fields: Off	When footage is transferred to video or originates from video, it contains two fields for every frame: an upper field and a lower field, to be exact. So for every frame of video, there are two fields. These two fields are "interlaced," meaning that they are blended and combined into a single frame during the video recording process. In playback on NTSC and PAL televisions, the fields are rendered sequentially, but sufficiently quickly so that the viewer sees a blended image. There are times when you want to separate one interlaced frame of video into two separate fields. The Separate Fields: Off setting does not separate the fields; it leaves them untouched.
	Separate Fields: Lower Fields First	When importing video footage, After Effects tries to guess which of the fields came first in the interlacing process. If the footage looks funny, use this option to reverse the "field order" (lower first or upper first) of the interlacing process. This problem is most often obvious when motion in video does not appear smooth.

continues on next page

The Interpret Footage Dialog Box *continued*

Category	Option	Description
Fields and Pulldown *continued*	Separate Fields: Upper Fields First	Same as the Lower Fields First setting, except that this places the upper field first.
	Motion Detect (Best Quality Only)	Increases the quality of rendered footage that has its fields separated.
	Remove Pulldown: Off	Pulldown becomes an issue with footage that originated as film (35 mm, 16 mm, or 8 mm that was shot at 24 frames per second) and was transferred to video using a Telecine process at 29.97 frames per second. If you choose to remove pulldown, After Effects will convert the video footage into 60 separate frames per second (each frame representing one video field). This setting is useful for rotoscoping live action (drawing on top of or tracing video footage). The choices in this pop-up menu determine which frames in the pulldown will be "whole frames" and which frames will be "split-field frames." Because of the uneven division involved in 3:2 pulldown, two out of every five frames are built from fields that span two different frames; these are the "split-field" frames.
	Guess 3:2 Pulldown	This option is important when your footage originated on film and was transferred to video using a Telecine process. After Effects' Guess 3:2 Pulldown process will convert every 4 film frames into 10 video fields, making the math for the transition from film to video work.
	Guess 24Pa Pulldown	Similar to 3:2 pulldown, this converts "progressive scan" (a mode used to more closely simulate film on video) imagery recorded at 23.976 frames per second to the correct number of interlaced video fields to make the video sync with footage brought in by other means.

continues on next page

The Interpret Footage Dialog Box

Category	Option	Description
Other Options	Pixel Aspect Ratio: D1/DV NTSC (0.9); D1/DV NTSC widescreen (1.2); D1/DV PAL (1.07); D1/DV PAL widescreen (1.42); Anamorphic 2:1 (2); D4/D16 Standard (0.95); D4/D16 Anamorphic (1.9)	Your computer graphics files produce images composed of square pixels, but many video formats use nonsquare pixels. There may be times when you incorporate live action into your After Effects project that was originally produced with a nonsquare format. That's okay—After Effects can mix square and nonsquare pixels, but you have to tell it what footage is not square during the import process. You do that with this option. By importing the footage with the proper setting (you must know how the footage was originally shot), you allow After Effects to preserve its pixel aspect ratio. When you output to a final movie, you can also choose whether to output square or nonsquare pixels, depending on the setting you use in the Time Sampling area of the Render Settings dialog box, accessed from the Render Queue. You'll learn about the Render settings in Chapter 18, "*Rendering Final Movies.*"
	Loop	You can set the number of times footage will repeat. The footage will become longer in the Timeline as a result.

2. ——————————Preparing for Parenting

In the last exercise, you practiced how to connect a child (**flames.mov**) to a parent (**rocket.psd**) layer. The child took on all the Transform properties that had been specified for the parent. It's also possible to animate children independently from their parents. You will learn how to do this in the following exercises. First, however, some preparation work has to go into this process. When planning this type of animation, you have to give thought to how pieces of artwork fit and move together. This often involves changing the anchor point of some of the pieces so that they rotate, scale, or move in the correct manner. In this exercise, you'll learn how to import a layered Illustrator file, and you will practice changing anchor points and parenting. Once the document is prepared properly, you'll learn to animate the parent and children independently in a subsequent exercise.

1. Create a new project. Double-click inside the empty **Project** window to bring forth the **Import Footage** dialog box. Navigate to the **chap_11** folder and choose **wavingmonkey.ai**. For the **Import As** option, choose **Composition – Cropped Layers**. The **wavingmonkey.ai** document is a layered Illustrator file. You can bring layered Illustrator files in as compositions in exactly the same way that you bring in layered Photoshop files.

NOTE | Composition Versus Composition-Cropped

When you bring in an Illustrator or Photoshop document using the **Import As: Composition** option, the layers are all brought in at a uniform size, and all anchor points are rooted to the center of the composition. This is the better mode for keeping nonmoving elements aligned. **Import As: Composition – Cropped Layers**, on the other hand, brings in each layer at the smallest possible size, with the anchor point rooted to the center of the artwork on each layer. This is the better mode for quickly manipulating layers for animation, since After Effects has less material to composite, and you have a smaller layer to haul around the screen.

2. Save the project file as **wavingmonkey.aep** to the **AE6 HOT Projects** folder that you created in Chapter 2.

3. Select the **wavingmonkey Comp 1** composition and choose **Composition > Composition Settings**—or press **Cmd+K** (Mac) or **Ctrl+K** (Windows)—and set the duration to four seconds (0:00:04:00). Click **OK**. Double-click the **wavingmonkey Comp 1** composition inside the **Project** window to open it. This will open the **Timeline** and **Composition** windows.

Select the pointing arm layer first

Next, click the Solo switch for that layer

4. Select the **pointing arm** layer, and click the **Solo** switch. This will cause all the other layers to turn off so you can see the arm layer all by itself. The anchor point needs to be moved to line up with the shoulder of the monkey. You'll do this next.

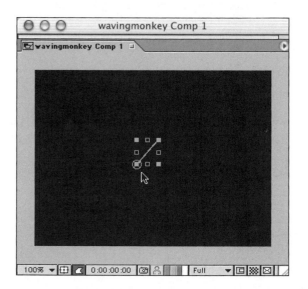

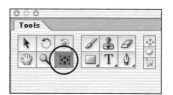

5. Using the **Pan Behind** tool, click and drag the **anchor point** inside the **Composition** window to match what you see here.

Note: The layer must be selected for the anchor point to be visible in the Composition window. Moving the anchor point will affect future animations, because the Transform properties Rotate, Scale, and Position all use the anchor point position as a reference point. This is why it is important to set the anchor points properly before animating; later changes to your anchor points will shift entire sections of your animation in ways that you may not have intended!

6. Click the **Solo** switch for the **pointing arm** layer to turn all the other layers off. The **Solo** switch made it easier to isolate this layer in order to see and move its anchor point.

7. Select the **pointing forearm** layer, click its **Solo** switch, and move its anchor point (by using the **Pan Behind** tool) to the position you see here. Click the **Solo** switch again to toggle the other layers back on once you complete this task.

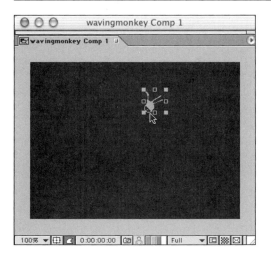

8. Select the **pointing hand** layer, click its **Solo** switch, and move its anchor point (by using the **Pan Behind** tool) to the position you see here. Click the **Solo** switch again to toggle it off once you complete this task.

You've finished changing the anchor points on the objects. If you think about your own shoulder, arm, forearm, and hand, and where those joints pivot, you'll see that you've just created the anchor points to mimic human (and monkey!) anatomy. Soon you'll animate the hand of the monkey, and you'll see how the anchor point adjustments play an important role in the success of your movie.

9. In the **Timeline**, using the **Pick Whip**, attach the **pointing arm** layer to the **monkey body** layer.

10. Next, you'll attach the **pointing forearm** layer to the **pointing arm** layer. As an alternative, you can use the **Parent** panel pop-up menu instead of the **Pick Whip** to achieve this. Click on the **Parent** panel menu for the **pointing forearm** layer, and select **3. pointing arm** from the list. The **3.** indicates that this is the third layer down in the stack. This tells the **pointing arm** layer to be the parent for the **pointing forearm** layer.

11. Next attach the **pointing hand** to the **pointing forearm** layer. Do this using the Pick Whip or the Parent panel menu item method—either way achieves the same result!

12. Save the project and leave it open for the next exercise.

In the first exercise, there was only one parent (the rocket) and one child (the flames). Here you can see that a layer can be the child to one layer and the parent of another! You'll see this come together in the next exercise.

3. ————————————Animating Children and Parents

In the first exercise, you saw how the animation of a parent affected the child. This exercise sets up a more complicated set of relationships. You've done the hard part of setting the anchor points and parenting. Now enjoy the fun of making it all move!

1. Lock the **background** layer by clicking the **Lock** switch. This prevents the background layer from being moved accidentally during the animation you are about to program.

2. In the **Timeline**, make sure the **Current Time Indicator** is at **0:00:00:00**. The easiest place to see this is **Current Time** display in the upper-left corner of the Timeline. Select the **monkey body** layer and set a position keyframe. There are many ways to do this—you could either twirl all the twirlies down and click the **Stopwatch** icon or press **Option+P** (Mac) or **Alt+Shift+P** (Windows). The Option or Alt keystroke shortcut sets the stopwatch and twirls down the Position property for you!

3. Select the **Selection** tool cursor from the toolbox (if it is still on the **Pan Behind** tool from the last exercise), and move the monkey to the left side of the branch, as you see here. This sets the start position for the monkey in a different place than before.

Notice that the monkey and all the child layers moved at the same time. Even though you set only the monkey body layer as the parent for the pointing arm layer, the pointing forearm and pointing hand layers moved as well. That's because they're all indirectly linked to the monkey body through the hierarchy of parenting. The pointing arm layer is the child of the monkey body layer. The pointing forearm layer is the child of the pointing arm layer, which is the child of the monkey body layer. The pointing hand layer is the child of the pointing forearm layer, which is the child of the pointing arm layer, which is the child of the monkey body layer. All the layers are ultimately related to the monkey body layer as the master parent.

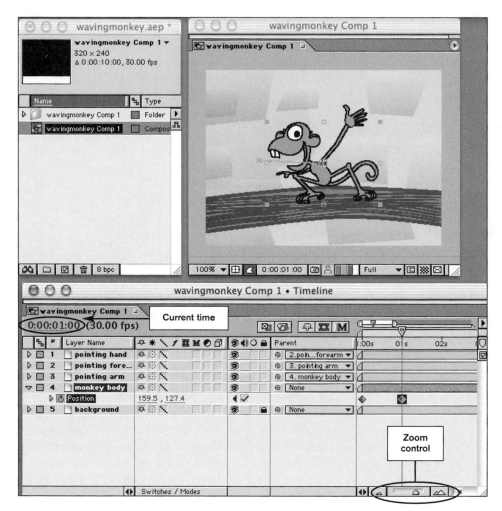

4. In the **Timeline**, move the **Current Time Indicator** to **0:00:01:00** (which may appear as **1s** depending on how far you are zoomed in). Move the monkey to the middle of the branch, as you see here. You should now see two keyframes set in your **Timeline**.

TIP | Moving to an Exact Time

With the **Zoom** control, you can see your Timeline broken down into single frames, or you can see an overview in seconds (or minutes, if your composition is long enough!). This is one way of finding the exact place you want to put your keyframe.

Another even faster way, if you know exactly when in the composition you want something to occur, is to simply click on the **Current Time** display and enter a new time in the format **seconds:frames**.

5. Move the **Current Time Indicator** back to **0:00:00:00**. Select the **pointing arm** layer and set a **Rotation** keyframe. (You really should know how to do this now on your own!) Notice that this **Rotation** keyframe is on **0:00:00:00** as well. Remember, a keyframe is always set on whatever frame the **Current Time Indicator** was on when you set it.

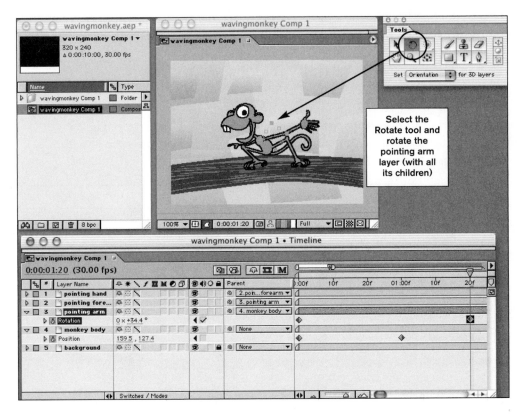

6. Move the **Current Time Indicator** to **0:00:01:20** (**1s, 20f** on the Timeline). Select the **Rotation** tool from the toolbox. Click and drag the arm on your screen so that it looks like what you see here. The pointing arm child will now animate independently from its parent, taking all its children with it.

As you rotate the pointing arm, notice that it rotates all the other children that are attached to it. The parent doesn't move because you haven't told it to. Children can be animated separately from their parents, but if the parent moves, so do the kids!

7. Move the **Current Time Indicator** to **0:00:00:00** and set a **Rotation** keyframe for the **pointing forearm** layer. This sets a start keyframe at **Frame 0**.

8. Move the **Current Time Indicator** to 0:00:01:20 and click to put a check in the **Keyframe** check box. This holds the start position for the **pointing forearm** layer so that it stays still from **0:00:00:00** to **0:00:01:20**.

9. Move the **Current Time Indicator** to **0:00:01:25** and, with the **pointing forearm** layer selected, use the **Rotation** tool to move it into the position you see here.

As you rotate the pointing forearm, notice that it rotates all the other children that are attached to it. The other parents don't move because you haven't told them to.

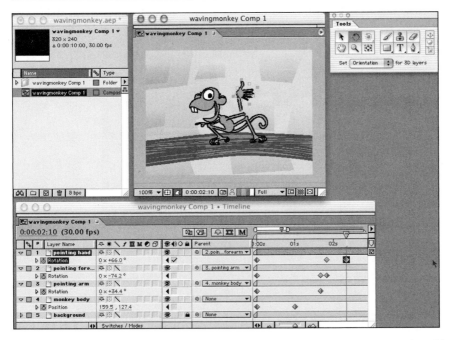

10. Move the **Current Time Indicator** to **0:00:0:00** and select the **pointing hand** layer. Set a **Rotation** keyframe. Using the **right arrow** next to the **Keyframe** check box on the **pointing forearm** layer, advance the **Current Time Indicator** to **Frame 0:00:02:05** and click to put a check in the **Keyframe** check box of the **pointing hand** layer. This is an easy way of advancing the **Current Time Indicator** through the keyframes on an already animated layer to ensure that the keyframes of the next layer you're animating will be accurately aligned. Checking the **Keyframe** box on the **pointing hand** layer sets the rotation so that it will not move at all from **0:00:00:00** to **0:00:02:05**.

11. Move the **Current Time Indicator** to **0:00:02:10**, and move the **pointing hand** layer with the **Rotation** tool as shown here.

This is the last child in the hierarchy. It can move all by itself without moving the other parents.

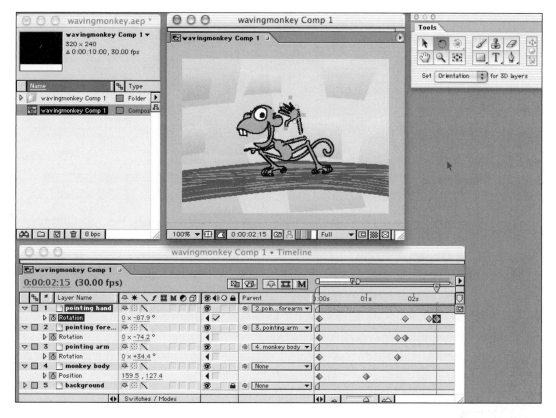

12. Move the **Current Time Indicator** to **0:00:02:15** and move the **pointing hand** layer with the **Rotation** tool as shown here.

13. Using the **Zoom** slider, zoom into the **Timeline** so you can get a closer look. Hold the **Shift** key and select the keyframes on **Frames 0:00:02:05** and **0:00:02:10** for the **pointing hand** layer. Copy them by pressing **Cmd+C** (Mac) or **Ctrl+C** (Windows).

14. Move the **Current Time Indicator** to **0:00:02:20** and **paste** the copied keyframes. Move the **Current Time Indicator** to **0:00:03:00** and **paste** again. Keep advancing the **Current Time Indicator** by 10 frames and pasting until you've pasted a few more times.

15. Rewind and use **RAM preview** to test your work. Try using the **Continuous Rasterization**, **Best Quality**, and **Motion Blur** switches and you'll see a big improvement in appearance. Don't remember how to do those things? Check the last chapter, or study this illustration for hints.

When you use RAM preview to test again, you'll see that it takes much longer to render but looks much better.

16. Save this project, and close it when you're finished looking at your handiwork.

4. ——————————Using a Null Object as a Parent

Null object is an intimidating term for an invisible object. Even the concept of an invisible object is a bit hard on the brain—why would anyone need or want something that wasn't visible? Our hope is that this exercise will provide a concrete example of when you might want to use a null object. In this example, you will create a null layer—in other words, a layer with an invisible object inside of it. The objects that are visible will be attached to the null layer, making them the children and the null layer the parent. The parent will be told to move, and the children will follow. The reason, in this example, to use the invisible object to control the movement of the visible objects is that they already move using Position keyframes. Adding the null object's movement to the already moving children achieves a compound movement that is otherwise incredibly difficult. (Before parenting, animators would create similar effects using nested compositions. You can visit some of these people in the finest insane asylums today.) You'll see what I mean as you work through this puzzle.

1. Open the **afilmby.aep** project from the **chap_11** folder. Double-click the **afilmby.ai** composition to open the **Composition** and **Timeline** windows. Select all the layers and press the **U** key. This is the keyboard shortcut that shows all the properties that have been animated in the composition. You will see that Position, Scale, Rotation, and Opacity properties have been applied. Deselect the layers so you don't see the motion paths. Play the composition to see what it looks like, and then click the **Rewind** button on the **Time Controls** panel to return to **Frame 0:00:00:00**. Select all the layers again and press **U**. This will collapse all the properties so your layers take up less space.

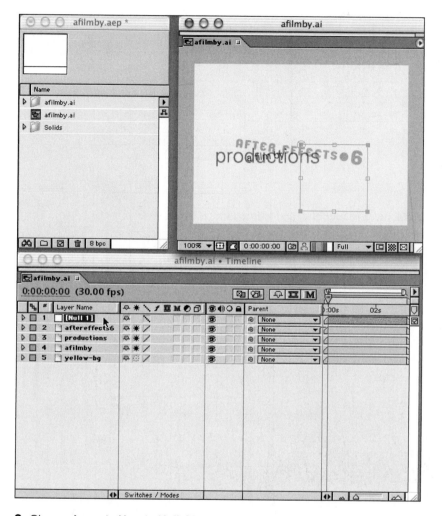

2. Choose **Layer > New > Null Object**. This puts a new layer called **Null 1** into the **Timeline**. Notice that an outlined box appears inside the **Composition** window. This is your null object. The box appears only in the **Composition** window. If you use RAM preview or make a movie (which you'll learn to do in Chapter 18, "*Rendering Final Movies*"), this outlined box will disappear. Meanwhile, however, the outlined box is important because you need to see the null object even though you don't want anyone else to see it.

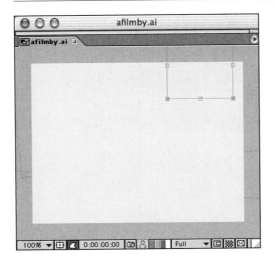

3. Attach the layers **aftereffects6**, **productions**, and **afilmby** to the **Null 1** layer.

4. Lock the **yellow-bg** layer so you don't accidentally move it. Select **Null 1** in the **Timeline**, and move it upward in the **Composition** window, as you see here. Because other layers are assigned to be children of the **Null 1** layer, they will move, too! Keep moving the box upwards until the text is offstage.

5. Set a **Position** keyframe for **Null 1** at **0:00:00:00**.

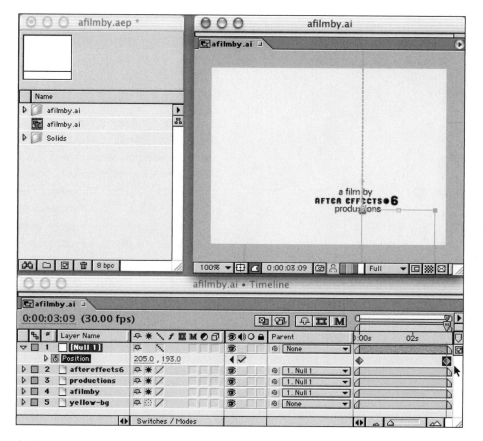

6. Move the **Current Time Indicator** to the last frame (**0:00:03:09**). Move the **Null 1** layer to the bottom of the screen, as you see in the **Composition** window here.

7. Use **RAM preview** to see the motion. The null object has allowed you to create compound motion—the type has its own motion, and the null object offers the opportunity to add another motion path to the animation. This would be very hard to do any other way. You can probably imagine how useful this would be for title sequences, type treatments, and other kinds of artwork.

8. Save and close the project; you're done!

That's a wrap for this chapter, folks! We hope you see the tremendous possibilities that parenting features offer, from both a practical and an aesthetic perspective. Now onward to the next chapter, where you'll learn about adding another powerful feature—effects.

12.

Paint

| Write On | Editing Paint Properties |
| Morphing Paint Strokes | Eraser Mask | Clone Tool |
| "Faking" Painting with the Scribble Effect |

chap_12

After Effects 6
H•O•T CD-ROM

In my opinion, and the opinion of many other seasoned After Effects veterans, the biggest complaint with past versions was that you couldn't type or paint directly in the program. Both complaints have been addressed in version 6 of the program, and these new features are welcome additions. You've already read the chapter on text, so you've seen how amazing the type features are in this version. Welcome to the chapter that addresses the new paint features! If you've ever used Photoshop's version of these tools, you might expect to feel right at home with them in After Effects. It's a lot more complex to paint over time, and there are many new things to learn with this new feature; many of which are not intuitive at first glance.

Paint in After Effects 6 is handled as vector artwork instead of bitmap artwork (which is the case in Adobe Photoshop). Painting with vectors has advantages and drawbacks. With the new Paint tool, each stroke and each erasure is recorded separately (even if you are only drawing a single frame!) so that you can modify its properties over time: from color to brush style to the shape of the stroke itself! With the time-enhanced Clone tool, you can copy parts of an image across space or time... or do both at once! This chapter covers it all—so dig in and stay tuned to learn some new things.

About Paint

Paint features in After Effects 6 are considered an effect, but are accessed through the Paint tools interface rather than the Effects menu. The new Paint tools include the Brush, Clone, and Eraser tools. All three have their own icons in the **Tools** palette, and all three share options in the **Paint** and **Brush Tips** palettes.

You can only use Paint tools in Layer Edit mode. To access a layer's Edit mode, double-click any layer in the Timeline window. The Composition window will change to display the selected layer, with the title of the layer followed by "(Layer in *Comp Name*)," with *Comp Name* replaced by the name of the Composition you're currently working in.

Once you're in the layer's Edit mode, you can use any of the Paint tools (and the modifiers in the Paint and Brush Tips palettes) to modify the layer. Once you've set down the initial stroke, you can use the main Timeline to modify Paint properties just as you would any other property.

The Paint tools are "nondestructive," meaning no permanent changes are made to your original image. It also means that all changes are recorded as individual modifications that can be changed over time.

I. ──────────Creating a Write-On

This exercise offers a first introduction to using the brand-spanking-new Paint tools. I didn't create a very elaborate-looking exercise because I'd rather show the principle of how to use the Paint tools, and leave it up to you to create a more complex project once you get the hang of how they work.

1. Open **paint.aep** from the **chap_12** folder. Save a copy to the **AE6 HOT Projects** folder you created on your hard drive.

2. Create a new comp by clicking on the **New Composition** button at the bottom of the **Project** window.

3. The **Composition Settings** window will appear. Name the comp **write on**, and set the **Duration** to **0:00:01:00** (01s). Click **OK**.

Solid Footage Settings

Name: Pale Purple Solid 1

Size

Width: 320

Height: 240   ☐ Lock Aspect Ratio to 4:3

Units: pixels

Pixel Aspect Ratio: Square Pixels

Width: 100.0% of comp
Height: 100.0% of comp
Frame Aspect Ratio: 4:3

(Make Comp Size)

Color

Cancel   OK

4. Create a new solid by choosing **Layer > New > Solid**. Choose a light color and click **OK**.

In order to use Paint, you must have a layer to work on first. Any layer will do—a movie, a still image, or a solid. In this exercise, you've been asked to create a solid so that you have a layer on which to paint.

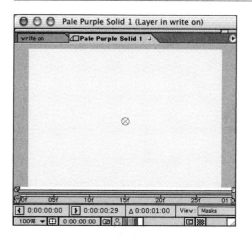

5. Double-click the **solid** layer in the **Timeline**. This will open the **Edit Layer** window. Notice that it appears within the Composition window? This makes it easy to confuse with the Composition window, but you'll learn how to toggle between the Edit Layer and Composition window in upcoming steps.

You might be wondering why you opened the Edit Layer window. So you can paint! You can't paint in any other window in After Effects. Don't know why—I didn't write the program, so don't blame me. :-)

6. Click the **Brush** tool in the **Tools** palette. In the **Paint** palette, choose a size **9** hard-edge brush from the pop-up menu and a dark color. For **Duration**, choose **Write On** from the pop-up menu.

You'll learn about the different duration types throughout this chapter. The Write On duration type memorizes the stroke you create and records it in real time as you draw with it. If you draw your artwork quickly, it will occupy less frames in the Timeline than if you take a long time to carefully create your stroke. You'll learn more about controlling the duration of the Write On in upcoming steps.

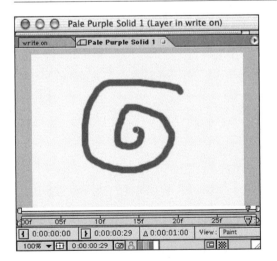

7. Click and drag your cursor in the **Edit Layer** window to create a spiral shape like what you see here. Once you release the mouse, the shape will disappear! Don't fear; it isn't really gone.

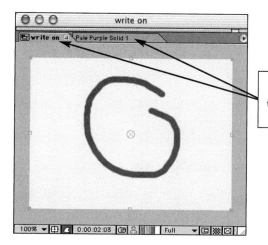

A separate tab appears for the Solid and the Composition. Switching between the two tabs toggles between the Composition mode and the Edit Layer Mode

8. Click the **write on** tab inside the **Composition** window. This switches you from **Layer Edit** mode into viewing the **Composition** window content. Press the **spacebar** to play the **Timeline** to see the stroke of the spiral appear. Most likely, it won't finish drawing itself on the screen. Why? Because the composition was only set for one second and you took longer than one second to draw the shape. You'll remedy that next.

Click the Keyframe Navigator arrow to find the hidden keyframe

9. Make sure that the **Current Time Indicator** is set to the first frame. In the **Timeline**, click the twirlies until you see the **Stroke Options** for **Brush 1**. Notice that Paint is considered an effect? It contains lots of properties that you'll learn about at the end of this exercise in a chart. See the keyframe for the **End** property? Note that the **Stopwatch** icon has been turned on even though you never touched it? Note that it is set to **0.0%**? These are automatic settings that are created when you choose the **Write On** duration type in the **Paint** palette.

10. Click the **Keyframe Navigator** to locate the second keyframe that was automatically created when you drew the spiral. How do I know there's another keyframe hidden from view? Because there's a right arrow on the **Keyframe Navigator**. Arrows appear only when there are keyframes to the right or left of where the **Current Time Indicator** resides.

11. My **Current Time** display shows a value of **0:00:05:03**. Your **Current Time** will vary according to how long it took you to draw your spiral. In the **Project** window, select the **write on** composition. Choose **Composition > Composition Settings** to access the **Composition Settings** window for this comp.

12. Change the **Duration** to match whatever value was in your **Current Time** display. Since mine was set to 0:00:05:03, I entered that amount in the Duration here. Click **OK** when you've entered the new value.

Drag on the Time Navigator End handle to view the entire expanded Timeline

13. Your **Timeline** will not look right. First, drag the **Time Navigator End** handle to the end of the composition in order to view the entire **Timeline**. Notice the keyframe on the last frame? There is a problem with seeing it play, however, because the duration of the **Solid** layer and the **Brush 1** layer are too short.

14. Drag the layer handles out until they go to the end of the comp. Press the **spacebar** or click **RAM Preview** and voilà! You will see the magnificent spiral appear to draw before your eyes. Sarcasm intended! Leave the **write on** composition open for the next exercise.

*The Write On duration type is dependent on how fast or slow you draw. Keyframes are automatically set to a start and end frame for the **End** property that is located under **Brush Options**. Every stroke becomes its own brush, which can easily get daunting if you create more than a simple spiral shape! That's because Paint treats each and every stroke as its own object. There's power in that that will soon be revealed to you, but it can also be cumbersome. You'll find yourself longing for the brushes you use in Photoshop, but those are bitmap brushes, not vector brushes. The beauty of vector brushes is that they can be edited and animated easily.*

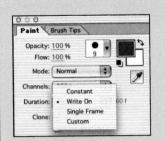

NOTE | Duration Options

The Duration settings are located in the Paint palette. They dictate how long a stroke remains on the screen by default. Here are the four options:

Constant: Paints the entire stroke beginning at the current time; the stroke will remain on the screen for the duration of the layer's existence.

Write On: The stroke is painted in "real time," beginning at the current time and finishing in approximately the same amount of time it took you to create the stroke. Any changes in the speed of your drawing mid-stroke won't be recorded; what is really going on is a simple interpolation between the start and end points of your stroke.

Single Frame: The stroke is painted only in the current frame. Use this mode for traditional frame-by-frame tracing, often called rotoscoping.

Custom: Paints the stroke beginning at the current time; the stroke will remain on the screen for the number of frames specified in the field next to the Duration pop-up.

Brush Stroke Options

Setting	Description
Start	Timing (measured by percent) where the brush begins.
End	Timing (measured by percent) where the brush ends.
Color	Where you set or animate color settings.
Diameter	Size of brush.
Angle	Angle of nib of brush. Different angle settings are only visible on noncircular brush nibs (tips).
Hardness	100% indicates a hard brush. Decreasing the percentage creates a feathered brush.
Roundness	100% indicates a round brush. Decreasing the setting will create an elliptical brush tip.
Spacing	Affects the spacing of the stroke. With a round brush, changing this setting can create a dotted line.
Channels	You can limit the channel to RGB, RGBA (RGB plus Alpha), or Alpha alone.
Opacity	Effects the transparency or opacity of a stroke.
Flow	Specifies how much the flow of brush marks vary in a stroke (works with the pressure-sensitive tablet—see the note that follows this chart).

NOTE | Pressure Sensitivity with Paint Tools

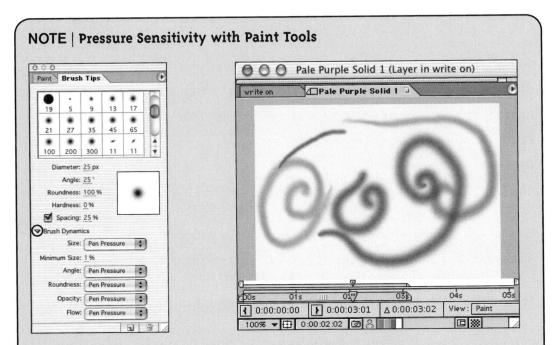

You need to access the Brush Dynamics settings to get pressure sensitivity to work. You must also own a tablet and stylus like the one I used here. Note the brush strokes inside the Edit layer window to the right and how they have thick and thin strokes and varying amounts of ink and opacity. This is all done through the Brush Dynamics settings.

You may or may not have heard of pressure-sensitive tablets. They are really cool—you will want one if you do much paint work in Photoshop or After Effects. I use a Wacom tablet (**www.wacom.com**). If you want to use pressure sensitivity in After Effects, click the twirly for **Brush Dynamics** and set the **Size, Angle, Roundness, Opacity**, or **Flow** to **Pen Pressure** to get this pressure sensitivity to work. Don't forget the tablet though—it won't work with a regular mouse!

2. ————————Editing a Paint Stroke

In this exercise, you'll work with the **write on** composition you just created. You'll see how to access an existing brush and change its attributes through the properties located under the Brush Options. Though this example is very simple, I hope you will understand the principle of it and be able to apply it to your own more complex work in the future.

1. Make sure that **Brush 1** is selected and that **Stroke Options** are visible. Move the **Current Time Indicator** to the first frame. Click the **Stopwatch** icons for **Color, Diameter, Angle, Hardness, Roundness, Spacing, Opacity**, and **Flow**. Read the chart that preceded this exercise to learn what each of these settings do.

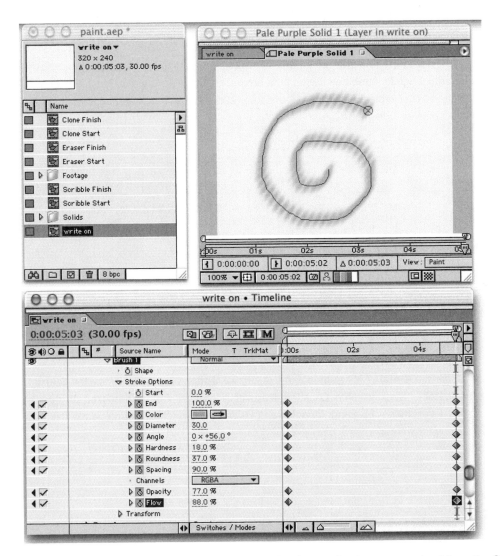

2. You don't have to be in **Layer Edit** mode to make these edits, but you can be. Move the **Current Time Indicator** to the last frame in the **Timeline**. Change the values in **Color** to a **light green**, **Diameter** to **30**, **Angle** to **56.0** degrees, **Hardness** to **18%**, **Roundness** to **37%**, **Spacing** to **90%**, **Opacity** to **77%**, and **Flow** to **88%**.

Each change you make will alter the appearance of the paint stroke. These properties can be animated by setting keyframes or changed throughout the composition by changing them and not activating the Stopwatch. Whether you animate or change these settings, it's good to know that they're there and can be changed at any time. Literally and figuratively!

3. Return to the **write on** composition to play the animation. You'll see the stroke write itself on and also change its visual characteristics based on the settings you made.

4. Close this composition, but leave the **paint.aep** project open.

3. ——————————Morphing Paint Strokes over Time

In the previous exercise, you controlled the placement, duration, and initial timing of paint strokes. In this exercise, you will modify the shape of a paint stroke over time. After Effects lets you "morph" (interpolate) only shapes that have been created with its Paint tools, however, so you will still have to trace over the shapes, even if your original footage is imported from Adobe Illustrator and started life as vector art.

1. Create a new composition, name it **morphing**, and set it to a **Duration** of **0:00:05:00**

2. Create a new solid layer by choosing **Layer > New > Solid**. Keep the same color you chose before, or chose another color of your liking.

3. Select the **Brush** tool from the **Tools** palette. Choose a smaller brush than before in the **Paint** palette (I chose **5**) and be sure to change **Duration** to **Constant**.

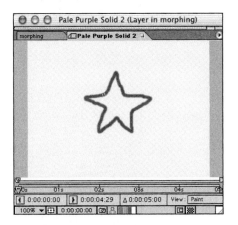

4. In the **Timeline**, double-click the solid layer to open the **Layer Edit** window. Make sure the **Current Time Indicator** is set to the first frame. Draw a star.

It's a bit hard to control the brush in After Effects since it's drawing vector artwork. This is a limitation of the program. A stylus and tablet, such as those that Wacom offers, is a helpful tool to gain better control. For now, a crude star will work to teach the principle of morphing brush strokes.

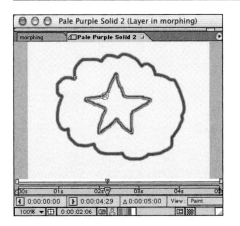

5. In the **Timeline**, click the **Stopwatch** for the **Shape** property. This will set a starting keyframe for this attribute. Move the **Time Marker** in the **Layer Edit** window to somewhere around **02s**. Notice that it also moves the **Current Time Indicator**. Make sure that you click the twirly for the solid layer to reveal **Brush 1** and the **Shape** property. Draw a cloud-like shape outside the star. When you let up off the mouse, the star will disappear.

This step is very important and easily overlooked. By selecting an existing paint stroke in the Timeline, you are telling After Effects that you want to modify the stroke rather than create a new one. The star shape has been replaced by the cloud shape on this frame. The star is still there on the first keyframe.

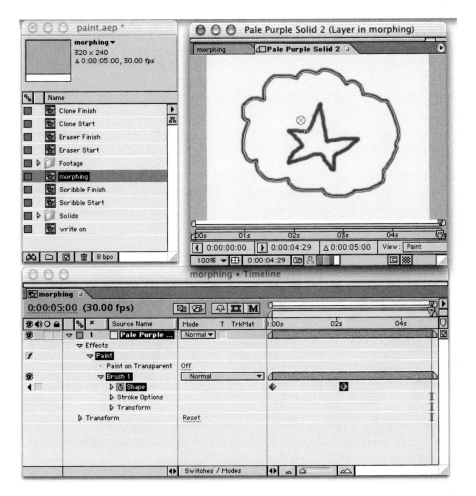

6. Move the **Current Time Indicator** to the last frame of the **Timeline**. Draw a star inside the cloud shape. This will add the third keyframe once you release the mouse, and the cloud shape will disappear. The cloud shape is still on the second keyframe, however.

---

7. In the **Composition** window, click the tab for **morphing**, which will return you to the composition and take you out of **Layer Edit** mode. Click **RAM Preview** and you'll see the three shapes you drew morph from one keyframe to another.

The paint and animation results might seem a little crude and uncontrolled to you. It does to me, too. This is the first version of a paint engine for After Effects, and it could use some more refinement, like Bézier handles on the paint strokes to be able to reshape them, or points to control the shape of the morph like you find in a lot of other morphing software programs. I'm sure these limitations will be improved upon in future versions.

---

4. —————————Creating a "Write On" Effect with the Eraser Tool

Using the Eraser tool is a great way of gradually hiding or revealing a layer over time. In this exercise, you'll be working with a layer that includes some text created from Photoshop and rasterized there, making it appear one stroke at a time. You could attempt a similar effect with the paintbrush, as you did in Exercise 1, but you could never paint each stroke as precisely as you can with the method you are about to learn. In this case, you will start with finished artwork, hide it, and then instruct After Effects to remove the eraser strokes over time.

1. From the **Project** window, double-click **Eraser Finish** and click **RAM Preview** to view its content. The letter **A** (in Adobe's **Giddyup** font) appears to draw itself on the screen. This finished composition shows the goal of this exercise, and once you see this preview, you can close this comp and open **Eraser Start** from the **Project** window.

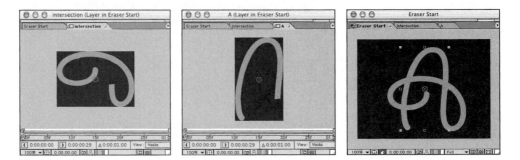

2. Notice that the composition includes two layers. In the **Timeline**, double-click the **intersection** layer to open its **Edit Layer** window. Double-click the **A** layer to open its **Edit Layer** window. In the **Composition** window, click the tab **Eraser Start**. This allows you to look at the two layers separately, as well as the composition, which combines the two layers causing them to appear as a single letter **A**.

Why separate the cross strokes from the main strokes of the letters? The reason will become apparent as you work through the exercise!

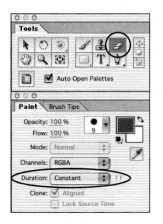

3. In the **Tools** palette, select the **Eraser**. In the **Paint** palette, make sure that **Constant** is set for **Duration**, and leave all the other settings alone from the last exercise.

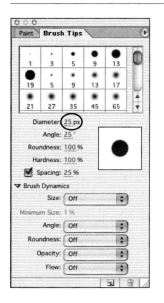

4. In the **Brush Tips** palette, change the **Diameter** to **25**.

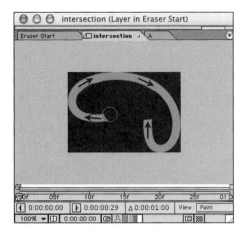

5. Make sure the **Time Marker** is at **0:00:00:00**. In the **Composition** window, click the **intersection** tab to bring up the **Edit Layer** window. Start erasing the image from the left side to the right side, following the shape of the font. Your stroke is being recorded, so it's important to make this stroke perfect. If you make a mistake, select the Paint effect from the Timeline (use your twirlies to find it!) and press the **Delete** key. It's important that you make the stroke follow the shape of the font, and do so with one brush stroke. When you come to the end of the shape, don't go beyond the end of the visible shape. Your next brush stroke will pick up where this one left off.

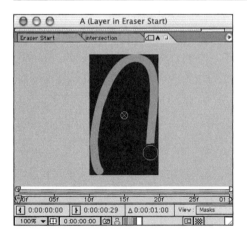

6. In the **Composition** window, click the **A** tab. Drag the eraser in this window and start erasing the image from the right side to the left side, following the shape of the font. Your stroke is being recorded, so it's important to make this stroke perfect. If you make a mistake, select the **Paint** effect from the **Timeline** (use your twirlies to find it!) and press the **Delete** key. It's important that you make the stroke follow the shape of the font, and do so with one brush stroke. Make sure you completely erase the shape on the screen.

7. In the **Timeline**, click the twirlies for the **intersection** layer until you see the **Stroke Options** for **Eraser 1**. Click the **Stopwatch** for **Start**. This will set a keyframe at the beginning of the composition.

8. Click the **Eraser Start** tab in the **Composition** window. In the **Timeline**, move the **Current Time Indicator** to **0:00:00:13**. Change the value of **Start** to **100%**. This will set a second keyframe, and you'll see the stroke appear in the **Composition** window.

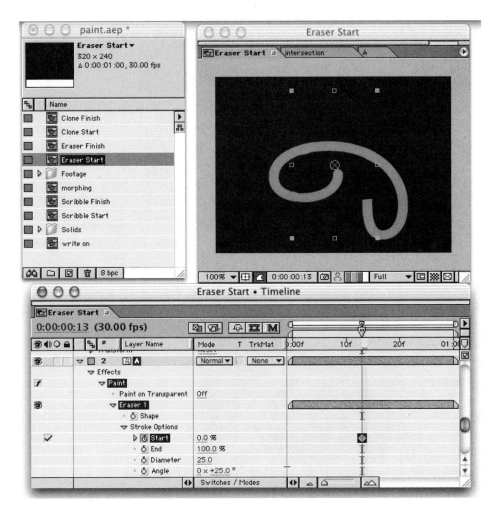

9. Make sure the **Current Time Indicator** is still set to **0:00:00:13**. Click the twirlies for the **A** layer until you see **Stroke Options** for **Eraser 1**. Click the **Stopwatch** for **Start**. You should see a keyframe appear for this layer at **Frame 13** on the **Timeline**.

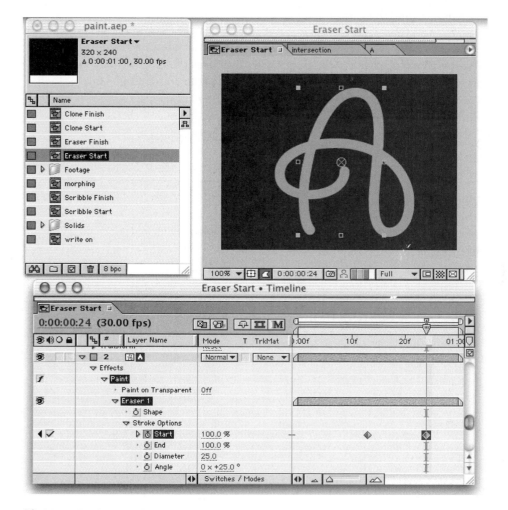

10. Move the **Current Time Indicator** to **0:00:00:24**. Change the **Start** value to **100%**.

11. Preview the animation by pressing the **spacebar** or by using **RAM Preview.**

You should see the text appear as if it is writing itself on. If you were to create an entire word using this technique, you might get a sense of how many layers and eraser strokes you would need. It is time consuming to make and plan paint effects as you see here, but the results are pretty cool and well worth it. I chose a single letter for this exercise to teach you the technique. Feel free to try something on your own that is more complicated and allot yourself lots of time!

12. Leave the project open, but close this composition; you won't be needing it again in this chapter.

MOVIE | eraser.mov

To view this exercise being performed, watch **eraser.mov** from the **movies** folder located on the **H•O•T CD-ROM.**

NOTE | Cumulative Eraser Effects

Did you figure out why it was important to separate out the intersecting strokes into two layers? Intersecting strokes make the write-on effect impossible to create in a single layer because the eraser is a paintbrush that, like all other Paint tools, layers its effect with each new stroke. The problem is that any area where your strokes overlap won't show up until both strokes have been removed. However, since eraser effects are only cumulative *per layer*, two erasures on different layers won't "hide" the contents of both layers. By hiding the intersecting strokes on one layer and the "main" strokes on another, each stroke can be fully hidden and then fully revealed without interference between the two.

5. _____Using the Clone Tool

The Clone tool has been a staple of Photoshop for what seems like forever—creating very funny effects like putting a third eye on a face, or a human face on a dog. Cloning is often used to remove wires in special effects movies, and is just as capable of creating a realistic-looking result as its comical counterpart. In After Effects, the Clone tool includes another dimension—that of time. In this example, you'll create a set of identical twins from a movie layer that has a single figure walking down a hiking trail.

1. From the **Project** window, open and play the **Clone Finished** composition to preview the end result of this exercise. Note the two women walking down this path? There is really only one woman in the original source footage. Close this comp and open **Clone Start** to get started.

2. Notice that there is only one woman on this movie layer? If you press the **spacebar** to preview the composition, you'll see that she is alone for the entire length of the layer. Move the **Current Time Indicator** back to the first frame. Double-click the **walk.mov** layer to open the **Edit Layer** window.

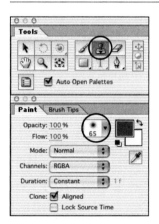

3. In the **Tools** palette, select the **Clone** tool. In the **Paint** palette, change the brush to a feathered **65**. I chose a large feathered brush for this clone exercise so it would be more forgiving than a small, precise hard-edged brush.

4. Maker sure the **Current Time Indicator** is on the first frame. **Option+click** (Mac) or **Alt+click** (Windows) on the woman's face. This sets the clone source point. Move your mouse to the left and start painting where you want the head to appear. The large feathered brush creates a soft edge to the image. Keep painting with one stroke until you get the entire figure drawn in to the left. It's important that you complete the clone with a single stroke; otherwise, you'll have multiple clone brush objects in the end, and they'll be harder to control than a single object.

5. Click the **Clone Start** tab and click **RAM Preview** to view the results. The duplicate stays in sync for a short time, but eventually, the offset between the original clone position and the speed at which the woman walks aren't in sync and the clone image walks off the screen. You'll fix this next!

6. Make sure the **Current Time Indicator** is on the first frame. Click the twirlies to reveal the **Stroke Options Clone Position** setting. Click the **Stopwatch** to set your first keyframe.

7. Move the **Current Time Indicator** to the last frame. Put your cursor over the **Y** value and scrub it until the woman's figure fits into the space of the clone shape. This will set a second keyframe. Click **RAM Preview** and miraculously she will fit! Close this comp when you're finished, but leave the **paint.aep** project open.

*Cloning can be tedious and difficult work. I intentionally picked a soft edge brush that would be more forgiving. On difficult projects, you might have to set the **Duration** setting in the **Paint** palette to **Single Frame** in order to create a different clone shape on every frame. This can take hours and be very tedious work. I often opt for the more forgiving feathered edge look, even if it isn't perfect, to save time and get quick results.*

MOVIE | clone.mov

To view this exercise being performed, watch **clone.mov** from the **movies** folder located on the **H•O•T CD-ROM**.

NOTE | Clone Alignment and Locking Source Time

By default, when you "sample" an area to be cloned, you are setting up a "virtual line" between the area you sample (when holding down **Option** or **Alt**) and the area you begin painting over (when you click without holding down the modifier key). This line moves with your painting so that the sampled area moves in alignment as you work across the area you're painting. This is shown visually by the two crosshairs that appear on the screen when the Clone tool is active: one for the source location, and one for the destination location.

Unchecking the **Clone: Aligned** box in the **Paint** palette "locks" the source area so that all of your destination painting is based on the single sample from where you first clicked. This is useful when you're trying to spread out a small, regular area of color across a wider area.

By default, the **Clone: Lock Source Time** box is unchecked, so the clone source is sampled for each video frame. This means that if something changes in the source area of your clone, that change will be reflected in the destination area of your clone as well. This is generally what you want when you're copying an area of action over time. However, if you're doing a "cover up" cloning to remove an unwanted object from a scene, you may want to sample all of the material from a single frame—perhaps a frame in which the offending object does not appear at all! In those cases, you want to check **Clone: Lock Source Time** so that the part of the image being sampled does not change as the video changes.

6. _____ "Faking" Painting with the Scribble Effect

This final project doesn't actually use any of the new Paint tools, but it introduces an effect that can be used to produce the "look" of an image being painted on the screen. This effect can also be used for a variety of custom transitions, but one of its simplest and most powerful uses is to make an object look like it's made out of animated paint strokes. In this exercise, you will "paint" a photograph of some flowers onto the screen by varying the strength of the Scribble effect over time.

1. In the **Project** window, double-click **Scribble Finished** to view the end results of this project. Once you are finished marveling at this painting effect that requires absolutely no brush work, close the composition. Open **Scribble Start** to get started.

NOTE | Preparing Images for Scribble

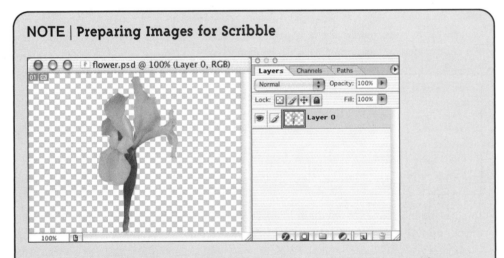

The artwork for the flower layer used in the Scribble composition originated from Photoshop. In After Effects, you don't see how it looks in Photoshop, but it's useful to look at it in Photoshop to understand how it was prepared. It started its life as a photograph from a digital camera. I opened it in Photoshop and used Photoshop's Eraser tool to create transparent pixels that form the outline of the flower. I then saved it as a Photoshop document and imported it into After Effects. I chose to Merge Layers when doing so, and After Effects honored the transparency information of the image.

```
                          Auto-trace

   Time Span
    ● Current Frame              Start: 0:00:00:01
    ○ Work Area                    End: 0:00:00:01
                              Duration: 0:00:00:01

   Options
    Tolerance:  [ 1 ]  Pixels   Threshold: [ 50 ]  %

    Channel: [ Alpha          ▲▼ ]   □ Invert

             □ Blur [ 0 ]  pixels before auto-trace
             □ Apply to new layer

  1 layer will be auto-traced.       ( Cancel )   ( OK )
```

2. In the **Timeline** window, select **flower.psd**. Choose **Layer > Auto-trace** and the **Auto-trace** dialog box will appear. Leave its settings as you see here and click **OK**. This will create a mask from the transparency information of the layer.

A mask is required to define the outline of the shape you wish to "draw" using the Scribble effect.

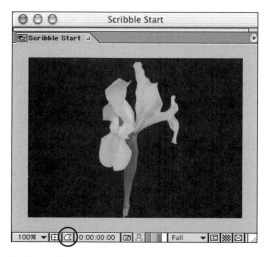

3. Turn off the yellow outlines of the mask by clicking on the **Toggle View Masks** button in the **Composition** window.

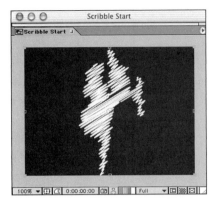

4. Choose **Effect > Render > Scribble**. The flower should turn into a loose, white scribble.

5. Twirl down the **Scribble** effect controls in the **Timeline**. Change the **Angle** property to **49%** and the **Stroke Width** property to **1.1**.

The Angle property affects the direction the stroke is drawn. The Stroke Width property affects how thick the stroke is.

6. Twirl down the **Stroke Options** beneath the **Stroke Width** property, and change the **Curviness** to **50%** and the **Curviness Variation** to **10%**.

The Curviness property affects how loopy the stroke is; the Curviness Variation determines whether the stroke appears uniform and controlled or more wild and varied.

7. Change the **Composite** property to **Reveal Original Image**. You should now see a rough, squiggly version of the flower on the screen. But wait, it gets cooler!

8. Make sure the **Current Time Indicator** is on the first frame, then click the **Stopwatch** icon next to the **End** property of the **Scribble** effect. Change the value of the **End** property to **0%**.

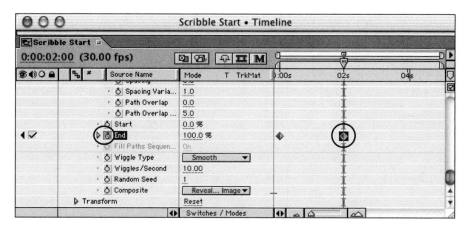

9. Move the **Current Time Indicator** to **0:00:02:00** and change the value of the **End** property back to **100%**.

10. Press the **spacebar** to preview the animation.

*Notice how even after the flower is drawn, the lines continue to wiggle as if the drawing is alive. The Wiggle parameters determine how the lines change over time; change the **Wiggle Type** to **Static** if you want the effect to appear to be a single, smooth line drawing.*

11. Now you are going to make the drawing appear to "fill in" a bit more after the initial scribble is in place. Move the **Time Marker** to **0:00:03:00 (03s)** and turn on the **Stopwatch** next to the **Curviness** property. A keyframe should appear at **0:00:03:00**.

Turning on the Stopwatch mid-animation means that the property value set in the first keyframe will apply from the beginning of the animation up through the first keyframe.

12. Move the **Time Marker** to **0:00:04:00 (04s)**, and change the **Curviness** property to **0%**. This should bring your lines together into a more solid flower.

13. Move the **Current Time Indicator** back to **0:00:02:00 (02s)** and click the **Stopwatch** for the **Spacing** property. Change the **Spacing** property to **13.1**. This should change your flower into a very loose line again.

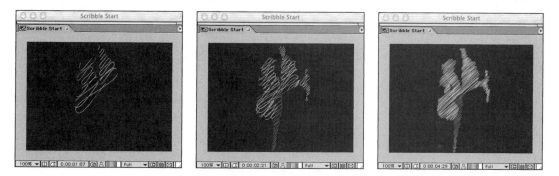

14. Move the **Current Time Indicator** to **0:00:03:00** (**03s**) and change the **Spacing** property to **3.1**. This should tighten up the flower's lines again, while still leaving them broadly curved.

15. Press the **spacebar** to preview your animation. The flower should now appear to be formed from a single scribble, which gradually resolves itself into a shimmering flower form.

As a hint, I actually prefer how this effect looks when the layer is rendered at "draft quality," but you should experiment with both draft and high quality settings for the layer to see which works better for your particular project.

Congratulations! With this chapter and the text layers chapter under your belt, you've now mastered the two biggest new features of After Effects 6. Hopefully, with these completely customizable non-destructive tools added to your kit, you're now more inspired than ever to play with the infinite options that After Effects 6 offers!

I3.
Masks

Simple Masks	Drawing Masks with the Pen Tool
Locking Masks	Applying Effects	Feathered Masks
Mask Modes	Animating Mask Shapes

chap_13

After Effects 6
H•O•T CD-ROM

Masks allow you to define transparent areas for footage items, and they play an important role in motion graphics design. You have already imported Photoshop and Illustrator images with transparent masked regions into After Effects. This chapter will show you how to produce masks in After Effects. Masks are useful for all kind of visual effects and are used often by professional animators.

You'll learn several useful and practical methods for creating, editing, and animating masks. You'll find these masking skills are used often in professional work—so no After Effects animator's training would be complete without it!

I. ————————Creating Simple Masks

A **mask** defines the boundary between transparent and opaque areas of a composition. When you draw a mask in After Effects, the area inside the boundary is completely visible, and the area outside the mask boundary is completely transparent. In addition to setting masked regions, After Effects allows you to set masked areas to have different levels of opacity. Masks can be used on still or movie footage.

After Effects allows you to create simple masks with the Rectangular or Oval Mask tools, or with complex masks using a Pen tool similar to the one in Illustrator and Photoshop. This first exercise will focus on making simple masks.

In the following exercise, you will learn to draw a simple mask and adjust its size. You will also learn to invert a mask. Inverting a mask reverses (or inverts) the transparent and opaque areas defined by the mask boundary.

> **1.** Open **Mask Project.aep** from the **chap_13** folder. Choose **File > Save As** and navigate to the **AE6 HOT Projects** folder you created in Chapter 2 to save a copy there.
>
> *Warning: If you get an error message saying that you don't have the Verdana font, don't worry. This project will still work properly; After Effects will simply substitute a font you do have.*

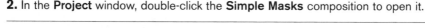

> **2.** In the **Project** window, double-click the **Simple Masks** composition to open it.

> **3.** Press the **spacebar** to preview the monkey animation.
>
> *You're going to place the monkey footage inside the rocket image, which is currently turned off in the Timeline window. In the following steps, you will turn the rocket layer on and draw a circular mask that will be used to make the port window transparent.*

4. Click the **Video** switch to display the **rocket.psd** layer in the **Composition** window. Observe the solid port window, which is where you will draw the mask to reveal the monkey animation.

This animation was set up for the purposes of this masking exercise. It was created in After Effects (remember the monkey animation from Chapter 11, "Parenting"?), saved as a QuickTime movie (which you'll learn to do in Chapter 18, "Rendering Final Movies"), and imported into this composition. I could have had you create all this yourself, but then it would have been another 30 pages before I could teach you about masking!

5. Make sure that your **Current Time Indicator** is on **Frame 0:00:00:01** and that the **rocket.psd** layer is selected. If the **toolbox** is not visible, choose **Window > Tools**.

6. Click and hold on the **Mask** tool in the **toolbox** to display the **Rectangular** and **Elliptical Mask** tools. Select the **Elliptical Mask** tool.

In the following steps, you will draw the mask in the Composition window and adjust the size of the mask. Go slowly with each step. If you want to undo something, use the Undo command by choosing **Edit > Undo**. *Alternatively, press* **Cmd+Z** *(Mac) or* **Ctrl+Z** *(Windows). After Effects' default preference settings will allow you 20 undos, which should be sufficient for any exercise in this book.*

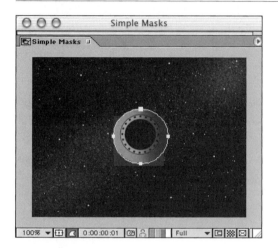

7. Hold down the **Shift** key and, in the **Composition** window, click just above and to the left of the port window of the rocket and drag to create a circular matte around the port window of the rocket. It will look as though the rocket has just disappeared, but don't worry! The mask immediately makes everything outside the mask path completely transparent. You'll fix this in the next step. Don't worry if your circle isn't perfectly matched to the shape of the port shape either. You'll fix this soon as well!

TIP | Using the Shift Key with Rectangular and Oval Masks

Holding down the **Shift** key creates a perfect circle when you draw with the **Elliptical Mask** tool. Likewise, when using the **Rectangular Mask** tool, hold down the **Shift** key to create a perfect square.

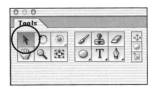

8. Click the **twirly** to the left of **rocket.psd** to display the **Mask** properties. In the **Timeline** window, observe that a mask has been added to the rocket layer. Click the **twirly** next to the **Masks** property. In the **Switches** panel, locate the **Inverted** switch and click the **check box** to invert the mask. Observe that the mask has been inverted so that it is now completely transparent inside the mask boundary and completely opaque outside the boundary. If the mask you drew doesn't fit properly, don't worry. You'll learn how to adjust its size and position next.

9. In the **toolbox**, select the **Selection** tool.

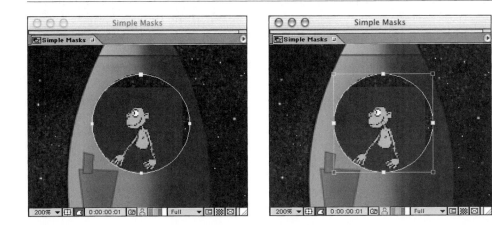

10. In the **Composition** window, set the **magnification** to **200%**. Double-click any **mask handle** to display the mask bounding box.

11. Hold down the **Shift** key and drag a **corner scale handle** to adjust the size of the circle mask to fit the port window. When done, click in an empty part of the **Timeline** window to hide the bounding box.

*If you need to reposition the mask, use the **Selection** tool. If you want to readjust the size of the mask, double-click any mask shape to display the bounding box and repeat the scale adjustment process.*

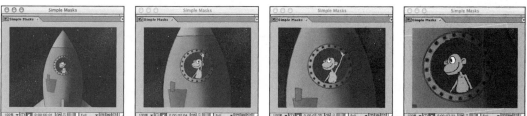

12. Set the **magnification** back to **100%**. Click **RAM Preview** or press the **spacebar** to view the properly masked animation. Notice that the monkey and rocket move together. They were animated to do this for you, using parenting!

13. Save your project. Close the **Simple Masks** composition and leave your project open for the next exercise.

Drawing Masks with the Pen Tool

In the previous exercise, you learned to create an oval mask using the Oval Mask tool. You can also draw custom masks using the Pen tool, which uses Bézier points to define a mask path. Masks drawn with the Pen tool can be either closed or open paths.

In a **closed path**, there is no definite beginning or end. A closed path is continuous; for example, a circle is a closed path.

An **open path** has different beginning and end points. A straight line is an example of an open path. You'll get to create an open path in the next exercise.

In the next exercise, you will learn to use the Pen tool to draw a free-form Bézier mask. The mask you create will have an open path.

TIP | Bringing in Masks from Illustrator

If you don't want to make masks in After Effects, you can copy and paste paths from Adobe Illustrator! Simply create your mask in Illustrator, select it there, and copy it. In After Effects, select the layer on which you want the mask applied and paste it there. The shape from Illustrator will not only paste into the Composition window, but the artwork on the selected layer will appear within the mask. It's that simple!

Working with the Selection Tool

The Selection tool has a great deal of functionality when used with paths. One of the tricks to working effectively with After Effects is to understand how the Selection tool works.

What might not be obvious when working with the Selection tool is that it does different things depending on what is currently selected. For example, if the entire mask is selected, the Selection tool will move the mask in the Composition window. However, if a single point or a group of points is selected, the Selection tool will change the shape of the mask. This can be a bit frustrating when you're adjusting a path.

Here's a possible scenario: The entire mask is selected and you click a point to select it individually, but After Effects won't let you select it. This behavior also causes a bit of frustration. You can develop a system, however, that will make these frustrations go away.

The first thing to do is to identify whether the entire mask or just individual points are selected before you attempt to drag a mask path. In a certain respect, this is the hardest part. Once you've trained yourself to become aware of the selection "state," the rest is easy.

The answer to the Selection tool dilemma lies in using keyboard commands that modify Selection tool functionality. There are three keys that will help you when using the Selection tool, and luckily they're easy to remember because you use them all the time:

Mac keys: **Command**, **Option**, and **Shift**

Windows keys: **Control**, **Alt**, and **Shift**

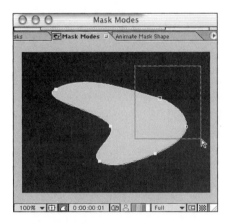

The first technique to learn is what to do if your entire mask is already selected and you want to change the "state" of the mask so you can select single points.

Hold down the **Shift** key and, with the **Selection** tool, draw a **marquee** around any point(s) you want to select. After that, the mask will be in the "individual point" selection state. You can just click any point within the marquee you want to select directly. Holding down the **Shift** key allows you to click unselected points and add them to your selected group.

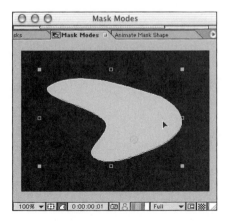

The second technique covers what to do if individual points are selected and you want to select the entire mask.

Press **Option** (Mac) or **Alt** (Windows) and click the mask. After that, the entire mask will be selected, and you can reposition it anywhere you want in the Composition window.

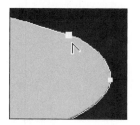 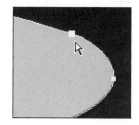

The third technique is to hold down the **Cmd** (Mac) or **Ctrl** (Windows) key to toggle between the **Selection** tool and the current **Pen** tool. For example, if the **Convert Control Point** tool is visible in the toolbox, it will become active if you hold down the **Cmd** (Mac) or **Ctrl** (Windows) modifier key while using the **Selection** tool. This can be handy when you are adjusting Bézier points and you want to convert their type from a straight point to a curved one, or vice versa.

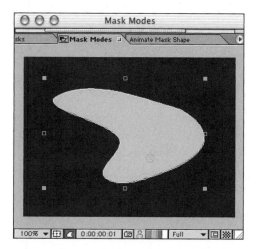

Finally, remember to **double-click** to display or hide the mask bounding box.

Knowing these techniques will make working with masks much less frustrating. You'll get some hands-on practice in the following exercises, and feel free to revisit this section as you gain more experience with masking in After Effects.

2. ——————Drawing Bézier Masks Using the Pen Tool

In Chapter 5, "*Keyframes, Animation, and Timeline*," you learned to use the Pen tool to adjust spatial keyframes in motion paths. The Pen tool can also be used to draw Bézier mask paths directly in the Composition window. In this exercise, you will open the Effects Mask composition, select the Pen tool, and draw a Bézier mask. After drawing the mask path, you will adjust the points to smooth the path.

1. In the **Project** window, double-click the **Effects Mask** composition to open it.

2. In the **toolbox**, select the **Pen** tool.

In the following steps, you will draw the mask path and save it for later. In the next exercise, you will combine that mask path with the text effect.

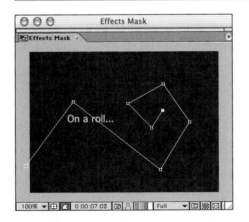

3. In the **Timeline** window, select the **Text Effect** layer. This is a solid layer that has the Text effect applied to it. In the **Composition** window, using the **Pen** tool, start on the right side and click from point to point to draw the mask path you see above, ending the path on the left side. When you click from point to point, you create a straight path.

You don't have to follow exactly what you see above; just do something that basically resembles this path, and it'll be fine.

In the following steps, you will smooth the mask path by converting each point from a straight path to a curved path.

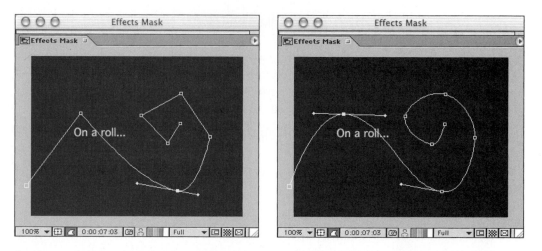

4. With the **Pen** tool still selected, **Option+click** (Mac) or **Alt+click** (Windows) over the **second point** from the right, and observe that the cursor changes to a caret (**^**) shape. This is the **Convert Vertex** tool. Click this same point again and observe that the point changes to a curved path.

5. Using this method, click each point—except the first and the last points in the path—and convert it into a curved path.

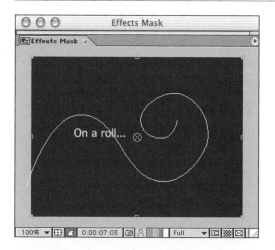

6. Select the **Selection** tool from the **toolbox** and adjust any points you like. Your finished mask path should be fairly smooth, so the text will flow nicely along the path when you animate it.

7. Save your project and leave it open for the next exercise. So far, you've learned how to create straight and curved paths. Upcoming exercises will build on these skills.

NOTE | Open Mask Paths

Open mask paths, like the one you just drew, are used only with effects. They act as a boundary for an effect, or they can define a path for an effect.

NOTE | Locking Masks

Knowing how to lock and unlock a mask is a nice skill to have, so you don't accidentally edit a mask after going to the trouble of creating it. To display the Lock switch for a mask, you must first display the mask properties.

Tip: You can display the Mask Shape property by pressing **M** (once) on your keyboard. This will also display the Lock switch for the mask.

The Lock column and the Lock switch for the mask are located in the **Switches** panel. Click the **Lock-box** icon to lock the mask. The icon changes to a lock to indicate that the mask is now locked.

3. _____Using Masks with Text Effects

In the following exercise, you'll apply a Path Text effect to the mask path you created in the last exercise. Once you apply the mask, you'll animate the text along the mask path. This combines techniques you learned from the last chapter with some you learned in this one. It's all starting to come together!

1. The **Effects Mask** composition should still be open from the last exercise.

2. In the **Timeline** window, select the **Text Effect** layer.

*To make this exercise more efficient, we've already applied the text effect to this solid layer. **Tip:** You can add a text effect to any kind of layer—a solid layer, still footage, or a movie.*

3. Choose **Effect > Effect Controls** to display the **Effect Controls** palette. As an alternative method, press **Cmd+Shift+T** (Mac) or **Ctrl+Shift+T** (Windows).

4. In the **Effect Controls** palette, click the **Path Text** twirly, and then click the **Path Options** twirly.

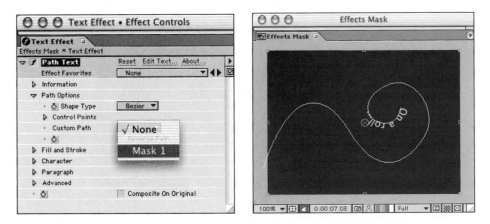

5. Locate the **Custom Path** option and click the pop-up menu to select **Mask 1**. Notice that the text conforms to the path. After Effects automatically assigns the name **Mask** to the mask you made in the last exercise.

6. You can change the mask's name to anything you want by selecting **Mask 1** in the **Timeline** window, pressing the **Return** (Mac) or **Enter** (Windows) key, and renaming it. For this exercise, you can leave it named **Mask 1**.

This text is oriented upside down. In the following step, you'll see how to reverse the orientation of the text by reversing the path.

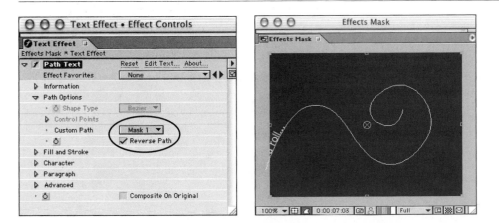

7. Click the **Reverse Path** check box. Notice that the text is now oriented right side up, just as it should be.

Reversing the path affects the text in two ways. One, it reverses the up/down orientation of the text. Two, it reverses the first/last point origin of the text. In the following steps, you'll learn to animate the text along the custom path, using the Left Margin option.

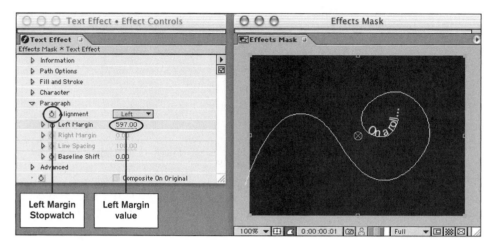

Left Margin
Stopwatch

Left Margin
value

8. In the **Timeline** window, make sure the **Current Time Indicator** is set to **Frame 1**.

9. In the **Effects Control** palette, click the **Path Options** twirly to hide those properties. Click the **Paragraph** twirly to display the Paragraph properties.

10. Click the **Left Margin Stopwatch** to turn on keyframes. Position your mouse over the **Left Margin** value so that you see the arrows. Clicking inside the value field and dragging to the right will increase the numbers. Do this until the text starts on the right, as shown in the image. The value (in this case **597**) relates to the relative position of the artwork, so it will be different for every path.

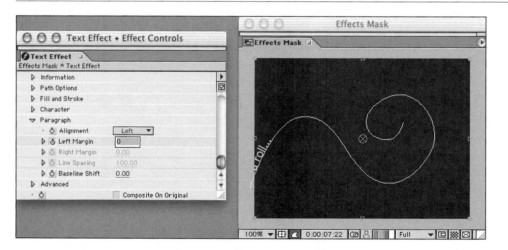

11. In the **Timeline** window, move the **Current Time Indicator** to the last frame. In the **Effect Controls** palette, set the **Left Margin** to **0**.

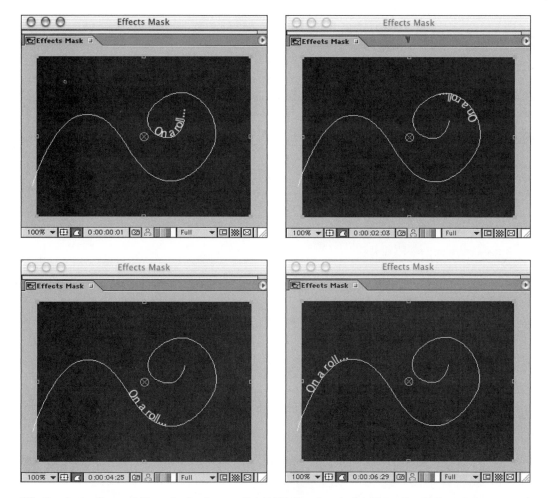

12. Scrub the **Current Time Indicator** or click **RAM Preview** in the **Time Controls** palette to see the results of the animation.

13. Close this composition, but leave the project open; you will need it for the next exercise.

4. —————————Creating Feathered Masks

So far, you've created a closed path (using the Elliptical Mask tool in Exercise 1) and an open path (using the Pen tool in Exercise 2). You can create closed paths using the Oval Mask tool, Rectangular Mask tool, or Pen tool. One of the benefits of creating a closed path is that it can be feathered, creating a soft-edged mask, which is what you'll get to try out next.

1. In the **Project** window, double-click the **Feathered Masks** composition to open it.

2. In the **Timeline** window, select the **Solid Yellow BG** layer. In the **toolbox**, select the **Oval Mask** tool. **Note:** You must always select the layer on which you want the mask applied before you create a mask. In fact, the mask tools in the toolbox are grayed out unless a layer in the Timeline is selected first!

Tip: Press **Q** *on your keyboard to toggle between the* **Oval** *and* **Rectangular Mask** *tools.*

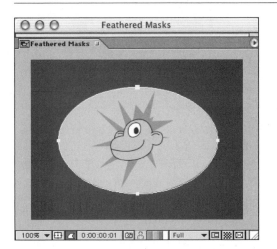

3. Draw an oval mask similar to the one shown here.

If you want to adjust the position of the mask, drag it with the **Selection** *tool.*

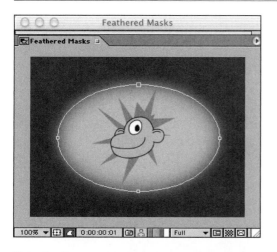

4. Press **MM** on your keyboard as a shortcut to display all of the **Mask** properties. Set the **Mask Feather** property to **30** pixels.

Note: The two separate values in this property represent the X-axis and Y-axis of your mask shape. They are locked by default, which is probably how you'll want to keep it for most feathering purposes. Since you haven't set the Stopwatch icon, this change will last for the duration of the composition. The only reason to set the Stopwatch icon is if you want a property to animate over time.

5. In the **Composition** window, notice that the mask path is in the center of the feathered transition.

*You can control the feathering along the mask path by using the **Mask Expansion** property. In the following steps, you will reduce the mask expansion. This will move the area from which the feathering originates.*

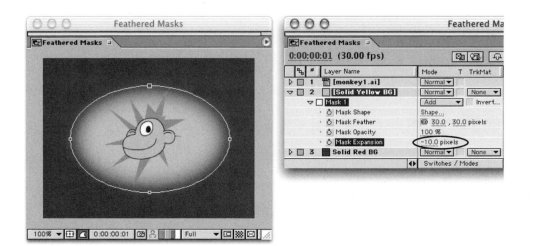

6. Set the **Mask Expansion** property to **–10 pixels**.

Positive numbers increase the mask expansion; negative numbers decrease it.

This is the end of the exercise. If you want to experiment more, you could try setting keyframes for the Mask Feather or Mask Expansion properties and changing the values over different keyframes. You can animate any of the Mask properties by clicking the Stopwatch icon, just as you can with any other After Effects property!

7. Save your project, and close the **Feathered Masks** composition. Leave your project open for the next exercise.

TIP | Deleting a Mask

How do you delete a mask? It's fairly simple. Hey, everything is simple in life if you know how to do it!

Select the mask by clicking its name in the **Timeline**. Press the **Delete** key. This will delete only the mask, not the layer itself!

5. ——————Using Mask Modes

More than one mask can be applied to a single layer. In fact, you can apply up to 127 masks to a single layer. Although there aren't many instances in which you'd use 127 masks on a layer, there are some interesting effects that can be derived from using multiple masks. When you use multiple masks on a single layer, you can work with **mask modes**. These modes change the appearance of the different mask shapes and can create effects that are quite beautiful and useful. In this exercise, you will learn to apply multiple masks and to use mask modes. You'll also learn to use mask opacity with mask modes.

This exercise works with a solid layer. It's amazing how many different "looks" you can get from a solid layer, especially when you're working with masking, feathering, and opacity. You will find that you might use Photoshop and Illustrator less, once you see the power of combining solid layers and masks.

1. In the **Project** window, double-click the **Mask Modes** composition to open it. This is an empty composition—not for long, though, because you are going to add content to it.

2. Create a new solid layer by choosing **Layer > New > Solid**. This opens the **Solid Footage Settings** dialog box. Pick a **yellow** color and click **Make Comp Size**. Then click **OK**. You should see a solid yellow layer that fits perfectly inside the Composition window.

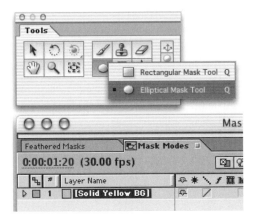

3. With the **solid** layer selected, press **Return** (Mac) or **Enter** (Windows) so you can rename it **Solid Yellow BG**. In the **toolbox**, select the **Oval Mask** tool.

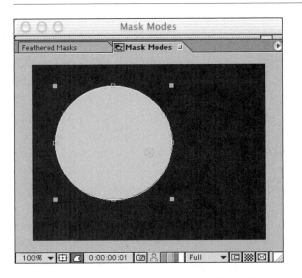

4. With the **Oval Mask** tool, draw a circle on the screen like the one shown here.

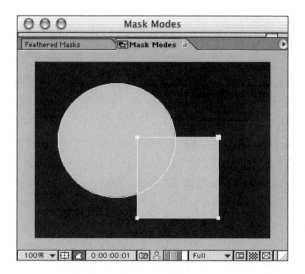

5. Select the **Rectangular Mask** tool. Hold down the **Shift** key and draw a square mask that overlaps the circle. **Note:** The **Shift** key constrains the rectangle mask to a perfect square. Don't worry too much about getting the positions to match exactly—the idea is to create two masks like the ones you see here.

6. Press **M** on your keyboard to display the **Mask Shape** property. Highlight each mask individually, and then press **Return** (Mac) or **Enter** (Windows) to type **Circle Mask** and **Square Mask** as the new names.

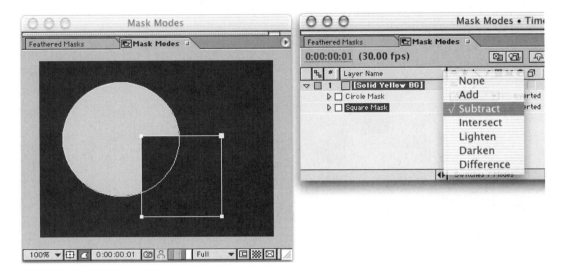

7. In the **Switches/Modes** panel, locate the **Mask Mode** pop-up menu for the **Square Mask**, which is set to **Add** by default. Choose the **Subtract** mode. Notice that the square mask is subtracted from the circle where they overlap.

This pop-up menu is automatically available in the Timeline as soon as you create a mask. Like many things in the Timeline, the Mask Mode menu in After Effects is context sensitive. Add a mask, and the menu appears.

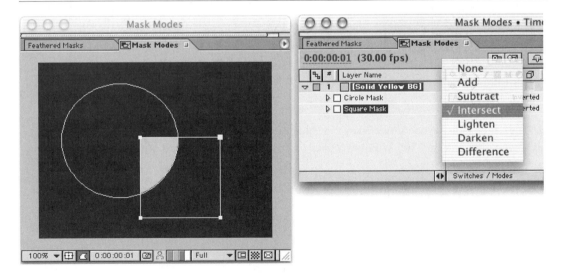

8. Choose the **Intersect** mode for the **Square Mask**. Notice that only the intersecting area of the masks is displayed.

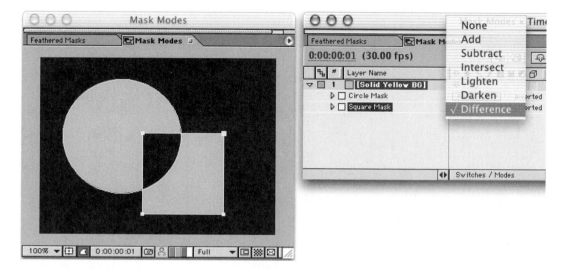

9. Choose the **Difference** mode for the **Square Mask**. Notice that only the areas of the masks that do not overlap are displayed.

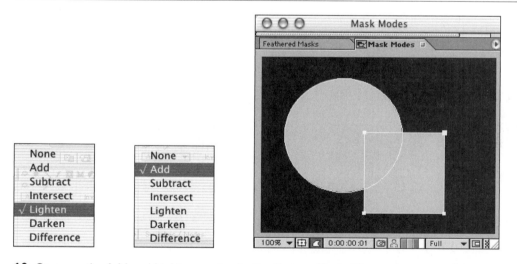

10. Compare the **Add** and **Lighten** modes for the **Square Mask**. The results appear the same.

Some modes work identically on the same artwork. Even though you used a solid layer for this exercise, you could have used a photograph or a movie as your source layer for the mask. If, instead of these solid shapes, you had photographic content that wasn't at full opacity, you would see a different effect if you selected Lighten.

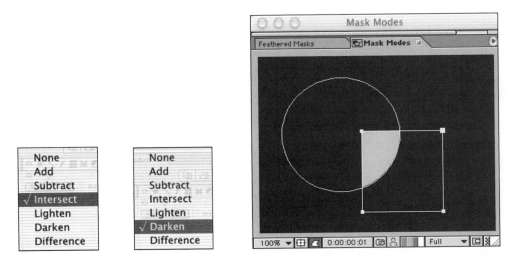

11. Now compare the **Intersect** and **Darken** modes for the **Square Mask**. The results of these modes also appear the same.

The Lighten and Darken modes take on greater significance when acting on masks that have opacities of less than 100%. In the following steps, you will draw a triangular Bézier mask and then adjust the opacity of all three masks. After that, you will reapply the Lighten and Darken modes, and observe the new results.

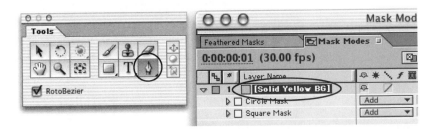

12. Set the **Square Mask** mode to **Add**. Make sure the **Solid Yellow BG** layer is selected, and then, in the **toolbox**, select the **Pen** tool.

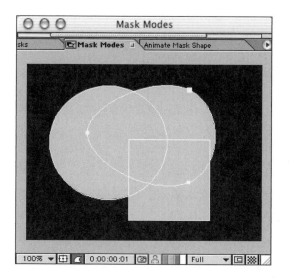

13. Draw a triangle that overlaps the circle and the square. Create this shape by clicking the three points to form the triangle.

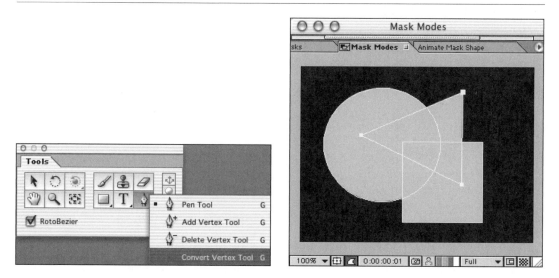

14. By clicking and holding the **Pen Tool** icon, select the **Convert Vertex** tool. Click the points you just created to give the triangle straight edges.

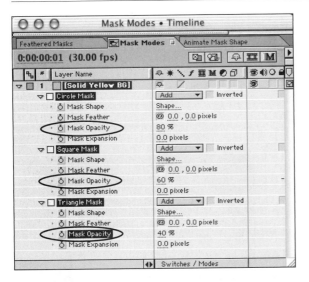

15. Select the new mask, and then press **Return** (Mac) or **Enter** (Windows). Type **Triangle Mask** as the new name. Press **Return** (Mac) or **Enter** (Windows) again to complete the renaming process.

16. Press **MM** on your keyboard to display the **Mask** properties for all the masks. Feel free to adjust the size of your **Timeline** window if you like.

17. Set the **Circle Mask** opacity to **80%**. Set the **Square Mask** opacity to **60%**. Set the **Triangle Mask** opacity to **40%**. After setting the opacity values, click the **twirly** next to each of the masks to hide the properties but still display the mask names. Readjust the height of your **Timeline** window if you like.

18. Click inside the **Timeline** but not on a layer to deselect everything. Alternatively, you can choose **Edit > Deselect All**, or press **Cmd+Shift+A** (Mac) or **Ctrl+Shift+A** (Windows) to deselect.

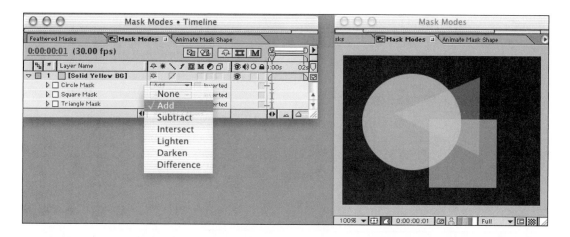

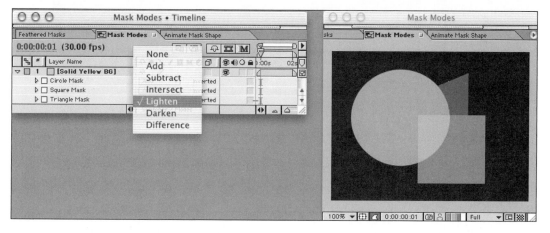

19. Change the **Triangle Mask** mode from its default (**Add**) to **Lighten**. Compare the results.

*The Add and Lighten modes display opacity values differently. In the **Add** mode, where multiple masks intersect, the opacity values of all intersecting masks are added together. In the **Lighten** mode, where multiple masks intersect, the highest opacity value is used.*

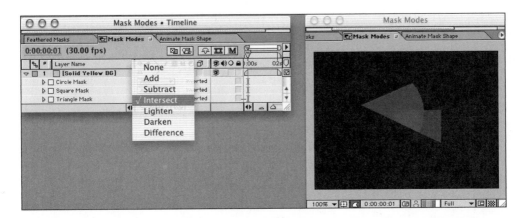

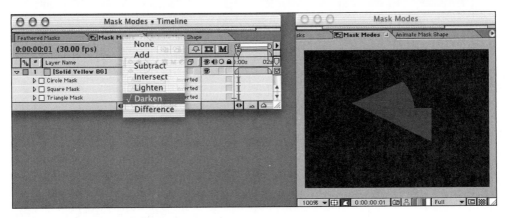

20. Set the **Triangle Mask** mode to **Intersect**, and then set it to **Darken**. Compare the results.

*Here again, the opacity values are processed and displayed differently. In the **Intersect** mode, the opacity of all intersecting masks is added together. In the **Darken** mode, opacity values are not added together—instead, a single opacity value is used for intersecting multiple masks.*

---

21. Save your project, and then close the **Mask Modes** composition. Leave your project open for the next exercise.

You don't need to worry about memorizing how each of these modes work. With experience you will intuitively understand the results you get from each mode.

Right now, it's primarily important to see what the Add, Subtract, Intersect, and Difference modes do. Of secondary importance is to see that the Lighten and Darken modes won't do anything for you unless you are using masks with opacity values of less than 100%.

Now that you've seen the modes and you have some first-hand experience, you'll be able to incorporate mask modes into your work.

TIP | Changing the Color of a Mask Outline

When working with multiple masks, it can be a good idea to change the color of mask outlines so you can easily identify each one in the Composition window.

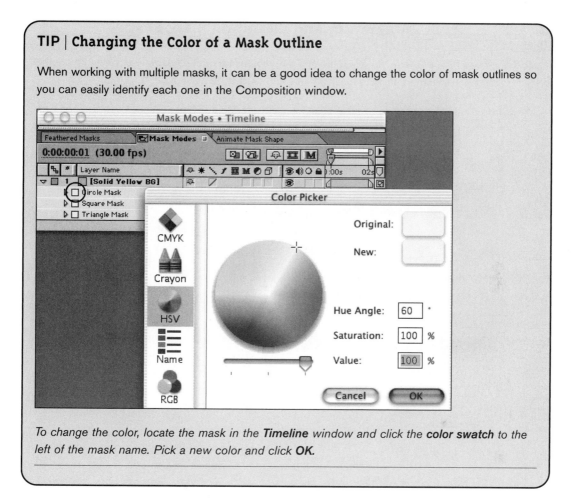

To change the color, locate the mask in the **Timeline** *window and click the* **color swatch** *to the left of the mask name. Pick a new color and click* **OK.**

6. _____Animating and Changing Mask Shapes

Mask shapes can be animated. The result creates the impression of one shape morphing into another. In this exercise, you'll learn to animate mask shapes and to change mask types.

1. In the **Project** window, double-click the **Animate Mask Shape** composition to open it.

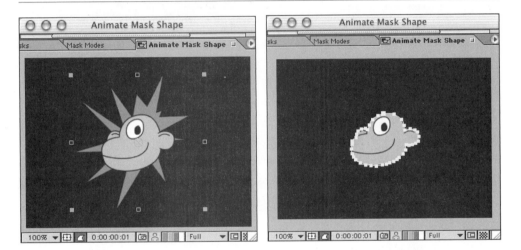

2. With **monkey1.ai** selected in the **Timeline**, select the **Pen** tool from the **toolbox**. Click around the monkey's head to create a mask that shows his head without the starburst, as you see above.

*Note: Click in an empty part of the Timeline to get rid of the mask selection so you can see whether you're happy with the mask. If not, using the **Selection** tool, double-click the monkey in the **Composition** window to see the mask handles. Using the **Pen** tool, you can modify the points from straight lines to curves or, using the Selection tool, you can move the mask. Keep up this process of clicking in an empty part of the Timeline to see it and fixing it until you're happy with the shape it's taken. This often takes some massaging—few people get it right without a little extra effort.*

3. Press **M** to reveal the **Mask Shape** property. Click the **Stopwatch** icon for the **Mask Shape** property. This will set a keyframe on the first frame.

*The shortcut **M** reveals only the property that has been set (Mask Shape), whereas the shortcut **MM** reveals all the different Mask properties. Since we are animating only the Mask Shape property, the shortcut key M is sufficient to show us what we need to see.*

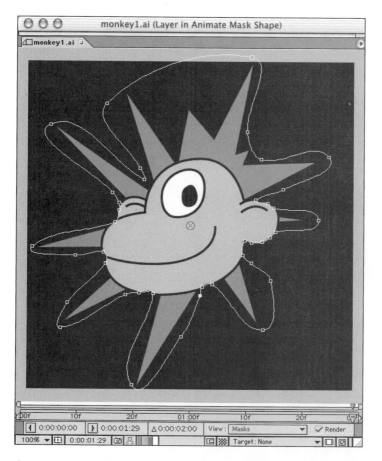

4. Move the **Current Time Indicator** to the end of the **Timeline**. Double-click the monkey artwork inside the **Composition** window to open the **Layer In Animate Mask Shape** window (see also the "Use the Layer In Window for Better Control" sidebar). Use the **Selection** tool to move the points of the mask outward, revealing the entire starburst shape. Close the **Layer In** window when you're finished.

If you look in the Timeline, you'll see that this change has set another keyframe. That's because the Stopwatch icon was on! Any change you make to the mask will create a keyframe as long as you move the Current Time Indicator to a new location. If you think about it, this is how all keyframes are created in After Effects. Set the Stopwatch, move the Current Time Indicator, make a change, and you have a new keyframe!

5. The effect you just created will be more impressive if you change the background color from black to something else. Choose **Composition > Background Color**, and pick a **bright orange**.

6. Click in an empty part of the **Timeline** to deselect the **monkey1.ai** layer. This will turn off the mask shape. Scrub the **Current Time Indicator** or press the **spacebar** to view the mask shape animation.

7. Save and close this project. You're finished trying out the mask exercises!

TIP | Use the Layer In Window for Better Control

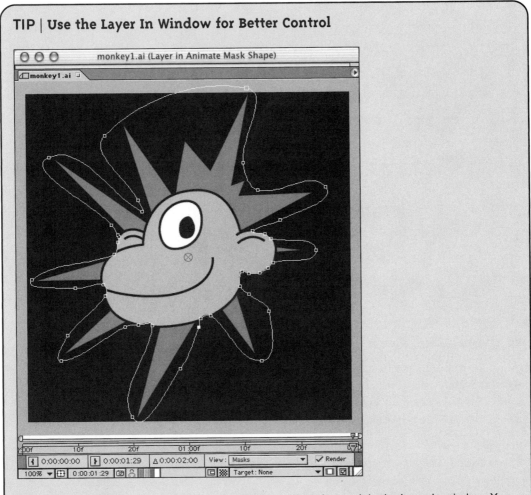

Sometimes, for really tight masking jobs, it's easier to view the mask in the Layer In window. You access this window by double-clicking on artwork in the Composition window.

This launches the Layer In window. It is more intuitive to move anchor points in this view, but you must close the view to see the results of your work, so it's a little inconvenient.

TIP | Toolbox Keyboard Commands

Drawing and adjusting masks often requires many trips to the toolbox. You can streamline your work process by using keyboard commands to access every tool in the toolbox.

Use these shortcut keys, and you'll find that you spend less time clicking on the toolbox and more time making creative choices.

Key	Tool
Toolbox Shortcut Keys	
V	Selection tool
W	Rotation tool
G	Pen tool
Q	Oval / Rectangular Mask tool (works only when a layer is selected)
C	Camera tools (works only when a 3D layer is selected, which you'll learn more about in Chapter 15, "*3D Layers*")
Y	Pan Behind tool
H	Hand tool
Z	Zoom tool

That's a wrap on another chapter! Masks are great tools for creating transitions, and you certainly have the experience now to create a vast array of masks for your projects. Practice on some footage of your own—don't stop with the examples in this chapter. Try masking all kinds of footage, and you'll be amazed by the different kinds of effects you can achieve.

14.

Track Mattes

chap_14

After Effects 6
H•O•T CD-ROM

The term **track matte** is new to any of you who've never used After Effects before. Actually, many experienced After Effects users do not use track mattes or know what they do. That's because the concept is slightly abstract—better explained with exercises than words!

Imagine that you had a movie that you wanted to appear within some text. This kind of effect would be perfect for a track matte. You would separate the text and movie onto two layers and use a track matte to tell After Effects to use the shape (or alpha channel) of the text as a mask for the movie. The cool thing about a track matte is that you can still animate the associated layers independently. This means that you could have a movie that scaled to different sizes, which also appeared inside moving text letters. This isn't just restricted to moving images inside text— it can work with any artwork that contains an alpha channel, which you'll learn more about in this chapter. It gets very exciting, and without further abstract description, let's get right to the heart of track mattes to try them out!

What Is an Alpha Channel?

Alpha channels are critical to working with track mattes. Why? Because a track matte has to use the alpha channel of footage in the Timeline in order to work. Not all footage items contain an alpha channel, but this chapter will help you identify when one exists and how to use it.

The term "alpha channel" sounds a lot more intimidating than it is. The simple explanation is that an alpha channel works invisibly to mask areas of a digital image created from Photoshop, Illustrator, and other programs that support this feature. If you work with Photoshop, we're sure you've created documents with alpha channels, even if you weren't aware that you were doing so. Any Photoshop or Illustrator layer containing artwork that employs transparent pixels uses an invisible alpha channel.

An image or movie that contains an alpha channel is also called a 32 bit. This stands for 8 bits for red, 8 bits for green, 8 bits for blue, and finally 8 bits for 256 shades of gray making up the masking channel. Add up all the bits and you get 32 bits. A 32-bit image or movie has the secret or extra power-packed value of the alpha channel.

Whenever you create a layer in Photoshop that has visible and transparent pixels, such as text, for example, the program generates an invisible mask called an alpha or transparency channel. The checkerboard background in Photoshop denotes this type of transparency.

If you could see the alpha channel, it would look like the image on the right. It works much like a film negative does: If you shine a light through it, the white areas expose the content, and the black areas mask it.

Interpret Footage

Interpretation for "six.psd"

Alpha

- ⦿ Ignore
- ○ Straight – Unmatted
- ○ Premultiplied – Matted With Color:

☐ Invert Alpha

[Guess]

Frame Rate

- ○ Use frame rate from file:
- ○ Assume this frame rate: 30

Fields and Pulldown

Separate Fields: [Off ▾]

☐ Motion Detect (Best Quality Only)

Remove Pulldown: [Off ▾]

[Guess 3:2 Pulldown]   [Guess 24Pa Pulldown]

Other Options

Pixel Aspect Ratio: [Square Pixels ▾]

Loop: [1] Times

[More Options...]

[Cancel]   [OK]

When you bring a file into After Effects, you can choose to merge layers, import a single layer, or import a Photoshop document as a composition. All of these methods preserve the alpha channel. In fact, if you don't want the alpha channel to be honored, you have to go through a little bit of effort. If you ever want to turn off an image's alpha channel, select the image in the **Project** window, choose **File > Interpret Footage > Main**, and select **Ignore**.

Masks and mattes in After Effects work in conjunction with alpha channels. The track matte feature in After Effects uses the alpha channel that resides in artwork created by Photoshop, Illustrator, or other software that support this feature.

Importing Alpha Channels from Photoshop Documents

Now that you know that alpha channels are essential to your track matte workflow, you might wonder how to prepare Photoshop artwork and import alpha channels properly. Since this is an After Effects book and not a Photoshop or Illustrator book, we've created the artwork for you to use in the exercises that follow. When you work on your own, however, you will be importing artwork that you've created in other programs. Photoshop and Illustrator files can be imported using a number of options.

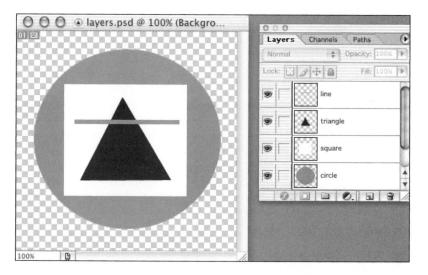

Adobe Photoshop and Illustrator files can contain layers that make up a complete image. This picture shows an image in Photoshop consisting of four individual layers. The Photoshop Layers palette lists each layer from top to bottom: line, triangle, square, and circle.

When you import the Photoshop file as **Footage**, you can choose to merge the layers or import each one individually. Choosing the Merged Layers option will combine all of the Photoshop layers into a single footage item. Choosing an individual layer will import only that layer as a footage item.

Individually imported Photoshop layers show up in the Project window with their original layer names followed by the name of the Photoshop file. Notice that the info for this footage states that it contains **Millions of Colors+ (Straight)**? This means that it contains a Straight alpha channel, which is the most common type. The different types of alpha channels are listed later in this chapter with more complete definitions.

You can also choose to import a Photoshop or Illustrator file as a **Composition** or **Composition – Cropped Layers**.

When you import a file as a composition, a new composition is automatically created in the Project window, and the layers are placed in the original stacking order. It's a real timesaver.

In all cases, alpha channel transparency from Photoshop and Illustrator files are imported appropriately into After Effects without you having to do anything special.

I. ———————————Creating a Track Matte

In the following exercise, you will learn to create a simple track matte that places a photograph inside some type.

1. Create a new project and name it **Track mattes.aep**. Save it in your **AE6 HOT Projects** folder on your hard drive.

2. Double-click inside the empty **Project** window to bring up the **Import File** dialog box. Navigate to the **chap_14** folder. Use your **Cmd** (Mac) or **Ctrl** (Windows) key to select the multiple filenames: **largeclouds.psd**, **sky.jpg**, and **sky.psd**. Click **Import**, and then click **OK** to merge the layers when prompted.

3. In the **Project** window, click the **New Comp** button, which will display the **Composition Settings** dialog box. Name the new composition **Sky Comp**, and enter the settings you see here. Click **OK**.

4. Drag the footage **sky.psd** and **sky.jpg** into the **Timeline** window. Make sure that the type layer, called **sky.psd**, is on top.

Click here to toggle to the Modes panel containing the track matte settings

5. Click **Switches/Modes** to toggle to the **Modes** panel, where you'll see track matte information. Notice that the switches disappear and that the column headings **Mode**, **T**, and **TrkMat** appear.

As you may recall, you learned what modes do in Chapter 8, "Layers." You'll work with the TrkMat and T settings shortly, and their meanings will be revealed. At the end of this chapter, you'll also learn about stencil modes, which you did not learn about in Chapter 8 because they work only with artwork that contains alpha channels.

Note: *The Switches/Modes toggle is part of every Timeline. All you have to do is click that area of your screen. You can toggle between these two groups of settings at any time.*

6. On the **sky.jpg** layer, change the **TrkMat** menu from **None** to **Alpha Matte "sky.psd."** Notice that the photograph now appears inside the type. The color you see behind the type is whatever color you have set your composition background color to be. The track matte layer is using the alpha channel from the layer directly above it. This is how track mattes work—you put the layer you want to pull the matte from above the layer that you want affected.

7. Drag **largeclouds.psd** from the **Project** window into the **Timeline** below **sky.jpg**. This layer's **TrkMat** option is automatically set to **None**, which means it is unaffected by the type. Since the **largeclouds.psd** file is now at the bottom of the layer stack, you see it instead of the background color that was there before.

8. Change the **TrkMat** option for **sky.jpg** from **Alpha** to **Alpha Inverted "sky.psd" Matte**. Notice that the type mask is now inverted. Be sure to change it back to **Alpha** when you're finished seeing the change.

Whether you select Alpha or Alpha Inverted as your TrkMat option is a creative decision that depends on the kind of look you're after. The nice thing about this feature is that it's so flexible. There's no harm in trying either setting. You'll learn about the luminance TrkMat settings in a later exercise. The artwork we've used in this exercise (the type) has a great alpha channel, so it doesn't need to rely on luminance.

9. Save this file and leave it open for the next exercise.

2. ——————Animating the Track Matte

Since anything and everything can be animated in After Effects, you haven't really touched the power of track mattes until you combine them with some keyframes and set some properties in motion. You'll see in this exercise that you can animate the matte, animate the contents of the matte, or do both!

1. With **sky.psd** selected, reveal the **Position** and **Scale** properties (Hint: remember **P** and **Shift+S**?), and change those settings to what you see here. Click the **Stopwatch** icon for both properties—you're going to be setting some keyframes! Change the **Scale** to **40%**, and the artwork should appear in the position you see here. You can click on the word **SKY** and just move it inside in the **Composition** window if you don't want to set it by numerics. This is the easiest way to set a position without thinking in numbers. :-)

2. Move the **Current Time Indicator** to the end of the **Timeline** (a great shortcut is to press the letter **K**). Change the **Scale** to **100.0%** and the **Position** to **156.0, 165.0**, as you see here. Two keyframes should now be set. Press the **spacebar** to see the effect of moving and scaling the type over time.

It's neat to see the type move through the cloud image of the track matte. Next you'll animate the photo of the sky for an even neater effect.

3. Move the **Current Time Indicator** back to the beginning of the **Timeline** (a great shortcut is to press the letter J). Select **sky.jpg** and press **P** for **Position**. Click the **Stopwatch** icon to set a keyframe. Change the **Y** position (the right value) to **−45**. This moves the image inside the type up on the screen.

4. Move the **Current Time Indicator** to the end of the **Timeline**. Change the **Position** property for **sky.jpg** to **166.0, 165.0**. Press the **spacebar** again to watch your work. Now, not only is the type moving, but the clouds are moving inside the type.

5. Move your **Current Time Indicator** to the end of the **Timeline** again. Select **largeclouds.psd** in the **Timeline**. Press **S** to reveal the **Scale** property, and click the **Stopwatch**. That will set a keyframe at the last frame of the **Timeline**. Move the **Current Time Indicator** to the beginning of the **Timeline** and change the **Scale** to **49%**. Make sure you have two keyframes set before you play the animation.

6. Press the **spacebar** or click the **Play** button or **RAM preview** to see your handiwork.

You could also put movie footage inside the type if you used a QuickTime movie instead of a still photo. The variations are endless!

7. Close this composition and save the project.

3. ————————— Luminance-Based Track Mattes

So far, you've had a chance to work with alpha channels and track mattes. This exercise will demonstrate when and why to use a luminance-based track matte. The term **luminance** in After Effects refers to footage that is measured in **grayscale** values. Source footage can originate from Photoshop, Illustrator, or a QuickTime source and can be in color or grayscale. If the artwork is in color, After Effects will convert the color values to grayscale values automatically for you behind the scenes. Basically, After Effects treats the grayscale value as it would an alpha channel—black in the grayscale image represents full masking, white represents full transparency, and the gray shades in between take on varying degrees of transparency. Why would you use a luminance track matte? They are generally used when you want to make a mask from artwork that doesn't have an alpha channel. It's a convenience to be able to choose from source artwork that contains either grayscale information or an alpha channel. The After Effects program is all about lots of choices to fit any creative needs that might arise!

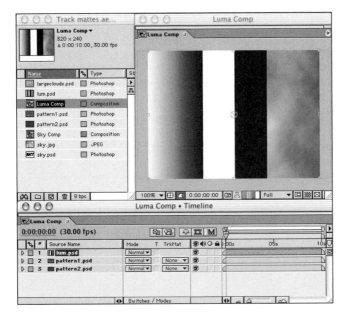

1. Create a new composition, using the same settings as the last exercise (After Effects is "sticky," meaning that all the settings from the last time you created a new composition are still set), and name it **Luma Comp**. Import the artwork **lum.psd**, **pattern1.psd**, and **pattern2.psd**. Click **OK** to merge layers. Drag **lum.psd**, **pattern1.psd**, and **pattern2.psd** from the **Project** window to the **Timeline**. Put the layers in the order you see here.

*Observe the **lum.psd** artwork and notice that it has some areas of pure black, some of pure white, and some mixed grays. This artwork is ideal for understanding how the luminance track matte works against different shades of gray.*

2. Change the **TrkMat** setting of **pattern1.psd** from **None** to **Luma Matte "lum.psd."** Observe that the areas that were pure black knock out **pattern1.psd** completely to reveal **pattern2.psd**. The areas that were pure white fully reveal **pattern1.psd** and hide **pattern2.psd**. The gradient gradually causes one pattern to reveal the other, and the mottled areas of gray show both patterns. The luminance mask is doing its handiwork!

3. Change the **TrkMat** setting for **pattern1.psd** to **Luma Inverted Matte "lum.psd."** Watch the mask change to the opposite of what it was before.

To summarize, luminance mattes are based on grayscale values. Use them when you have source artwork that contains lights and darks, and you want to use that artwork as a mask. Remember that you can use movie footage as well as still footage as your mask source. The effects you can achieve with this technique are endless!

4. Close the **Luma Comp** and save this project. You'll make another new composition for the upcoming exercise.

4. ——————————Soft-Edged Track Matte with a Masked Solid Layer

This track matte stuff gets even better. You can combine the masking skills you learned in Chapter 13, "*Masks*," with what you've learned in this chapter. You'll create a soft-edged matte from a solid layer and feather its edges. Then you'll use that layer to mask another layer. It's easier than it sounds—just try it!

1. Create a new composition and name it **Soft Comp**. Drag **sky.jpg** from the **Project** window into the **Timeline**.

Solid Footage Settings

Name: |glow|

Size

Width: |320|

Height: |240|

☐ Lock Aspect Ratio to 4:3

Units: | pixels ▲▼ |

Pixel Aspect Ratio: | Square Pixels ▲▼ |

Width: 100.0% of comp
Height: 100.0% of comp
Frame Aspect Ratio: 4:3

(Make Comp Size)

Color

[ ] [🖊]

(Cancel) (OK)

---

2. Create a new solid layer by choosing **Layer > New > Solid**. In the **Solid Footage Settings** dialog box, name the solid layer **glow**. The color doesn't really matter, because ultimately the solid layer won't be visible. Pick a bright green for the heck of it, to make sure you remember how to set the color of a solid layer.

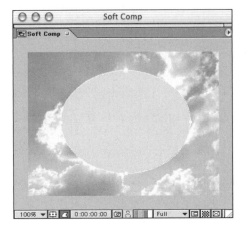

3. Make sure the layer named **glow** is selected, and then using the **Elliptical Mask** tool, draw a circle on the solid layer. It will become masked in the shape of a circle, as you see here.

4. Press **MM** to reveal all of the **Mask** properties. Change the **Mask Feather** to **48** pixels, and click in an empty area of the **Timeline** to turn off the bounding box around the circle.

5. On the **sky.jpg** layer, change the **TrkMat** to **Alpha Matte "glow."** The **sky.jpg** layer will appear inside the glow.

When you create a mask on a solid layer, you also create an alpha channel without realizing it. In this instance, the track matte is using the alpha channel from the masked solid layer. This is a very useful technique, because it's so convenient to make masks from solid layers. You don't have to leave After Effects and go to Photoshop to make the glow artwork this way. Time to animate!

6. With **glow** selected, press **M** to hide the **Mask** properties. Click the **Lock** switch for **sky.jpg** so you don't accidentally move it.

7. With **glow** selected, press **Option+P** (Mac) or **Alt+Shift+P** (Windows) to set a keyframe for the **Position** property. Drag the artwork in the **Composition** window as you see here.

8. Move the **Current Time Indicator** to **Frame 20**, then to **Frame 40**, and then to the end of your **Timeline**, and move your artwork accordingly to create a motion path like the one you see here. This is a good refresher for you to remember how to set multiple keyframes.

---

9. Play the animation and notice that the glow passes over the static cloud image, panning the image as it moves. Sometimes this is what you want, but sometimes you want the artwork to move with the glow. You can do that too—you'll learn this next.

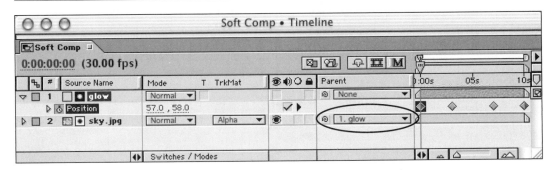

10. Unlock the **sky.jpg** layer in the **Timeline**. In the **Timeline**'s **Options** menu, choose **Columns >
Parent** to show the **Parent** panel.

11. Move the **Current Time Indicator** back to **Frame 1**. Set the **Parent** panel menu for **sky.jpg** to
glow. Now play the animation. It's not as interesting as the previous one, but who knows? You might
want to do this in an animation you'll make in the future.

12. Close this composition and save the project.

Other Masking Modes

You learned about modes in Chapter 8, "*Layers.*" Modes are used to composite two or more images together to create interesting artistic effects. There were a couple of modes that weren't discussed there, because they dealt specifically with masking. I find we use masking modes less often than track mattes, but there are times when they are useful. Although the following examples are not hands-on exercises, you have all the artwork shown here in the project you created in this chapter, and you can try them if you want to. Examples and definitions follow in this section.

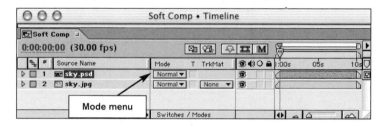

Modes are located next to the T and TrkMat columns of the Modes panel. A Mode menu appears for each layer in the Timeline, and its default is set to Normal. For the most part, modes have nothing to do with masks or alpha channels. A few modes do, however, and they are located toward the bottom of the Mode menu.

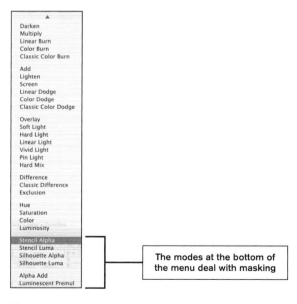

The stencil modes, in general, cut through multiple layers so that you can see all the layers beneath the layer containing the stencil. The source artwork sits on top in the stacking order of layers in the Timeline, and the mode is applied to this source layer.

STENCIL ALPHA MODE

Stencil Alpha mode: Cuts through all the layers beneath it (the source footage must contain an alpha channel). In this case, the top layer is set to Stencil Alpha, and the bottom two layers show through.

STENCIL LUMA MODE

Stencil Luma mode: Cuts through all the layers beneath it (the source footage will be treated as grayscale; if it's in color, it will be converted). In this case, the top layer is set to Stencil Luma, and the bottom two layers show through.

Silhouette mode: In general, blocks out all layers beneath it, allowing you to cut a hole through several layers at once. The source artwork sits on top in the stacking order of layers in the Timeline, and the mode is applied to this source.

SILHOUETTE ALPHA MODE

Silhouette Alpha mode: The artwork with an alpha channel punches a hole all the way through to the background color of the composition. It cuts through every layer below it in the composition.

SILHOUETTE LUMA MODE

Silhouette Luma mode: The grayscale artwork (source artwork in color will be converted to grayscale) punches a hole all the way through to the background color of the composition. It cuts through every layer below it in the composition.

The modes **Alpha Add** and **Luminescence Premul** are described in your user manual. These modes require complicated compositions that are too detailed to stage in the context of this book. We find that only advanced users ever require these features, and they are rarely used even by them!

NOTE | The Preserve Underlying Transparency Option

There is another option in the Modes panel. The Preserve Underlying Transparency option is a single check box. Locate the option by finding the letter **T** at the top of the column. (Think "T" for transparency in this case.)

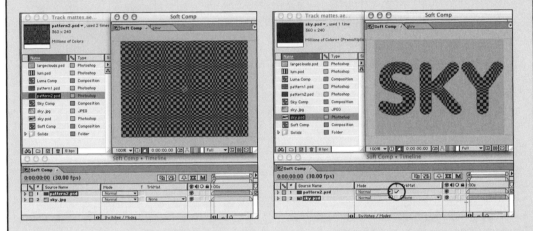

With this check box turned on for the top layer, the alpha channel from the layer beneath is used to mask the artwork. The Preserve Underlying Transparency option works only if the artwork below the layer with the T option checked contains an alpha channel.

continues on next page

NOTE | The Preserve Underlying Transparency Option *continued*

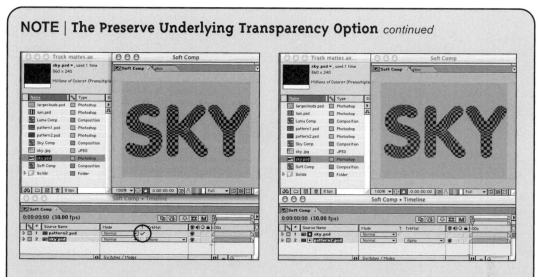

Here's a side-by-side comparison with the same artwork using two different techniques. The example on the left uses Preserve Underlying Transparency, and the example on the right uses a track matte. The results are identical, but the layer order in the Timeline is different.

To use the Preserve Underlying Transparency option, just click the check box. This option has an identical function to alpha channel–based track mattes; it just accomplishes that function differently. I usually use whichever method is most convenient based on the stacking order (though it's also easy to move the stacking order!)

I hope you enjoyed the techniques that you learned in this chapter. Feel free to experiment and try other combinations of artwork for your track mattes. I suggest that you use track mattes with QuickTime movies as source footage, or that you practice working with masked solid layers as your source for track mattes. Honestly, the possibilities are infinite. A little imagination is all you need to combine with the skills you've just learned.

See you at the next chapter, "3D Layers." Rest up, because it's a huge new area for you to learn that will open even more doors for artistic expression.

I5.

3D Layers

Making 3D Layers	3D Views
Custom Camera Views	Lighting	Material Options
Adding and Animating Cameras	Animating the Point of Interest
Camera Options and Settings	Previewing 3D

chap_15

After Effects 6
H•O•T CD-ROM

It's safe to say that working with 3D layers will probably inspire you creatively. Seeing your images move in three-dimensional space, complete with gorgeous lighting, shadows, and camera work, is exciting for anyone working with After Effects. However, there is a lot of new territory to cover for those of you who have never worked in a 3D environment before. Getting to know your way around different views and looking at artwork from the top, left, right, bottom, and front is uncomfortable at first, because it isn't familiar. Likewise, moving artwork along a new axis and dealing with cameras and lights aren't intuitive either. Thankfully, you'll get to try everything firsthand in this chapter, which should demystify the process.

3D in After Effects

At heart, After Effects is a program designed to combine two-dimensional images. As you've seen, you can import a variety of digital image formats as footage into After Effects. All of these footage files have an **X axis** (providing the ability to move from side to side) and a **Y axis** (for the ability to move up and down). These two axes are the two dimensions of movement.

Other programs that are entirely 3D in nature have the capability to build, animate, and render three-dimensional models. These specialized programs have a different purpose. They are designed to create three-dimensional *objects* that reside in a three-dimensional "world" inside a computer.

After Effects should not be confused with these 3D programs. Artwork in After Effects is two-dimensional and has no depth. By activating a **3D layer** in After Effects, you allow your 2D objects to reside and move in After Effects' 3D world. Basically, After Effects offers a 3D viewing and lighting environment, just like any 3D program would, in which you can move 2D objects. The real difference between After Effects and true 3D programs is the lack of a modeling application. This simply means that you can't create true 3D objects that have thickness and depth; you can create only 2D artwork and move it in a 3D space.

When a 2D object is turned with its side toward the viewer, it disappears completely. That's because 2D objects have no depth. The effect of moving 2D artwork in 3D space is very similar to what you could achieve with a skew tool in a 2D drawing program. The difference is that when you see the artwork in motion, the movement looks as though it is occurring in 3D space. This type of believable 3D motion is very hard to simulate with a simple skew tool.

What does all this mean? It means that as you design your 3D work in After Effects, you have to keep in mind that you are working with 2D objects. There's no thickness in a 2D object when it is displayed in perspective. However, the realistic perspective results that occur inside After Effects' 3D environment are quite astounding. As well, the three-dimensional lighting and shadows provide benefits that can be fully appreciated only when seen in action.

You can do amazing work in After Effects. By understanding the way its 3D layers work, you can create images of striking believability, imaginative stylization, and stunning beauty.

Overview of Making 3D Layers in the Timeline

Basically, all you have to do to turn a regular layer into a 3D layer is click a switch in the Timeline.

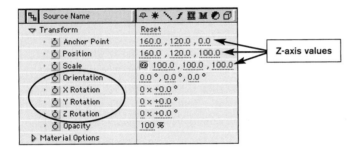

Z-axis values

Once you've converted a layer to a 3D layer, additional Transform properties and options are shown in the Timeline:

- The Anchor Point, Position, and Scale properties display a **Z-axis** option.

- The Orientation property is added.

- Rotation values are separated into X-, Y-, and Z-axis properties.

What is the **Z axis**? Just as the X axis (side to side) and Y axis (up and down) define two-dimensional space, three-dimensional space includes a Z axis. The X axis is the horizontal dimension, the Y axis is the vertical dimension, and the Z axis is the distance, or depth, dimension. With this coordinate system, you can place objects in After Effects' 3D world and use the axis values to define their exact position.

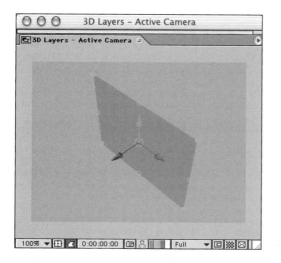

When you select a 3D layer, you'll see three arrows extending from the anchor point. Each arrow is color-coded. The **red** arrow is the **X axis**, the **green** arrow is the **Y axis**, and the **blue** arrow is the **Z axis**.

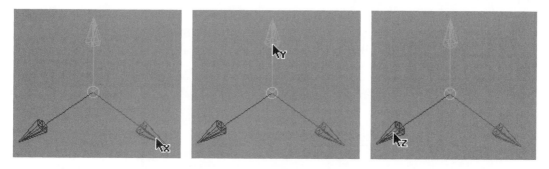

You can move an object by holding the Selection or Rotation tool over any handle. The letter X, Y, or Z will appear next to the pointer, identifying the axis and allowing you to drag the object.

In the following exercise, you'll learn to turn a layer into a 3D layer. You'll also learn to use 3D Transform options.

I. ————————————Making 3D Layers

In this exercise, you'll work with a prepared composition that contains two layers, and you'll learn how to convert them to 3D layers. You'll also use the Position and Rotate properties for each layer. Feel free to take your time and become comfortable with each step.

1. Open **3D_Project.aep** from the **chap_15** folder. Save it in your **AE6 HOT Projects** folder on your hard drive.

2. Double-click the **Making 3D Layers** composition to open it. This composition has two simple layers: an Illustrator file called **monkey1.ai** and a solid layer named **Gray Solid**.

3. In the **Timeline** window, locate the **3D cube** icon in the **Switches** panel. This is the **3D Layers** switch. Click this switch for the **monkey1.ai** layer.

*Note: If this panel is still showing Track Matte information, it is still set to the Modes panel from the last chapter. Click **Switches/Modes** to toggle it back to the **Switches** panel.*

4. Click the twirly for the **monkey1.ai** layer to display the properties. Display the **Transform** properties, if they aren't already showing. Place your cursor over the **X Rotation** degrees value, and drag back and forth to see the effect.

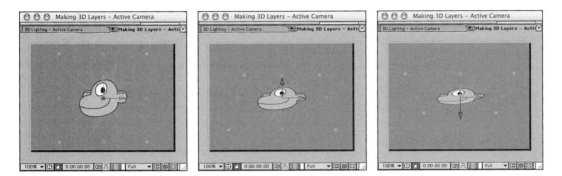

5. Notice that the layer rotates around the X axis. When you are done, return the **X Rotation** value to **0** degrees.

6. Place your cursor over the **Y Rotation** degrees value, and drag back and forth to see the 3D rotation around the Y axis. Return the **Y Rotation** value back to **0** degrees when you are done.

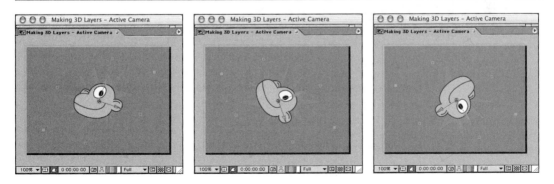

7. Now drag the **Z Rotation** degrees value and observe the image as it rotates around the Z axis. When you are done, return the **Z Rotation** value to **0** degrees.

Next, you'll set keyframes to animate the 3D layer.

NOTE | The Orientation Property

▽ Transform	Reset
› ⦵ Anchor Point	243.0 , 246.0 , 0.0
› ⦵ Position	160.0 , 120.0 , 0.0
› ⦵ Scale	⊚ 40.0 , 40.0 , 40.0 %
› ⦵ Orientation	0.0 ° , 0.0 ° , 0.0 °
› ⦵ X Rotation	0 × +0.0 °
› ⦵ Y Rotation	0 × +0.0 °
› ⦵ Z Rotation	0 × +0.0 °

There is another property in the Transform group called **Orientation** that works to rotate a 3D layer. However, it can get confusing if you start using the Orientation property in conjunction with the X Rotation, Y Rotation, and Z Rotation properties to rotate layers.

For this reason, we recommend using the X Rotation, Y Rotation, and Z Rotation properties for animating 3D rotation while learning After Effects. That way, you'll develop a consistent approach to working in 3D.

Later, after you've had a fair amount of experience with 3D, use the Orientation property when you need to set an object in 3D space but do not need to use keyframe animation. The Orientation property moves your object along the shortest rotational path in 3D space. For this reason, Orientation is best used to set a position and leave it, rather than for keyframe animation. If you attempt to use keyframe animation with Orientation, the layer may move in ways you do not intend.

8. Click the **Stopwatch** for the **X Rotation** and **Y Rotation** properties to set keyframes on **Frame 0**. Accept the default value of **0** for both properties.

9. Move the **Current Time Indicator** to **0:00:00:29**. Set the **X Rotation** value to **−30** degrees, and set the **Y Rotation** value to **30** degrees.

10. Scrub the **Current Time Indicator** or click **RAM Preview** to view your 3D layer in action.

In the following steps, you'll turn the Gray Solid layer into a 3D layer and set property options for it.

11. Hide the **monkey1.ai** properties by clicking the **monkey1.ai** twirly. Click the **3D Layers** switch for the **Gray Solid** layer.

12. Display the properties for the **Gray Solid** layer and then display its **Transform** properties by clicking those twirlies. Set the **Position Z-axis** value to **100**. **Note:** 2D layers do not have a Z-axis Position property. This extra field appears only when you set the 3D Layers switch for a layer.

In the Composition window, the Gray Solid layer will get smaller because it is moving away from the Active Camera 3D view, which you'll learn more about in future steps. In After Effects, you view 3D layers from several angles. In the following steps, you'll switch the 3D view to see your layers from another viewpoint.

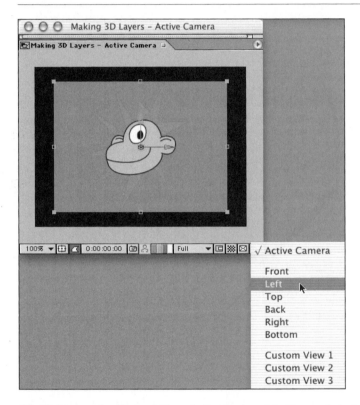

13. Make sure the **Current Time Indicator** is set to **Frame 0**. In the **Composition** window, click the **3D View** pop-up menu and select the **Left** view. If you can't locate the pop-up menu, it's likely because it's hidden. Use the **resize tab** on the bottom right of the **Composition** window to make it a little wider, which should reveal the **3D View** menu at the bottom right. Alternately, you can access the 3D view settings anytime by choosing **View > Switch 3D View** on the menu toolbar.

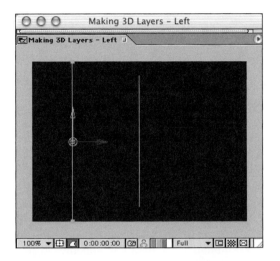

14. Observe the **Left** view. The **Gray Solid** layer is selected and is positioned 100 pixels along the Z axis behind the **monkey.ai** layer. Since the monkey.ai and Gray Solid layers are 2D objects without depth, you will see only a line representing each object's position. It may help you to click each of the two lines to look at the 3D layer handles. The red X-axis handle is pointing directly toward you, the green Y-axis is pointing straight up, and the blue Z-axis is pointing to the right, toward the normal view (the Active Camera).

You will learn all about 3D views in the next section. Here we wanted to give you a preview of seeing your 3D layers from the left side to help you visualize the layers in depth during this exercise.

15. Select the **Active Camera** view from the **3D View** pop-up menu in the **Composition** window to return to the default view. This is the most important view because it is what After Effects will render if you preview or make a movie.

In a future exercise, you'll learn that you can have more than one camera! To begin, however, it's important to understand the principle of an invisible camera through which you are viewing your scene.

16. In the **Timeline** window, click the **Stopwatch** for the **X Rotation** and **Y Rotation** properties to set keyframes for **Frame 0** of the **Gray Solid** layer. Accept the default value of **0** for both properties.

17. Move the **Current Time Indicator** to **0:00:00:29**. Set the **X Rotation** value to **−30** degrees, and set the **Y Rotation** value to **30** degrees.

18. Click **RAM Preview** in the **Time Controls** panel to view your 3D animation. Although this result may look just like a simple skew effect to you, After Effects is moving this flat artwork in true 3D space. More-realistic 3D results come later in this chapter, when you learn to animate the lighting and camera.

19. Save your project and leave it open for the next exercise.

Overview of 3D Views

The previous exercise gave you a brief introduction to **3D views**. These views allow you to see 3D layers from different angles in your Composition window. When you first start working with 3D layers, it can be a little disorienting to see any 3D view other than the default view, which is called Active Camera view. With a little experience, though, you'll quickly get comfortable with using different 3D views.

Active Camera is the view that will be rendered when you preview or create a final movie; this is the view that you should use to evaluate your work. The other 3D views are available to aid you in positioning your layers accurately in 3D space.

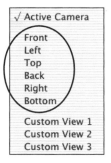

The Front, Left, Top, Back, Right, and Bottom views are **orthogonal views**. An orthogonal view shows the position of your layers but does not show perspective. This can take some getting used to. Again, with a little experience, you'll feel comfortable with these views.

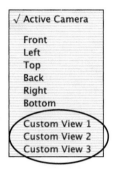

There are three custom views that show your layers in perspective. These views look more natural because they use perspective. They are also quite useful because you can adjust each view position to your liking.

You'll find yourself using all the views, however, because working in 3D space requires that you view objects from many positions while creating your design. You'll also see that orthogonal views, without perspective, are useful because they give you a good idea of object relationships, proportions, and positions. Perspective changes the size of objects, which can be a hindrance at times. For these reasons, the orthogonal views are valuable.

In the following exercise, you'll learn to use each view and to move layers in space using the various 3D views. As you'll soon see, using 3D views is the best way to position objects accurately in your 3D world.

2. _____Using 3D Views

In this exercise, you'll check out all of the 3D views. The purpose of doing so is to become familiar with each view and how it shows object relationships in the Composition window. By the end of this exercise, you'll be able to relate your objects' positions to each view and understand the view options.

The three custom views can be positioned anywhere you like. You'll learn to create your own custom views at the end of the exercise.

You'll also learn to move and position layers in space using 3D views. This is one of the main tasks when working in 3D. For most people who are new to 3D, positioning objects in 3D space is one of the hardest concepts to get comfortable with.

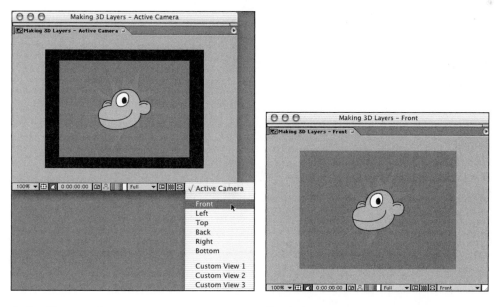

Active Camera view   _Front view_

1. The **Making 3D Layers** composition should still be open. If it's not, open that file now. Make sure the **Current Time Indicator** is set to **Frame 0** and the **Gray Solid** layer is selected. Select the **Front** view from the **3D View** pop-up menu in the **Composition** window. Compare this view to the Active Camera view.

In Active Camera view, the Gray Solid layer looks smaller than it does in the Front view. That's because there is no perspective in the Front view. When the perspective is taken away, the width (the X axis) and height (the Y axis) are displayed at their full values.

2. Now select the **Back** view from the **3D View** menu. You are looking at the back of the Gray Solid layer, so you can't see the monkey.ai layer. Again, the width and the height of the Gray Solid layer are displayed without perspective.

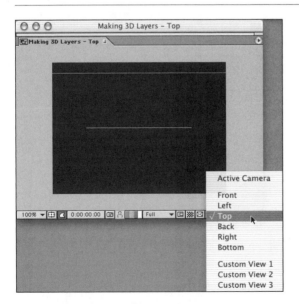

3. Select the **Top** view. You are looking down on the monkey.ai and Gray Solid layer. Note that the Gray Solid layer is selected, so its axis handles are visible. Those handles appear only on layers that are selected.

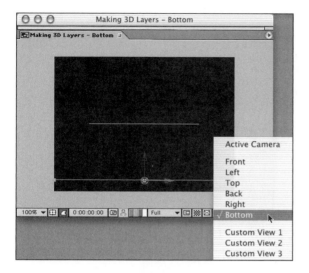

4. Select the **Bottom** view. Now you are looking up at the two layers. The Gray Solid layer is still selected, so its axis handles are visible.

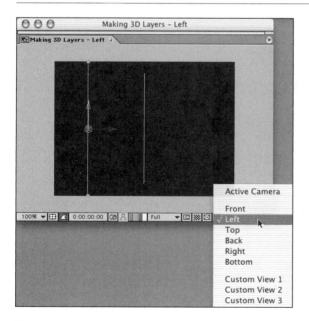

5. Select the **Left** view. You will see the side of the graphic again. The Gray Solid layer is still selected, so its axis handles are visible.

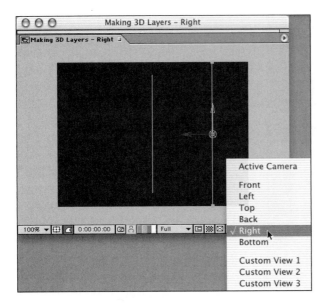

6. Select the **Right** view. This is another side view, from the right side. The Gray Solid layer is still selected, so its axis handles are visible.

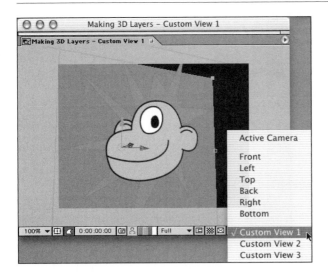

7. Select **Custom View 1**. Notice that this view has perspective. This is After Effects' default Custom View 1. You will learn to create your own custom views soon.

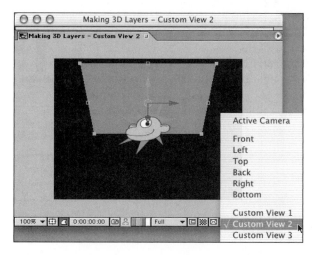

8. Select **Custom View 2**. The default view looks down from the center of the 3D world.

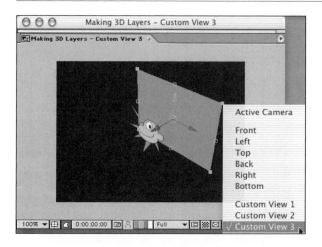

9. Select **Custom View 3**. The default viewpoint is located above and to the right of center.

You've looked through all the possible views for this composition now. These views are available to compositions that contain 3D objects. They make sense to use only when viewing 3D layers, because they are very helpful when you're positioning your objects in 3D space.

10. Save your project. Leave the **Making 3D Layers** composition open for the next exercise.

At this point, you should be able to make some sense out of each view. If you are having trouble with this, it's okay. Understanding the 3D views is the hardest part of learning 3D in After Effects. With repetition, you'll be able to understand where you are in the 3D world using each view.

3. ─────────Changing Custom Camera Views

In the previous exercise, you became familiar with views and learned how they can help you see the 3D environment. You can easily change any of the custom camera views while you are working. This exercise will show you how.

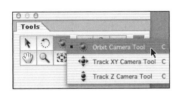

1. Select **Custom View 1** from the **3D View** menu.

2. In the **toolbox**, select the **Orbit Camera** tool. In the **Composition** window, drag the cursor across the window to orbit your view, as you see here.

Note: This tool is simply changing the view, not moving the artwork!

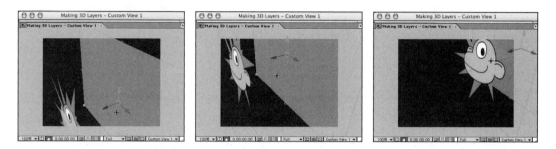

3. Select the **Track XY Camera** tool to change your view in the X axis or the Y axis. As before, this tool is simply changing the view. The artwork remains in the same position.

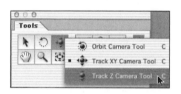

4. Select the **Track Z Camera** tool from the **toolbox** and experiment with changing your view in the Z axis, as you see here. The Z axis controls how close or far the camera view is from your artwork. Once again, note that this tool changes only the view of the artwork, not its position.

That's all there is to it. If you toggle between Custom View 2 and Custom View 1, you'll see that Custom View 1 is just where you left it. It will be set to the last view you created until you change it again.

View	Window	Help	
New View			⌥⇧N
Zoom In			.
Zoom Out			,
Resolution			▶
Show Rulers			⌘R
Hide Guides			⌘;
✓ Snap To Guides			⇧⌘;
Lock Guides			⌥⇧⌘;
Clear Guides			
Show Grid			⌘'
Snap to Grid			⇧⌘'
View Options...			⌥⌘U
Hide Layer Controls			⇧⌘H
Reset 3D View			
Switch 3D View			▶
Set 3D View Shortcut			▶
Switch To Last 3D View			
Look At Selected Layers			⌥⇧⌘\
Look At All Layers			
Go To Time...			⌘G

5. To reset the view to the default, choose **View > Reset 3D View. Note:** Any change you make to a custom view is permanent until you change it again. Resetting the view will set it back to the default, unless you change it again.

---

6. Save the project and close this composition. You won't be using it again in this chapter.

Multiple Views

This feature allows you to have multiple views of the same Composition open, and each window can have its own view settings.

To add a new view, choose **View > New View**.

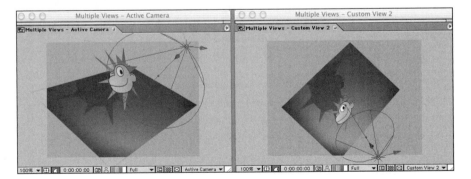

Once you create another view, you can set the 3D view and the magnification of the new window. Shown here are Active Camera and Custom View 2. This Composition already has a light applied to it. Doesn't it look cool? You'll learn to do this very soon!

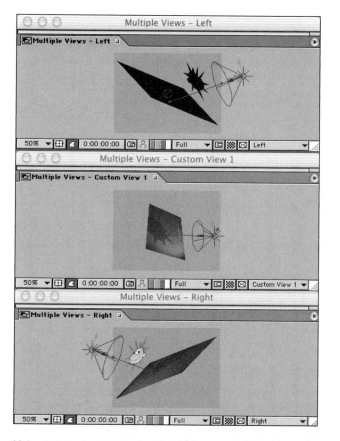

Using this technique, you can add as many different views as you wish. The reason to have multiple views is to get a better idea of how your artwork is positioned in 3D space.

4. Lighting in 3D

So far, everything you've looked at has been very flat. You might still be wondering why 3D is such an exciting feature if you can achieve a lot of the same effects more easily using a simple skew tool in an illustration program. Adding lights is when working in 3D starts to get magical.

In After Effects, a light is a special type of layer. When you add a light, it shows up in the Timeline window, just as any other layer does. However, lights have their own set of properties, all of which can be keyframed for animation, of course!

After Effects offers several types of lights, but in general, you'll probably use the Spot type most often. It provides many options and the greatest range of control. In the following exercise, you'll learn how to add lights, adjust the options, and position lights within your compositions.

1. In the **Project** window, double-click the **3D Lighting** composition to open it. You'll see that it already contains three layers, two of which have 3D layers turned on. Press the **spacebar** or click the **RAM Preview** button in the **Time Controls** panel to see that the layer **6** has already been animated in 3D. Select layer **6** and press the **U** shortcut key to see which properties have been animated for this layer. You'll see that keyframes have been set for the **Y Rotation**. When you're finished observing the animation, rewind the Timeline to **0:00:00:00**.

You should know how to do this kind of animation based on the first exercise in this chapter. If you want to practice, turn the 3D Layers switch off in the Timeline, then turn it back on to reprogram this animation on your own! Since this exercise is focused on lighting, I've chosen to do the animation work for you, but don't let that stop you from gaining more practice!

2. Deselect layer **6** by clicking off it in an empty space in the Timeline Window. Choose **Layer > New > Light**.

Light Settings

Name: Light 1

Settings

Light Type: ✓ Spot
- Parallel
- Point
- Ambient

Intensity:

Cone Angle: 90   degrees

Cone Feather: 50   %

Color: [ ]   [✎]

☐ Casts Shadows

Shadow Darkness: 100   %

Shadow Diffusion: 0   pixels

Note: Shadows are only cast from layers with 'Casts Shadows' enabled to layers with 'Accepts Shadows' enabled.

Cancel   OK

3. In the **Light Settings** dialog box, click the double arrow next to **Light Type** to see the pop-up menu. Notice that there are four types of lights.

---

4. Select each type from the menu and observe that only the Spot type offers the Cone Angle and Cone Feather options.

Settings

Light Type: Parallel

Intensity: 100   %

Cone Angle: 90   degrees

Cone Feather: 50   %

Parallel light is directional, unconstrained light from an infinitely distant source. This type is best used when you want light to fall evenly on all objects, and you want the light to come from a specific direction.

Settings

Light Type: Spot

Intensity: 100   %

Cone Angle: 90   degrees

Cone Feather: 50   %

Spot light is constrained by a cone. The Spot type is the most useful because you can control all aspects of the light.

Settings

Light Type: Point
Intensity: 100 %
Cone Angle: 90 degrees
Cone Feather: 50 %

Point *light is unconstrained, omnidirectional light. This type is best when you need something like a bare light bulb that lights up whatever is nearby.*

Settings

Light Type: Ambient
Intensity: 100 %
Cone Angle: 90 degrees
Cone Feather: 50 %

Ambient *light has no source and casts no shadows. It contributes to the overall brightness of your composition. It is best used as a secondary light to bring up the general lighting level for all objects. Use it sparingly, if at all.*

5. From the **Light Type** pop-up menu, select the **Spot** light option. Make sure the **Casts Shadows** option is checked. Click **OK**.

Notice that the light has taken effect on the two layers that have 3D turned on. 3D must be activated on a layer for the light to have an effect. Also notice that even though you turned on the Casts Shadows option, no shadow is cast on the background. You'll fix this next.

6. In the **Timeline** window, select layer **6** and press **U** again. This closes the twirly. Manually, click the twirlies for layer **6** until you see the **Material Options** properties. Click the **Casts Shadows** property to select the **On** value. Click the twirlies for the **Pale Lime Green Solid 1** layer to display its **Material Options** properties. Change the value in **Accepts Shadows** to **On**. In the **Composition** window, notice that the 6 layer now casts a shadow. The shadow is quite hard-edged and not very attractive yet. You'll fix this soon.

*Note: The layer named **after effects** hasn't been turned into a 3D layer, so it does not cast any shadows. Only 3D layers cast shadows in After Effects. You can control whether some layers are 3D and some are not by clicking the 3D Layers switch for each layer, as you did in Exercise 1. For this exercise, leave the **after effects** layer alone and do not convert it to 3D.*

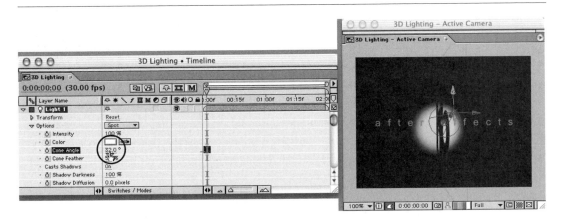

7. In the **Timeline** window, click the twirly to display the **Light 1** layer properties, and then click the twirly to display the **Options** properties. Drag across the **Intensity** value to see the effect of changing the intensity. Intensity is how bright you want the light to be. When you're done, set the **Intensity** value back to **100%**.

8. Drag across the **Cone Angle** value to see the effect of changing it. Observe that the cone angle constrains the light in degrees. When you're done, return the **Cone Angle** value to **90%**.

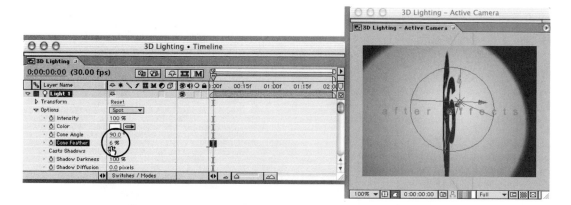

9. Drag the **Cone Feather** value and observe how the edge of the light gets softer or harder. When you're done, return the **Cone Feather** value to **50%**.

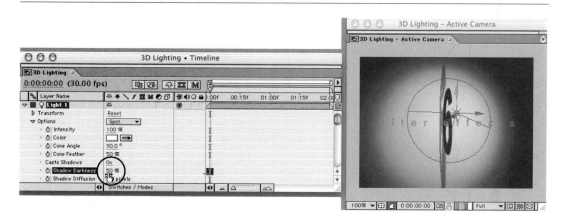

10. Set the **Shadow Darkness** value to **50%**. Observe the results in the **Composition** window.

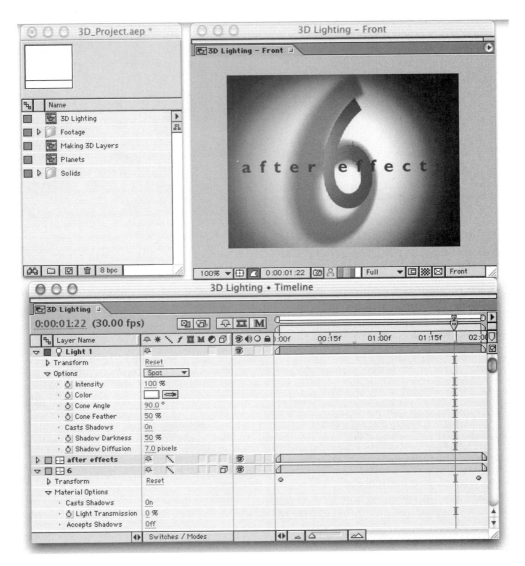

11. Move the **Current Time Indicator** to **0:00:01:22** to see the effect that the lighting has on the **6** as it animates. Set the **Shadow Diffusion** property to **7** pixels. Shadow diffusion softens the edges of the shadow. If the shadow still looks bad, make sure that the **Pale Lime Green Solid 1** layer is set to high quality. Note that you haven't set any keyframes, meaning that you're making a global change to the Shadow Diffusion over the entire composition. Leave the **Current Time Indicator** at **0:00:01:22** to see the position of the **6** layer at this point in its animation. Because it is turned toward the camera view, you can see the lighting changes better.

In the following steps, you will learn to position the light using the axis arrow handles.

12. Leave the **Current Time Indicator** at **0:00:01:22**, and in the **Composition** window, drag the red **X-axis** handle to move the light to the far left of the composition. Locate the **Point of Interest** control. (It's the round icon with the cross mark that extends from the center of the light.) Drag this control to fully illuminate the **6**. The default position of the light was center screen. Lighting effects are always more interesting if they are set to an angle, like you just learned how to do!

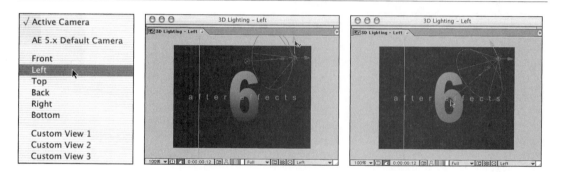

13. Select the **Left** view from the **3D View** pop-up menu in the **Composition** window. Drag the green **Y-axis** handle up to the top. Drag the **Point of Interest** control to fully illuminate the **6**.

*The text in the **after effects** layer does not change in this view because it is a 2D layer. Only 3D layers are affected by changing views.*

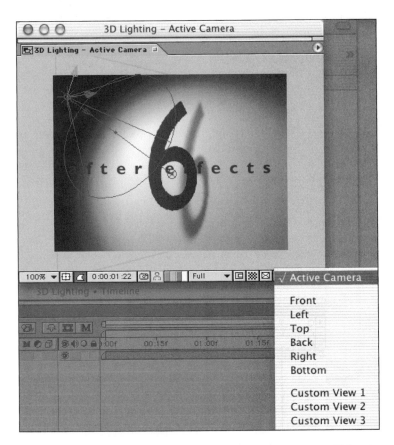

14. Select the **Active Camera** view from the **3D View** menu. This takes you back to the view you'll see when previewing or rendering a final movie. Click **RAM Preview** in the **Time Controls** panel to play the animation. Since this composition is complex, it may take a few minutes to render. You can also use the various RAM preview options discussed in earlier chapters to help it render faster.

Lights can be colors other than white. In the following steps, you'll change the color of Light 1 to red. Then you'll add a green light and a blue light to your composition.

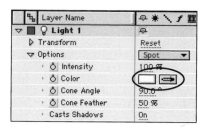

15. In the **Timeline** window, click the **Light 1** layer's **Color selector** block. Change the color to **red**.

You can have more than one light in a composition. Using multiple lights can create interesting shadows and colored effects. Next, you'll learn to add extra lights.

Light Settings

Name: [Light 2]

Settings

Light Type: [Spot]

Intensity: [100] %

Cone Angle: [90] degrees

Cone Feather: [50] %

Color: [ ] [ ]

☑ Casts Shadows

Shadow Darkness: [100] %

Shadow Diffusion: [0] pixels

Note: Shadows are only cast from layers with 'Casts Shadows' enabled to layers with 'Accepts Shadows' enabled.

[Cancel] [OK]

16. Choose **Layer > New > Light**. In the **Light Settings** dialog box, click the **Color selector** block. Change the color to **green**. Back in the **Light Settings** dialog box, accept the current settings by clicking **OK**.

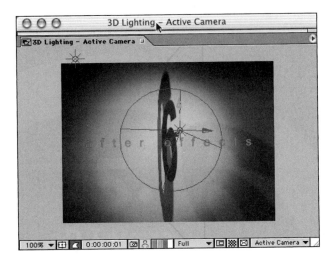

Observe the new two-color light. Its position is fine, so you don't need to adjust it.

17. Select **Layer > New > Light**. In the **Light Settings** dialog box, click the **Color selector** block. Change the color to **blue**. Back in the **Light Settings** dialog box, accept the current settings by clicking **OK**.

18. Drag the red **X-axis** handle to the far right. Drag the green **Y-axis** handle to the bottom. Drag the **Point of Interest** control to the center of the **6**. Get a sense of how moving these settings provides different lighting effects.

19. Click **RAM Preview** in the **Timeline Controls** panel to view your animation. **Note**: This takes a long time to display.

In this exercise, you merely set lights in a single position and did not set keyframes for them. Notice, however, that every light has properties, and every property has a Stopwatch icon. Any time you see that Stopwatch icon, it means that a property can be animated! This exercise was just a starting point that helped you begin to learn about lights. Take some time on your own to set up some lighting animation to better understand the feature.

20. Save your project, and leave the **3D Lighting** composition open for the next exercise.

NOTE | Using the Intensity Property with Lights

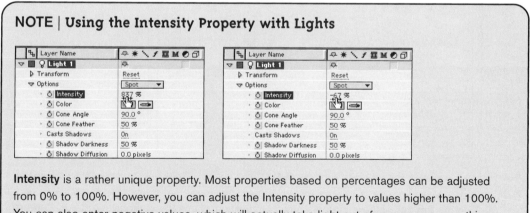

Intensity is a rather unique property. Most properties based on percentages can be adjusted from 0% to 100%. However, you can adjust the Intensity property to values higher than 100%. You can also enter negative values, which will actually take light out of your scene, something like a black hole. Used judiciously, both high values and negative values can be beneficial ways of controlling light in your scene.

5. ——————Adding and Animating a Camera

So far in this chapter, you have been working with a camera view that was set up by After Effects, called Active Camera view. All compositions that contain 3D layers employ a single, default Active Camera view. Once you add 3D layers to your composition, this Active Camera view appears and displays 3D perspectives on 2D objects, including the capability to control lights and cast shadows.

You probably didn't realize that it is possible to add a new camera to your composition. This may sound odd at first. Why would you want or need to have more than one camera?

The most common reason to add a camera is because the default camera cannot be animated. This means that you *could* move the artwork or lights in 3D, but you *could not* animate the point of view of those objects with the default camera. When you add a new camera layer manually, it contains properties that can be keyframed. Setting keyframes for the camera layer makes it possible to create animations with camera views, not just by moving artwork and lights.

In the following exercise, you'll learn to add a camera, position it in your 3D world, set keyframes on its position, and animate it through your 3D world.

1. In the **Project** window, create a new composition. Name the composition **Basic Camera Comp,** and use the settings you see here.

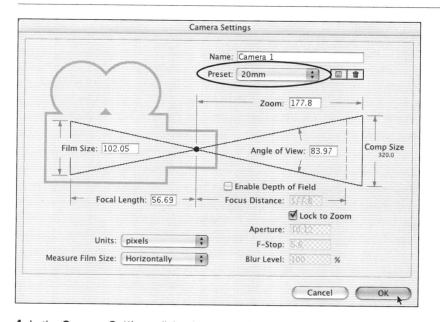

2. Add the artwork **monkey1.ai** from the **Footage** folder located in your **Project** window to the **Timeline**. Change the **Scale** property to **30%**, and click the **3D Layers** switch for the layer to set it to 3D.

3. Choose **Layer > New > Camera**. This opens the **Camera Settings** dialog box.

4. In the **Camera Settings** dialog box, set the **Preset** option to **20mm** and click **OK**. This view should look different from the default camera because you've changed the lens setting. When you add your own camera, you have access to a lot of new controls that affect the outcome of the movie.

The Camera Settings dialog box might seem very intimidating. It's different from most dialog boxes because of the picture and all the new terminology. A chart describing the options in this dialog box follows at the end of this exercise. The 20mm lens preset you chose provides a very wide-angle lens view, which is going to look like a fish-eye lens, if you know what that is. Basically, setting the lens to a lower number will produce a more dramatic perspective that will be more obvious when you get close to objects. If you are not familiar with photography or cameras, that's okay. If you are, you will probably marvel at these settings, which emulate those of conventional movie cameras.

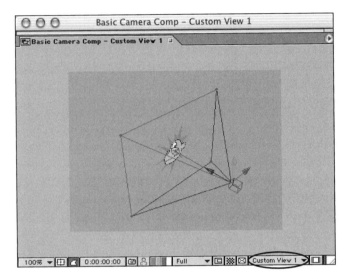

5. Select **Custom View 1** from the **3D View** menu in the **Composition** window. This view allows you to see the camera you just added. **Note:** The camera layer must be selected in the Timeline window in order to see the new camera. You cannot see the outline of the camera if you are in Active Camera view. That is why we suggested that you change the view to Custom View 1.

6. Click the twirly for the **Camera 1** layer, then click the twirly for **Transform** to see the camera properties. This exercise focuses on ways to move the camera while getting feedback from the view in the Composition window and the property values in the Timeline.

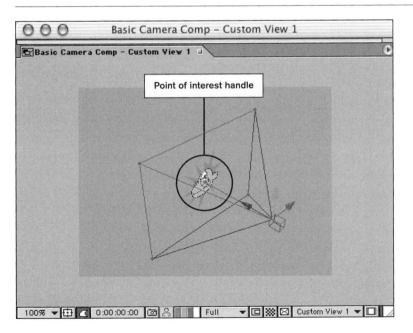

7. In the **Timeline** window, move the **Position X axis** value back and forth and notice that the camera appears to pivot and rock from side to side in the Composition window. Move the **Position Y axis** value back and forth and notice that the camera appears to pivot and rock up and down. It's pivoting on the point of interest, which has been set by default on the center of the Composition window.

Any time you add a new camera to a 3D composition, the new camera will place its point of interest in the center of the screen, just as it has done here. You had a little experience with the Point of Interest setting when you worked with lighting earlier. This setting tells a camera or a light where to point itself.

The point of interest is the origin point on the Camera layer from which all X, Y, and Z values are based. It is what causes the camera to pivot.

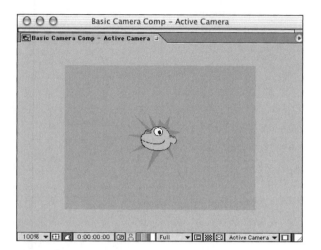

8. Change from **Custom View 1** to **Active Camera** view and move the **X** and **Y** values again to see how the pivot effect looks from this view. You won't see the outline of the camera any longer, because After Effects doesn't show you the camera in Active Camera view. What you will see, which is almost more important, is how this movement will appear in the final rendering or preview of this composition.

The custom view lets you see the camera, whereas Active Camera view shows you what the camera is seeing. It's extremely important to be aware of this distinction so that you cannot only position the camera properly but also accurately gauge what the camera is going to see. For this reason, you will change views often when staging camera animations.

NOTE | Active Camera Versus New Cameras

In this exercise, you have added a new camera, called Camera 1. When you choose Active Camera view, you are seeing what Camera 1 sees. If you added more than one camera to this composition, Active Camera view would show the results of whatever camera was selected in the Timeline. Because you have only one camera in this Timeline, whenever you choose Active Camera view, you see the point of view of Camera 1.

9. Make sure that you are in **Active Camera** view and that the **Current Time Indicator** is set to **Frame 0**. Set the **Stopwatch** for the **Position** property. Move the **X** position to **0.0**, and move the **Y** position to **277.0** for the **Camera 1** layer. Leave the **Z** position alone. Lock the **monkey.ai** layer so you don't accidentally move it.

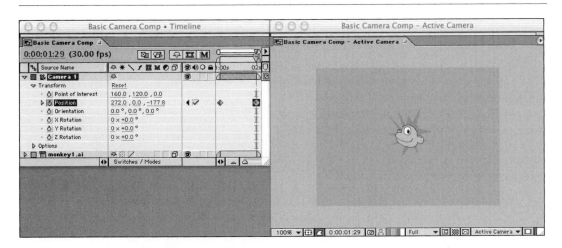

10. Move the **Current Time Indicator** to **Frame 59**. Change the **X** position to **272.0** and the **Y** position to **0.0**. Preview the animation by pressing the **spacebar** or clicking **RAM Preview**.

11. Save the project and close this composition. You won't be using it again in this chapter.

You could have made the animation you just created by using a camera (which you just did) or by moving the object. This exercise was not intended to show you how to create an interesting animation but instead was geared to point out some issues of moving the camera. In particular, you should now be aware of the impact that the Point of Interest, Active Camera view, and Position settings have on camera animations. The next exercise kicks your awareness of moving and animating cameras up another notch.

6. _____Animating the Point of Interest

The last exercise contained only a single 3D object. However, you would rarely create a camera animation to view a single object. Camera animations are much better suited for flying by multiple 3D objects, because the camera creates a sense of space and depth that can't be achieved simply by moving the objects themselves. This exercise builds on the previous one, adding complexity as it deals with handling multiple objects and animating the point of interest. The first part of the exercise shows you how to set up a composition that contains multiple objects set at different depths along the Z axis of the 3D environment. The second part deals with getting your camera to fly by the objects along a path you control.

1. Create a new composition and name it **planet comp**. Use the settings you see here.

2. Import **redplanet.psd**, **cyanplanet.psd**, **blueplanet.psd**, and **yellowplanet.psd** into the **Project** window from the **chap_13** folder. Choose to **Merge Layers** when prompted.

3. Drag **redplanet.psd**, **cyanplanet.psd**, **blueplanet.psd**, and **yellowplanet.psd** from the **Project** window into the **Timeline**, and arrange them in the order you see here. When you drag these images into the Timeline, each image is automatically centered in the Composition window. It will look as though only one image is in the Composition window, because all the planets are the same size and they are stacked right on top of one another, obscuring all layers but the top one. You'll soon fix this by moving them in 3D space. Click the **3D Layers** switch for each layer to turn it into a 3D object.

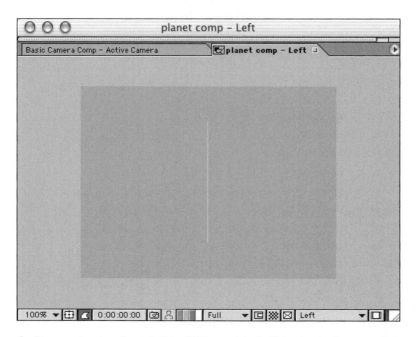

4. Change the view from **Active Camera** to **Left**. This shows the artwork from the left side. Again, this shows the four layers stacked right on top of one another, which causes them to look like a single line.

You'll be moving the layers next to position them farther apart on the Z axis. The Z axis represents depth. By moving the objects on their Z axes, you will be spreading them apart in 3D space, as you might see planets in a telescope, or better yet from a spaceship!

5. Select **cyanplanet.psd** in the **Timeline**. You'll see the layer's axis handles appear in the **Composition** window. Click the blue **Z-axis** handle (your cursor arrow will show a small **z**, indicating that this is the Z axis), and drag the artwork to the right in the **Composition** window. Your screen should look like the one here.

Note: Selecting the image in the Timeline first causes its selection handles to appear, making it easier to isolate in the composition. This is a great technique for positioning artwork in 3D space, since by default, all artwork is on the same Z axis until you move it. You will often encounter overlapping artwork, and this technique helps you isolate it in order to move it.

6. Select **redplanet.psd** in the **Timeline** window. This causes its selection handles to appear in the **Composition** window. Move it to the right, as you see here.

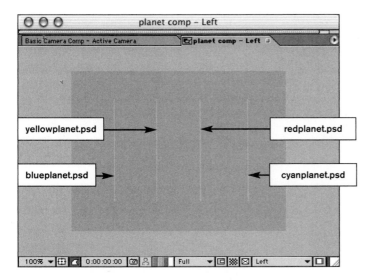

7. Repeat this process with **yellowplanet.psd** and **blueplanet.psd** until your Composition window looks like this one.

8. Change the view from **Left** to **Top**. This allows you to view the artwork from above. You are going to move the artwork from this view next. Drag the **Composition** window to make it larger so you can see the gray work area around the screen. Drag your artwork into the positions you see here.

Your artwork is now positioned so that a camera can fly around the objects and look at them. That's what you'll learn to do next.

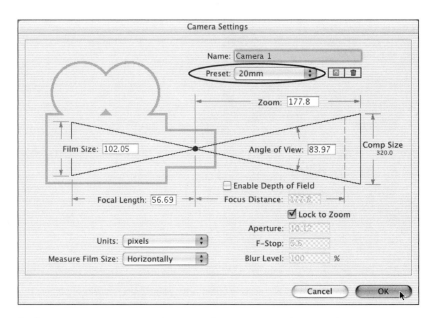

9. Choose **Layer > New > Camera**. This opens the **Camera Settings** dialog box. We explain the settings in this dialog box in a chart at the end of this exercise. For now, make sure the **Preset** option is set to **20mm** and click **OK**.

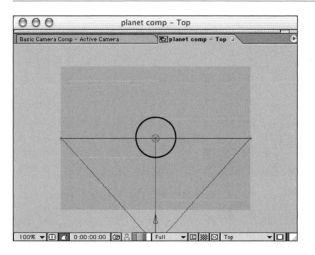

10. Camera 1 appears in your **Timeline** and also in the **Composition** window. Adding a camera to your composition is the only way to animate a camera. As you can see, the camera has handles similar to the ones 3D objects have. However, it also has a triangular shape attached to it that simulates the field of view from the lens. The Point of Interest is circled in the screen here. It indicates which way the camera is pointed—currently straight ahead.

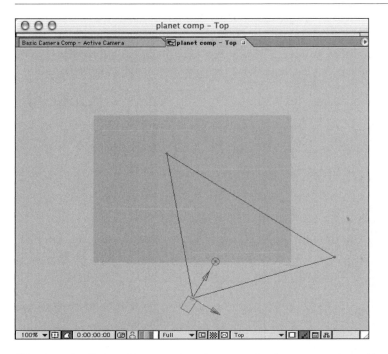

11. In the **Timeline**, click the twirly for **Camera 1**. Click the **Transform** twirly, and then click the **Stopwatch** icon for the **Point of Interest** and **Position** properties.

You have now set the keyframes to be active. Next, you'll move the camera to set it for this first keyframe.

12. Move the **Point of Interest** handle to match what you see here. You have moved the camera to face the **cyanplanet.psd** object.

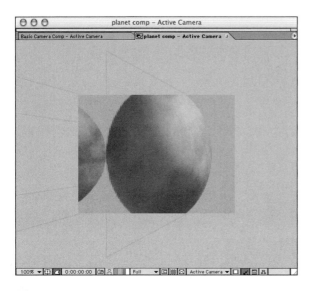

13. Change the view to **Active Camera** to see what the camera sees.

Notice the distortion in the closest planet—it doesn't look circular. That's because the camera is basically looking at a piece of flat artwork from an oblique angle, causing it to distort. You'll fix this later, after getting the camera animation set up.

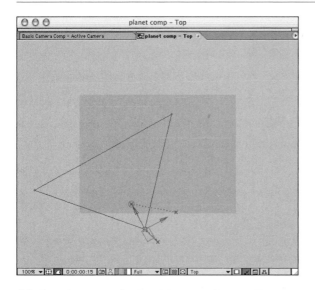

14. Return the view to **Top**. Move the **Current Time Indicator** to **Frame 15** and change the **point of interest** to match what you see here. Move the camera's position as well by moving the **rectangle** icon closer to the **Point of Interest** handle.

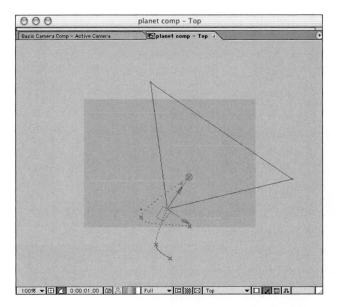

15. Move the **Current Time Indicator** to **Frame 30**. Move the camera to match what you see here by moving the **point of interest** and **camera** position.

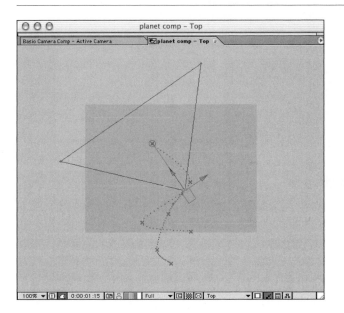

16. Move the **Current Time Indicator** to **Frame 45**, and move the **point of interest** and **camera** to match what you see here.

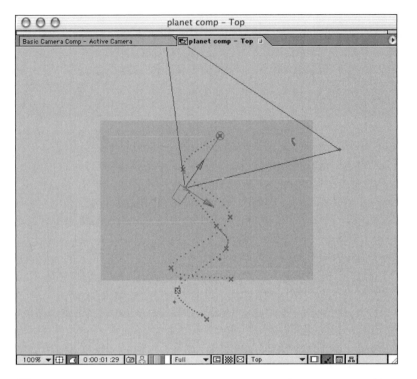

17. Move the **Current Time Indicator** to **Frame 59**. Move the **point of interest** and **camera** to match what you see here.

---

18. Move the **Current Time Indicator** to the first frame, change the view to **Active Camera**, and press the **spacebar**. Your camera should fly through the path of planets! The only problem is that the planets all look like cardboard cutouts, rather than being round! You'll fix this next.

---

19. In the **Timeline**, select **cyanplanet.psd**, **redplanet.psd**, **yellowplanet.psd**, and **blueplanet.psd** by holding down the **Shift** key and clicking each layer.

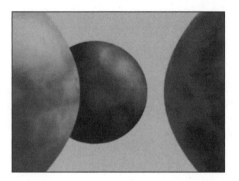

20. Choose **Layer > Transform > Auto-Orient**. The **Auto-Orientation** dialog box opens. Choose **Orient Towards Camera** and click **OK**. This tells each object to face the camera as it moves by.

21. Test your movie again by pressing the **spacebar**. Voilà—all the planets are now circles! Change the view to **Top** and scrub the **Current Time Indicator** to see what After Effects is doing behind the scenes. It's causing each planet to rotate as the camera flies past. Pretty amazing!

22. Save the project and close this composition. You won't be using it again in this chapter.

Camera Settings Dialog Box

In the last exercise, you had a chance to add a camera to your composition, and you briefly saw the dialog box for the camera. As promised, here's a handy chart that describes the numerous features found in this dialog box.

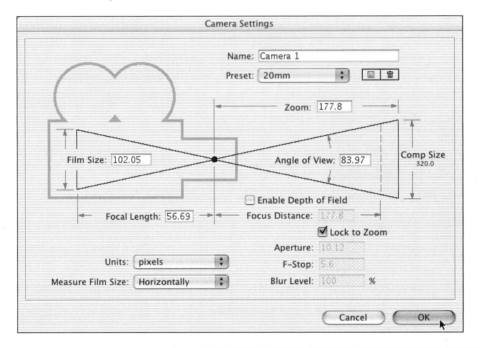

Camera Settings	
Setting	**Description**
Name	After Effects will automatically name your camera for you, or you can give your camera a name. This name will appear in the Timeline layer that represents the camera object.
Preset	The camera ships with a menu of different presets. These presets emulate different 35mm lens settings with different focal lengths. The angle of view, zoom, focus, distance, focal length, and aperture are all stored with each preset. You can create your own custom camera presets by changing the settings and clicking the Disk icon to save them.
	continues on next page

Camera Settings *continued*

Setting	Description
Angle of View	The focal length, film size, and zoom settings all determine the angle of view. You can create wide-angle lens settings or more narrow lens settings, depending on what value is entered.
Enable Depth of Field	Affects the distance range in which the image is in focus. Images outside of the distance range are blurred. This setting is used to create realistic camera-focusing effects.
Focus Distance	Specifies the distance from the camera's position at which objects appear in focus.
Aperture	Increases or decreases the size of the lens. This setting affects depth-of-field blur as well as f-stop positions.
F-Stop	Indicates the ratio of focal length to aperture. Analog cameras specify aperture size using the f-stop measurement. If you specify a new value for this setting, the value for Aperture changes dynamically to match it.
Blur Level	Indicates the amount of depth-of-field blur in an image. A setting of 100% creates a natural blur as dictated by the camera settings. Lower values reduce the blur.
Film Size	Relates directly to the composition size. When you specify a new value for film size, the zoom changes to match the perspective of a real camera.
Focal Length	The distance from the film plane to the camera lens. The camera's position represents the center of the lens. When you specify a new value for the focal length, the zoom changes to match the perspective.
Units	The units of measurement in which the camera setting values are expressed.
Measure Film Size	The dimensions used to depict the film size.
Zoom	The distance from the position of the camera to the image plane.

7. ————————————Camera Options and Settings

You might have noticed that—besides the Transform properties—there is another set of camera properties, named Options.

The **Options properties** are based on physical camera options. In everyday life, actual cameras have lenses, apertures, shutters, and other components that work together to allow cameras to take photographs. Each camera you create in After Effects can have its own lens settings, aperture settings, and other features that allow you to adjust the way your 3D world is "photographed."

If you've done a bit of photography in the past, these camera terms are probably familiar to you. If you've never studied photography, these terms are probably a bit of a mystery. That's okay; you don't have to know photography. In this exercise, you'll learn the function of each option by adjusting the settings and observing the results.

1. Open the **Planets** composition and make sure that **Active Camera** view is set in the **Composition** window. Use **RAM Preview** to watch the animation. A camera move using Transform settings is already programmed for you, and all the planets were set up in 3D space ahead of time. You'll be changing the animation using features in the **Options** menu.

2. In the **Timeline** window, display the properties for the **Camera 1** layer, and then display the **Options** properties by clicking the corresponding twirly. Observe the following options: **Zoom**, **Depth of Field**, **Focus Distance**, **Aperture**, and **Blur Level**.

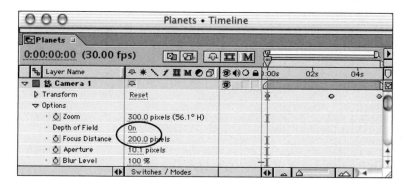

3. Change the **Zoom** setting to **300**. Click **RAM Preview** again and notice how much more dramatic the perspective is. The neat thing about changing the zoom is that it is a lot easier than animating the Transform properties of the camera, and it often has more impact on the overall perspective.

4. Toggle the **Depth of Field** setting **On** and **Off**, and notice that the planets get blurry and come back into focus. Make sure the setting is **On** before continuing. Change the **Focus Distance** from **100** to **200**. Observe the planets come more into focus, but notice that far away, planets are less focused.

The Focus Distance property can be controlled only when the Depth of Field option is enabled. In real life, all camera lenses have depth of field. This means that not everything is in focus at the same time. A real lens can focus only within a certain range of depth. This range where everything is in focus is called the depth of field. In computer graphics, a virtual lens does not have depth of field— everything can be in focus at the same time. The Depth of Field property in After Effects provides more realistic camera focusing effects for your projects.

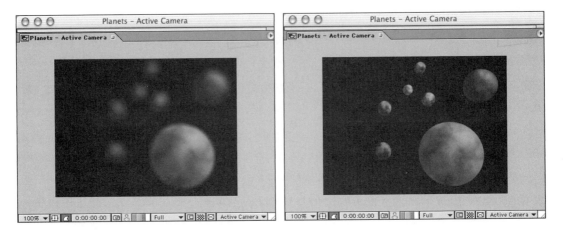

5. Drag the **Blur Level** value left and right to see the range of blur level setting. When you're done, return it to **100%**.

Blur Level allows you to control how much focus blur is applied to the objects in your scene. This is not related to a real camera setting. A real camera's focus blur is determined by the physical characteristics of the lens and cannot be changed. The Blur Level option in After Effects is a computer graphics setting that gives you another means of controlling the focus blur. Blur Level values can be set greater than 100%.

6. Click **RAM Preview** to see the **Depth of Field** property and its associated settings in action.

7. Save your project and leave the **Planets** composition open for the next exercise.

8. _____Previewing Draft 3D and Wireframe Interactions

Your computer has to work hard to create 3D images. Previewing an image or rendering a final movie will take longer whenever 3D layers are involved. Lights, shadows, and depth-of-field options take longer to process, and they slow down previews. You can speed up previews in After Effects 3D by using two buttons.

The **Draft 3D button** (in the Timeline window) disables lights, shadows, and depth of field. Clicking on this button allows you to work in Draft mode, which is After Effects' low-quality setting. You'll still see your objects in 3D, and your previews will be faster.

The **Wireframe Interactions button** (in the Timeline window) allows you to move your objects in the Composition window as wireframe objects, which won't render color, texture, fills, gradients, and so on. This setting enables much quicker interactivity while dragging objects. Wireframe preview is suitable for many positioning purposes and will speed your workflow.

In this exercise, you'll learn to use the Draft 3D button and the Wireframe Interactions buttons to speed up previews of your 3D work.

1. The **Planets** composition should be open from the preceding exercise. In the **Timeline** window, locate and click the **Draft 3D** button. Notice that the **Depth of Field** effect becomes disabled in the **Composition** window.

The Draft 3D button disables lights, shadows, and depth of field.

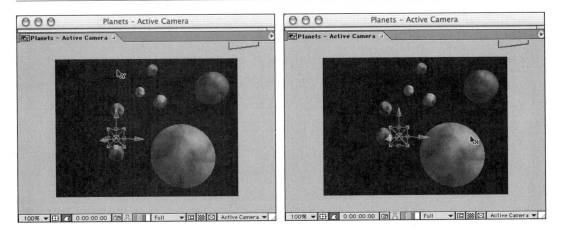

2. Click the **Wireframe Interactions** button.

3. Select the **Planet 5** layer in the **Timeline**. In the **Composition** window, drag the green **Y-axis** handle up to a position similar to that shown in the first image. Drag the red **X-axis** handle to the right as shown. Notice that the **Planet 5** object is displayed as a simple wireframe while it is being the moved.

If you turn the Wireframe Interactions button off and move the artwork again, you'll see that the object looks solid and maintains its color, texture, gradient, and so on. The Wireframe Interactions button is useful for when you are positioning objects in 3D and you want to go a little faster.

4. Click **RAM Preview** and observe that the preview renders relatively quickly. As After Effects is building the RAM preview, the motion might appear jerky, but it will build the preview faster and play it back smoothly once it's finished.

5. Save your project and close After Effects.

> ### NOTE | Zaxwerks 3D Invigorator
>
> Of particular interest to After Effects users is a third-party plug-in called 3D Invigorator. Unlike After Effects' 3D objects, which never have true depth, objects built with this plug-in are true 3D models created within After Effects from vector artwork. Check out the plug-in at **http://www.zaxwerks.com**.

If this was a hard chapter for you, don't think badly of yourself (or me!). Honestly, there's a very big learning curve to this subject, and the more you practice, the easier it will become. Take a break and get ready for one of the most advanced aspects of After Effect—expressions.

16.

Expressions

Adding Expressions	Creating Property Relationships
Multiplying Expression Values	Effects and Expressions
Disabling Expressions	Deleting Expressions	Expressions Library
Converting Expressions to Keyframes

chap_16

After Effects 6
H•O•T CD-ROM

The word **expression** is a mathematical and programming term that describes the creation of a new value that is based on an old value. What this might mean to you as an After Effects user is that you can use expressions to take the value from one property and apply it to another property. One example of this that you'll learn to create in this chapter is how to make the blur of some lettering get more blurry as the letters become more spaced apart. Being able to base the reaction of one property on the transformation of another is only achievable through expressions. It makes for interactive animations that react to physical changes in the artwork.

Expressions are written in JavaScript, but the beauty is that you don't have to know how to write any code at all to use them because After Effects will automatically write them for you. However, to make expressions more than minimally useful, you will want to know how to modify the expressions that After Effects creates, which is fairly easy once you learn a few rules. This chapter will show you some practical examples of using expressions and will also teach you how to make modifications to them.

I. ————————————Adding Expressions and Creating Relationships

Chapter 11, "*Parenting*," introduced you to the Pick Whip tool for creating parent-child relationships. The Pick Whip is also used to create expression relationships. In this exercise, you'll learn how to add an expression to a layer's Scale property and create a one-to-one relationship with another layer's property.

1. Open **Expressions Project.aep** from the **chap_16** folder. Save a copy of it in your **AE6 HOT Projects** folder on your hard drive.

2. Double-click the file **Creating Expressions Comp** to open it. This composition contains two layers with distinct names, yet identical artwork, and no keyframes. You are going to animate one layer and learn to apply an expression to the other layer.

3. In the **Timeline** window, display the **Scale** property for both layers. You can do this by selecting both layers with the **Shift** key and then pressing **S** on your keyboard. Select the **Scale** property for **rocket_2**.

4. Choose **Animation > Add Expression**. Alternatively, press **Option+Shift+=** (Mac) or **Alt+Shift+=** (Windows) and click the **Stopwatch** icon. This will not set a keyframe; instead, it will set an expression. A new icon appears in the **Switches** panel of the **Timeline** that includes a **Pick Whip** icon in the middle. The icon to the left is called the **Post-Expression Graph** button, which turns on a value graph for the expression (not demonstrated in this chapter, but useful to see the velocity of changes to the property), and to the right is the **Expression** language menu, which you will learn about later in the chapter.

5. Click the **Pick Whip** icon for the **rocket_2 Scale** property and drag it to the **rocket_1 Scale** property.

The expression field appears automatically as soon as you apply the expression from one layer to another

6. Notice that a JavaScript expression is automatically written in the **rocket_2 Expression** field.

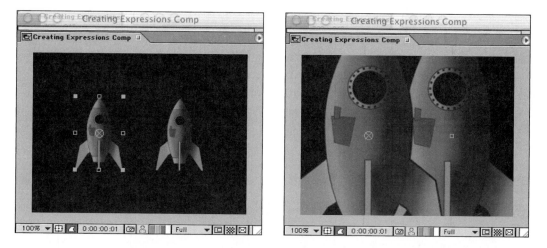

7. Drag the **rocket_1 Scale** value back and forth to change it. Observe that both rockets now scale equally when the **rocket_1** value is changed because the **rocket_2** value is tied to the value **rocket_1** via the expression.

This is pretty neat, but couldn't you do the same thing with parenting? Yes! This is a very simple example of creating an expression, but it doesn't really reveal the power of expressions yet. In following exercises, things will get more exciting—I promise!

8. Set the **rocket_1 Scale** property back to **20%**. Save your project and leave this composition open for the next exercise.

WARNING | Unique Layer Names

Expressions use a layer's name to refer to layer objects. You should give layers unique names before using expressions. Without unique layer names, expressions can refer to the wrong layer object. Rename layers, if necessary, to ensure that all layers have unique names. To rename a layer, simply select the layer name and press **Return** (Mac) or **Enter** (Windows).

2. _____Creating Property Relationships

In this exercise, you'll continue to work with the same layers and composition to build on what you've learned so far. The first expression you created borrowed the Scale property from one layer and applied that value to another. Since this same result could also have been achieved with parenting, you may not be too impressed at this point. Now, however, you are going to tell After Effects to take the value of the Scale property for one layer and apply it to the Rotation property of another layer. Once completed, if you move the scale from one layer to 30 percent, the other layer will rotate 30 degrees. That is something you cannot do with parenting!

1. The file **Creating Expressions Comp** should be open from the last exercise. Select the **rocket_2** layer and press **R** on your keyboard to display the **Rotation** property.

---

2. Option+click (Mac) or **Alt+click** (Windows) on the **Rotation Stopwatch** icon. Notice that an expression is enabled for the **Rotation** property on the **rocket_2** layer. You can tell that the expression is active because the word "rotation" appears within the **Expression** field on the layer.

3. Click the **Pick Whip** icon for the **rocket_2 Rotation** property and drag it to the **rocket_1 Scale** property.

4. Drag back and forth over the **rocket_1 Scale** value. Notice that the **rocket_2** layer scales and rotates, and the **rocket_1** layer just scales.

Making a rocket rotate based on the scale of another rocket is not a very practical example of when to use expressions, but it illustrates their power. Future exercises in this chapter offer more practical uses, now that you've learned the basic principle!

5. Save your project, and leave the composition open for the next exercise.

3. ———————Multiplying Expression Values

As you've seen, once you use the Pick Whip to create property relationships, JavaScript code is automatically written in the Expression field. If you wish, you can edit and modify this code. This allows you to create fairly sophisticated relationships between properties.

In this exercise, you will learn a simple way of modifying an expression by multiplying its values. You can use this same method to add, subtract, multiply, or divide the value of an expression. Although it might sound intimidating to write your own code, you'll soon see that this method is quite straightforward.

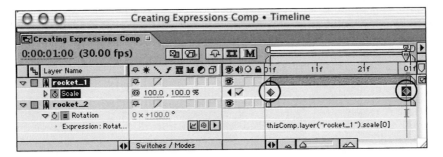

1. Make sure the **Time Marker** is at **Frame 1**, and that the **Scale Property** is showing for the **rocket_1** layer. Set the **Scale Property** to **20%**. Click the **Stopwatch** icon for **Scale** to set a beginning keyframe. Move the **Time Marker** to **00:01:00**, and set a keyframe for the **Scale** property by changing the **Scale** to **100%**.

You are doing this so you can see how the expressions you've created interact with keyframes and with properties that change over time. Once you set the second keyframe, you'll see both rockets grow in size. The expression is doing its job!

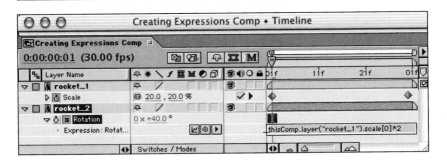

2. Move the **Time Marker** back to **Frame 1**, click in the **rocket_2 Rotation Expression** field, and place your cursor at the end of the line of code. Type ***2** and then either press **Enter** on your numeric keypad or click outside the **Expression** field to activate the expression.

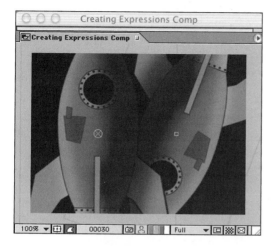

3. Scrub the **Time Marker** and notice that the rotation of **rocket_2** is doubled.

4. Save your project and close **Creating Expressions Comp**. Leave your project open for the next exercise.

NOTE | Math Operations Using Expressions

In the last exercise, you added an asterisk and a value at the end of the line of JavaScript code to multiply the value for the Rotation property by 2. This method allows you to easily modify the automatically generated JavaScript code. The following chart lists the symbols to use for other simple math operations in JavaScript expressions. As you can see, they are just standard math symbols.

Simple Math Operations	
Symbol	**Operation**
+	Add
–	Subtract
*	Multiply
/	Divide

Use these symbols to perform simple math operations on expression values. You can change an action to its opposite—for example, clockwise to counterclockwise rotation—by using *–1 (or any other value).

4. ──────────Text, Effects, and Expressions

Expressions can be used to control the options or parameters of Effects properties, as well as those of Transform properties. In this exercise, you will see an example of using a text layer and the Fast Blur effect.

1. Create a new composition and name it **blur**. Make the duration **0:00:02:00**.

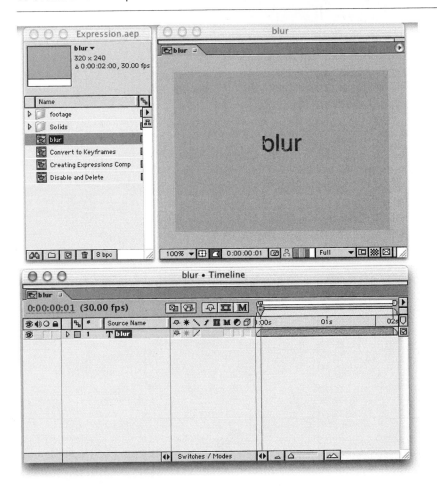

2. Create a new text layer by choosing **Layer > New > Text**. The text insertion cursor will be blinking inside the **Composition** window. Type the word **blur** on the screen. A new text layer will appear inside the **Timeline** called **blur** (once you click off the text). Make sure the text is center justified by clicking on the center icon in the **Paragraph** window (not shown here).

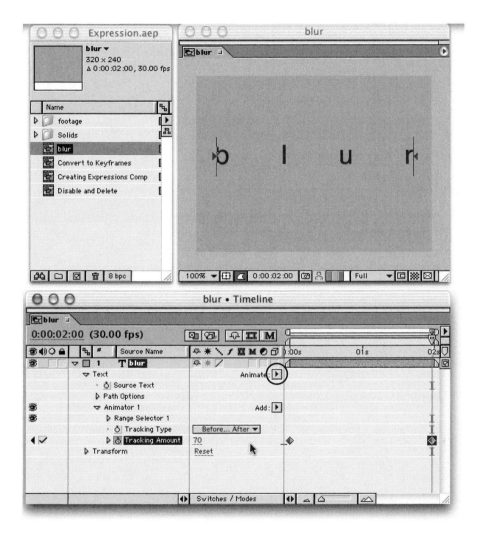

3. Make sure the **Current Time Indicator** is on the first frame in the **Timeline** window. Click the twirly for the text layer to reveal the **Text** properties. Select **Tracking** from the **Animate** menu. Properties for **Animator 1** will appear, including a **Tracking Amount** property. Activate the **Stopwatch** for the **Tracking Amount** property. This should create a keyframe on **Frame 0:00:00:00**. Move the **Current Time Indicator** to the last frame (press **End** on your keyboard). Change the **Tracking Amount** to **70**. Your screen should look like the picture you see here.

4. Choose **Effect > Blur & Sharpen > Fast Blur**. This adds the **Fast Blur** effect to the **Basic Text** effect, though it won't look any different yet. That's because you haven't applied any settings to the Fast Blur effect. That will come in a later step.

5. In the **Timeline**, click the twirly next to **Effects**. Click the twirly next to **Fast Blur** to reveal its settings. Next, you'll create an expression.

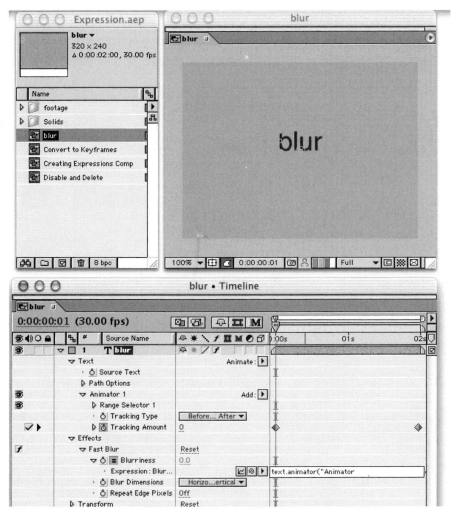

6. Move the **Current Time Indicator** back to **Frame 0:00:00:00**. **Option+click** (Mac) or **Alt+click** (Windows) on the **Stopwatch** for **Blurriness** to add an expression. You'll see JavaScript code appear immediately for the **Blurriness** value. Drag the **Blurriness Pick Whip** to the **Tracking Amount** value. More code will be added to the JavaScript field.

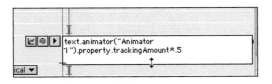

7. At the end of the JavaScript code, type ***.5**. This multiplies the **Tracking** value by **.5** and applies the resulting blur to the **Blurriness** property. You won't see any change at first, because the value inside the first keyframe of the **Tracking** value is **0**.

```
text.animator("Animator
1").property.trackingAmount*.5
```

If you have trouble getting to the end of the JavaScript code, you can expand the text field by placing your cursor at the bottom of the field. The cursor will change to an up and down arrow. Dragging the text field with this arrow will expand what it shows.

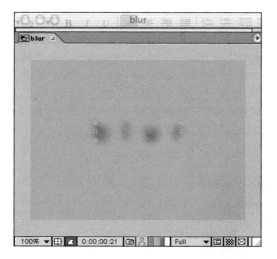

8. Move the **Current Time Indicator** to a frame in the middle of the composition, and you'll see that the amount of tracking directly affects the amount of blur. Try changing the **Tracking** value to something else, like **.2** or **.7**, and scrub the **Timeline** to see the result. You'll be able to pick a value that is pleasing to you this way.

Note: When you scrub, you have to let go of the mouse to see the blur effect render—it doesn't render as you scrub.

What's neat is that you didn't use any keyframes for the Fast Blur effect. After Effects is collecting values for the blur based on how much the Tracking Setting values are. This makes for motion that is synchronized—the blur amount directly relates to the tracking amount. You can use expressions to control all types of Effects properties and values; this is just a taste of the sort of results this kind of programming achieves.

9. Close the **Blur** comp. Leave your project open for the next exercise.

5. _____Disabling an Expression

After Effects will sometimes disable an expression if it contains an error. You can also choose to disable an expression manually. You may want to disable a complex expression to speed up your previews. Or you may have several expressions chained together and want to debug the chains. Or you may simply be unsure as to whether you want to use an expression or not, and choose to disable it until you decide.

In this exercise you'll learn how to disable an expression. Enabling an expression is equally easy.

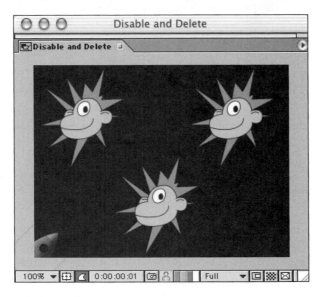

1. Double-click the **Disable and Delete** composition to open it.

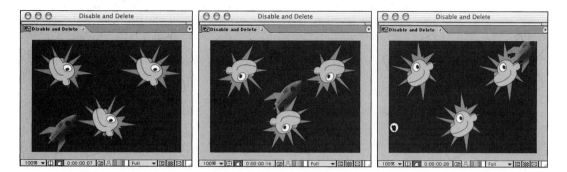

2. Scrub the **Time Marker** and notice that the monkeys rotate as the rocket position animates.

All of the monkey layers have expressions that chain to the first monkey's Rotation value. In the following step, you will disable the first expression in the chain. This will disable all rotations of the monkey layer.

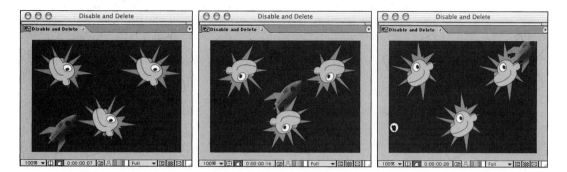

3. Select the **monkey_1** layer and press the **R** key. This does the same thing as clicking its twirly to locate its properties, only it isolates the **Rotation** property so your screen is less cluttered. Click the **Enable Expression** switch next to the **monkey_1 Rotation** property. This switch looks like an equal symbol. Notice that it changes to an equal symbol with a slash through the center when switched off.

4. Observe, in the **Composition** window, that the monkey images no longer rotate when you scrub the **Time Marker**. The chain of expressions are disabled.

Disable means to temporarily turn off, but the good news is that it doesn't mean the work is forever lost as if it was deleted. Re-enabling the expression is easy as you'll see in the next step.

5. To re-enable the expression, click the **Enable Expression** switch so that it appears as an equal symbol.

6. Save your project, and leave the composition open for the next exercise.

NOTE | Deleting Expressions

Deleting an expression is very simple. There are three possible ways to do it.

- Choose **Animation > Remove Expression**.

- **Option+click** the = sign (Mac) or **Alt+Click** the = sign (Windows).

- **Option+click** the **Stopwatch** icon (Mac) or **Alt+click** the **Stopwatch** icon (Windows).

JavaScript's Expressions Library

If you know JavaScript, you can use the Expressions library to write your own JavaScript expressions.

To access the library menu, click the **Expression language menu** icon for an expression.

You can select from the entire library of JavaScript language elements used by After Effects. An experienced JavaScript programmer could have a blast with all these options. If you don't know JavaScript, you can ignore these options or decide to learn what they mean by reading a JavaScript book!

6.————Converting Expressions to Keyframes

After Effects obtains the values for an expression frame-by-frame during the rendering process. In essence, expressions are calculated "live." If you have a particularly complex expression, this can slow down rendering time. You can convert expressions to keyframes to speed up rendering. In this exercise, you'll select a property that already has an expression, and you'll learn to use the **Convert Expression to Keyframes** option.

1. Open the **Convert to Keyframes** composition.

2. Click **RAM Preview** in the **Time Controls** palette, and notice that the rocket moves through the **Composition** window as the dial makes a complete rotation.

The rocket layer has an expression that references the dial layer. In the following steps, you will convert the rocket expression to keyframes.

3. Select the **rocket.psd** layer **Position** property. It doesn't matter where your **Current Time Indicator** is in the **Timeline**.

4. Choose **Animation > Keyframe Assistant > Convert Expression to Keyframes**.

5. Observe the keyframes created from the expression. Also notice that the expression is now disabled, as demonstrated by the **Enable Expression** icon with the slash through it.

6. In the **Composition** window, observe the motion path created by the keyframes.

7. Save and close your project. You're finished!

That's it for this chapter. You've gotten a sampling of the power of expressions. If you like working with expressions, the sky's the limit. They are truly boundless tools that can be combined in infinite new ways.

17.

Audio

Adding Audio to Your Compositions	Previewing Audio
Adding Markers and Comments	Audio Palette
Adjusting Volume Levels	Audio Effects

_chap_17_

After Effects 6
H·O·T CD-ROM

Most professional animation and motion graphics work contains music, narration, sound effects, or all of these at once. After Effects is primarily a tool for motion graphics and animation, but it would not be complete if it didn't offer the opportunity to include audio. Audio files can be used simply as a "guide track" to help you choreograph moving images, or they can be used to create the final audio track for your movie.

It's important to understand that After Effects is not designed to be an audio authoring tool. Other programs are better equipped to record and process a finished music track.

However, if you want to combine a finished music track with sound effects, narration, and animation, After Effects is a great tool for the job. You can import a prerecorded track, fit it to your image, make volume adjustments, and output the final audio track with your movie. The audio capabilities of After Effects shine as a finishing tool.

Overview of Audio in After Effects

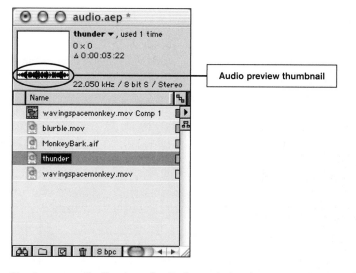

Audio preview thumbnail

You import audio files into the Project window just as you import any other file—by choosing **File > Import**. When you select audio footage in the Project window, rather than seeing the little image preview, you see a waveform indicating that the footage is audio-only.

Audio file formats supported by After Effects include QuickTime movies, AIFF (a popular Mac audio file format), and WAV (a popular Windows audio file format). These and other audio files supported by QuickTime, including MP3, AU, and Mac Sound (Mac OS only), can be imported directly into After Effects. Once imported, audio footage can be used as layers in your compositions.

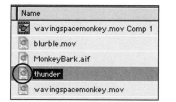

The QuickTime movie icon looks the same for images or for audio. Please refer to the section on importing QuickTime movies in Chapter 3, "*The Project*," if you need more information.

You can preview audio footage from the Project window by double-clicking on the audio items. This opens a little audio player and allows you to hear the audio track before you place it in your composition.

I. ——————Adding Audio to Your Compositions

In this exercise, you will learn to use the **Audio switch** and to view audio **waveforms** in the Timeline window.

1. Copy the **chap_17** folder from the **H•O•T CD-ROM** to your hard drive. Open the **audio.aep** project file from the **chap_17** folder. Navigate to your **AE6 HOT Projects** folder and save a copy of the document there so you won't alter the original.

2. Double-click on **wavingspacemonkey.mov Comp 1** to open it.

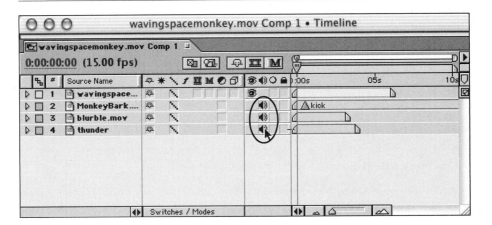

3. In the **Timeline** window, click the **Audio** switch for the **MonkeyBark.aif**, **blurble.mov**, and **thunder** layers.

4. Click on the twirly for the **thunder** layer to display the **Audio** properties. Then click on the **Audio >
Waveform** twirly to reveal the **Waveform** graph.

*The waveform is a graphical representation of recorded sound. In the image above, the two squiggly
lines represent the left and right stereo tracks. Each squiggly line represents the frequency and volume of the audio track.* **Tip:** *The Audio switch must be on to see the waveform.*

5. Save and leave the composition open for the next exercise. You'll learn how to preview the sound next!

2. ——————Previewing Audio

One of the least intuitive parts of After Effects, strangely enough, is previewing sound. In this exercise, you will learn how to preview audio using the Time Controls panel and the **Audio Preview** command. You will also learn to preview sound in the Timeline by dragging the Current Time indictor. It sounds simple, and it is. It's just easier to figure out when someone shows you how to do it.

1. In the **Time Controls** panel, make sure the **Audio** button is on, and then click **RAM Preview**. The first few seconds of your audio is previewed along with the animation. Notice that the audio and image must be rendered first, which causes a slight delay. When you are done previewing, click anywhere or press any key on your keyboard to stop the preview.

*Warning: If you have turned the sound down on your computer, you may not hear the audio. If this is the case, locate the **Sound** control panel for your operating system and check the sound levels.*

2. Move the **Current Time Indicator** to the middle of the composition. Choose **Composition > Preview > Audio Preview (Here Forward)**. When you want to stop the preview, click anywhere or press any key.

Notice that the audio plays immediately from the current Current Time Indicator position forward. No prerendering is necessary using this preview method. The image does not move using this method, so you cannot use it to check synchronization, but it's the quickest way to hear all of your audio tracks.

3. Press the **period** key on the numeric keypad. This is the keyboard shortcut to the **Audio Preview (Here Forward)** command. Click anywhere or press any key to stop the preview.

4. In the **Timeline** window, scrub the **Current Time Indicator** while holding down the **Cmd** (Mac) or **Ctrl** (Windows) key. Notice that the audio previews. Stop scrubbing the **Current Time Indicator** to stop the preview.

*Note: Scrubbing audio can result in jerky playback. It's best to use **RAM Preview** with the **Audio** button turned on for smooth movement and sound. If you stop moving the **Current Time Indicator** while keeping the mouse button depressed, a short section of audio will loop.*

5. Leave the composition open for the next exercise.

TIP | Setting the Audio Preview Duration

You can set the **audio preview duration** in the Preferences window. You might want to limit the duration if you have a long piece and you want to concentrate on how a small part of it is sounding and synchronizing with your live action or animation.

Choose **After Effects > Preferences > Previews**. In the **Preferences** dialog box, set the **Duration** option to the desired time and click **OK**. This will cause the audio preview to last for a specified length of time. The audio preview will be cut short if the audio footage is longer than the amount of time entered in this setting.

3. —————————Adding Markers and Comments

When working with audio layers, it's often helpful to add **markers** as references to emphasize beats in the music or passages of narration. These markers help to visualize where beats in the music occur and can be used to synchronize sound with motion events.

After Effects offers an easy way to add markers while listening to audio. In this exercise, you will learn to add markers while listening to an audio layer. We've already added one marker with a comment to the layer used in this exercise. You will add more.

1. In the **Timeline** window, hide the **thunder** layer properties. Click the **Solo** switch for the **MonkeyBark.aif** layer to solo the layer. You learned about the Solo switch in Chapter 8, "*Layers*."

2. Select the **MonkeyBark.aif** layer. Display the **Audio** and **Waveform** properties by clicking those twirlies.

3. Press the **period** key on your numeric keypad to preview the **MonkeyBark** audio track. While listening to the audio track, press the **asterisk** key on the numeric keypad each time you hear a major beat. Click anywhere or press any other key to stop the preview.

Tip: *If you want to delete a marker,* ***Ctrl+click*** *(Mac) or* ***right-click*** *(Windows) it to delete.*

Notice that a marker has been added at each press of the asterisk key. They look like small pyramids in the Timeline. These markers provide a helpful guide when you are setting animation keyframes that you want to match up perfectly with audio beats.

Warning: *The markers may not appear as quickly as you would like. This has to do with the processor speed of your computer and the fact that After Effects just doesn't seem to do this task very quickly. If this technique doesn't work, there could be different causes. One is that the layer must be selected for this process to work. Also, if* ***Num Lock*** *is pressed on your keyboard, the feature will not work. If you work on a laptop and don't have a numeric keypad, you can add a marker manually. Do this by choosing* ***Layer > Add Marker****. Here too, a layer must be selected to access this feature. In addition, this process is not useful for timing to the beats of the audio, because it is too slow. You can, however, move a marker once it's created.*

4. Double-click on any one of the markers you just added to create a comment. This opens the **Marker** dialog box. Anything you enter in the **Comment** field will show up on the **Timeline** as a comment. Other features of this dialog box are listed in a chart at the end of this exercise.

5. Save your project, and leave this composition open for the next exercise.

The Marker Dialog Box

The Marker dialog box allows you to do more than simply enter a comment for the purpose of adding sound notations. You can access the Marker dialog box by double-clicking on any marker you've created. Here's a chart that explains the features of this dialog box.

Marker Dialog Box Options	
Setting	**Description**
Comment	Adds a comment to the marker, allowing you to write notes to yourself inside the Timeline.
Chapter	A chapter marker is a QuickTime-only feature that offers the capability to jump to a certain part of a QuickTime movie. You can add the chapter name easily to After Effects by filling in this field. To program the chapter, please visit **http://developer.apple.com/ quicktime/** to learn about advanced programming and development for QuickTime.
Web Links	If you create a Web link, your user can click on the part of the movie that contains the link and be transported to its destination. This is a QuickTime-only feature.
URL	Indicates the Web site that you want users to be taken to when they click the Web link. This is a QuickTime-only feature.
Frame Target	Allows you to set up the destination Web page in a separate window from the QuickTime movie containing the Web link. The target naming conventions are part of standard HTML targeting. You can learn more about this and other advanced features of QuickTime at the Apple Web site. This is a QuickTime-only feature.

The Audio Palette

Occasionally, you will need to fix a sound that you've chosen to work with in your After Effects project. You can use the **Audio** palette to make changes to your audio files. Again, we want to reiterate that After Effects is not a good sound-editing tool. The Audio palette is reserved for small, simple audio needs.

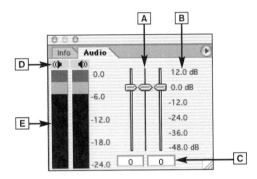

To access the Audio palette, choose **Window > Audio**. The Audio palette has several tools that allow you to work with volume levels. The following chart describes these tools.

Audio Palette Controls	
Setting	**Description**
A. Volume Level controls	The Volume Level controls are used to adjust the volume.
B. Level units	The Level units indicate the change of volume in decibels.
C. Level values	The Level values indicate the exact value of each Volume Level control.
D. Audio Clipping Warning icons	The Audio Clipping Warning icons indicate when the audio is being "clipped"; when these icons are red, the audio level is loud enough to cause loss of audio data.
E. VU meter	The VU (**V**olume **U**nit) meter offers feedback about the volume of your audio; it displays the volume range as the audio plays.

While you're previewing audio, the VU meter will display green, yellow, and red volume levels. Green audio levels during playback indicate that your volume level is perfectly safe. Yellow peaks indicate caution, but your levels are still safe. Red peaks during playback indicate that your audio levels may be in danger of being clipped. If your audio is clipped, the Audio Clipping Warning icons will turn red.

When audio is clipped, some of the audio frequency data is lost. However, if you are very familiar with digital recording techniques, you may be comfortable with some audio clipping. The safe rule of thumb is to keep the levels high enough that your audio bounces into the red zone occasionally, but never so high that audio data is clipped. If you follow this guideline, your audio will be safe while maintaining maximum fidelity, clarity, and richness of tone.

If you intend to use After Effects to finish the audio for your final movie, we recommend that you learn more about digital audio and work with other tools besides After Effects. You'll find a list of audio-related resources at the end of this book in the "*Resources*" appendix.

4. —————————Adjusting Volume Levels

In this exercise, you will learn to adjust the **Master Volume Control** slider and the **left** and **right channel** sliders.

1. In the **Timeline** window, make sure the **MonkeyBark.aif** layer is selected.

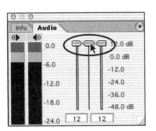

2. If the **Audio** palette is not already open, choose **Window > Audio**. Drag the **Master Volume** control (the center slider) up to **12.0 dB**.

The center slider is the Master Volume control. It moves both the left and right channels equally from their current position.

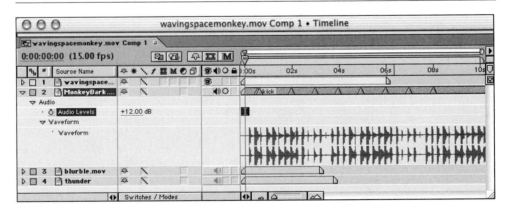

3. In the **Timeline** window, notice that the waveforms grow larger when you increase the volume.

4. Press the **period** key on your numeric keypad to preview the audio.

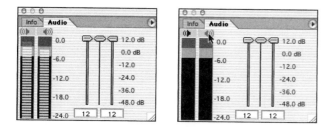

5. In the **Audio** palette, watch the **VU** meter while the audio previews. Both the left and right channels are too loud, which has caused the **Audio Clipping Warning** icons to turn red. Click on each **Audio Clipping Warning** icon to reset it to black.

Note: Previewing audio does not alter your original audio footage data. Volume settings affect only the preview and output of audio data. It is perfectly safe to preview your audio files with clipping. You will learn how to output a final audio file in the upcoming Chapter 18, "Rendering Final Movies."

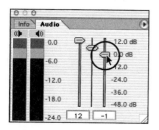

6. Drag the **right channel** slider to approximately **–1.0 dB**.

Note: The audio layer must be selected, or you cannot adjust the channel slider.

7. Notice that the **right channel** waveform shrinks as the volume decreases.

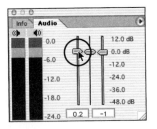

8. Drag the **left channel** slider to approximately **0.0 dB**.

9. Press the **period** key on your **numeric keypad** to preview the audio. Both channels are set about as loud as possible without clipping.

10. Save your project and close it.

TIP | Setting Volume Level Keyframes

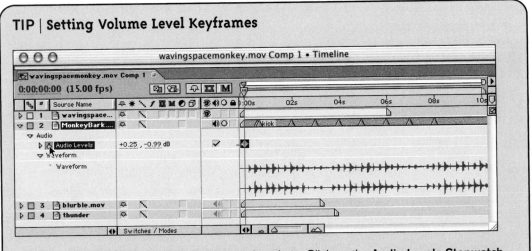

You can set keyframes for Volume Level control settings. Click on the **Audio Levels Stopwatch** icon to enable keyframes for the **Volume Level** controls. This is useful if you want to fade sound in or out or animate a sound effect by increasing or decreasing its levels on separate keyframes.

TIP | **Production Bundle Audio Effects**

In the production bundle, there are audio effects that you can add to audio layers. Choose **Effect > Audio** and choose an audio effect from the menu. Listen to the results, practicing the previewing techniques that you learned in this chapter. As stated previously, you can animate these audio effects as well.

BONUS MOVIE | **render_audio.mov**

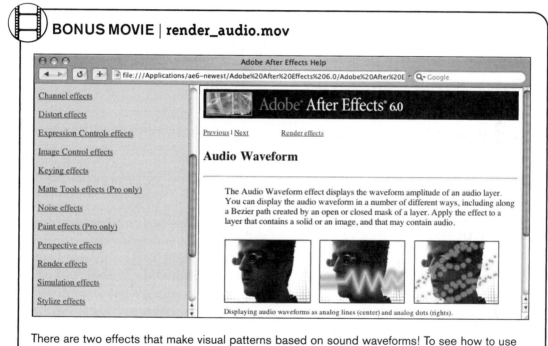

There are two effects that make visual patterns based on sound waveforms! To see how to use these effects, watch the bonus movie called **render_audio.mov** from the **movies** folder located on the H•O•T CD-ROM. Special thanks to Paavo Stubstad for providing his music for this exercise. If you're interested in contacting Paavo, he can be reached at Paavo@ojai.net.

You're all done with a short and sweet chapter on audio. Rock on. Next, you'll learn how to render your final movies.

18.

Rendering Final Movies

Render Queue	Render Settings	Output Module Settings
Rendering Audio	Saving an Alpha Channel or Motion Mask
Rendering for the Web	Saving RAM Previews
Creating and Using Rendering Templates	Collecting Files
Creating Macromedia Flash Output

chap_18

After Effects 6
H•O•T CD-ROM

Throughout this book, you've learned how to preview movies for your own viewing. This chapter focuses on making movies that are the final product of your work. In After Effects, you can create many types of movie output from a single composition. For example, you can output a single composition to video, motion picture film, CD-ROM, streaming video on the Web, GIF animation, HDTV, and many other output types. The variety of choices available are one of the great strengths of After Effects.

The process of outputting your project is called **rendering**. Just as an artist renders a painting, After Effects follows your instructions and renders the final movie. Each pixel of your image and each audio signal is determined and rendered to the output type of your choice.

This chapter was saved until late in the book because it's a complicated subject. Although all the output choices After Effects offers are wonderful, they also require careful explanation. Don't be intimidated, though; this is a necessary step in your After Effects education, and you will always have this chapter available to refer to if you get stuck on a future project.

QuickTime Versus AVI/Video for Windows

If you use a Mac, you have likely heard of QuickTime, and if you use Windows, you've likely heard of AVI/Video for Windows. When rendering movies, After Effects defaults to producing QuickTime in its Mac version and AVI/Video for Windows in its Windows version.

In our opinion (and it is shared by the majority of video professionals), QuickTime is the superior format because of its versatility. QuickTime is used much more often than AVI/Video for Windows in professional video production. This is because of its versatility and resolution capabilities.

QuickTime is used on projects ranging from low-end Web and multimedia presentations to feature-film formats that are shown in movie theaters. AVI/Video for Windows is best suited for the low end of the publishing spectrum—it is ideal for Web movies. One of the benefits of the AVI/Video for Windows format is that so many more consumers own PCs than Macs. If you surf the Web much, you will find that the low-end video formats of AVI/Video for Windows, Real Video, and QuickTime all vie for market share. Since the majority of end users have PCs, the majority of people can view AVI/Windows without installing other players such as Real Video or QuickTime. For this reason, many Web publishers prefer to render in AVI/Video for Windows format instead of QuickTime or Real Video.

It is possible to create movies in many formats through After Effects. In the first few exercises of this chapter, you will learn to create movies in your default file type—either QuickTime (Mac) or AVI/Video for Windows (Windows). After that, you'll learn to create movies using any file type. You'll find helpful charts throughout this chapter that will assist you in your decisions about which file formats and settings to use for various types of projects.

Compression and Decompression

When you render a movie in After Effects, you are not only creating a final product, but you are also creating settings for compression and decompression. The term for this in video production is called a codec (short for **co**mpression/**dec**ompression). Many settings affect the quality of your movies, such as dimensions, colors, and sound. The codec, however, deals specifically with how the video is rendered. Some codecs compress the size of the movie to be small enough for Web delivery; other codecs are reserved for very high quality film production. Sometimes your client will tell you which codec to use, and sometimes you'll have to figure it out on your own. As a student of After Effects, however, you can and should conduct a lot of your own codec experimentation. Using a Sorenson codec might produce better colors than a Cinepak codec, for example. If you want to get an in-depth education about compression, I suggest the *Compressions Principles* CD-ROM by Sean Blumenthal. Visit **http://www.lynda.com/products/videos/cpcd** to learn more.

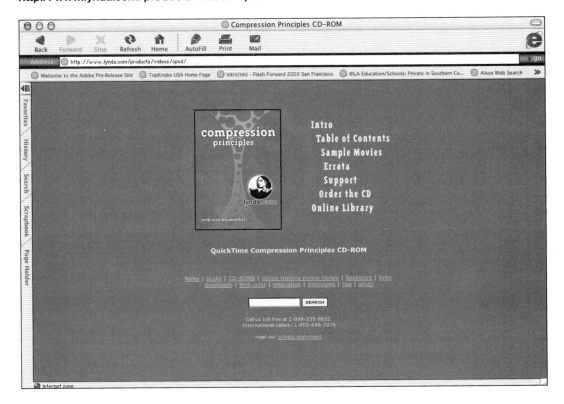

The Render Queue Window

In this chapter, you'll work with a part of After Effects that you haven't learned about yet—the **Render Queue** (the term "queue" means to wait your turn, and is pronounced like the letter Q). This is the window that offers feedback about how you are rendering your final movies. It's possible to render a single composition or to add multiple compositions to the Render Queue and have After Effects render each composition in the order you specify.

The settings in the Render Queue window do not affect your composition, but how that composition will be published for use outside of After Effects (for video, digital video, Web, and so on). As well, you can make movies that you bring back as footage items into an After Effects project.

The Render Queue can render multiple compositions at once

Each item in the Render Queue can be set to the type of output you want. Because there are many output types available, and each output type has its own set of options, rendering is a fairly substantial subject for those with no previous experience in producing digital movies. Sometimes, the best way to learn is by doing, so the hands-on exercises should help you through the learning curve. To begin, you'll learn how to render a single composition. Later, you'll learn how to render multiple compositions at once.

I.————————Using the Render Queue Default Settings

Macintosh versions of After Effects default to producing a QuickTime movie; Windows versions default to producing an AVI movie. This exercise will walk you through the basics of rendering a movie, using the program's default settings to output a movie. Later in this chapter, you'll learn to change these settings, but for now, this exercise will give you the satisfaction of learning the basic rendering steps.

1. Copy the **chap_18** folder from the **H•O•T CD-ROM** to your hard drive.

2. Open the **Rendering.aep** project from the **chap_18** folder.

3. Choose **File > Save As**. Navigate to your **AE6 HOT Projects** folder and click **Save**.

4. Double-click the **Popcorn Planets** composition to open it. Preview this movie to see what it contains.

5. Choose **Composition > Make Movie**, or use the shortcut keys **Cmd+M** (Mac) or **Ctrl+M** (Windows). The **Render Queue** will open. Locate the **Output To** field, and click the underlined **Popcorn Planets.mov** (Mac) or **Popcorn Planets.avi** (Windows) name. You will be prompted to save the movie. On a Mac, After Effects will prompt you to save it as **Popcorn Planets.mov**; on Windows, it will prompt you to save it as **Popcorn Planets.avi**. Navigate to your **Desktop** to save it there, and click **OK** (**Save** in OS X).

You can save the movie anywhere on your hard drive. I'm just suggesting where to save it, so you can find the movie easily once it's rendered.

6. Observe that there are all kinds of settings in this window. For now, you'll leave these settings as they are. Simply click the **Render** button.

7. Notice that the **Current Render** status bar becomes active, along with messages showing the elapsed time, the estimated time remaining, and other information about the rendering process. This feedback shows you that the movie is being rendered!

8. When the movie has finished rendering, you'll hear a sound bite of a bell ringing if your sound is turned on. After hearing the sound, locate your **Popcorn Planets.mov** or **Popcorn Planets.avi** movie on the Desktop (if that's where you saved it), and double-click it to open the QuickTime or AVI/Video for Windows player. Click the **Play** button and view the movie.

Note to some Windows users: This file might have to be played in Windows Media Player. If necessary, right-click on the movie icon to choose **Open With** > **Windows Media Player***.*

9. When you're finished watching the movie, return to After Effects. In the **Render Queue** window, select the **Popcorn Planets** composition name and press **Delete** (Mac) or **Backspace** (Windows) on your keyboard to delete the rendered composition from the Render Queue. Alternatively, choose **Edit >** **Clear**. Close the **Render Queue** window.

10. Save the project to your **AE6 HOT Projects** folder and close the **Popcorn Planets** composition. Leave the project open for the next exercise.

NOTE | Deleting Compositions from the Render Queue

It's not necessary to delete the composition from the Render Queue. I make this suggestion only because After Effects does not automatically delete compositions for you. It leaves rendered compositions displayed in the queue in the event that you need to check the settings or statistics for that render. It's up to you to delete rendered compositions when you no longer need to refer to them. You may choose to delete rendered compositions simply to clean out your Render Queue, because it can be confusing to see rendered and unrendered compositions in the same window. Rendered compositions will not be rendered again, even if they are left in the queue.

TIP | Close the Composition Window

Although you can view the results in the Composition window while rendering is in progress, this slows down the rendering. Before starting your render, close the Composition window to make the rendering go as fast as possible. Select the movie you want to render from the Project window and then press **Cmd+M** (Mac) or **Ctrl+M** (Windows). Everything from Step 5 onward in the previous exercise will stay the same, but the process will go faster.

2. _____Changing the Render Settings

The settings in the Render Queue window are at the heart of outputting final movies. In this exercise, you'll learn to change some of these settings. The focus of this exercise is to teach you how to make a low-resolution test movie. Many After Effects professionals render movies at small sizes to test their work before outputting a final movie at high-resolution settings. At the end of this exercise is a chart that outlines the scope of all the render options and indicates when you would use each one.

1. In the **Project** window, select (but do not open) the **Atmosphere** composition, and then choose **Composition > Make Movie**, or use the shortcut **Cmd+M** (Mac) or **Ctrl+M** (Windows). The **Render Queue** will open. Locate the **Output To** field, and click the underlined **Atmosphere.mov** (Mac) or **Atmosphere.avi** (Windows) name. Navigate to your **AE6 HOT Projects** folder and save the movie there.

Feel free to open and preview the Atmosphere composition before you render it. Remember to close the composition before you render it, however, because it takes longer to render a composition that is open.

2. Click the underlined words **Current Settings** to open the **Render Settings** dialog box.

3. In the **Render Settings** dialog box, notice that there are three groups of settings: **Composition**, **Time Sampling**, and **Options**. To read about these choices, check out the chart at the end of this exercise. Meanwhile, I'll walk you through changing some of the settings.

4. In the **Composition** section, click the **Quality** pop-up menu. Select **Draft** quality.

*Best quality is generally used for final output. Draft quality is generally used when you need to do a test movie and you don't want to wait for Best quality to render. Wireframe quality will render wireframe outlines of each layer; it is extremely quick but lacks detail. These are the same settings available in the Quality switch in the composition's Timeline. The default is **Current Settings**, which pulls the setting used in your composition. Therefore, if your composition's Quality switch is set to Best, Current Settings will use that setting, and you don't have to make a change here.*

5. Click the **Resolution** pop-up menu and select **Half** resolution. After you make this change, notice that the **Size** indicates the composition size, with the half size in parentheses.

*The Resolution default is **Current Settings**, which uses the resolution that you set for your composition. You would generally choose a smaller size for your resolution when you are making test movies in order to speed up the rendering time and to get a quick sense of what your movie will look like.*

6. In the **Time Sampling** options, click the **Time Span** option and select **Length of Comp**. Click **OK** to close the Render Settings dialog box.

*The Time Span setting is an important option. The default is **Work Area Only**. You learned to set the work area in Chapter 7, "Previewing Movies." However, in most cases, you'll probably want to output the entire composition. For this reason, you should make it a habit to check this option each time you set up a composition to be rendered. The chart at the end of this exercise explains all of the settings in the Render Settings dialog box.*

7. In the **Render Queue** window, click **Render**.

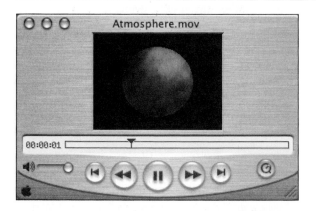

8. When your render completes, locate the **Atmosphere.mov** (Mac) or **Atmosphere.avi** (Windows) movie and double-click to open it. Click the **Play** button to view the results.

9. In the **Render Queue** window, select the **Atmosphere** composition name and press **Delete**, or **Backspace** on Windows, to remove it from the Render Queue. Alternatively, select **Edit > Clear**. Close the **Render Queue** window.

10. Save your project and leave it open for the next exercise.

The Render Settings Dialog Box		
Options	**Settings**	**Description**
COMPOSITION SETTINGS		
Quality	Current Settings, Best, Draft, Wireframe	**Best** quality takes the longest to render; use it for final output. Use **Draft** quality for rendering test movies, when speed of rendering is more important than quality. **Wireframe** quality renders only wireframe outlines of each layer. It is extremely quick but lacks detail. **Current Settings**, the default, uses the Quality setting in your composition.
Resolution	Current Settings, Full, Half, Third, Quarter, Custom	These terms relate to the original size setting in the composition that is being rendered. When you choose one of the sizes, the Size field displays the dimensions in pixels. The **Custom** setting allows you to enter your own settings. After Effects artists generally pick smaller resolution settings when they want the movie to render faster, since it takes less time to render a lower-resolution movie.
Proxy Use	Current Settings, Use All Proxies, Use Comp Proxies Only, Use No Proxies	Proxies are an advanced feature that allows you to set up dummy footage that can later be swapped with real footage. They are often used as a faster method of working by professionals who are creating high-resolution movies. The idea is that you make a low-resolution "proxy" of your footage, and once you're happy with how everything looks, you replace the proxy footage with the final footage. To learn more about proxies, refer to the After Effects manual.
Effects	Current Settings, All On, All Off	**Current Settings** uses the effects that you have active in your composition. You can also choose to render with all effects on or with all effects off (overriding the composition setting). Movies render more quickly with effects off, so consider using **All Off** if you need to speed up rendering.

continues on next page

	The Render Settings Dialog Box *continued*	
Options	**Settings**	**Description**
TIME SAMPLING SETTINGS		
Frame Blending	Current Settings, On For Checked Layers, Off For All Layers	Frame blending can be used only on moving footage and is set in the Switches area of the Timeline. It creates an effect of a cross dissolve (one image fading out while another image fades in) and is usually used in footage that has been time-stretched. To learn more about frame blending and time stretching, refer to the After Effects user manual.
Field Rendering	Off, Upper Field First, Lower Field First	Field rendering is used only in video projects, not for film or the Web, because it deals with video fields that are present only in video footage and output. Use this option if you are outputting to NTSC or PAL video, for example. Before you can accurately set this option, you will need to know whether your video hardware (camera and recording deck) uses *upper field first* or *lower field first*. If you are not outputting to video, leave this option set to **Off**.
Time Span	Length of Comp, Work Area Only, Custom	The default time span is Work Area Only. You learned to set the work area in Chapter 7, "*Previewing Movies*." You will usually want to set this to **Length of Comp** to output the entire composition. The **Custom** setting allows you to specify time spans that aren't tied to the length of the composition or the work area.
Motion Blur	Current Settings, On For Checked Layers, Off For All Layers	The Motion Blur setting defines how you want to treat motion blur in the rendered output. Motion Blur must be activated in the Switches panel of the Timeline. You learned about this panel in Chapter 8, "*Layers*."
Frame Rate	Use comp's frame rate, Use this frame rate	You can choose to use the composition's frame rate or set a different frame rate. Sometimes you'll choose to raise or lower the frame rate of your movie to save rendering time or disk space.
OPTIONS SETTINGS		
Use storage overflow		If your hard disk fills up before the render is complete, this option, when selected, will use another hard disk that you specify as the overflow volume. To specify overflow volumes, choose **Edit > Preferences > Output**.

(3.) ————————Working with the Output Module

In the last exercise, you worked with the Render settings in the Render Queue. This time, you'll learn to work with the **Output Module** that's also located in the Render Queue. Here you'll learn to choose a format and set format options.

1. In the **Project** window, select (but do not open) the **3D Text** composition.

2. Choose **Composition > Make Movie**, or press **Cmd+M** (Mac) or **Ctrl+M** (Windows). The **Render Queue** will open. In the **Output To** field, click the underlined **3D Text.mov** (Mac) or **3D Text.avi** (Windows) name. Save your movie to the **AE6 HOT Projects** folder. Locate the **Output Module** field and click on the underlined word **Lossless**. This opens the **Output Module Settings** dialog box.

At the end of this exercise, you will find a chart that lists most of the features found inside this dialog box. For now, you'll learn to change the settings appropriate to this exercise.

The Output Module Settings dialog box will open.

Composition Layer Effect Help

3D Text - Active C

Output

Based on "Lossless"

Format:
Embed:
Post-Render Action:

▲
PCX Sequence
PICT Sequence
PNG Sequence
Photoshop Sequence
Pixar Sequence
√ QuickTime Movie
SGI Sequence
TIFF Sequence
Targa Sequence
Windows Media

☑ **Video Output**

(Format Options...)

Animation Compressor
Spatial Quality = Most (100)

me Number

☐ **Stretch**

	Width		Height
Rendering at:	320	x	240
Stretch to:	320	x	240
Stretch %:		x	

Custom

Stretch Quality: High

☑ Lock Aspect Ratio to 4:3

☐ **Crop**

☐ Use Region of Interest   Final Size: 320 x 240

Top: Left: Bottom: Right:

☐ **Audio Output**

(Format Options...)

44.100 kHz   16 Bit   Stereo

(Cancel)   (OK)

3. In the **Composition** settings, click the arrow to the right of the **Format** option, and observe the different available output formats. Make sure **QuickTime Movie** is selected. **QuickTime Movie** is the default format on a Mac; **AVI/Video for Windows** is the default format on Windows.

The "Output Format Types" chart at the end of this exercise explains all the format types and their uses.

4. Click the **Embed** option and observe the available options. For this exercise, leave the selection to **None**.

*If you are working with other Adobe products, such as Premiere, you can use the **Embed** option to create a link to the original After Effects project. The **Project Link** option will embed a link only. The **Project Link and Copy** option will embed a link and a copy of the project in the output file. When you use an embedded output file in Premiere, you can use the Edit Original command to easily reopen the project in After Effects.*

5. In the **Video Output** settings, click the **Format Options** button. The **Compression Settings** dialog box opens.

If a format other than QuickTime is selected, other sets of options are displayed. After Effects does a great job of providing the appropriate options for all supported formats.

6. In the **Compression Settings** dialog box, click the **Compressor** pop-up menu that says **Animation**. Observe all the available compressor types. For this exercise, leave the compressor type set to **Animation**.

The Animation setting represents the Animation compressor. The Animation compressor is used to preserve high-quality visuals, but it can also result in large files, which aren't suitable for certain kinds of output, such as the Web. The "QuickTime Compressors" chart at the end of this exercise explains all of the compressor types and their uses.

7. Click the **Depth** option that says **Millions of Colors**. Observe all the depth options available. For now, leave the setting at **Millions of Colors**.

8. Set the **Quality** slider to **High**.

The Animation compressor offers a full range of quality. **Best** *quality will result in lossless output, which means that there will be no loss of image quality.* **Least** *quality will probably show image degradation due to compression. Other compressors may or may not offer a range of quality settings as an option.*

9. Observe the **Motion** section in the **Compression Settings** dialog box. These options allow you to set the number of frames per second, add a QuickTime key frame (not the same as an After Effects keyframe), and, for streaming video, limit the data rate. For this exercise, leave these settings as they are and click **OK**.

A key frame in QuickTime sets a reference for the compressor. Reference frames are not highly compressed. The more QuickTime key frames you set, the larger your output file. Keyframes in After Effects are different from key frames in QuickTime.

10. Back in the **Video Output** options of the **Output Module Settings** dialog box, click the **Channels** option and notice that you can select RGB only, Alpha only, or RGB + Alpha as your output. For this exercise, make sure that **RGB** is selected. This is the most common setting. If you wanted to export a mask or a movie with a mask, you would choose one of the other settings. You'll get a chance to do this at the end of this chapter.

11. Click the **Depth** option and notice that the color bit depth is set to **Millions of Colors**. This option is redundant with the **Colors** option under **Format Options**. If you change the setting in either place, they both change. Again, leave it set to **Millions of Colors**.

12. Click the **Color** option and notice the choices of **Straight (Unmatted)** and **Premultiplied (Matted)**. For this exercise, leave the setting at **Premultiplied (Matted)**.

A straight alpha channel is sometimes known as unmatted alpha. With a straight alpha channel, the effects of transparency are not visible until the image is displayed in an application that supports straight alpha. Many 3D programs support straight alpha channels.

The majority of time, you will want a premultiplied alpha, also known as matted alpha with a background color. The colors of semitransparent areas, such as feathered edges, are shifted toward the background color in proportion to their degree of transparency. For most purposes, the Premultiplied option is used.

13. Observe the **Stretch** options. If you needed to stretch your output to a larger size, you would do it here by clicking the **Stretch** check box and typing in the size you want. For this exercise, leave the Stretch options untouched.

*Stretching in After Effects will scale the movie to be larger or smaller, depending on the values you enter. I do not recommend that you stretch your final output because the image quality will be severely degraded. If you have to provide a larger output than anticipated for your project and you must use the Stretch options, be sure to set the **Stretch Quality** to **High**. In general, avoid using the Stretch options, if at all possible.*

14. Observe the **Crop** options. If you needed to crop pixels off of any side of your composition, you would do it here by clicking the **Crop** check box and typing in the number of pixels that you wish to crop. For example, typing 10 in each box would remove 10 pixels on each side of the output. For this exercise, leave the Crop options untouched.

15. Observe the **Audio Output** options. If you needed to output audio in your QuickTime movie, you would specify it here by clicking the **Audio Output** check box and selecting appropriate options. In this exercise, leave the Audio options untouched. Click **OK** to complete the Output Module settings for your render.

You will learn how to use the audio output options in the next exercise.

16. In the **Render Queue** window, click **Render**.

This composition is fairly complex and will take a few minutes to render. Watch the estimated time remaining, and take a short break if you'd like while the rendering completes.

17. When the rendering completes, double-click the QuickTime movie to play it in the QuickTime player.

18. In the **Render Queue** window, select the **3D Text** comp name and press **Delete** on your keyboard to delete the rendered composition from the **Render Queue**. Alternatively, select **Edit > Clear**.

19. Save your project and leave it open for the next exercise.

The Output Module Settings Dialog Box

You got to work with the Output Module in the previous exercise. This module is a very important part of After Effects. It is where you choose exactly the type of format you wish to output and the options for the format type. For example, you can choose to output a sequence of TIFF images, a QuickTime movie, or an animated GIF file, to name just a few of the format choices available.

The Output Module Settings dialog box.

Here is a chart that describes the numerous features in this important dialog box.

Output Module Settings Dialog Box	
Setting	**Description**
FORMAT SETTINGS	
Format	Allows you to choose the format for your movie. See the "Output Format Types" chart that follows this one for a description of the available formats.
Embed	Allows you to set your movie so that it can be opened using Edit Original in programs that support this feature, such as Adobe Premiere. This allows you to launch an After Effects movie from within Premiere by double-clicking on the movie file. Any changes made to the movie in After Effects will appear in the Premiere project.
Post-Render Action	**Import into Project When Done** causes the finished movie to be imported into the current project when it's finished rendering.
VIDEO OUTPUT SETTINGS	
Format Options	Opens another dialog box that lets you specify format-specific options. For example, QuickTime will have different options than TIFF.
Channels	Allows you to set how many channels your movie will have. Most movies are rendered in RGB, although you can also render in RGB+Alpha, which stores the movie and an alpha channel.
Depth	Sets the bit depth of the movie. This option controls whether the movie is in grayscale, in color, or in color with an alpha channel.
Color	Specifies how colors are treated in the alpha channel. The options are **Straight (Unmatted)** and **Premultiplied (Matted)**. The Premultiplied option is used for most purposes. These options are discussed in Chapter 11, "*Parenting*."
Stretch	This group of options specifies the dimensions of your final movie. If you enter dimensions that differ from the composition settings, you can choose to do so at a Low or High quality.

The following chart describes the format choices that appear on the Format pop-up menu.

Output Format Types	
Format	**Use**
Amiga IFF Sequence	A format designed for the Amiga computer.
Animated GIF	A very popular Web file format, often used for Web banners, cartoons, buttons, and simple animated graphics. GIF stands for **G**raphics **I**nterchange **F**ormat.
BMP Sequence	Microsoft Windows bitmap format.
Cineon Sequence	The Cineon file format was developed by Kodak. It is the standard file format used for professional motion picture visual effects.
Electric Image IMAGE	Electric Image is a 3D animation package. IMAGE files can be used as texture maps or cards within Electric Image.
FLC/FLI	Autodesk's "Flic" animation format was designed for Autodesk Animator and Animator Pro.
Filmstrip	The Photoshop filmstrip format was developed to contain a series of animating images that can be brought into Photoshop. This is a single file that can contain many images.
JPEG Sequence	JPEG is the popular Web file format used for continuous-tone images such as photographs. Use this format if you need to output a single image or group of images to the Web.
MP3	MP3 is an audio file format used extensively on the Web and in personal audio players.
PCX Sequence	PC Paintbrush format. You might choose this format if you needed to get a sequence of images from After Effects into another program that supports PCX.
PICT Sequence	PICT is a Macintosh image file format. You might choose this format if you needed to get a sequence of images from After Effects into another program that supports PICT.

continues on next page

Output Format Types *continued*	
Format	**Use**
PNG Sequence	PNG is a cross-platform image file format utilizing lossless compression. Images can include an alpha channel. It is a public domain format that can be used to transport images between computers or to store images with very good compression. You might choose this format if you needed to get a sequence of images from After Effects into another program that supports PNG.
Photoshop Sequence	Use this format to output a single file or a sequence of images to Photoshop.
Pixar Sequence	Pixar format is sometimes used in professional motion picture and television work with proprietary software applications. You might choose this format if you needed to get a sequence of images from After Effects into another program that supports Pixar.
QuickTime Movie	The Apple QuickTime format is a cross-platform standard for distributing movies. QuickTime is a container file that will hold various types of audio, moving pictures, Web links, and other data. This is probably the most useful format for most digital artists working in After Effects.
SGI Sequence	This file format is used by SGI computer workstations. It is usually used only by scientific or visual effects facilities.
TIFF Sequence	Tag Image File Format (TIFF) is a cross-platform image file format used for lossless compression. Images can include an alpha channel. Use this format to transport images between computers or to store images with fairly good compression.
Targa Sequence	Targa is an image file format used on PCs that have Targa hardware. It has also been widely used for scanners and imaging software.

The following chart describes the compressor types available in the Compression Settings dialog box.

QuickTime Compressors	
Compressor	**Use**
Animation	Use this compressor when you have large areas of solid color, such as cartoons or graphics. The size will be large, and it is best for film or video projects, not the Web or CD-ROM.
BMP	BMP is a Windows image file format with medium-quality compression. Use this compressor to transport images between computers.
Cinepak	Use this option to compress 24-bit movies intended for CD-ROMs.
Component Video	This compressor can be used to output through an analog video card, if your computer has one.
DV-NTSC	Use this codec to transfer digital video to an external digital video recorder. NTSC is the standard used in North America.
DV-PAL	Use this codec to transfer digital video to an external digital video recorder. PAL is the standard used in most of Europe.
Graphics	The Graphics compressor creates 8-bit images and is intended primarily for still images.
H.261 & H.263	These codecs were developed for video conferencing. H.263 can be used for streaming Web video as well.
Motion J-PEG A, Motion J-PEG B	These compressors are useful for creating video files that work with Motion J-PEG hardware such as capture and playback cards.
None	This selection means that no compression will be applied. Selecting this results in very large, lossless files.
Photo–JPEG	This compression scheme is intended for images that contain gradual color changes. It offers a range of quality settings.
Planar RGB	A lossless compression scheme intended for large areas of solid color. Use as an alternative to the Animation compressor.
	continues on next page

QuickTime Compressors *continued*	
Compressor	**Use**
PNG	PNG is a cross-platform image file format utilizing lossless compression. Images can include an alpha channel. Use this compressor to transport images between computers.
Sorenson Video	Useful for compressing 24-bit movies to be used as streaming video on the Web. It can also be used to compress movies for CD-ROMs. It produces better picture quality and smaller files than Cinepak.
TGA	TGA is for use with Targa hardware.
TIFF	TIFF is a cross-platform image file format used for lossless compression. Images can include an alpha channel. Use this compressor to transport images between computers.
Video	This compressor is useful for capturing analog video. It supports both spatial and temporal compression of 16-bit movies with fairly high quality. Use it as an alternative to the Component Video compressor.

4. ———————Rendering Audio

Just as you can use various image compression schemes, you can also use audio compression to output audio files. In this exercise, you will learn to select audio compression and render audio.

1. In the **Project** window, select (but don't open) the **Orbit Down** composition.

2. Choose **Composition > Add To Render Queue**. Alternatively, press **Cmd+Shift+/** (Mac) or **Ctrl+Shift+/** (Windows).

Note: The Add to Render Queue command is another way to begin the process of making a movie. It is used often because you can add multiple compositions to the queue at once this way. In this example, however, I am simply showing this as an alternative method to the Make Movie command you've used in earlier exercises.

3. In the **Render Queue** window, click on the underlined word **Lossless**.

4. In the **Output Module Settings** dialog box, make sure the **Format** is set to **QuickTime Movie**. QuickTime is one of the only formats that can include audio. Click the **Audio Output** check box, and then click the **Format Options** button in this option group.

5. In the **Sound Settings** dialog box, click the **Compressor** option, select **MACE6:1**, and then click **OK**.

See the "Audio Output Settings" chart at the end of this exercise for information on each audio compressor type. I have chosen MACE 6:1 here because it is a good all-purpose audio compression choice.

6. Accept the default **Rate, Size,** and **Use** options and click **OK**.

Rate specifies the audio sample rate in kilohertz; the higher the sample rate, the better the quality. High-quality settings are generally selected if you're going to put the movie on broadcast video. Lower audio sample rates are used when the file size is a concern, such as for Web, multimedia, or DVD output. A variety of standard sample rates can be selected from the small drop-down menu. The Size option refers to the bit depth. Just as images can have 8 bits or 16 bits per channel, audio channels are also in sizes of 8 bits and 16 bits. A high bit rate will sound better but will result in a larger file size. The Use option allows you to specify Mono for one audio channel or Stereo for two audio channels.

7. In the **Output Module Settings** dialog box, click **OK**. You will be returned to the **Render Queue** window.

8. Click the **Render** button in the **Render Queue** window.

9. When your movie finishes rendering, play the movie in the QuickTime player. You should hear audio with it!

10. In the **Render Queue** window, select the **Orbit Down** composition name and press **Delete**, or **Backspace** in Windows, on your keyboard to delete the rendered composition from the **Render Queue**. Alternatively, choose **Edit > Clear**.

11. Save your project and leave it open for the next exercise.

The following chart will help you sort out the various audio output settings available in the Sound Settings dialog box.

Audio Output Settings

Setting	Description
Format	Identifies the format type. File formats include QuickTime, Video for Windows, and file types available from plug-in file format modules.
Embed	Allows you to include information in the output file that links to the source project in After Effects. See the After Effects Help menu for more detailed information.
Post-Render Action	Requests an action for After Effects to perform after the composition is rendered. See About Post-Render Action options in the After Effects Help menu.
Format Options	Opens a dialog box that contains format-specific information. For example, if QuickTime is your format, Format Options opens a QuickTime Compression dialog box. (See Choosing Compression Options in the After Effects Help menu.)
Starting #	Sets the number for the starting frame of a sequence. For example, if this option is set to 38, After Effects names the first frame filename_00038.psd (or whatever format is specified). The Use Comp Frame Number option adds the starting frame number in the work area to the starting frame of the sequence.
Channels	Specifies the output channels contained in the rendered movie. After Effects creates a movie with an alpha channel if you choose RGB+Alpha, which translates to a depth of Millions of Colors+.
Depth	Sets the color depth for the rendered movie. Choose from color or grayscale options.
Color	Sets how colors are treated with the alpha channel. Choose from either Premultiplied (Matted) or Straight (Unmatted). (See Importing footage containing an alpha channel in the After Effects Help menu.)
Stretch	Sets the size of your rendered movie. Select Lock Aspect To if you want to retain the existing aspect ratio. Select Low Stretch Quality when rendering tests, and select High Stretch Quality when rendering a final movie.
Crop	Used to add or subtract pixels to the edges of the rendered movie. Type positive values to crop (subtract), and type negative values to add pixels. Select Region of Interest to render only the region of interest selected in the composition or layer window.
Audio Output	Sets the sample rate, sample depth (8 Bit or 16 Bit), and playback format (Mono or Stereo). Choose a sample rate that corresponds to the capability of the output format. Choose an 8-bit sample depth for playback on the computer, and a 16-bit sample depth for compact disc and digital audio playback or for hardware that supports 16-bit playback, an alternative to the Component Video compressor.

5. ————————Saving Alpha Channels or Motion Masks

Sometimes it's useful to output only the alpha channel for a composition. Perhaps you want to bring some type that you designed in After Effects into another program, such as Apple's Final Cut Pro or Adobe's Premiere. Those programs will honor the alpha channel output by After Effects. In addition, many 3D programs use alpha channel information from QuickTime movies to create interesting texture effects. You can even bring the finished movie back into After Effects itself, and it will honor the alpha channel.

In this exercise, you will learn to output only the alpha channel of a composition.

1. In the **Project** window, double-click the **Alpha Mask** composition to open it.

2. Click **RAM Preview** to preview the animation in color. Notice that the color circles have feathered edges. The circles and edges were all created in After Effects as solid layers, and I used mask settings with feathering to create the shapes. Whenever you create masks in this way in After Effects, the program creates an alpha channel for the composition. When you're done observing, close the **Composition** window.

Tip: Remember, rendering is faster with the Composition window closed.

3. Choose **Composition > Make Movie**, or press **Cmd+M** (Mac) or **Ctrl+M** (Windows). The **Render Queue** will open. In the **Output To** field, click the underlined **Alpha Mask.mov** (Mac) or **Alpha Mask.avi** (Windows) name. Navigate to the **AE6 HOT Projects** folder where you've been saving your work.

4. In the **Render Queue** window, click the underlined word **Lossless** next to **Output Module**.

5. In the **Output Module Settings** dialog box, make sure that **QuickTime Movie** is selected as the **Format**. Click the **Channels** option and select **RGB+Alpha**. This tells After Effects that you want to make a movie that includes an alpha channel. Accept all other default settings and click **OK**.

6. In the **Render Queue** window, click **Render**.

7. When the movie has been rendered, open the **AE6 HOT Projects** folder on your hard drive to locate and play the movie in the QuickTime player.

It looks like a normal movie, identical to what you saw in the Composition window. The difference occurs when you combine this movie with another movie by bringing it back into an After Effects composition or into another program, such as Apple Final Cut Pro or Premiere. When you do that, all the black areas will become transparent and the three colored circles will float on top of the other content with the feathered edges preserved. You'll get to bring this movie file back into After Effects soon to see what I mean.

8. Return to After Effects. In the **Render Queue** window, select the **Alpha Mask** composition name and press **Delete**, or **Backspace** in Windows, on your keyboard to delete the rendered composition from the **Render Queue**. Alternatively, choose **Edit > Clear**. Close the **Render Queue** window.

9. Double-click inside the **Project** window to access the **Import File** dialog box. Navigate to the **AE6 HOT Projects** folder, and import the **Alpha Mask.mov** movie that you just rendered.

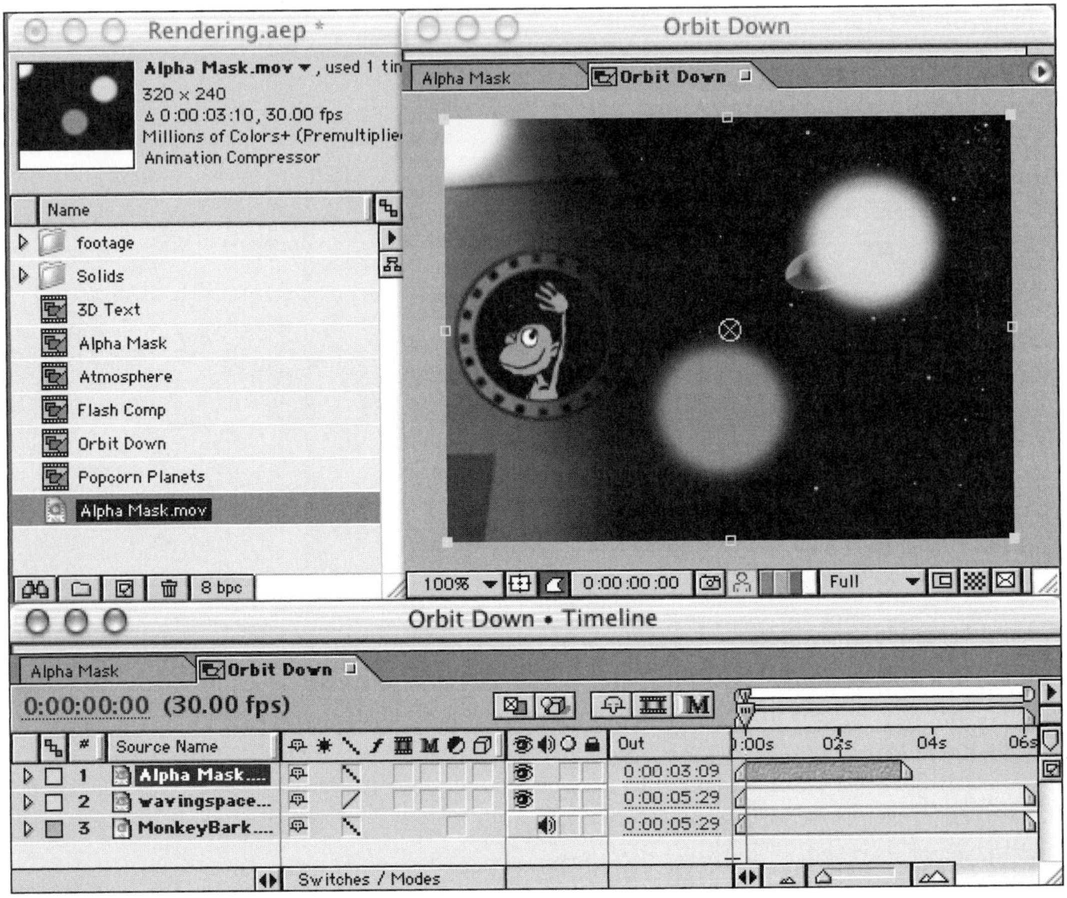

10. Open the **Orbit Down** composition from the **Project** window. Drag **Alpha Mask.mov** into the **Orbit Down Composition** window. Make sure it is positioned above the other layers—it should be listed first, as shown here.

Notice that the circles appear to float over the rest of the layers. That's because you rendered the movie with its alpha channel, and the circles are masked as a result. During the course of this book, you've worked with lots of movie files in various compositions that were created for you. This is how it was done—by rendering the alpha channel. Sometimes you want to render a movie for a layer element instead of for a final output element, as you did in this exercise. Doing so makes sense when you have a lot of layers and your composition is getting bogged down trying to render everything at once.

11. Save the project and close the **Orbit Down** composition. You won't be needing it again.

How Can You See the Alpha Channel of a Composition?

When you want to render a movie with an alpha channel, you first have to know whether the composition contains an alpha channel. As described in previous chapters, it's easy to bring artwork into After Effects from Photoshop or Illustrator and have it preserve the transparency. When you render a composition, however, you are rendering all the layers inside your composition, and some layers might have transparency, and some might not. For this reason, it becomes important to know what the alpha channel of the composition looks like before you choose to render a composition with it.

When you open the Alpha Mask composition from the **Render.aep** project that you just worked with, you can't tell right away that the composition contains an alpha channel. You might be wondering, as you progress to creating your own projects, how you'll know whether a composition contains an alpha channel.

Show Alpha Channel button

Every Composition window has a row of red, green, blue, and white colored buttons at the bottom. To see the alpha channel, click the white button, as shown here. This is the **Show Alpha Channel** button. The other buttons let you view the R, G, or B channels. You might want to open some of the other compositions in this project and click on those buttons to check them out. The majority of the compositions in the **Render.aep** project you are working with in this chapter will show a solid white alpha channel if you click on the **Show Alpha Channel** button. That's because they use images as backgrounds that take up the entire screen, so the alpha channels for the composition look completely white. Try turning off background layers, and you'll see shapes emerge in the alpha channel.

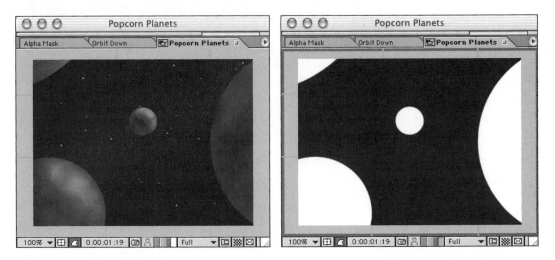

For example, try opening the **Popcorn Planet** composition and clicking the **Show Alpha Channel** button. The entire composition will turn white. If you turn off the last layer in this composition (**space_backdrop.psd**) and click the **Show Alpha Channel** button again, you'll see the shapes of the planets appear in white. Before you turned off the last layer, it was showing the alpha channel for the background layer. If you wanted to put these planets over some live action, you would need to turn the background layer off and render the composition with its alpha channel, as you learned to do in the last exercise. You could then bring the movie back into After Effects, where the planets would composite perfectly over the other layers you put into the composition. Likewise, you could take this movie to Premiere or Final Cut Pro, and the planets would mask over other footage.

In general, the white areas of the alpha channel are used to reveal the image in the document, and the black areas mask that image.

After Effects for the Web

I'm assuming that once you get into After Effects, you might want to put a portfolio of your work on the Web. This isn't a hands-on exercise, but I'll cover some of the important issues related to Web delivery in this section.

When creating for the Web, I recommend that you work with the QuickTime format because it has more features that are Web savvy than the AVI format. In the **Output Module Settings** dialog box, make sure that the **Format** is **QuickTime Movie**. Click the **Format Options** button.

In the **Compression Settings** dialog box, for the **Compressor** type select **Sorenson Video**, which is the best choice for compressing 24-bit movies as streaming video.

Next, experiment with the **Quality** setting. The lower the quality, the smaller the file will be. When publishing for the Web, always lower the frames per second to 15 or less. You can also change the key frame rate to make smaller Web movies. Recall that key frames in QuickTime are different from keyframes in After Effects. Adobe recommends a **3:1 formula** to come up with a key frame rate. For example, if you choose a frame rate of 15, multiply it by 3, for a value of 45. To enter 45 as the key frame rate, check the **Key frame every** check box, and enter 45 for the value. The data rate varies depending on the speed of your end user's system. Sample data rates are: 28K modem = 2.5K per second, 56K modem = 4.0K per second, ISDN = 12K per second, and T1 = 20K per second. It's better to set your data rates for slower modems so that everyone can see your work, not just those with high-speed Internet access.

You might also want to set your resolution to **Half**, **Third**, or **Quarter**. Every bit of savings you can eke out of the file will save your end users precious downloading time.

TIP | HTML Needed for QuickTime Movies

After Effects doesn't write HTML, as some other Adobe products do. Therefore, it's up to you to write this code yourself. This is the HTML code we use to put QuickTime movies on our Web site. Feel free to use it, if you need to! If you don't know how to write HTML at all, see the resources listed in the back of this book in the "*Resources*" appendix.

```
<embed src="yourmovienamehere.mov" width="640" height="496" autoplay="true"
loop="true" controller="true" playeveryframe="false" cache="false" bgcolor=
"#FFFFFF" kioskmode="false" targetcache="false" pluginspage=
"http://www.apple.com/quicktime/" align="middle">
</embed>
```

Note: Make sure you replace the src footage where I wrote "yourmovienamehere.mov" with your own movie name!

TIP | Adding Output Modules

You can add additional Output Modules to any item in the Render Queue. This will allow you to output more than one version from the same item, using the same Render settings.

To add an **Output Module**, select the **composition name** in the **Render Queue** window.

Choose **Composition > Add Output Module**.

Another Output Module is added to the item, and you can create different output settings by clicking on its settings and changing them. When you click **Render**, After Effects will actually create multiple movies with different settings.

6. ——————————Saving RAM Previews

RAM previews can be saved as movie files. This allows you to save a permanent movie file quickly and easily, without making a visit to the Render Queue window. (Although the Render Queue will open quickly, you can't make any changes to settings there.) Most After Effects artists save RAM previews to be able to view them again and again, to show one to a client as a quick rough, or to import them back into a project as source footage for compositions.

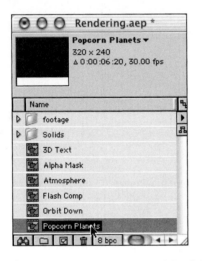

1. In the **Project** window, double-click the **Popcorn Planets** composition to open it.

Note: The composition must be open to save a RAM preview.

2. Choose **Composition > Save RAM Preview**. Once you choose this menu setting, After Effects appears to play the composition for you. While it is playing, it is rendering the composition, and it will prompt you when it is finished.

3. When the RAM preview ends, in the **Output Module Settings** dialog box, navigate to your **AE6 HOT Projects** folder to save the movie. Notice that the **Render Queue** pops up, and your movie renders as if you had selected **Make Movie**.

4. After your movie renders, open and view it in the QuickTime or AVI player. You might be wondering why you would ever use this feature. It's a matter of personal preference; in essence, it does the exact same thing as **Make Movie**.

5. In the **Project** window, notice that the rendered RAM movie is automatically imported as footage. You might want to keep it there, or you might want to drag it to the **Trashcan** icon at the bottom of the **Project** window if you don't need to use it.

6. Save your project and leave it open for the next exercise.

7. ——————————Creating and Using Rendering Templates

As you've seen, the Render settings can get quite complex. Wouldn't it be neat if you could come up with your favorite settings and save them so you could access them when needed? You can! **Rendering templates** store predefined settings, and they're easy to make. Both the Render settings and the Output Module settings have a few default templates that you can choose from a drop-down menu. These templates have specific settings for rendering and output. Better yet, you can create your own templates with exactly the settings you need. This means that you can store the settings that you use often and have them appear via a drop-down menu. When you create a template, you can give it a name that is meaningful to your work style. In this exercise, you'll learn how to create rendering templates and choose rendering templates at output.

1. In the **Project** window, select the **Popcorn Planets** composition.

2. Choose **Composition > Make Movie**. Alternatively, press **Cmd+M** (Mac) or **Ctrl+M** (Windows). The **Render Queue** will open. In the **Output To** field, click the underlined **Popcorn Planets.mov** (Mac) or **Popcorn Planets.avi** (Windows) name. Navigate to your **AE6 HOT Projects** folder and save it there.

3. In the **Render Queue** window, click the arrow next to the **Render Settings** option and select **Make Template** from the drop-down menu.

4. In the **Render Settings Templates** dialog box, locate the **Settings Name** entry box and type **Quick Study** as the name for the template. Click **Edit**. The **Render Settings** dialog box opens.

5. In the **Render Settings** dialog box, click the **Quality** menu and select **Draft**. In the next few steps, you are going to create settings for a low-quality, quick-rendering, rough draft movie.

6. Click the **Resolution** menu and select **Quarter**.

7. Click the **Time Span** menu and select **Length of Comp**.

8. For the **Motion Blur** option, select **Off For All Layers**. Click **OK** to return to the **Render Settings Templates** dialog box.

In the following steps, you will create a second template to be used when rendering high-end movies.

9. In the **Render Settings Templates** dialog box, click **New**.

10. For the **Quality** option, select **Best**.

11. For the **Resolution** option, select **Full**.

12. For the **Motion Blur** option, select **On For Checked Layers**. Click **OK**.

These arrows allow you to access different templates, if you have multiple templates defined

13. In the **Settings Name** entry box, type **High End** for the name of the new template. Click **OK**.

14. In the **Render Queue** window, click the **Render Settings** drop-down menu and notice that the **High End** and **Quick Study** templates have been added to menu. Select the **Quick Study** template and then click the **Render** button.

15. When the movie is rendered, locate the output file and view it in your movie player. Go back and see if you can add another movie to the **Render Queue**, but this time, use the **High End** template you just created. Reread the steps if you can't figure this out—but I know you can! Most After Effects artists love this template feature, because it allows them to easily set up the exact render they want for their specific needs.

16. Save your project and leave it open for the next exercise.

TIP | Output Module Templates

You create Output Module templates using the same process you use to create Render Settings templates.

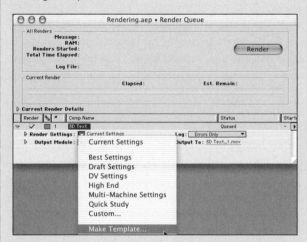

You must first add a composition to the **Render Queue** by choosing **Composition > Make Movie**. Before rendering a movie, click the **Output Module** drop-down menu and select **Make Template**.

In the **Output Module Templates** dialog box, give your new template a name and click **Edit**. Select the settings you want in the **Output Module Settings** dialog box. Once you've selected the options, click **OK** to close the **Output Module Settings** dialog box, and then click **OK** again to close the **Output Module Templates** dialog box. Your new Output Module template will now show up in the Render Queue window in the drop-down menu for the Output Module option.

8. _____Collecting Files

A very important automated command is available in After Effects that you will undoubtedly use frequently to help organize your work. The command is called **Collect Files**. It allows you to automatically create a copy of all the footage used for a project, along with a copy of the project file itself, and place the copies in a single folder at the location of your choice. I cannot overstate the usefulness of this command, which makes it very easy to collect all of the files for a project in the form of a copy that you can use to archive, render, or transport the project. In this exercise, you will learn to use the Collect Files command. Note that this feature can be applied to an entire project or to an individual composition.

1. Choose **File > Save**. Alternatively, press **Cmd+S** (Mac) or **Ctrl+S** (Windows). This saves your project.

Note: You must save your project before using the Collect Files command. Otherwise, you'll see a prompt window notifying you that your project must be saved before collecting files and giving you the option to save the project.

2. Choose **File > Collect Files**.

3. In the **Collect Files** dialog box, click the **Collect Source Files** option, make sure **All** is selected, and then click **Collect**.

The All option will collect the project file and all the footage items used in the project. It will also generate a report.

4. In the **Collect Files into a Folder** dialog box, navigate to the **AE6 HOT Projects** folder and click **Save**.

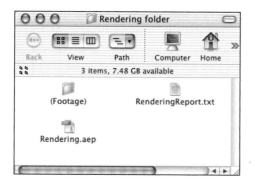

5. Once the collection process is complete, locate the folder and open it to see the project file and footage file copies inside.

Writing Macromedia Flash Files

It's pretty easy to output After Effects movies to the Macromedia Flash file format (SWF). The question is, why would you want to use After Effects for this purpose?

Macromedia Flash supports sound, graphics, motion, and interactivity. For this reason, the scope of what you can create in Macromedia Flash is different from the scope of what you can create in After Effects. You can create an entire Web site in Macromedia Flash, with working buttons and forms for visitors to fill out.

Adobe After Effects has different capabilities and strengths. It is a stronger tool for creating bitmap motion graphics, due to its superior blending, blurring, masking, and keyframing features.

The advantage to outputting After Effects movies in the Macromedia Flash format is that you may not know how to create motion in Macromedia Flash, but you know how to do so easily in After Effects. For this reason, After Effects is attractive because you are more skilled at producing animation in it than you might be in Macromedia Flash. As well, After Effects has much more sophisticated motion control capabilities than Macromedia Flash, through the presence of keyframable effects and the independent Transform and Mask properties in the Timeline. For this reason, you might want to use After Effects because you are able to achieve a different kind of animated image than you are in Macromedia Flash.

In addition, many After Effects production companies use Macromedia Flash to create their Web sites because the format is so much more visually liberating than HTML. This is because you can produce full-screen animation and use any font you want in Macromedia Flash, which is untrue of HTML.

It's important to understand that After Effects outputs pixels, and the Macromedia SWF format for Macromedia Flash distinguishes between vectors and pixels. If you use only vectors in your Macromedia Flash work, your file sizes will be quite small and will download more quickly than if you use pixel-based artwork. Anything that includes live action, an effect, or blur in After Effects is treated as pixel-based artwork in Macromedia Flash. This almost ensures that the download will be larger if you choose to incorporate After Effects work in your Macromedia Flash work.

It is possible to output vectors only from After Effects. The key is to use vector-based artwork from Illustrator or to use solid layers and nonfeathered masks. You should also avoid effects, blurs, and live action. The truth is, however, that After Effects is best suited for pixel-based animation, and most people will want to use live action, effects, masks, and blurs freely in their After Effects work.

After Effects offers you a choice to ignore pixel-based artwork when you output to the Macromedia Flash format. You can also choose to rasterize frames that contain unsupported features and add them to the SWF file as JPEG-compressed bitmaps. If you add bitmaps for each frame, however, the file size of the Flash movie will be larger, making it less efficient and less appropriate for the Web. This following exercise will walk you through some of the issues firsthand.

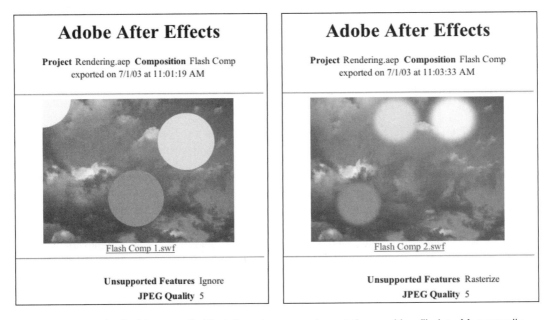

Once you output in the Macromedia Flash format, you can import the resulting file into Macromedia Flash. The program accepts both SWF and QuickTime, so you could also elect to output QuickTime format from After Effects for Macromedia Flash work. You might choose to experiment with your specific content to see whether it's better to output your After Effects work as SWF or QuickTime.

9. Outputting the Macromedia Flash Format

This exercise walks you through the steps to create Macromedia Flash SWF output as your final movie format. You'll see that it's quite easy, and that you are given a choice of ignoring pixel-based effects in order to write pure vectors for a smaller file size.

1. Open and play the **Flash Comp** from the **Project** window to see what it looks like. This composition includes a solid layer with feathered masks. This example was chosen because it is a good candidate for trying different settings when outputting to the **Macromedia Flash (SWF)** file format. Close the **Flash Comp,** but leave it selected in the **Project** window.

2. Choose **File > Export > Macromedia Flash (SWF).** Unlike the other movies you have made in this chapter, the **Macromedia Flash (SWF)** format is supported only through **Export** menu, not through the **Render Queue.**

3. Navigate to your **AE6 HOT Projects** folder and click **Save.**

4. In the **SWF Settings** dialog box, notice the **Images** group of options. For this exercise, leave the **JPEG Quality** at the default settings.

This setting affects any pixel-based content, such as a photograph or live action footage. Choosing higher quality results in larger files.

5. Click to see the **Unsupported Features** menu, and notice that you can choose to ignore unsupported features or to rasterize them. For this exercise, keep the **Ignore** setting.

*The **Rasterize** option will convert any unsupported features as JPEG images and will increase the file size.*

6. Notice the **Audio** section. In this exercise, there is no audio, so leave the option unchecked.

*Audio is encoded in Flash files using MP3 compression. If you use audio in your Web project, and you want to create the smallest files possible, keep the **Sample Rate** low (11.025 or 22.050 kHz) while still maintaining acceptable quality. Mono audio will create less data than stereo. A lower **Bit Rate** will also reduce file size.*

7. Click the **Loop Continuously** check box, which causes your movie to play over and over. Click the **Prevent Import** check box, which prevents the output SWF file from being accessed by someone else who could then modify your content.

8. Take note of the remaining options, and then click **OK**.

*The **Include Object Names** option will include the names of any layers, masks, and effects that exist in your Composition. This will increase the file size. The **Include Layer Marker Web Links** option allows any layers that have markers with Web links to be included and active in the Macromedia Flash output file. The **Flatten Illustrator Artwork** option merges Illustrator artwork. See the tip at the end of this exercise for more information about this option.*

TIP | Illustrator Files

Adobe Illustrator files are vector files (though Illustrator files can contain bitmaps, too) and are supported as an export item. However, be aware that After Effects supports only stroked paths and/or filled paths in CMYK or RGB color spaces.

9. When the export is finished, an SWF file and an HTML file will be created. Open the **HTML** file in a Web browser.

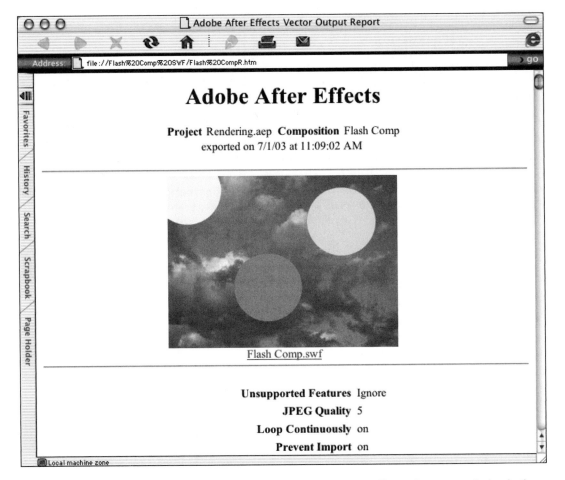

10. If you have the Flash plug-in installed in your Web browser, you will see the output playing in the HTML page. Scroll down the page and notice the report created regarding your Flash output. When you are done viewing the animation, close the browser. This HTML file is created to help you preview the final SWF file and its settings only. It is likely that you would want to bring the SWF file into Macromedia Flash or Adobe Live Motion, and thus would discard the HTML.

11. Save and close your After Effects project. You're finished with this chapter!

This was a big chapter with a lot of technical information. You can always refer to it again as you begin outputting your own projects. By completing this chapter, you have covered all the rendering basics, and you are prepared to discover each detail necessary for the type of output your projects require. As usual, the more you use the rendering tools, the more you will learn.

I hope you enjoyed working through this book, and that it turned you on to the tremendous possibilities that After Effects holds. All I can say is the more you create, the more confidence you'll build. Be sure to check out the "Resources" appendix for other training and reference resources. Enjoy!

A

Resources

H•O•T

After Effects 6

This appendix offers helpful information and resources related to After Effects, video, audio, and motion graphics.

You might be surprised to see that I recommend training resources other than ours. The beauty of After Effects is that this program is so deep and vast that you will always be hungry to learn something new. Like most deep programs, there are many ways to accomplish the same tasks, many different approaches to creating content, and many experts in the field who can teach you new techniques. Dive in!

Books About After Effects

Creating Motion Graphics with After Effects, Volume 1
Authors: Chris and Trish Meyer
Publisher: CMP Books
ISBN: 1578201144

A great reference book for After Effects professionals, written by two of the industry's most respected experts. Especially useful if you want to learn about high-end video and film projects.

Creating Motion Graphics with After Effects, Volume 2
Authors: Chris and Trish Meyer
Publisher: CMP Books
ISBN: 1578202078

Includes more advanced techniques than Volume 1, including alpha channels, Macromedia Flash, paint, and text.

After Effects in Production
Authors: Chris and Trish Meyer
Publisher: CMP Books
ISBN: 1578200776

A project-based book with intermediate to advanced projects contributed by top After Effects luminaries.

Adobe After Effects 6 Classroom in a Book
Author: Adobe Creative Team
Publisher: Adobe Press
ISBN: 0321193792

This book wasn't published at the time of this writing, but I found it listed on Amazon.com. I recommend it because past editions have been a good learning resource.

Creative After Effects 5.0
Author: Angie Taylor
Publisher: Butterworth-Heinemann
ISBN: 0240516222

A project-based book with all exercises developed by one or two authors (offers good continuity). Covers lots of interesting techniques.

After Effects 5.5 Magic
Authors: Nathan Moody and Mark Christiansen
Publisher: New Riders
ISBN: 0735711445

A project-based book that features advanced techniques; especially strong on the subject of After Effects expressions.

CD-ROMs About After Effects

Learning After Effects 6
Author: Lynda Weinman
Publisher: lynda.com
Time: 6 hours
http://www.lynda.com/products/videos/ae6cd/
If you liked the QuickTime movies in this book, try this CD-ROM: It has six hours worth of movies to watch! It covers all the same topics as this book, in more depth in some cases.

After Effects 5.0 Six-Volume Set
Author: e-trainingdirect
http://www.e-trainingdirect.com/cdeffects.html

Videos About After Effects

Total Training for After Effects 6 Four-Volume Set
Author: Brian Maffit and Steve Holmes
Publisher: Total Training
Time: 16 hours
http://www.totaltraining.com

VideoSyncrasies: The Motion Graphics Problem Solver
Authors: Chris and Trish Meyer
Publisher: Desktop Images Publishers
http://www.desktopimages.com/

After Effects Boot Camp
Author: Taz Goldstein
Publisher: Desktop Images
http://www.desktopimages.com/

Online Communities and Resources

http://www.uemedia.com/CPC/designinmotion/
Design in Motion: The Art, Technology, and Business of Motion Design

http://www.creativecow.net
Professional forums

http://www.dv.com
DV magazine and DV Expo site

http://www.adobe.com
In-depth education for Web, print, and DV professionals

http://www.digitalproducer.com/aHTM/HomeSet.htm
News, tools, and techniques for content creation

http://www.mgla.org/
Motion Graphics Los Angeles Users Group

http://www.uemedia.com/CPC/2-pop/
The Digital Filmmaker's Resource Guide

http://www.media-motion.tv/
After Effects discussion group

Online Resources for Audio and Video Formats

http://cit.duke.edu/resource-guides/tutorial-web-multimedia/06-audio-formats.html
Center for Instructional Technology at Duke University

http://www.kendavies.net/resources/webaudio.html
Ken Davies Music Publications

http://www.apple.com/quicktime/
QuickTime reference guide

http://www.sorenson.com/
Sorenson compression site

HTML and QuickTime Links

http://www.apple.com/quicktime/authoring/embed.html
QuickTime authoring/developer site

http://www.faculty.de.gcsu.edu/~flowney/quicktime/TS/QT4Ed/
QuickTime for educators

http://www.nd.edu/PageCreation/TipsAndHints.html
University of Notre Dame tips on Web authoring

Related lynda.com Training Products

QuickTime Compression Principles with Sean Blumenthal
http://lynda.com/products/videos/cpcd/

Learning QuickTime Pro with Sean Blumenthal
http://lynda.com/products/videos/lqt5procd/

Learning Illustrator 10 with Bruce Heavin
http://lynda.com/products/videos/illus10cd/

Learning Photoshop 7 with Bruce Heavin
http://lynda.com/products/videos/ps7cd/

B

Troubleshooting

H·O·T

After Effects 6

This appendix is the first place to check if you're having a problem with any of the exercises in this book. You might also want to check the book's Web site (**http://www.lynda.com/ books/hot/ae6**) to see if any errata have been posted. As a last resort, email us with your problems— **ae6hot@lynda.com**. Please realize that, due to the huge amount of email we receive, we cannot help you with your own After Effects projects; our support covers only issues related to the exercises in this book. Please allow 72 hours for us to get back to you with an answer (longer over holidays or week- ends). For tech support on After Effects questions, please contact Adobe or join one of the discussion groups listed in the "Online Communities and Resources" section of the "*Resources*" appendix.

Why Do I Get a Gray Frame at the End of a Composition?

The After Effects Timeline often shows a gray frame if you manually move the Time Marker to the end. This is because the Timeline often extends one frame beyond the true end of the composition. Move to the last frame by pressing the **End** key on the keyboard or by clicking the **Last Frame** button on the **Time Controls** panel.

Why Does My RAM Preview Stop Short?

For RAM preview to work properly, you must have enough RAM in your computer. The amount of RAM you need varies depending on how complex and large your After Effects project is. The good news is that RAM is a lot less expensive than it has been in the past!

QuickTime Isn't Working—What Should I Do?

Try going to the Apple Web site and downloading the latest QuickTime plug-in. Make sure that After Effects is not open while you do this. If you are using Windows XP, make sure you have installed the latest updates. This is accomplished by choosing **Start > All Programs > Windows Update**. There have definitely been some updates that affected QuickTime compatibility, so don't neglect to try this!

What Can I Do When the "Missing Footage" Error Message Appears?

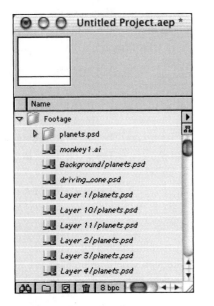

The missing footage will appear inside the **Project** window (you might have to click twirlies to find it) as italicized text. If you double-click on the name of the missing footage inside your **Project** window, After Effects will let you navigate to your hard drive to locate the missing footage.

Why Is My Movie Playback Jerky?

When you play a QuickTime movie on your hard drive, it will be jerky if you don't have a fast enough processor or enough RAM. If this is a movie you created from After Effects, you might want to render it again using a higher compression method. **Tip:** Try using the Sorenson or Graphics compression types and a lower frame rate with fewer keyframes.

Why Do I Get an "Untitled" Warning?

When you open a project file that was created in After Effects 5 into After Effects 6, you will encounter the warning shown here.

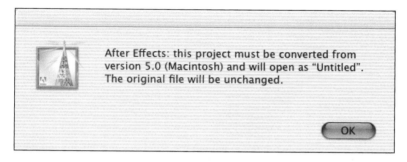

Click **OK**, and the project will open as originally intended, except that it will appear as an untitled project until you save it.

What If I'm on a Laptop and the Keyboard Shortcuts Don't Work?

Not all keyboard shortcuts work on a laptop. For the **Home** key, press **Shift+Option+left arrow** (Mac) or **Shift+Alt+left arrow** (Windows). For the **End** key, press **Shift+Option+right arrow** (Mac) or **Shift+Alt+right arrow** (Windows).

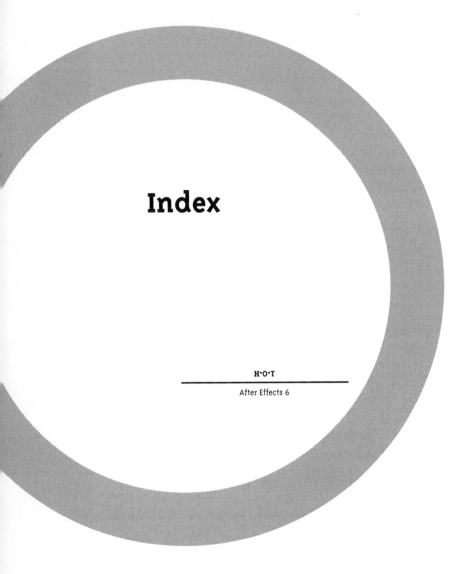

Index

H·O·T

After Effects 6

Symbols

A

D

E

Visit Peachpit on the Web at www.peachpit.com

- Read the latest articles and download timesaving tipsheets from best-selling authors such as Scott Kelby, Robin Williams, Lynda Weinman, Ted Landau, and more!

- Join the Peachpit Club and save 25% off all your online purchases at peachpit.com every time you shop—plus enjoy free UPS ground shipping within the United States.

- Search through our entire collection of new and upcoming titles by author, ISBN, title, or topic. There's no easier way to find just the book you need.

- Sign up for newsletters offering special Peachpit savings and new book announcements so you're always the first to know about our newest books and killer deals.

- Did you know that Peachpit also publishes books by Apple, New Riders, Adobe Press, Macromedia Press, palmOne Press, and TechTV press? Swing by the Peachpit family section of the site and learn about all our partners and series.

- Got a great idea for a book? Check out our About section to find out how to submit a proposal. You could write our next best-seller!

You'll find all this and more at www.peachpit.com. Stop by and take a look today!

Keep Learning

with More Hands-On Training Books:

Adobe Photoshop Elements 2
Hands-On Training

Adobe Photoshop CS ImageReady
CS Hands-On Training

Macromedia Dreamweaver
MX 2004 Hands-On Training

Macromedia Flash MX 2004
Hands-On Training

- Learn by doing.
- Follow real-world examples.
- Benefit from exercise files and QuickTime movies included on CD-ROM.
- Many other titles to choose from.

Visit http://www.lynda.com/books/

lynda.com ™

Hands-on Training Books, CDs & Online Movie Library.